STOP

This is the back of the book!

This manga collection is translated into English but oriented in right-to-left reading format at the creator's request, maintaining the artwork's visual orientation as originally published in Japan. If you've never read manga in this way before, take a look at the diagram below to give yourself an idea of how to go about it. Basically, you'll be starting in the upper right corner and will read each balloon and panel moving right to left. It may take some getting used to, but you should get the hang of it very quickly. Have fun!

1
I KNOW ALL ABOUT IT.
HOW HE'S A MONSTER THAT EATS HUMAN FLESH.
2
I KNOW IT ALL TOO WELL.
3
......
......
4
AND I KNOW THAT YOU CONTINUE TO PROVIDE HIM WITH HIS MEALS.
5
!
6
I PASSED THEM AT THE GATES OF THE CITY.
7
A PRISON WAGON FULL OF WOMEN AND CHILDREN.
8
I...I AM THE MAYOR!
IT IS MY DUTY TO PROTECT THIS TOWN!
9
PROTECT THIS TOWN? DON'T YOU MEAN PROTECT "MYSELF"?

ベルセルク

BERSERK ⑮

BY
KENTARO MIURA
三浦建太郎

TRANSLATION
DUANE JOHNSON
LETTERING AND RETOUCH
REPLIBOOKS

DARK
HORSE
MANGA

PRESIDENT AND PUBLISHER
MIKE RICHARDSON

US EDITORS
CHRIS WARNER
FRED LUI

COLLECTION DESIGNER
DAVID NESTELLE

English-language version produced by
DARK HORSE COMICS and DIGITAL MANGA PUBLISHING.

BERSERK vol. 15 by KENTARO MIURA

Dark Horse Manga
A division of Dark Horse Comics LLC
10956 SE Main Street
Milwaukie OR 97222

DarkHorse.com

To find a comics shop in your area, go to comicshoplocator.com

First edition: January 2007

ISBN 978-1-59307-577-4

20 19 18 17 16 15 14 13
Printed in the United States of America

BERSERK

ベルセルク⑮

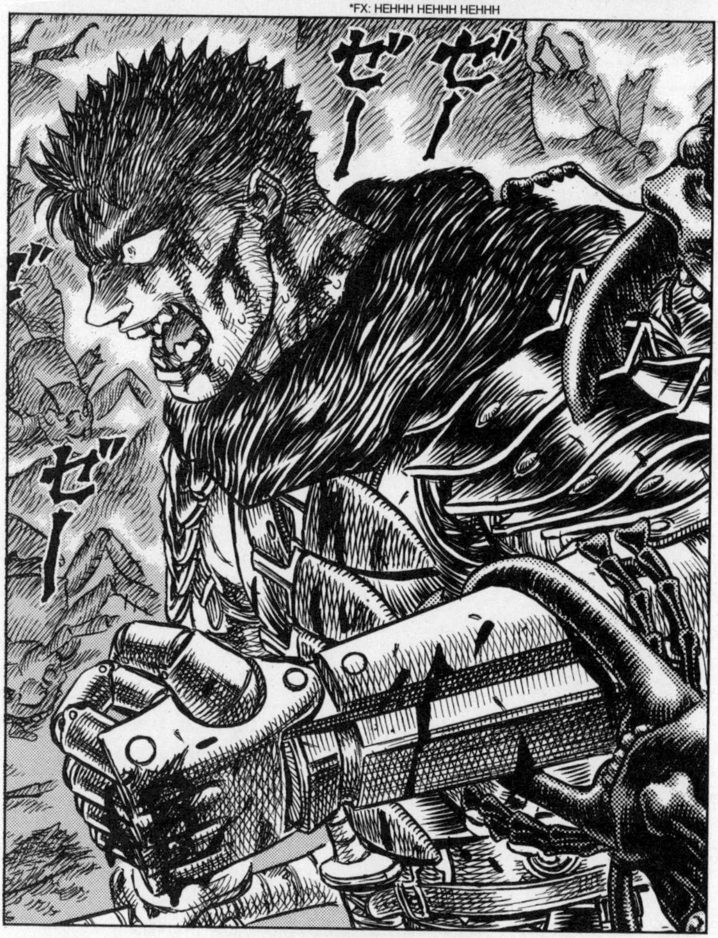
ゼー
ゼー
ゼー

*FX: HEHHH HEHHH HEHHH

三浦建太郎

CONTENTS

**CONVICTION ARC
LOST CHILDREN CHAPTER**

QUEEN...5

ELF FIRE 27

RED-EYED PEEKAF...47

THE RECOLLECTED GIRL................................69

THE WORLD OF WINGED THINGS.................89

GUARDIANS, CHAPTER 1 109

GUARDIANS, CHAPTER 2 131

PURSUERS 151

THE MISTY VALLEY, CHAPTER 1.................171

THE MISTY VALLEY, CHAPTER 2.................191

COCOONS...213

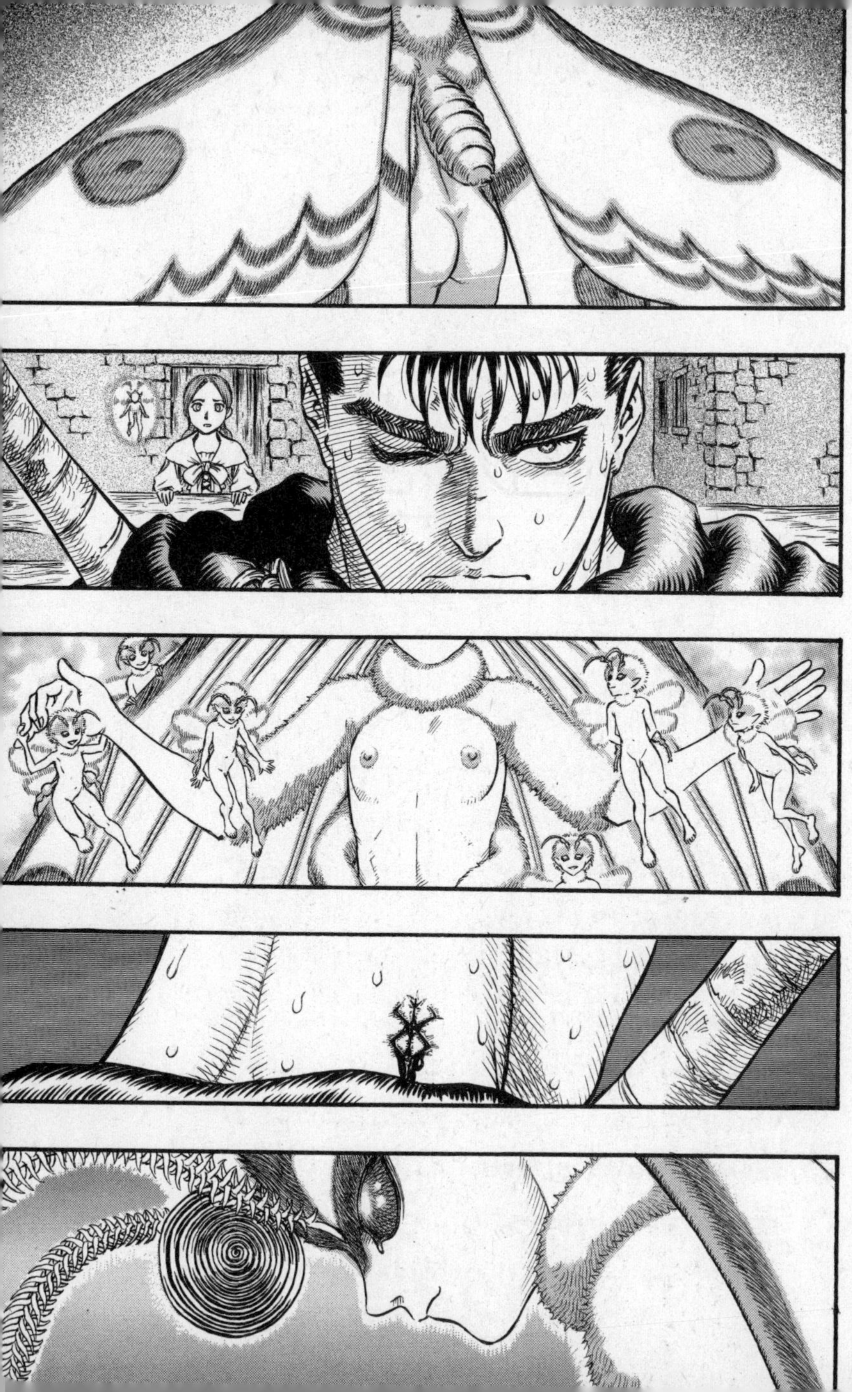

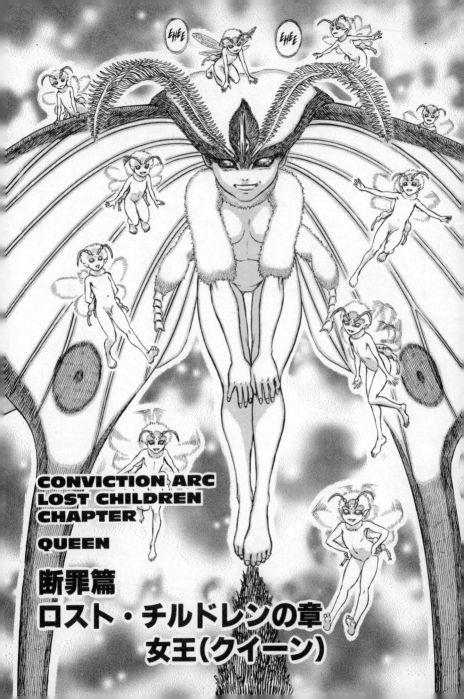

CONVICTION ARC
LOST CHILDREN
CHAPTER

QUEEN

断罪篇
ロスト・チルドレンの章
女王（クイーン）

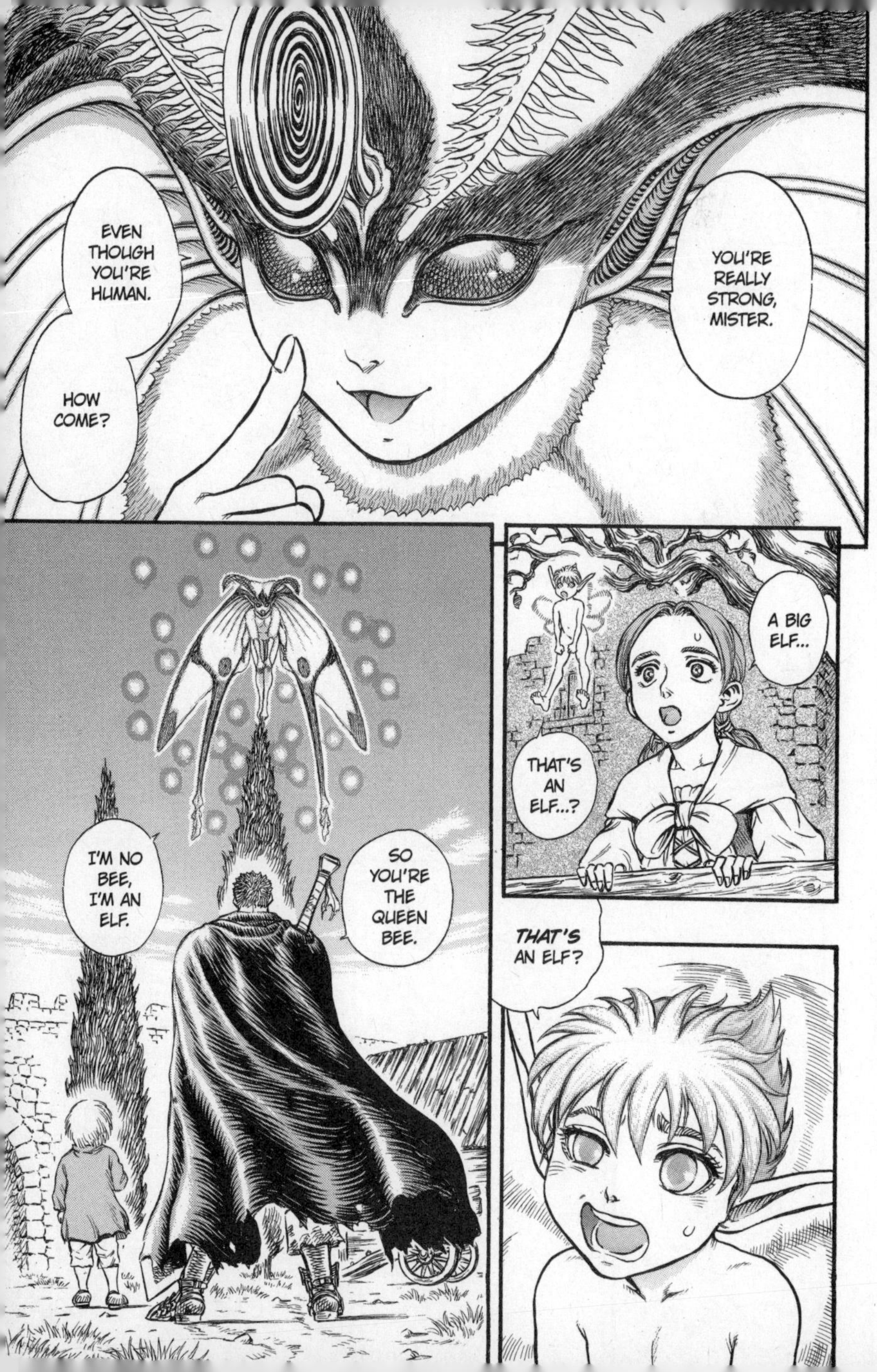
YOU'RE REALLY STRONG, MISTER.
EVEN THOUGH YOU'RE HUMAN.
HOW COME?
A BIG ELF...
THAT'S AN ELF...?
THAT'S AN ELF?
SO YOU'RE THE QUEEN BEE.
I'M NO BEE, I'M AN ELF.

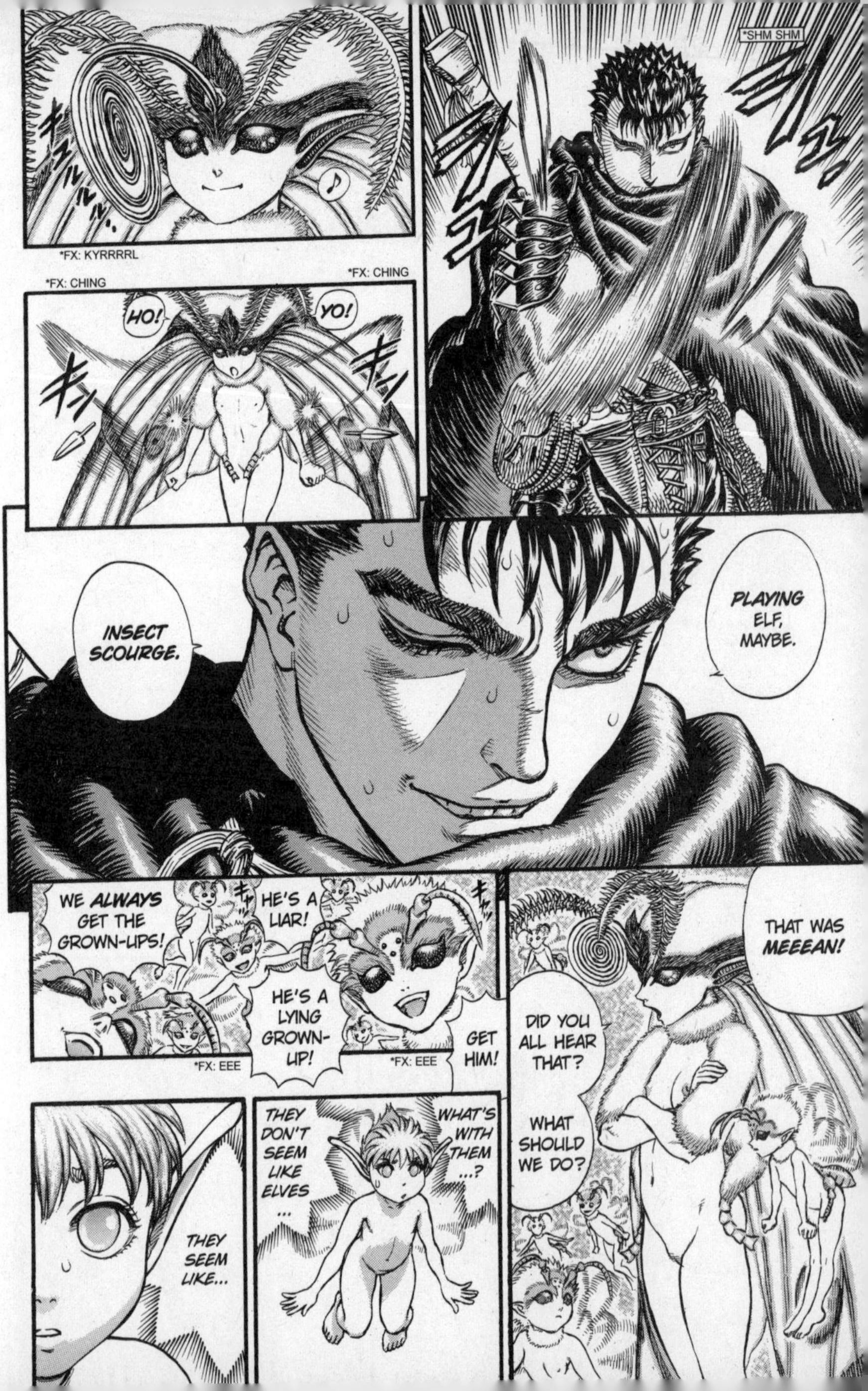
*SHM SHM
*FX: KYRRRRL
*FX: CHING
HO!
YO!
*FX: CHING
PLAYING ELF, MAYBE.
INSECT SCOURGE.
THAT WAS MEEEAN!
DID YOU ALL HEAR THAT?
WHAT SHOULD WE DO?
GET HIM!
HE'S A LIAR!
HE'S A LYING GROWN-UP!
WE ALWAYS GET THE GROWN-UPS!
*FX: EEE
*FX: EEE
WHAT'S WITH THEM ...?
THEY DON'T SEEM LIKE ELVES ...
THEY SEEM LIKE...

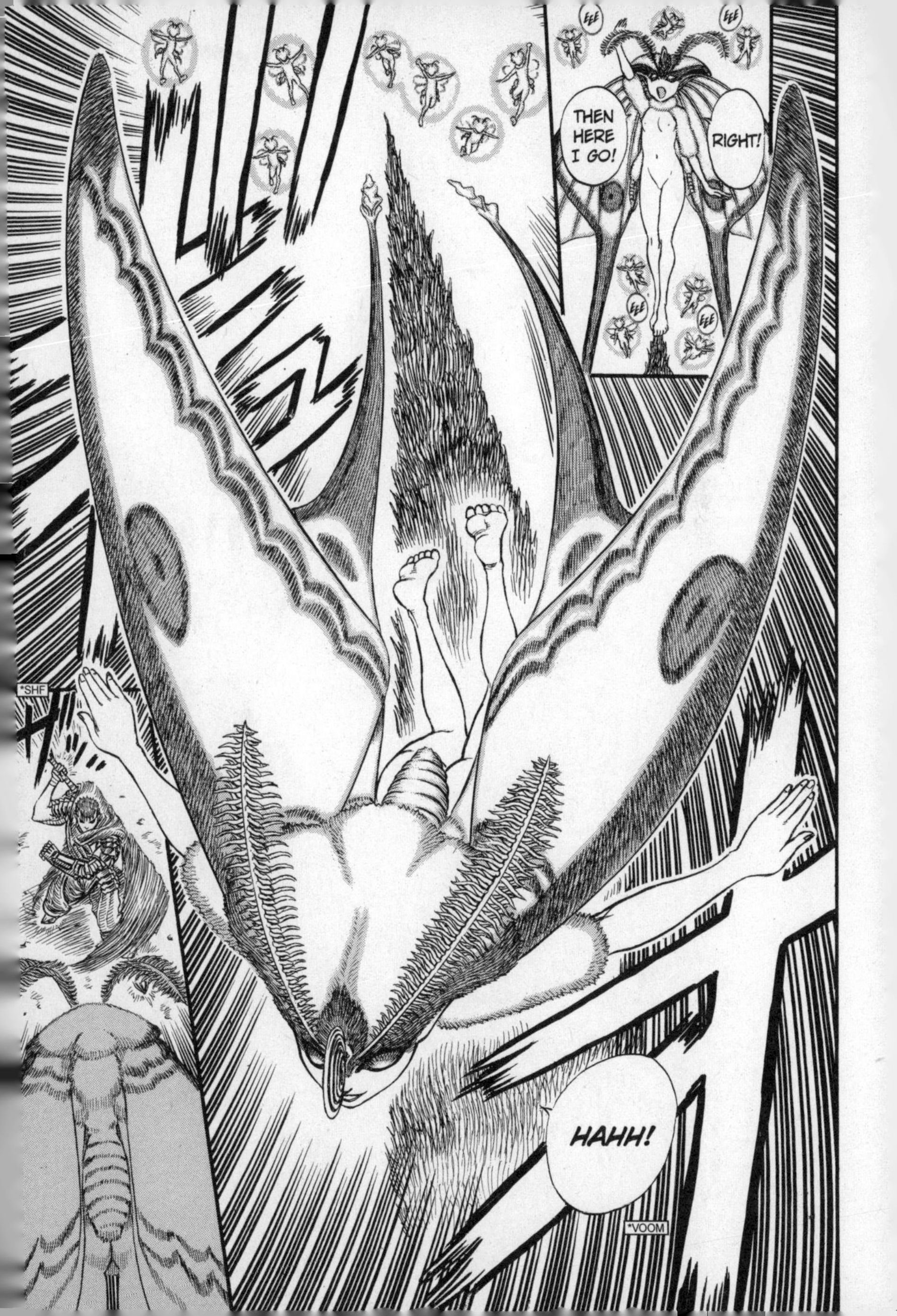
RIGHT!
THEN HERE I GO!
*SHF
HAHH!
*VOOM

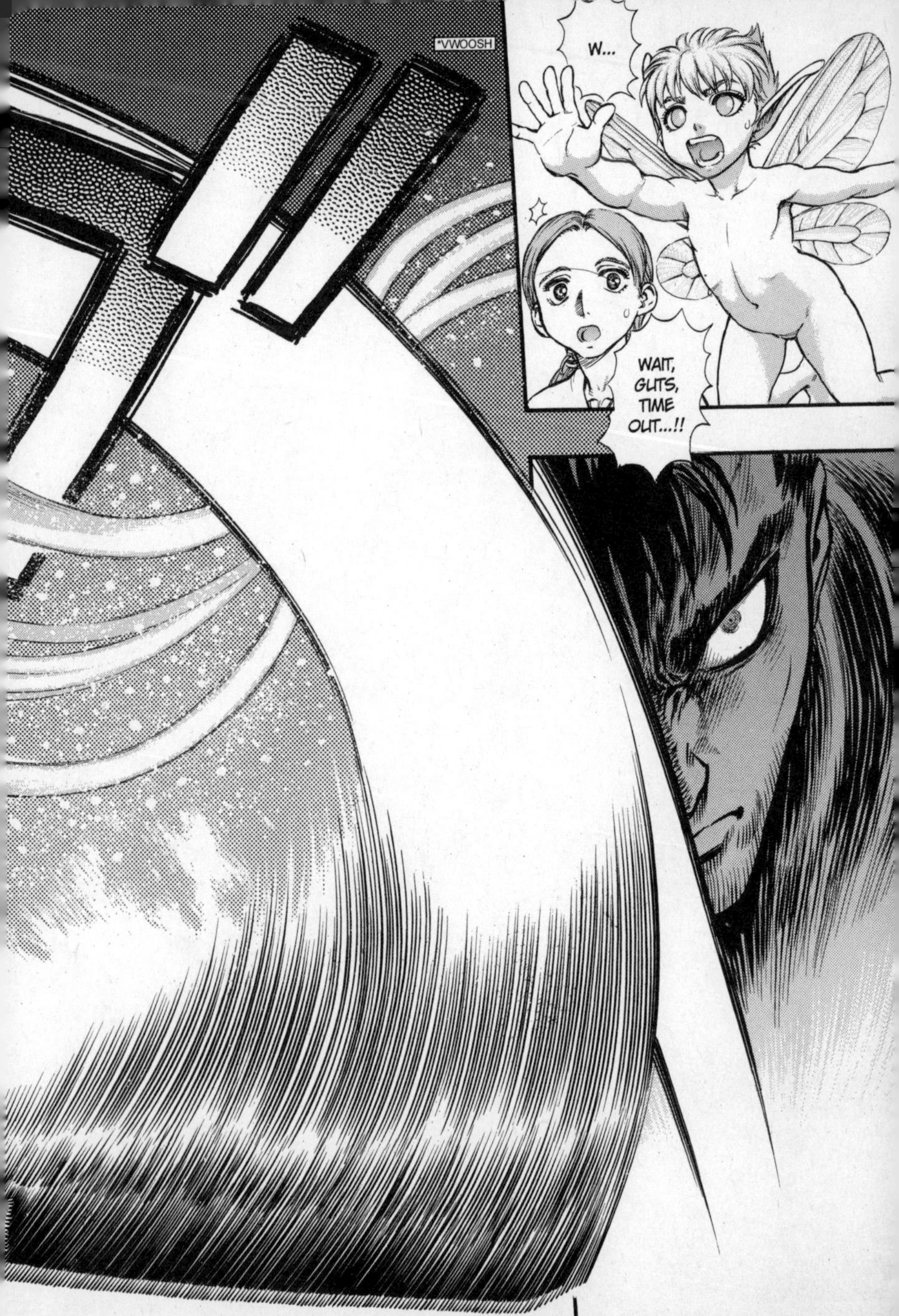
W...
WAIT, GUTS, TIME OUT...!!
*VWOOSH

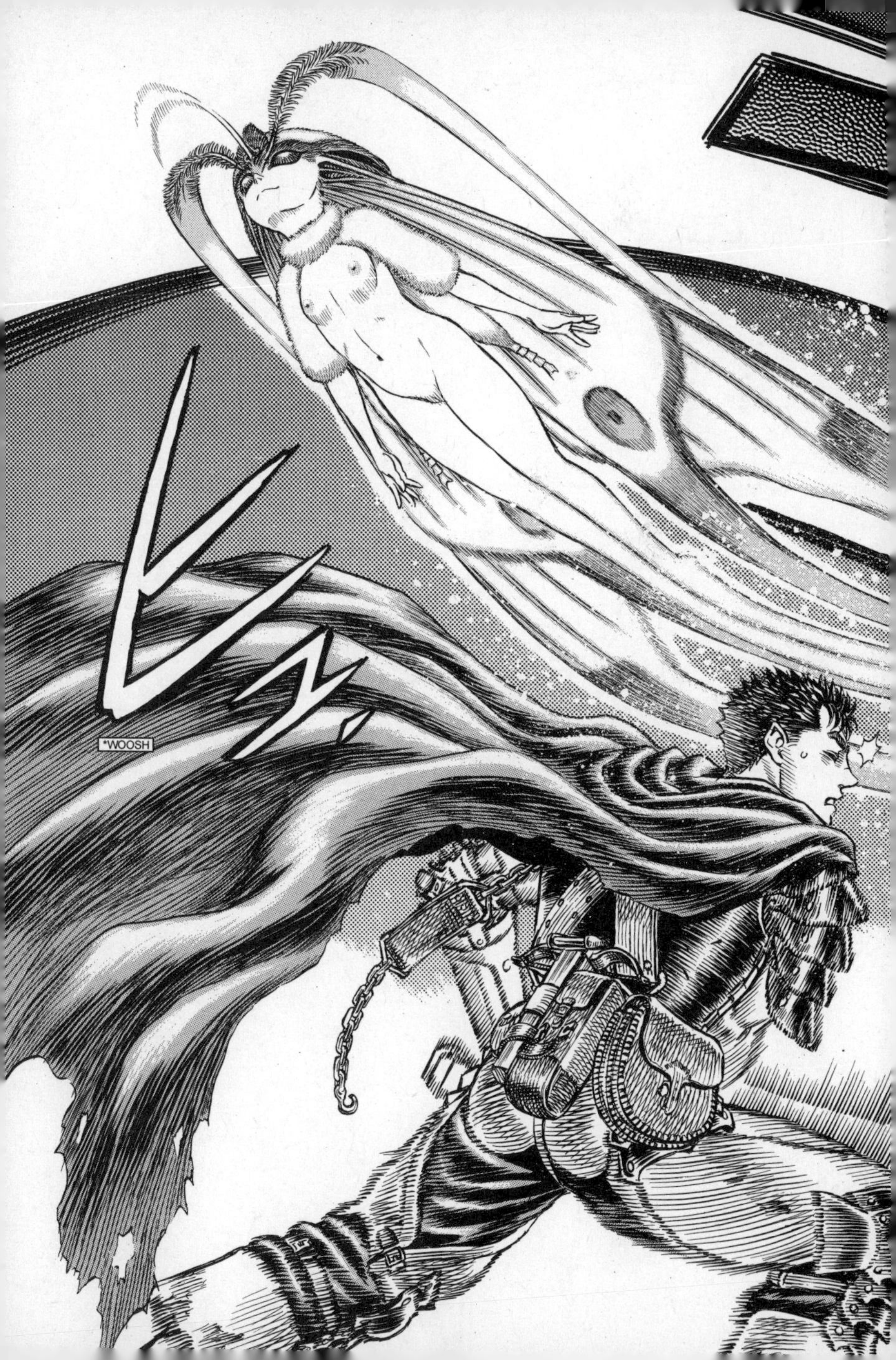
*WOOSH

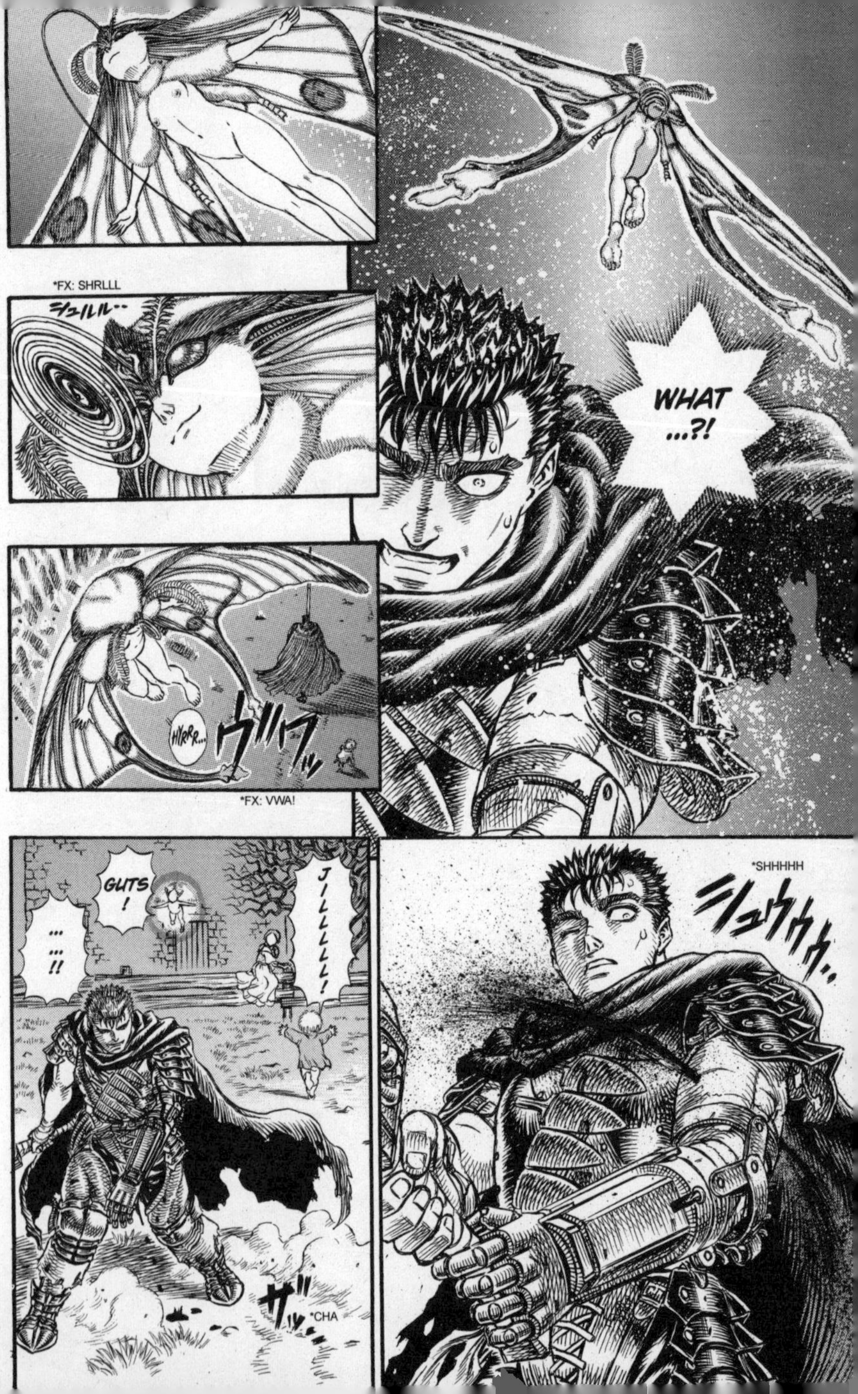
WHAT ...?!
*FX: SHRLLL
シュルル‥
HYRRR...
*FX: VWA!
*SHHHHH
シュウウウ‥
J-ILLLLLL!
GUTS!
... ... !!
*CHA

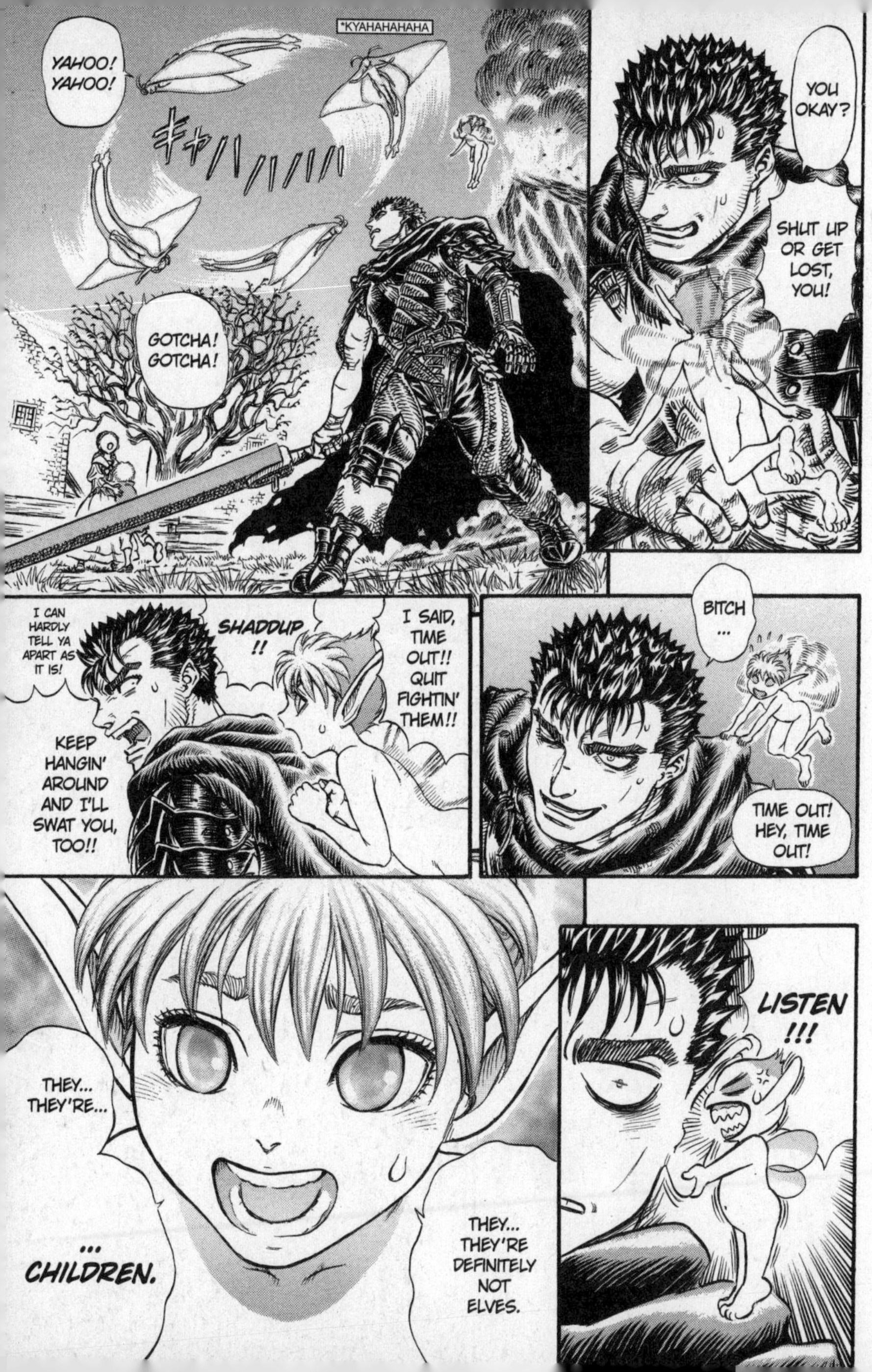
YOU OKAY?
SHUT UP OR GET LOST, YOU!
*KYAHAHAHAHA
YAHOO! YAHOO!
キャハハハハ
GOTCHA! GOTCHA!
BITCH...
TIME OUT! HEY, TIME OUT!
I SAID, TIME OUT!! QUIT FIGHTIN' THEM!!
SHADDUP!!
I CAN HARDLY TELL YA APART AS IT IS!
KEEP HANGIN' AROUND AND I'LL SWAT YOU, TOO!!
LISTEN!!!
THEY... THEY'RE...
... CHILDREN.
THEY... THEY'RE DEFINITELY NOT ELVES.

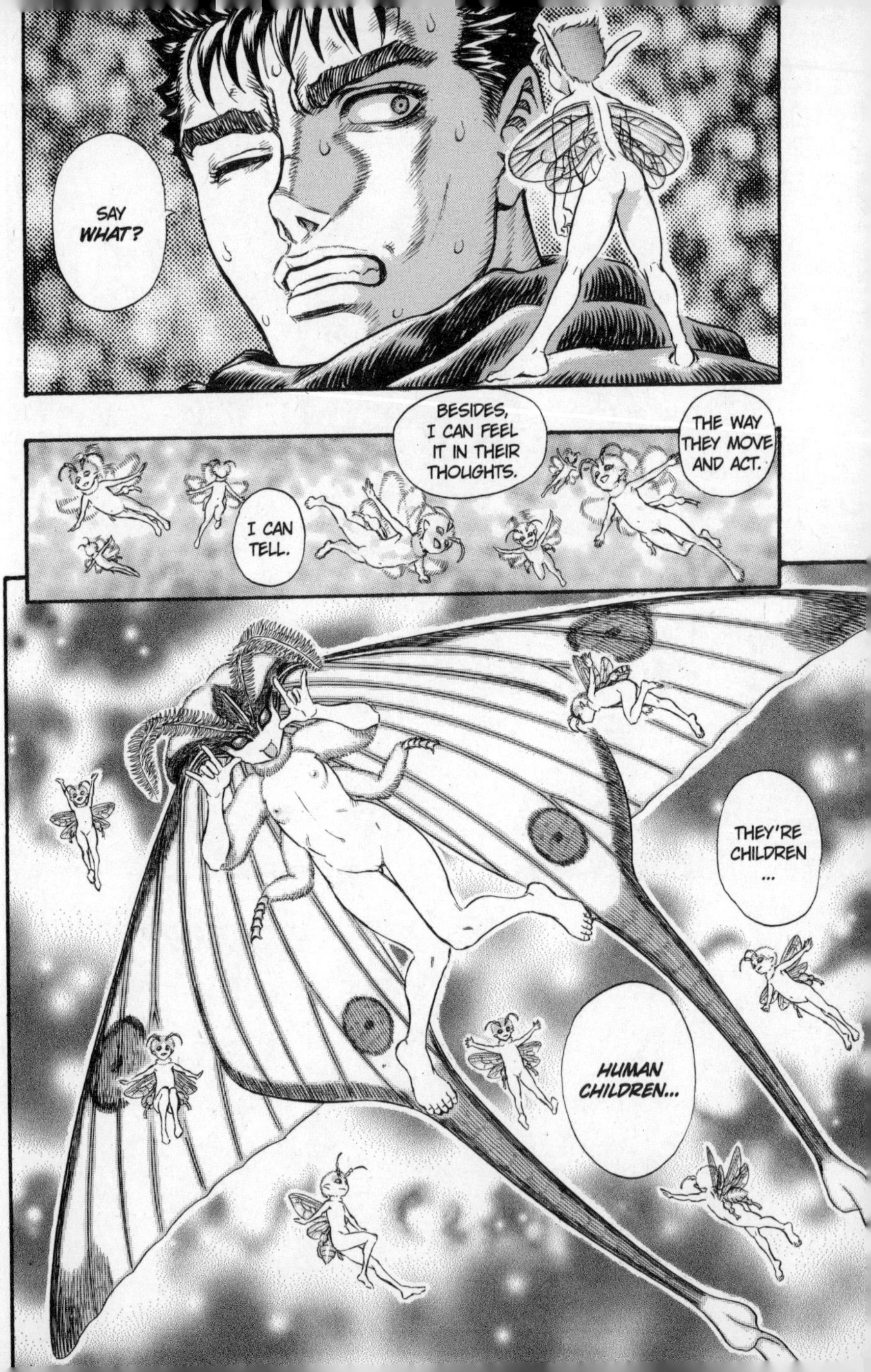
SAY WHAT?
THE WAY THEY MOVE AND ACT.
BESIDES, I CAN FEEL IT IN THEIR THOUGHTS.
I CAN TELL.
THEY'RE CHILDREN ...
HUMAN CHILDREN...

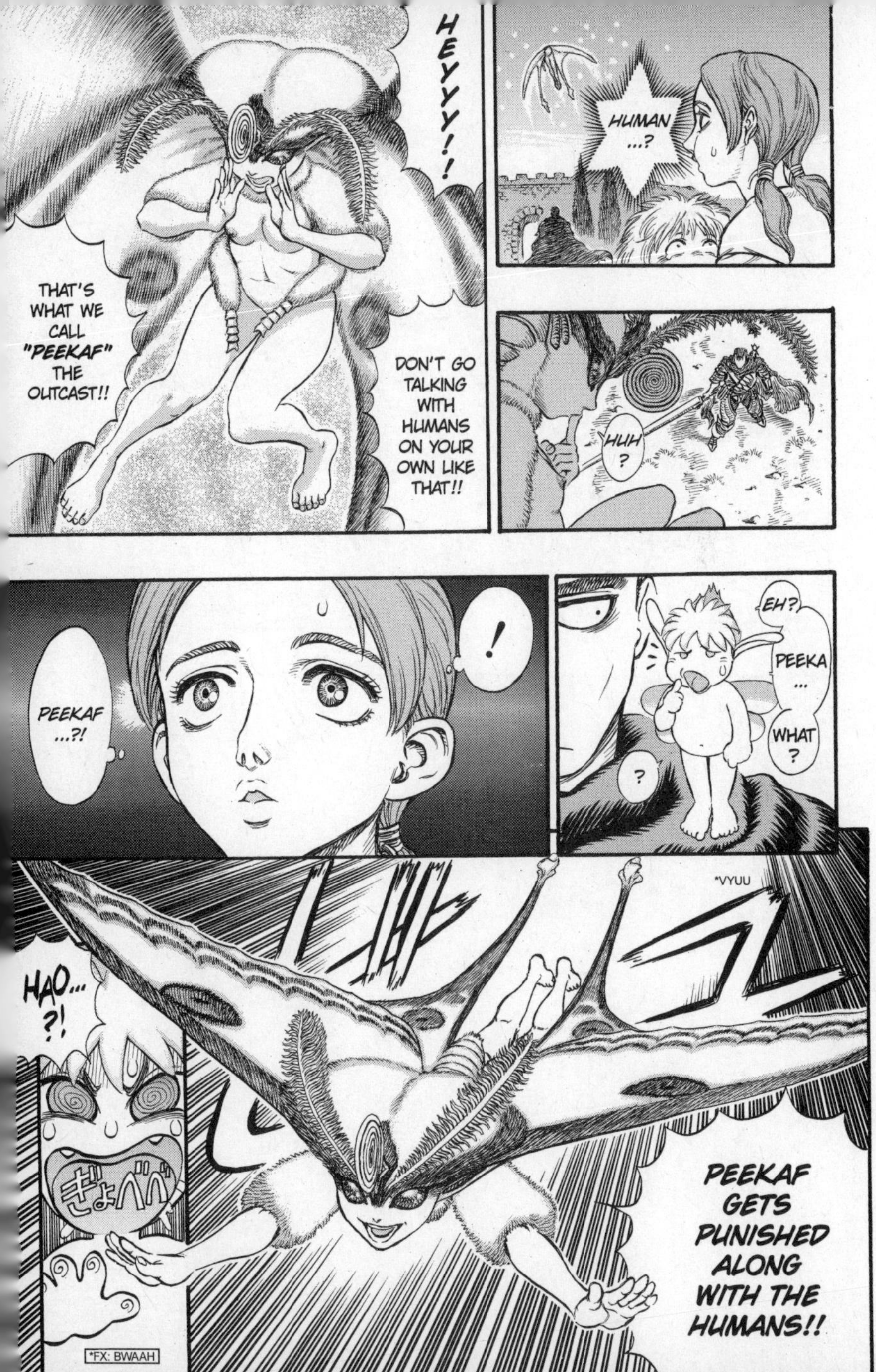

HUMAN ...?
HUH ?
HEYYY!!
DON'T GO TALKING WITH HUMANS ON YOUR OWN LIKE THAT!!
THAT'S WHAT WE CALL "PEEKAF" THE OUTCAST!!
EH?
PEEKA ... WHAT ?
?
!
PEEKAF ...?!
*VYUU
HAO... ?!
ぎょべべ
PEEKAF GETS PUNISHED ALONG WITH THE HUMANS!!
*FX: BWAAH

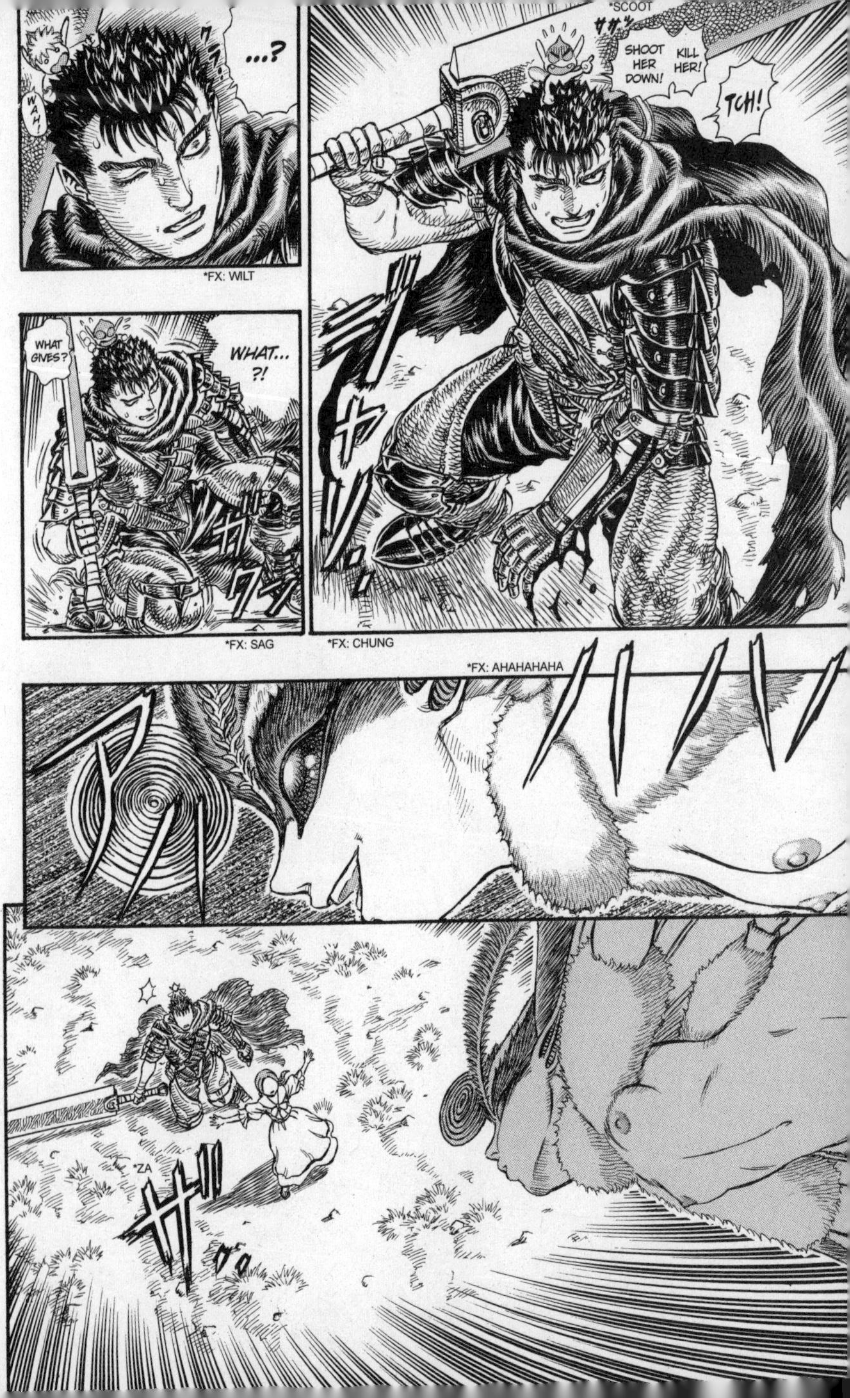
*SCOOT
KILL HER!
SHOOT HER DOWN!
TCH!
*FX: CHUNG
...?
WAH!
*FX: WILT
WHAT...?!
WHAT GIVES?
*FX: SAG
*FX: AHAHAHAHA
*ZA

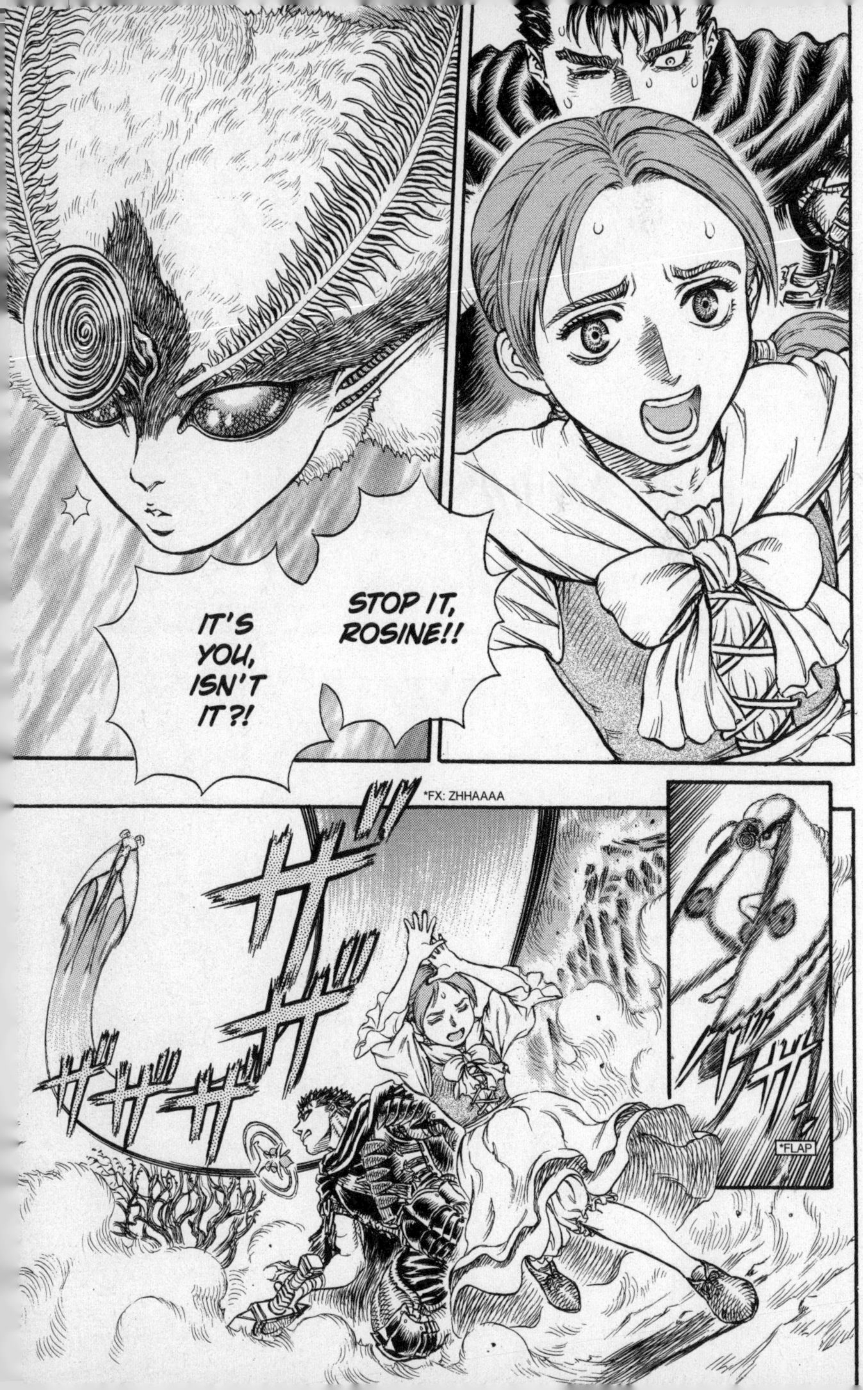
STOP IT, ROSINE!!
IT'S YOU, ISN'T IT?!
*FLAP
*FX: ZHHAAAA

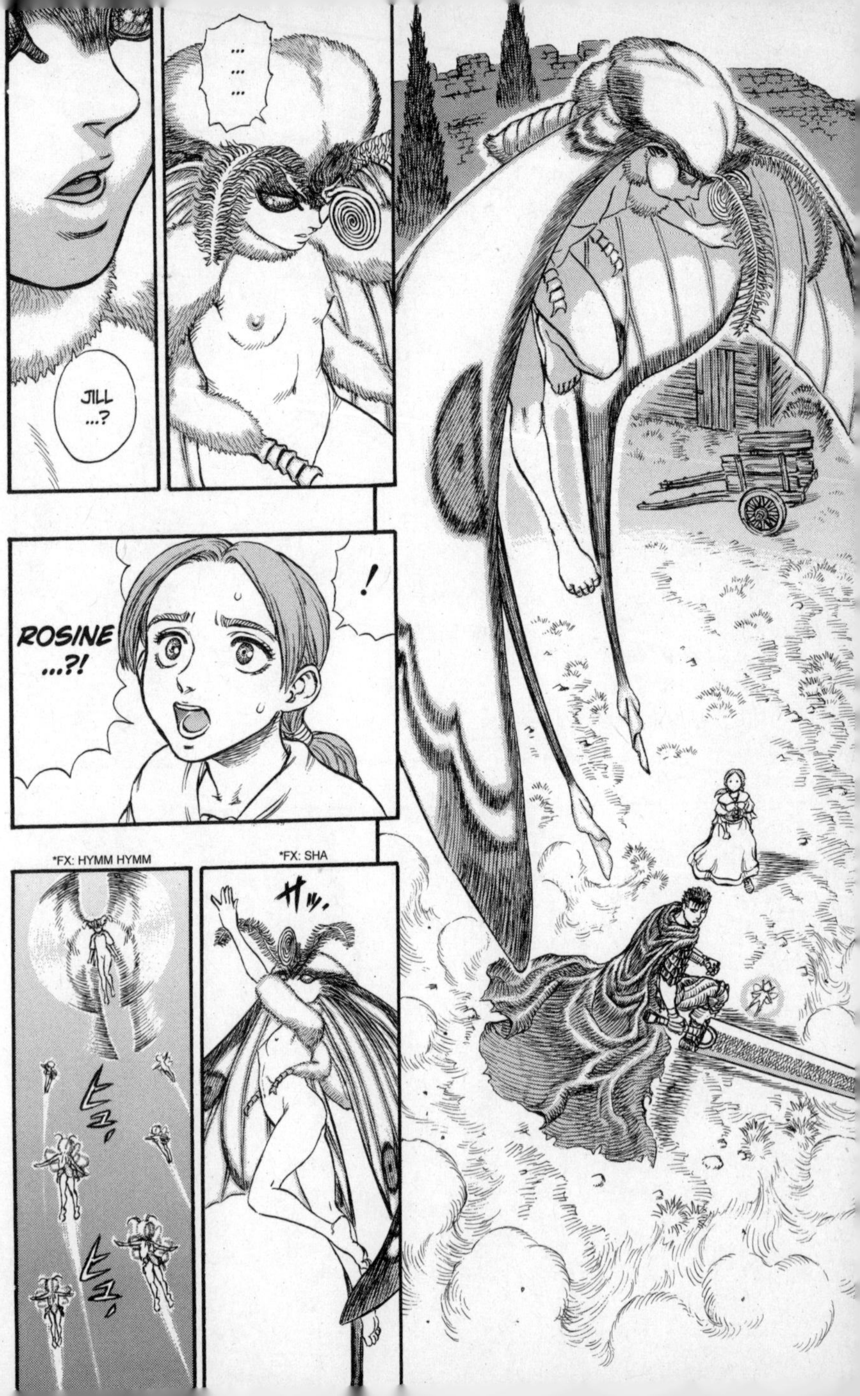
...
...
...
JILL ...?
!
ROSINE ...?!
*FX: SHA
*FX: HYMM HYMM

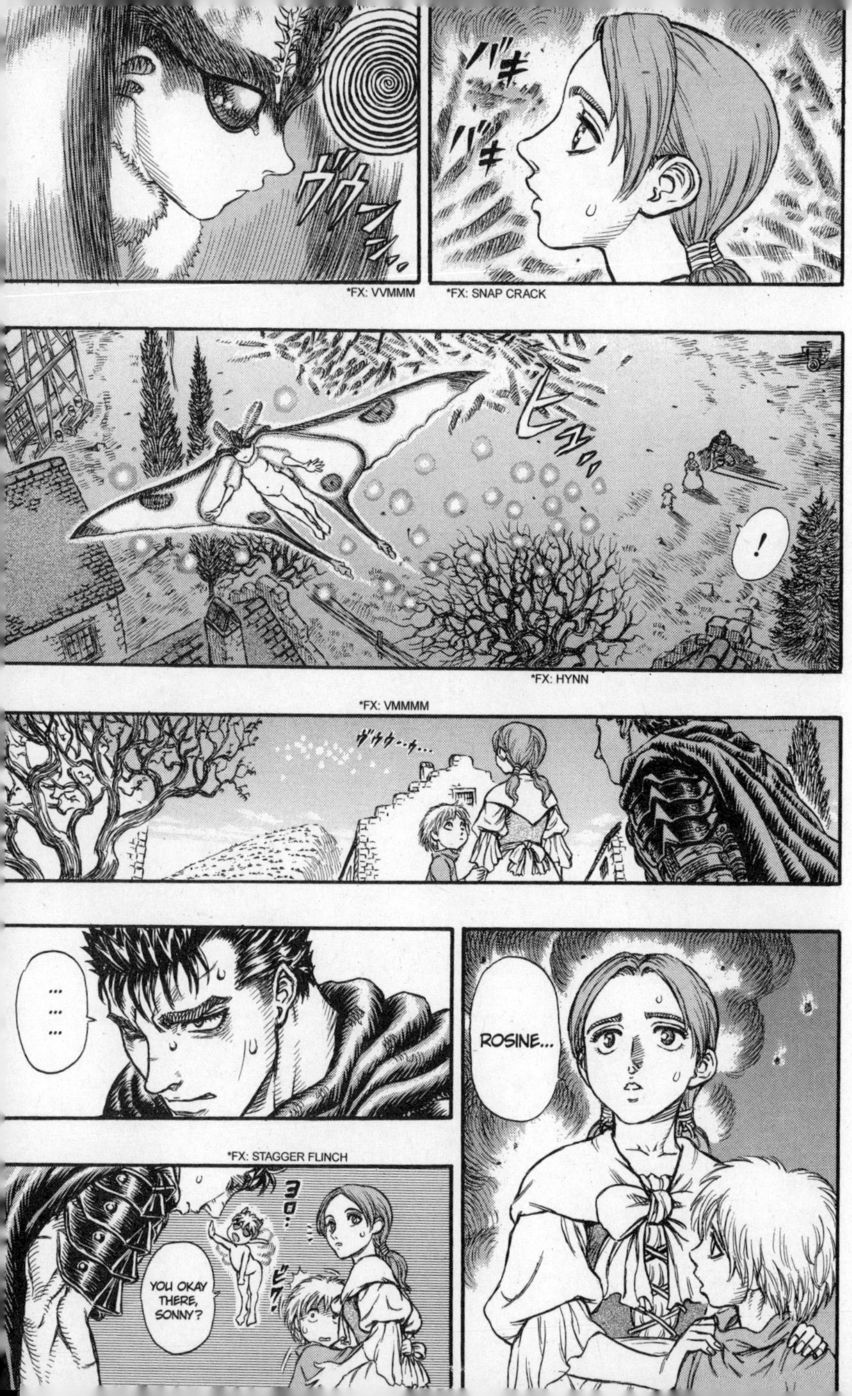

バギ バキ
*FX: SNAP CRACK
*FX: VVMMM
!
*FX: HYNN
*FX: VMMMM
ROSINE...
...
...
...
YOU OKAY THERE, SONNY?
*FX: STAGGER FLINCH

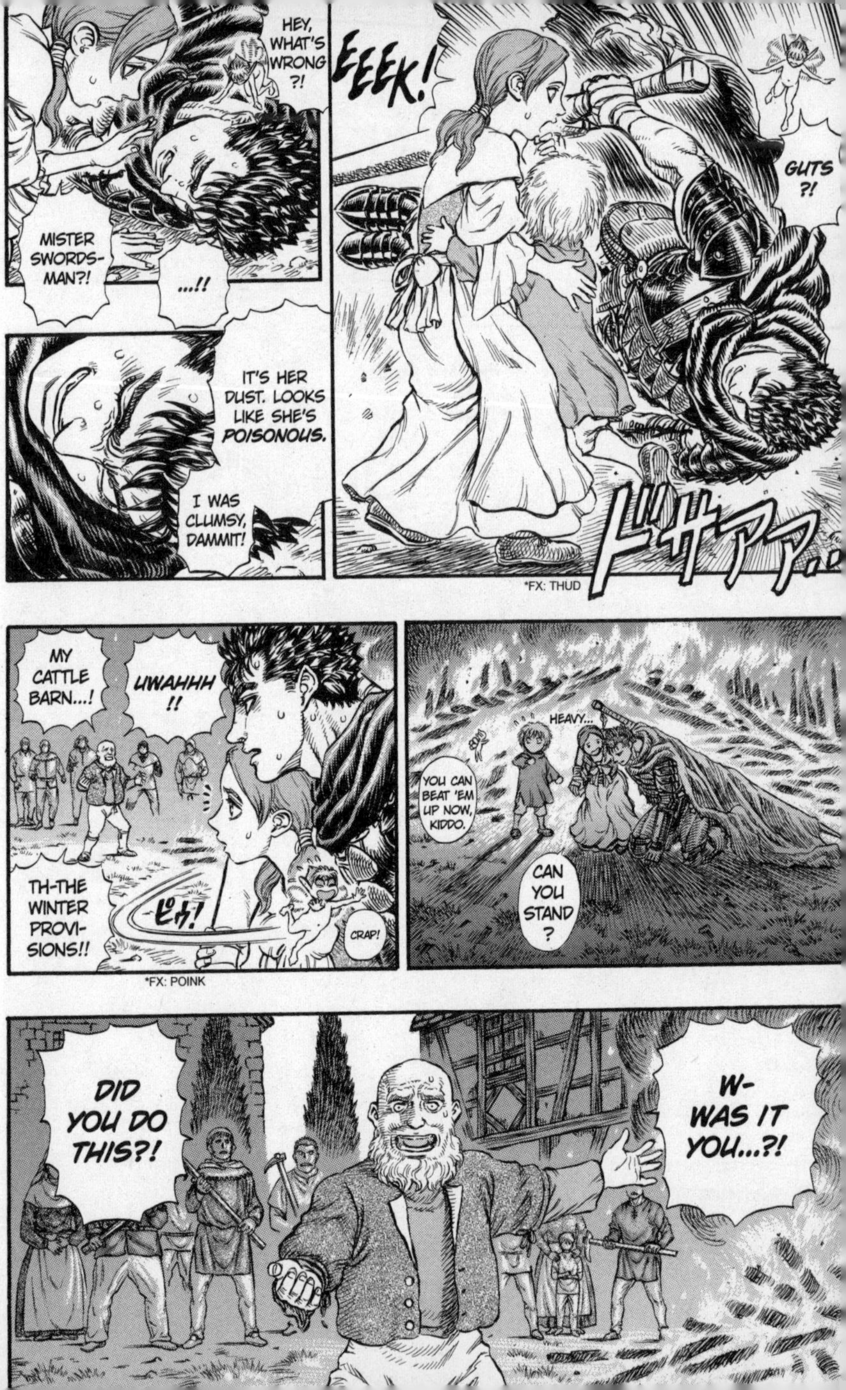
EEEK!
GUTS ?!
ドサアア..
*FX: THUD
HEY, WHAT'S WRONG ?!
...!!
MISTER SWORDS-MAN?!
IT'S HER DUST. LOOKS LIKE SHE'S POISONOUS.
I WAS CLUMSY, DAMMIT!
HEAVY...
YOU CAN BEAT 'EM UP NOW, KIDDO.
CAN YOU STAND ?
UWAHHH !!
MY CATTLE BARN...!
TH-THE WINTER PROVI-SIONS!!
ピゥ!
CRAP!
*FX: POINK
W-WAS IT YOU...?!
DID YOU DO THIS?!

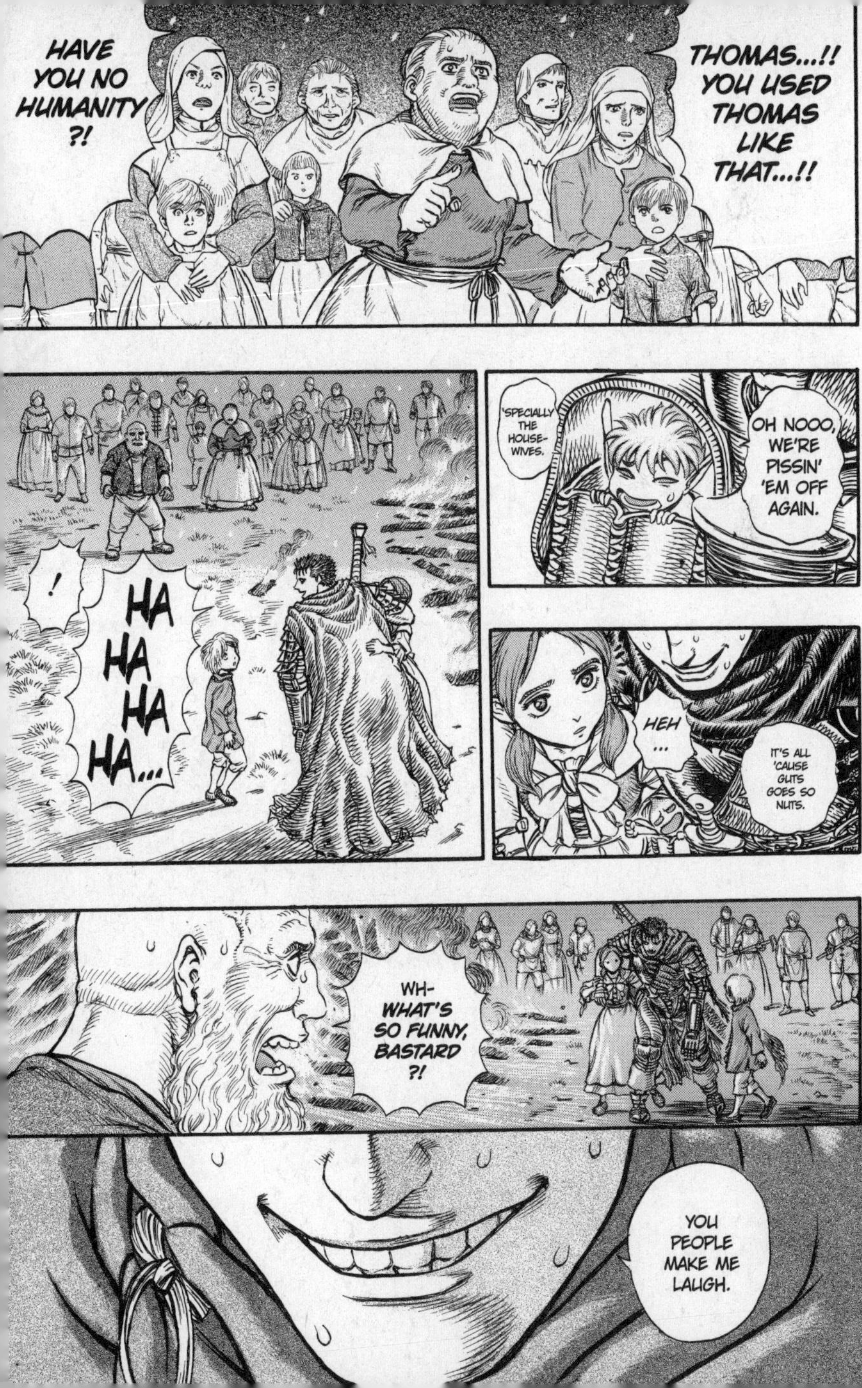
THOMAS...!! YOU USED THOMAS LIKE THAT...!!
HAVE YOU NO HUMANITY ?!
OH NOOO, WE'RE PISSIN' 'EM OFF AGAIN.
'SPECIALLY THE HOUSE-WIVES.
HEH ...
IT'S ALL 'CAUSE GUTS GOES SO NUTS.
HA HA HA HA...
!
WH- WHAT'S SO FUNNY, BASTARD ?!
YOU PEOPLE MAKE ME LAUGH.

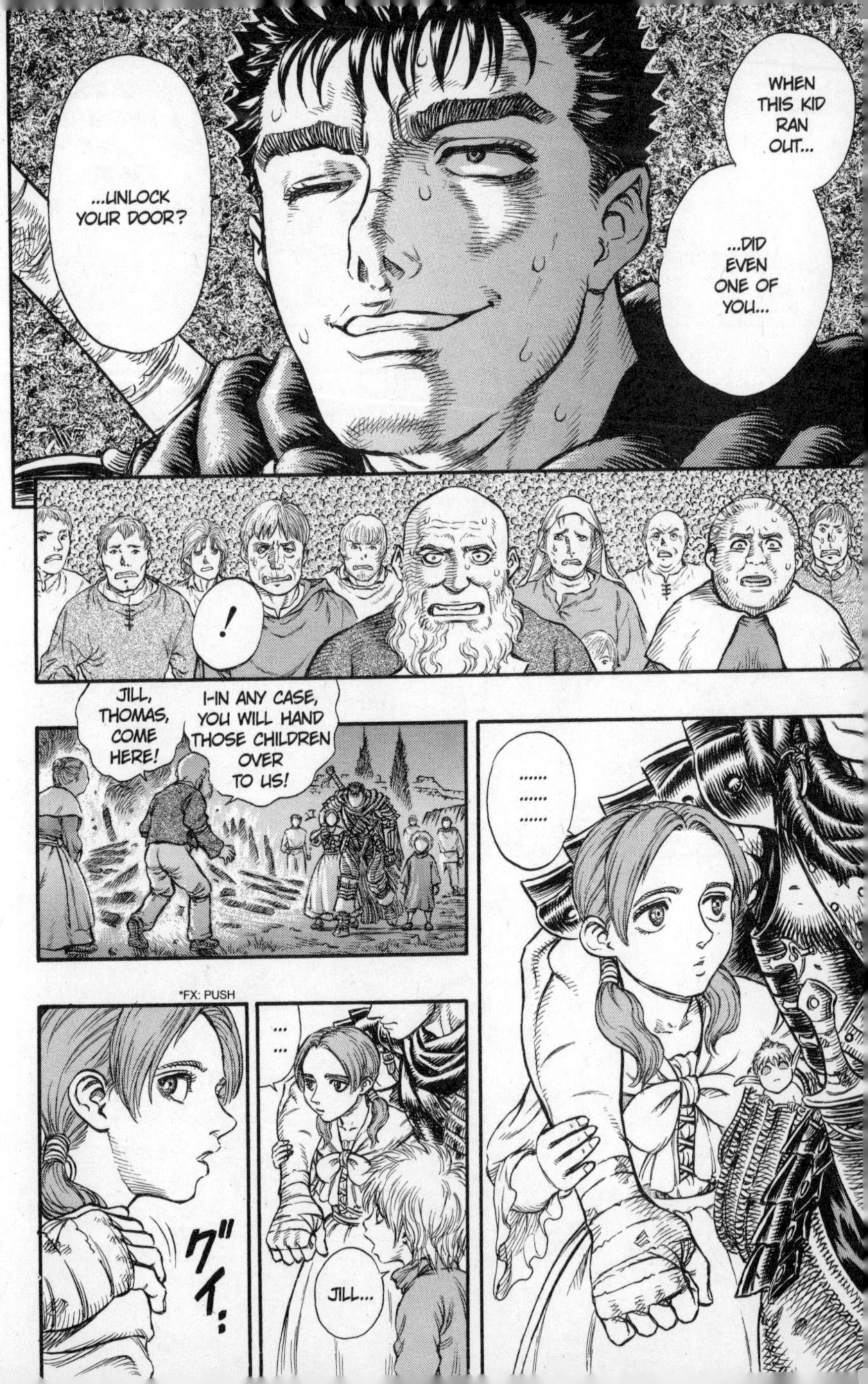
WHEN THIS KID RAN OUT...
...DID EVEN ONE OF YOU...
...UNLOCK YOUR DOOR?
!
......
......
......
I-IN ANY CASE, YOU WILL HAND THOSE CHILDREN OVER TO US!
JILL, THOMAS, COME HERE!
...
...
JILL...
グイ
*FX: PUSH

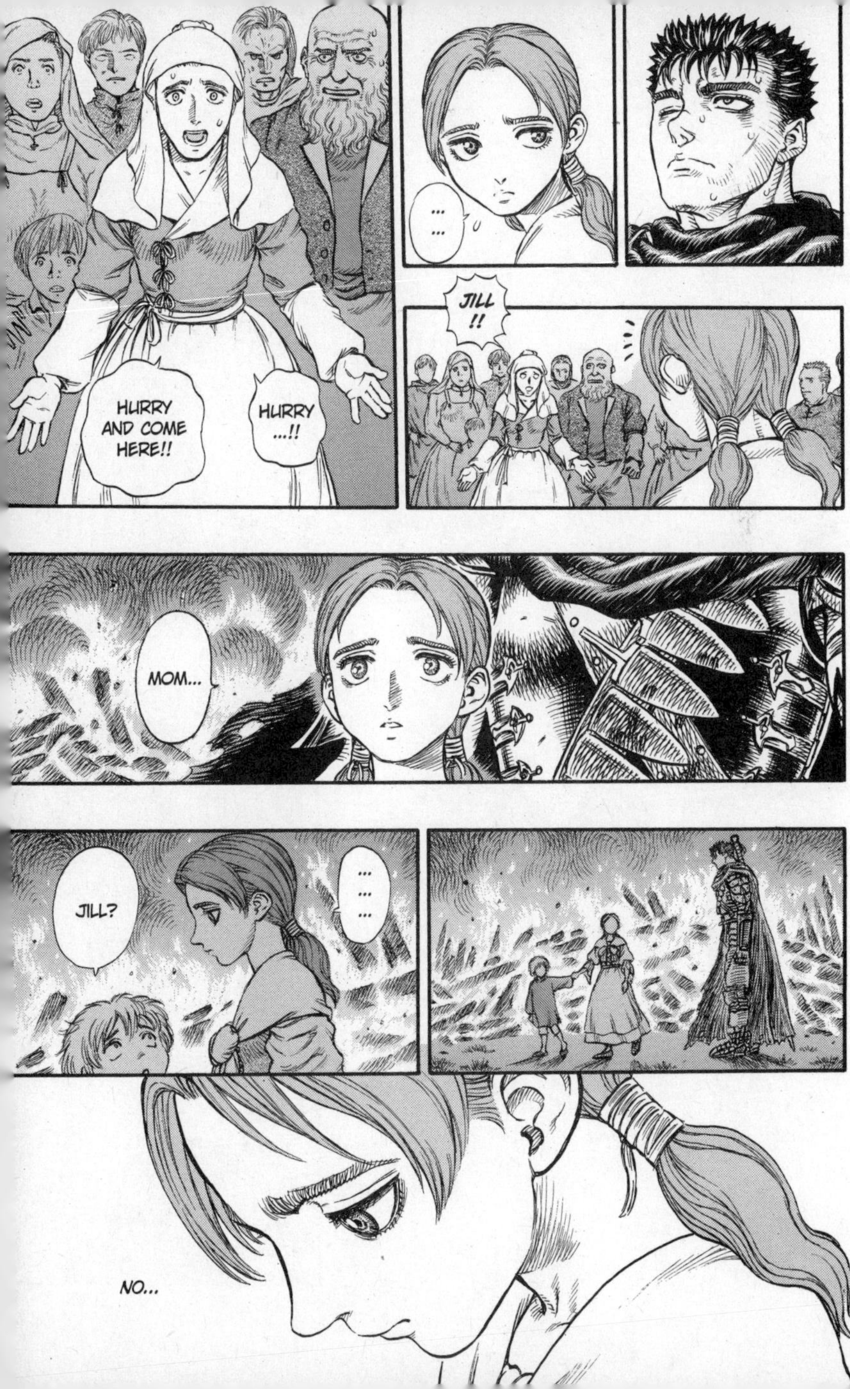
... ...
JILL !!
HURRY ...!!
HURRY AND COME HERE!!
MOM...
... ...
JILL?
NO...

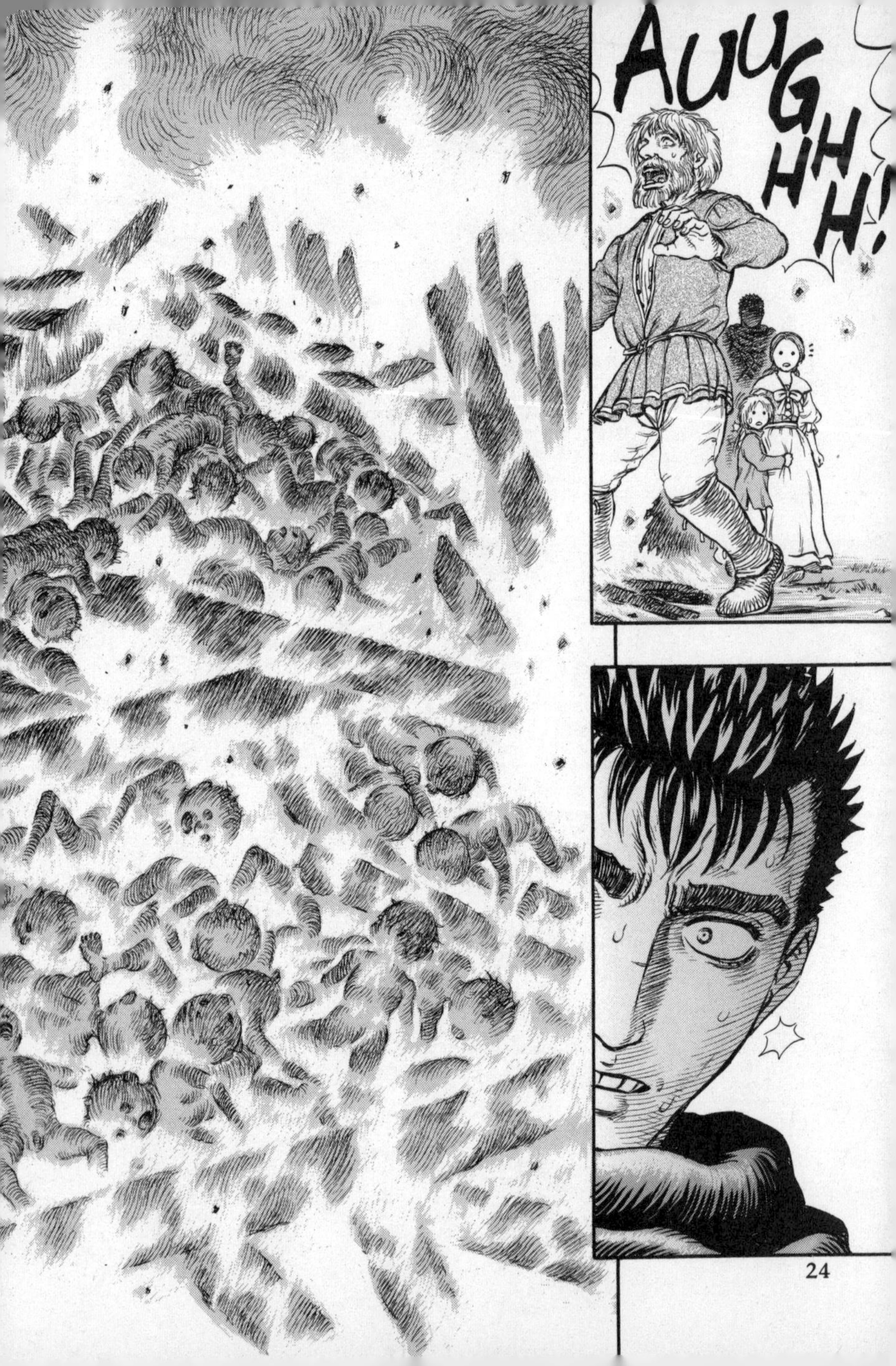
AUUGHHHH!

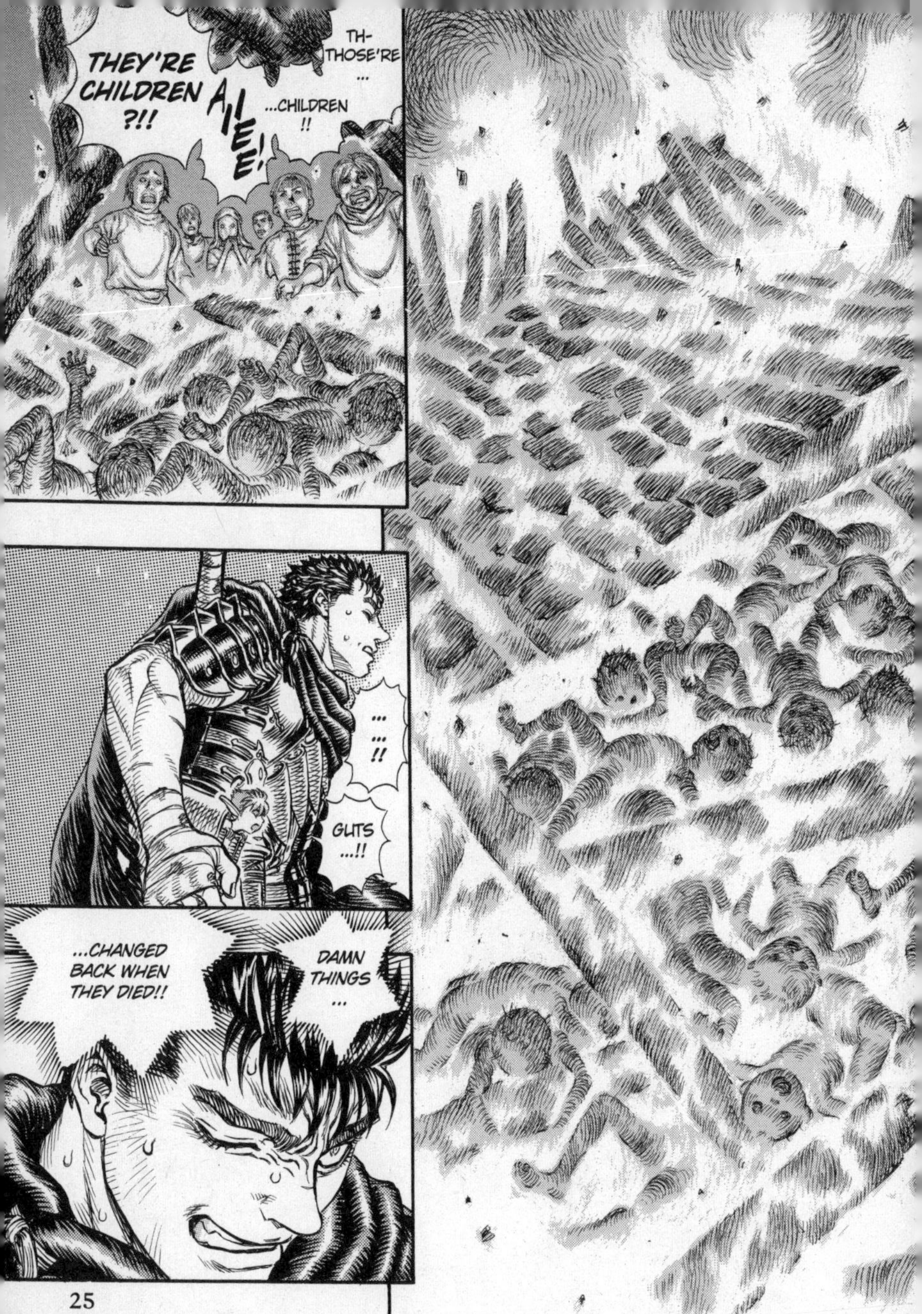
TH- THOSE'RE ...
...CHILDREN !!
AIEEE!
THEY'RE CHILDREN ?!!
... ... !!
GUTS ...!!
DAMN THINGS ...
...CHANGED BACK WHEN THEY DIED!!

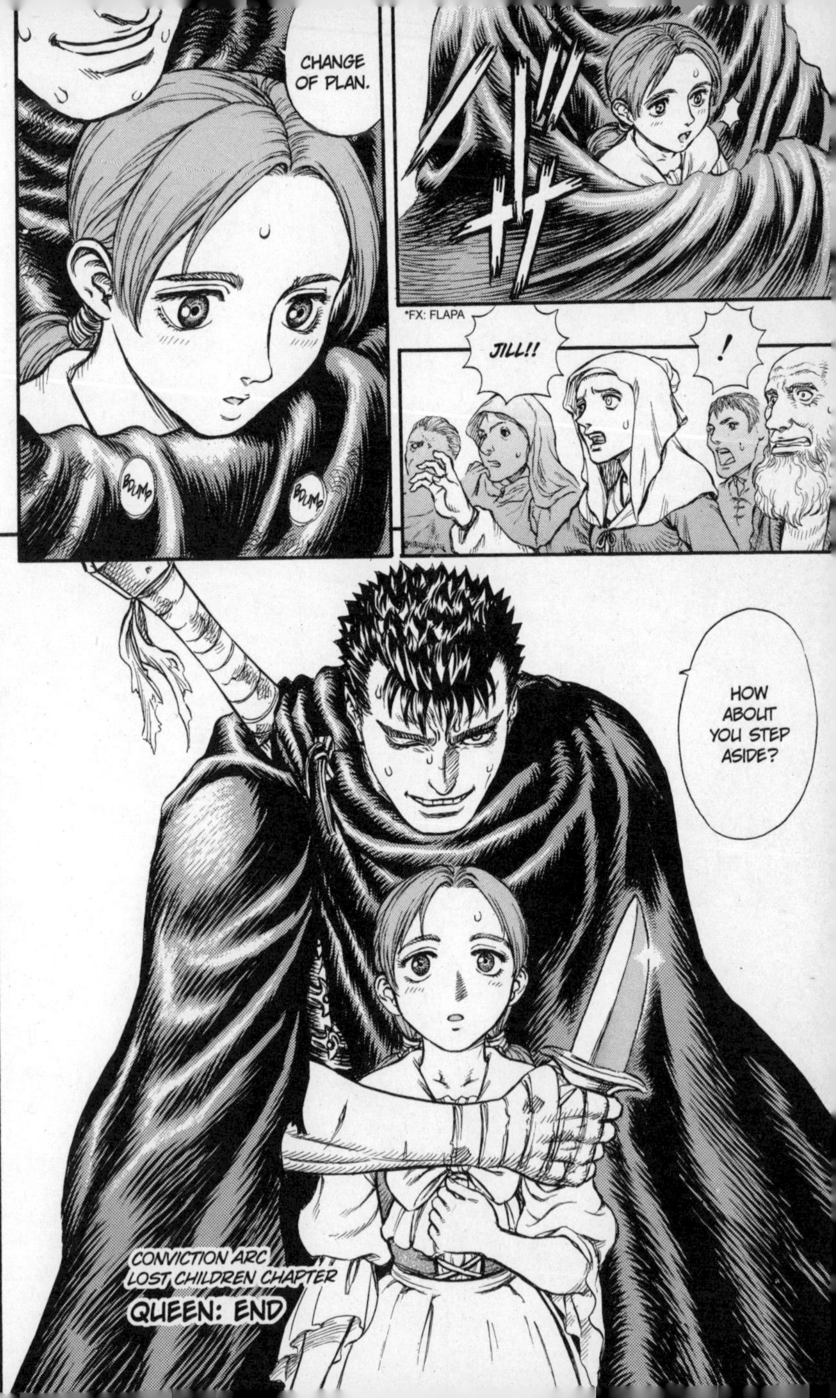

*FX: FLAPA
!
JILL!!
CHANGE OF PLAN.
BOUMP
BOUMP
HOW ABOUT YOU STEP ASIDE?
CONVICTION ARC
LOST CHILDREN CHAPTER
QUEEN: END

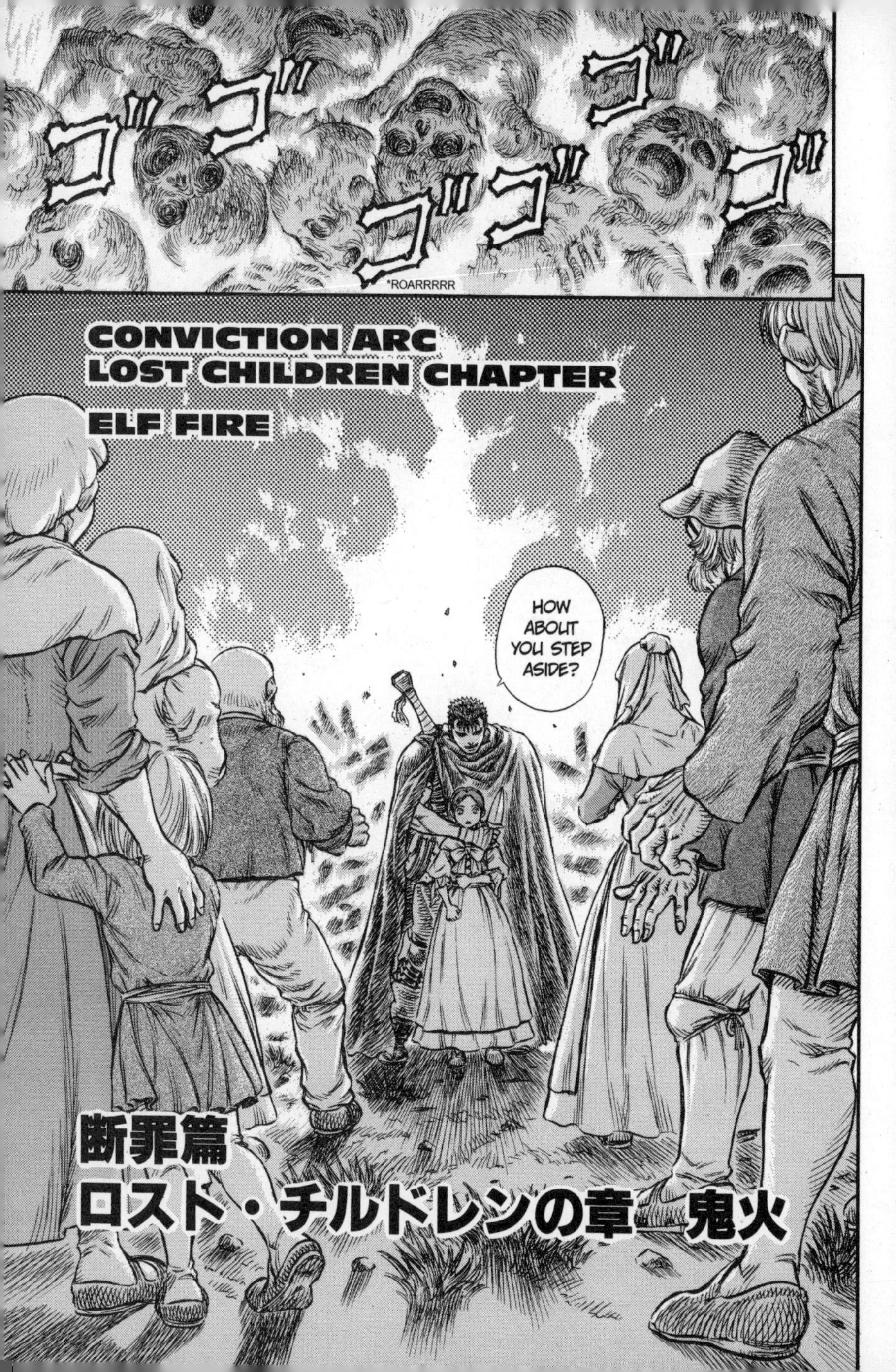
ゴゴゴゴゴゴ
*ROARRRRR
CONVICTION ARC
LOST CHILDREN CHAPTER
ELF FIRE
HOW ABOUT YOU STEP ASIDE?
断罪篇
ロスト・チルドレンの章 鬼火

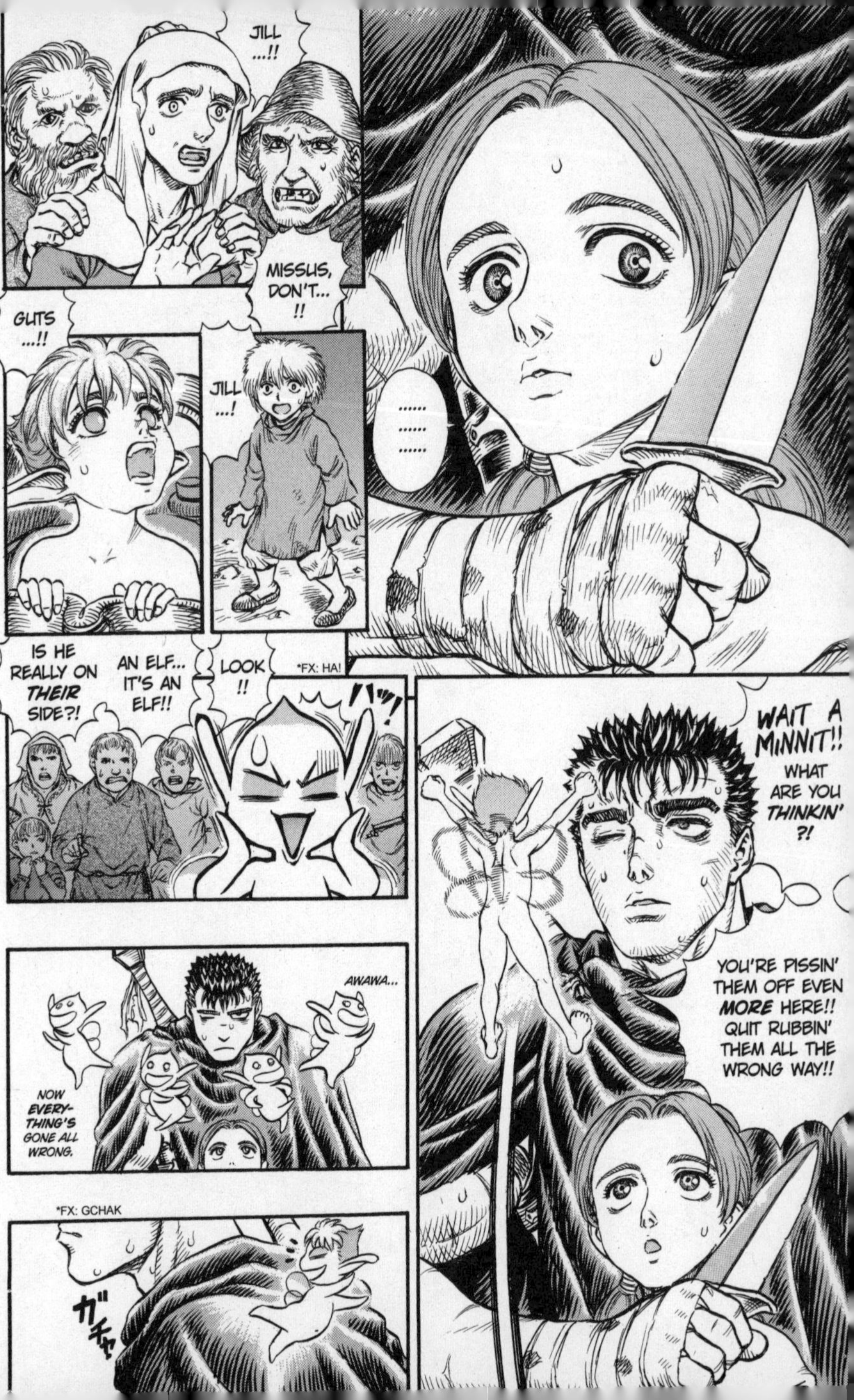

......
......
......
JILL
...!!
MISSUS, DON'T...
!!
JILL
...!
GUTS
...!!
WAIT A MINNIT!!
WHAT ARE YOU THINKIN'?!
YOU'RE PISSIN' THEM OFF EVEN MORE HERE!! QUIT RUBBIN' THEM ALL THE WRONG WAY!!
*FX: HA!
LOOK!!
AN ELF... IT'S AN ELF!!
IS HE REALLY ON THEIR SIDE?!
AWAWA...
NOW EVERY-THING'S GONE ALL WRONG.
*FX: GCHAK

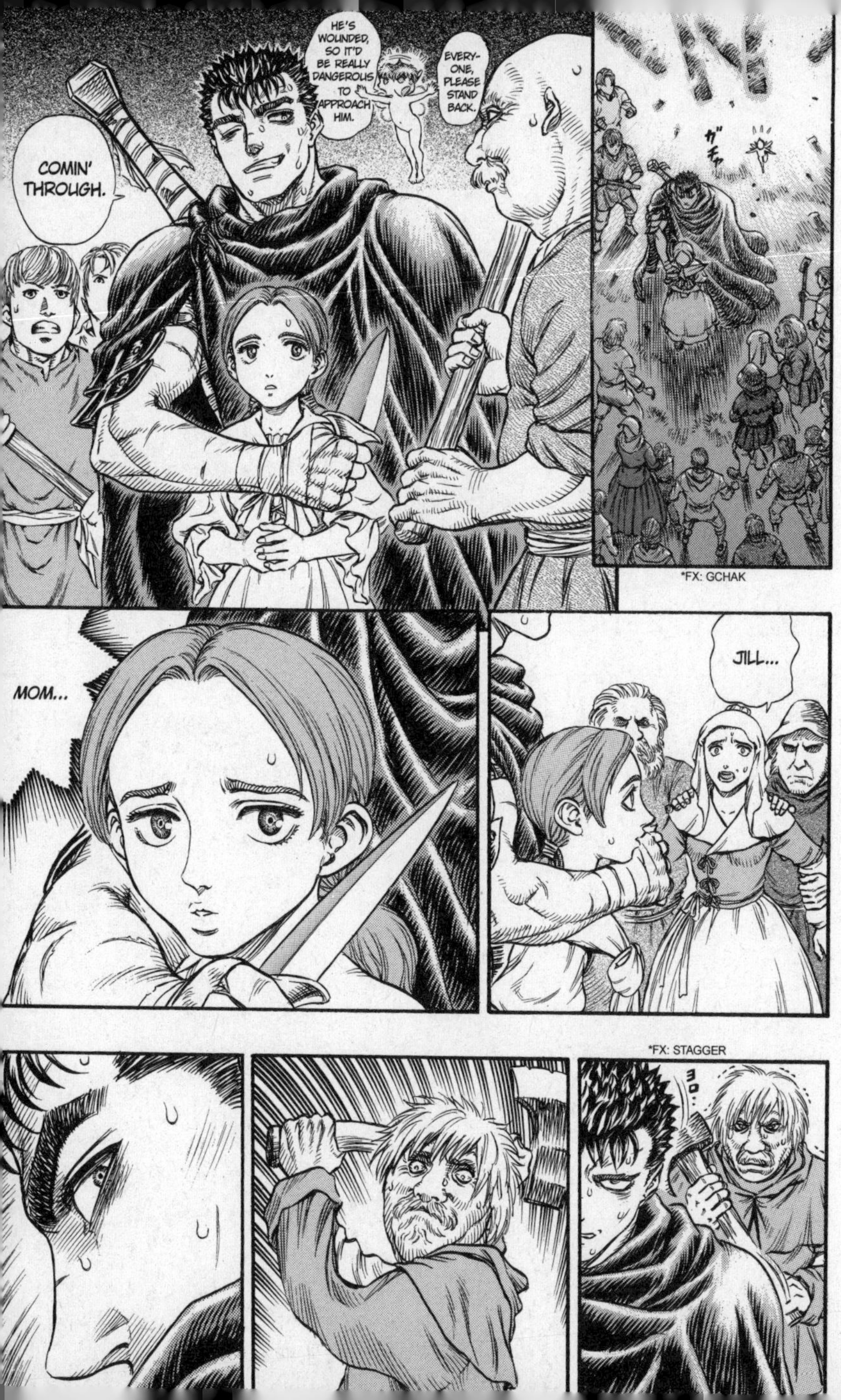
*FX: GCHAK
EVERY-ONE, PLEASE STAND BACK.
HE'S WOUNDED, SO IT'D BE REALLY DANGEROUS TO APPROACH HIM.
COMIN' THROUGH.
JILL...
MOM...
*FX: STAGGER

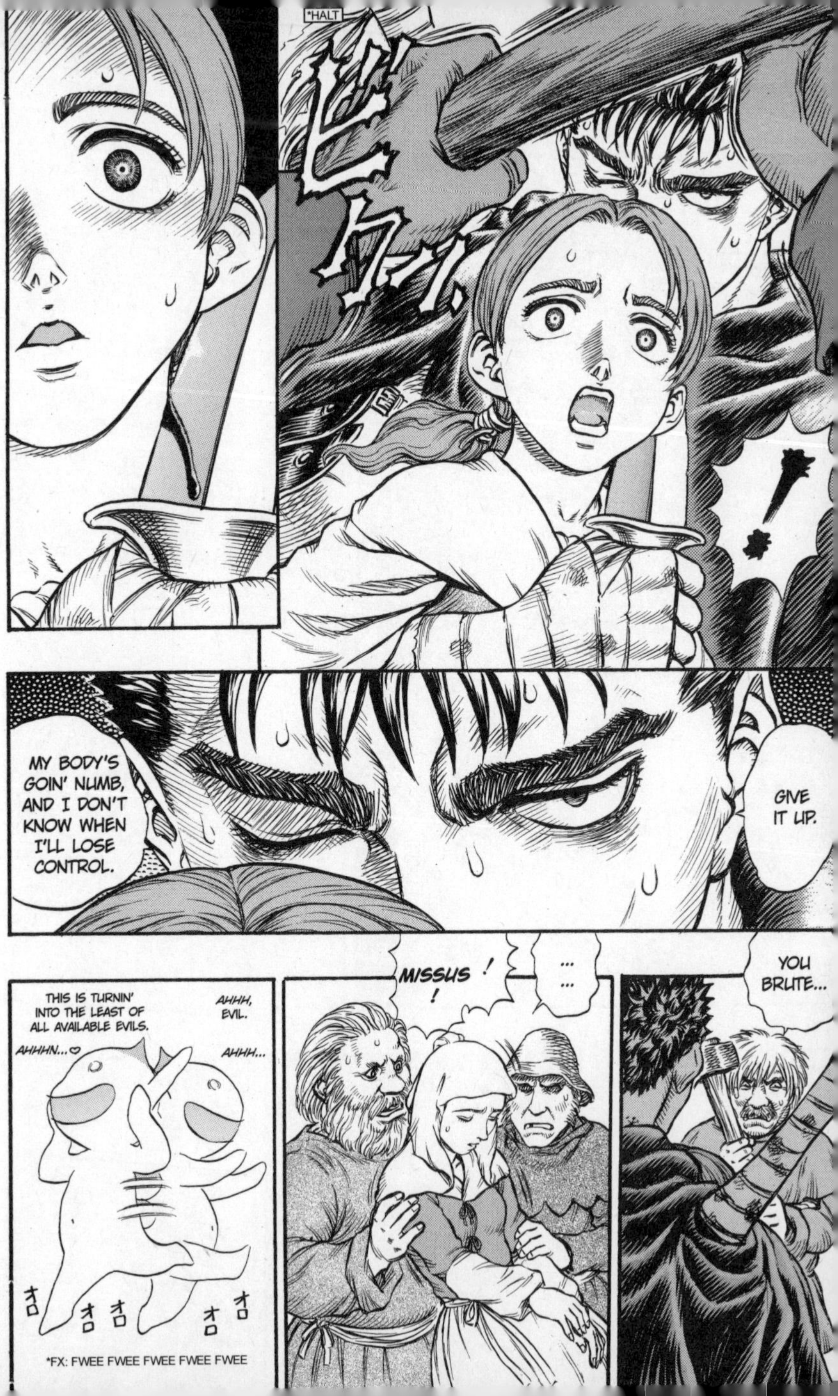
*HALT
GIVE IT UP.
MY BODY'S GOIN' NUMB, AND I DON'T KNOW WHEN I'LL LOSE CONTROL.
YOU BRUTE...
...
...
MISSUS!
!
AHHH, EVIL.
THIS IS TURNIN' INTO THE LEAST OF ALL AVAILABLE EVILS.
AHHH...
AHHHN...♡
*FX: FWEE FWEE FWEE FWEE FWEE

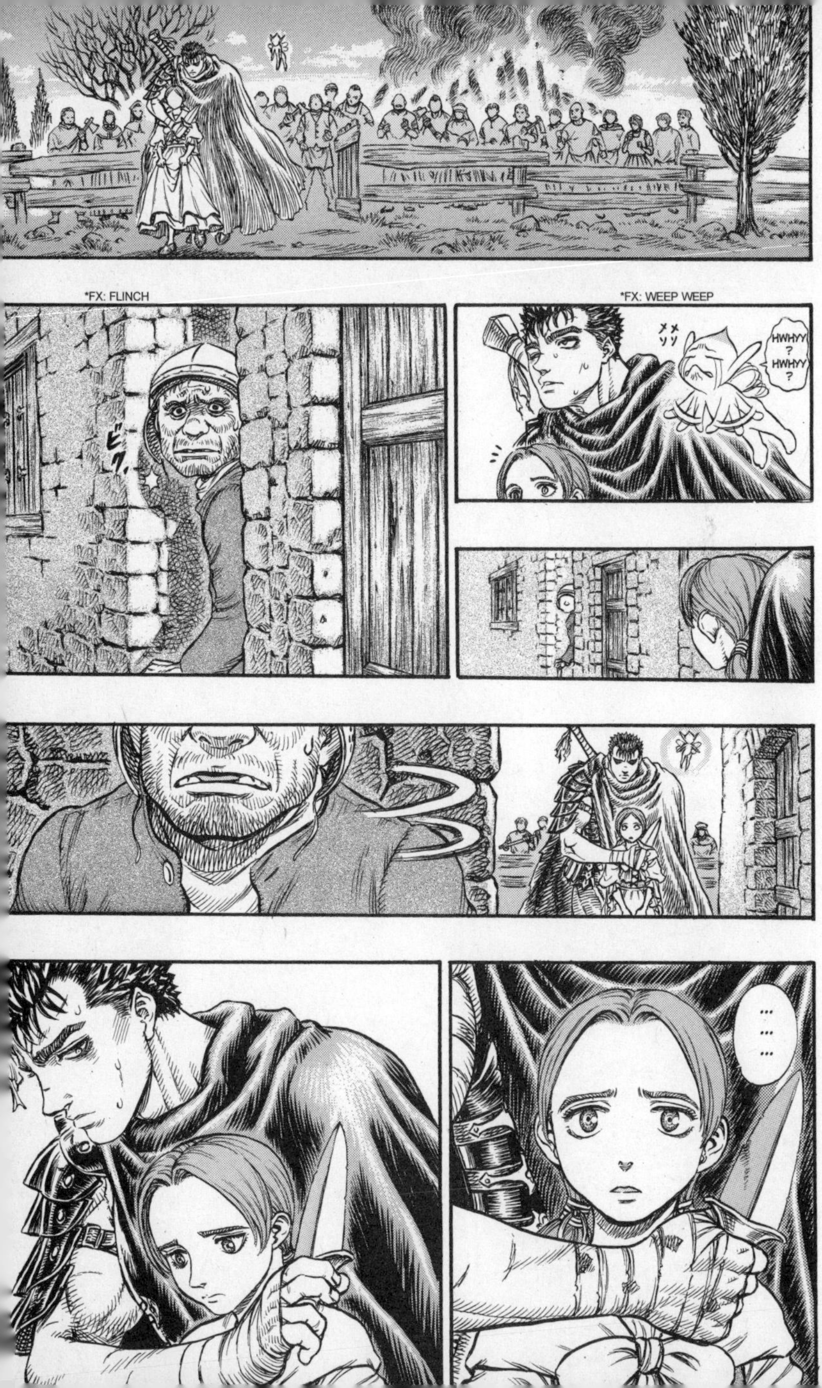
*FX: WEEP WEEP
メソメソ
HWHYY? HWHYY?
*FX: FLINCH
ビクッ
...
...
...

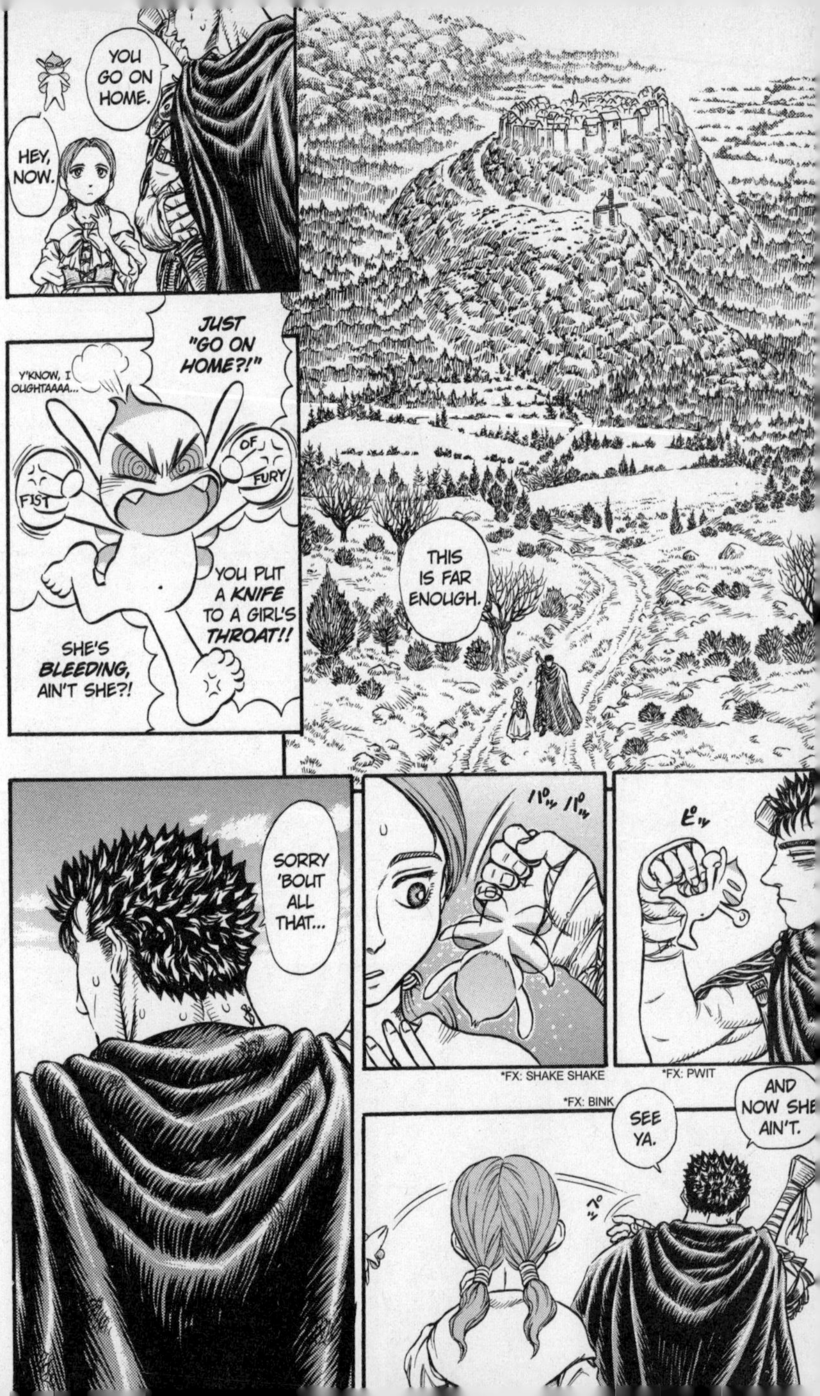

THIS IS FAR ENOUGH.
YOU GO ON HOME.
HEY, NOW.
JUST "GO ON HOME?!"
Y'KNOW, I OUGHTAAAA...
FIST
OF FURY
YOU PUT A KNIFE TO A GIRL'S THROAT!!
SHE'S BLEEDING, AIN'T SHE?!
ピッ
*FX: PWIT
パッ パッ
*FX: SHAKE SHAKE
AND NOW SHE AIN'T.
SEE YA.
*FX: BINK
SORRY 'BOUT ALL THAT...

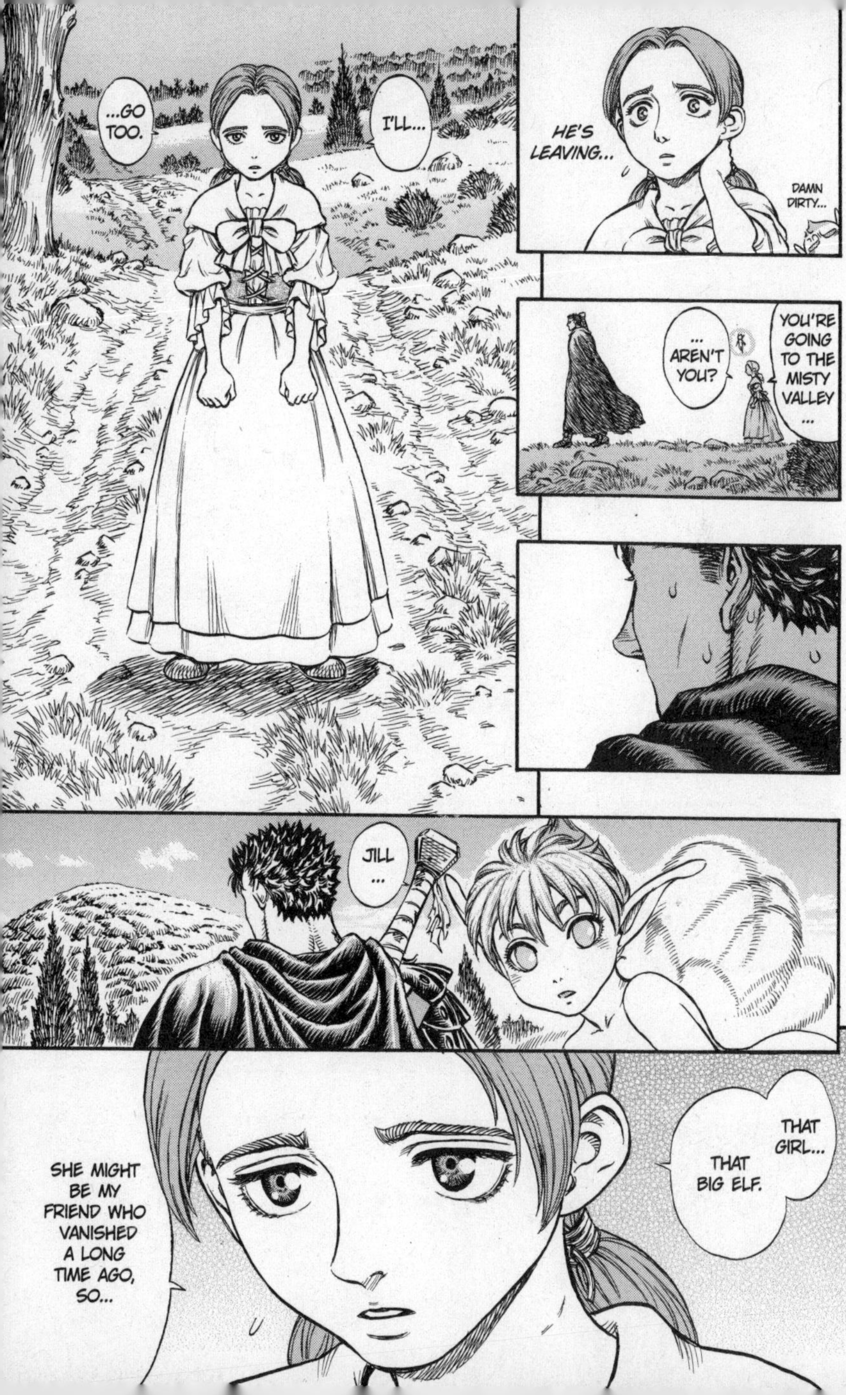
HE'S LEAVING...
DAMN DIRTY...
YOU'RE GOING TO THE MISTY VALLEY...
...AREN'T YOU?
I'LL...
...GO TOO.
JILL...
THAT GIRL... THAT BIG ELF.
SHE MIGHT BE MY FRIEND WHO VANISHED A LONG TIME AGO, SO...

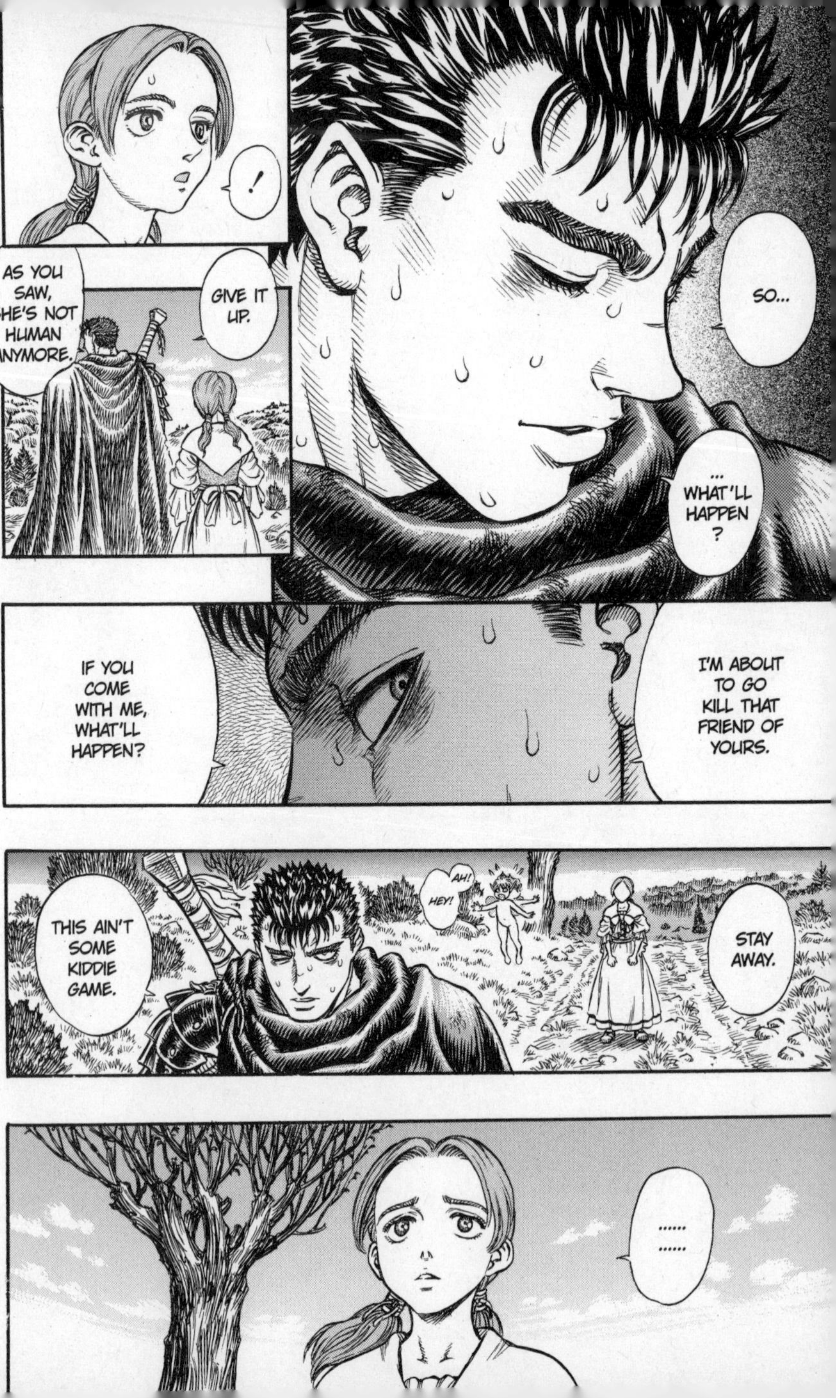
SO...
...WHAT'LL HAPPEN?
!
GIVE IT UP.
AS YOU SAW, SHE'S NOT HUMAN ANYMORE.
I'M ABOUT TO GO KILL THAT FRIEND OF YOURS.
IF YOU COME WITH ME, WHAT'LL HAPPEN?
STAY AWAY.
AH! HEY!
THIS AIN'T SOME KIDDIE GAME.
......
......

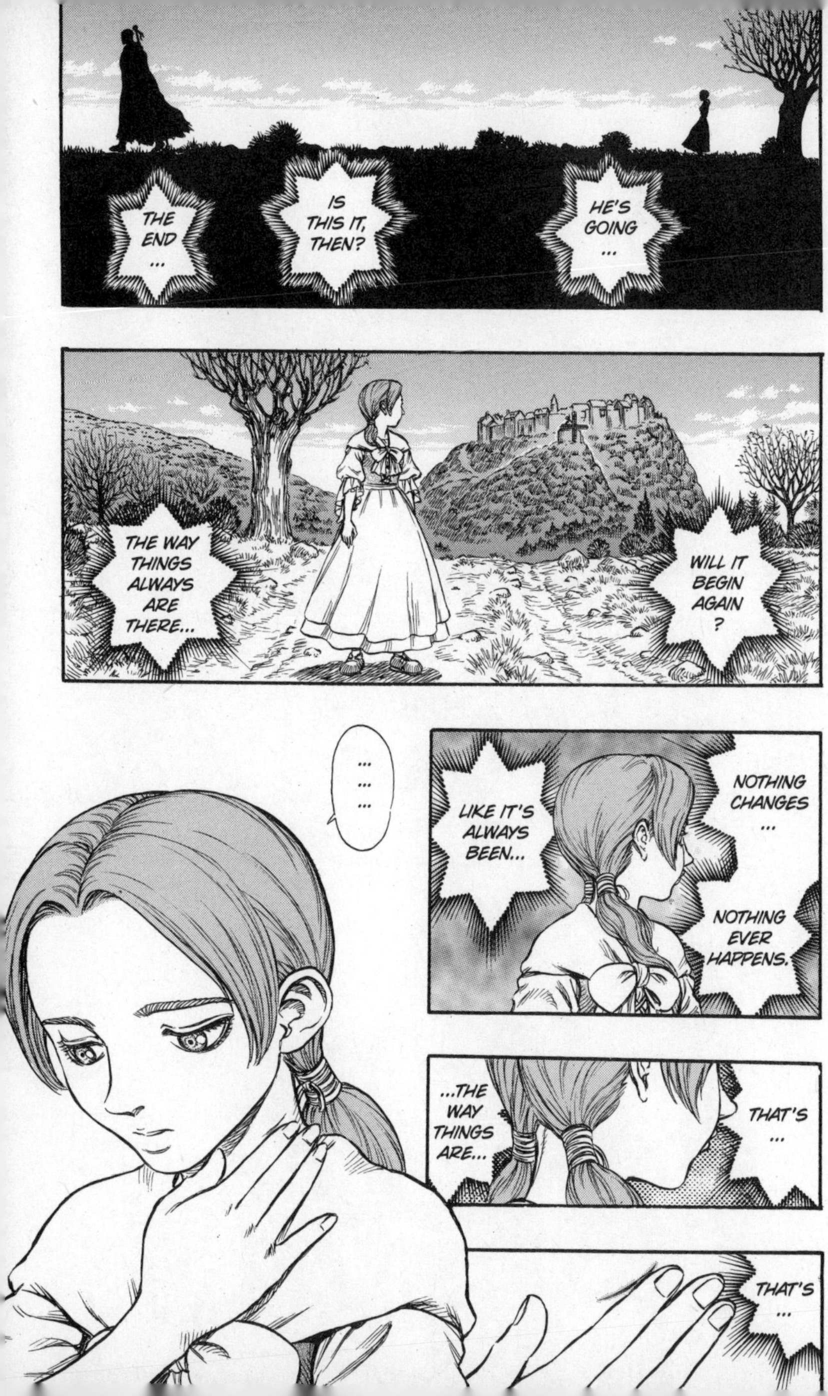

HE'S GOING ...
IS THIS IT, THEN?
THE END ...
WILL IT BEGIN AGAIN ?
THE WAY THINGS ALWAYS ARE THERE...
NOTHING CHANGES ...
NOTHING EVER HAPPENS.
LIKE IT'S ALWAYS BEEN...
THAT'S ...
...THE WAY THINGS ARE...
THAT'S ...
... ...

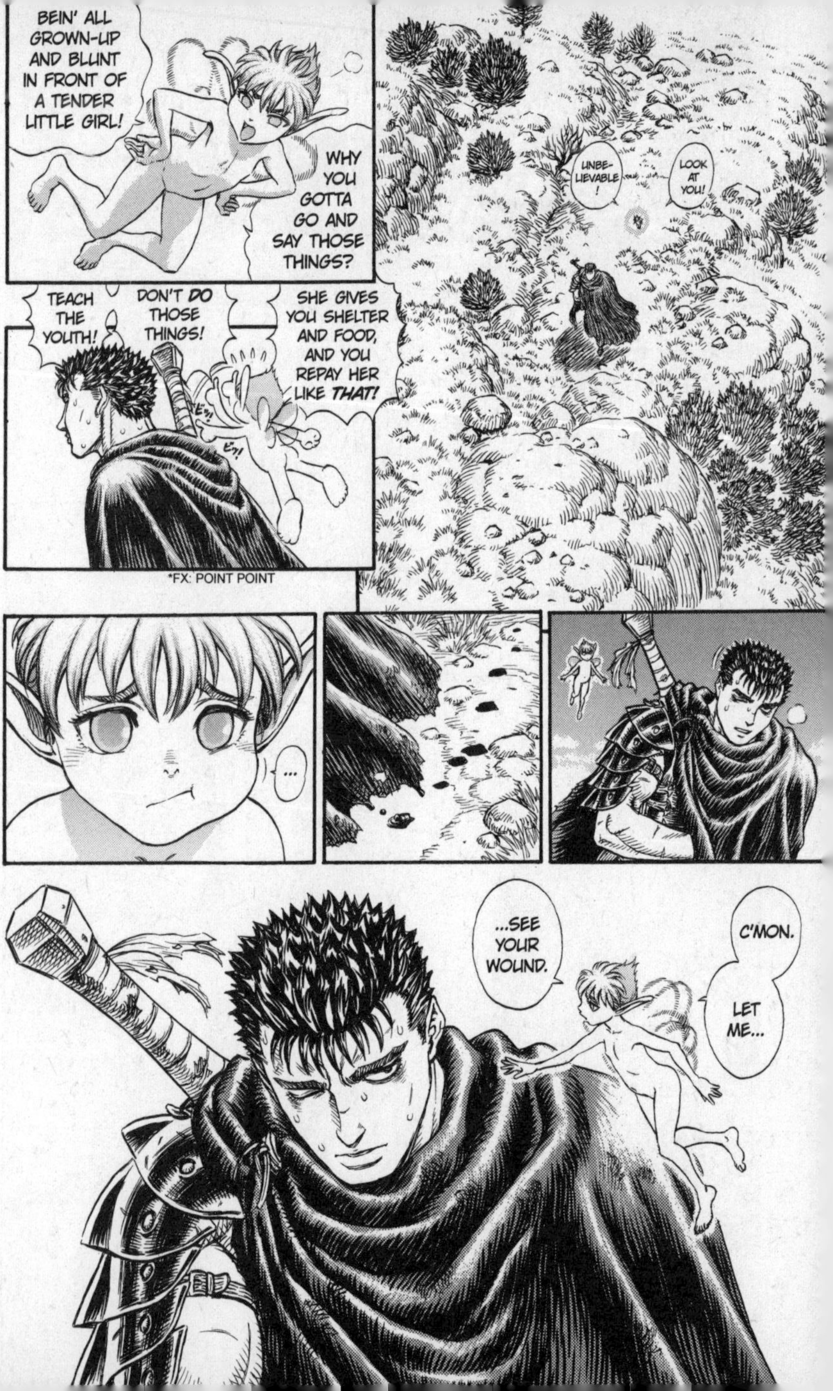
LOOK AT YOU!
UNBE-LIEVABLE!
BEIN' ALL GROWN-UP AND BLUNT IN FRONT OF A TENDER LITTLE GIRL!
WHY YOU GOTTA GO AND SAY THOSE THINGS?
SHE GIVES YOU SHELTER AND FOOD, AND YOU REPAY HER LIKE *THAT!*
DON'T *DO* THOSE THINGS!
TEACH THE YOUTH!
*FX: POINT POINT
...
C'MON.
LET ME...
...SEE YOUR WOUND.

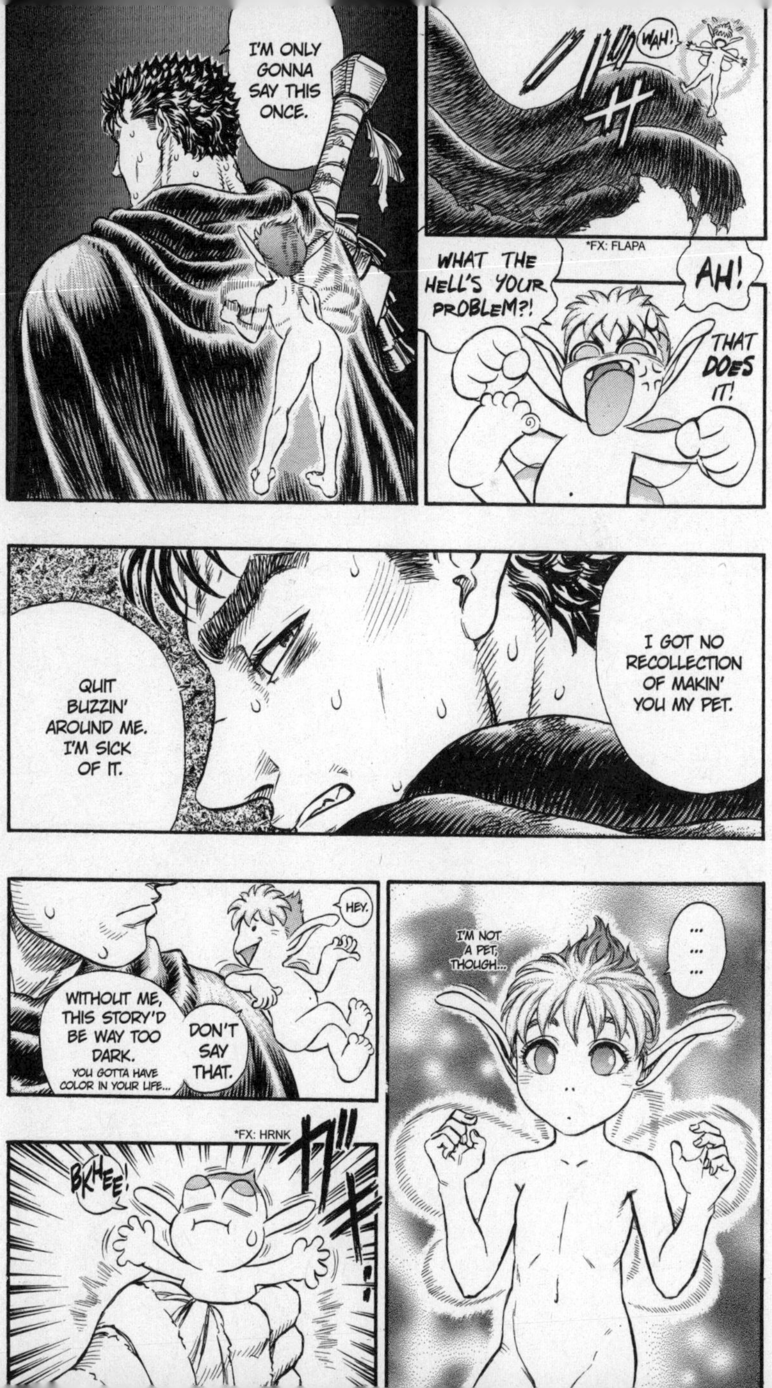
WAH!
*FX: FLAPA
AH!
WHAT THE HELL'S YOUR PROBLEM?!
THAT DOES IT!
I'M ONLY GONNA SAY THIS ONCE.
I GOT NO RECOLLECTION OF MAKIN' YOU MY PET.
QUIT BUZZIN' AROUND ME. I'M SICK OF IT.
...
...
...
I'M NOT A PET, THOUGH...
HEY.
WITHOUT ME, THIS STORY'D BE WAY TOO DARK.
YOU GOTTA HAVE COLOR IN YOUR LIFE...
DON'T SAY THAT.
*FX: HRNK
BKHEE!

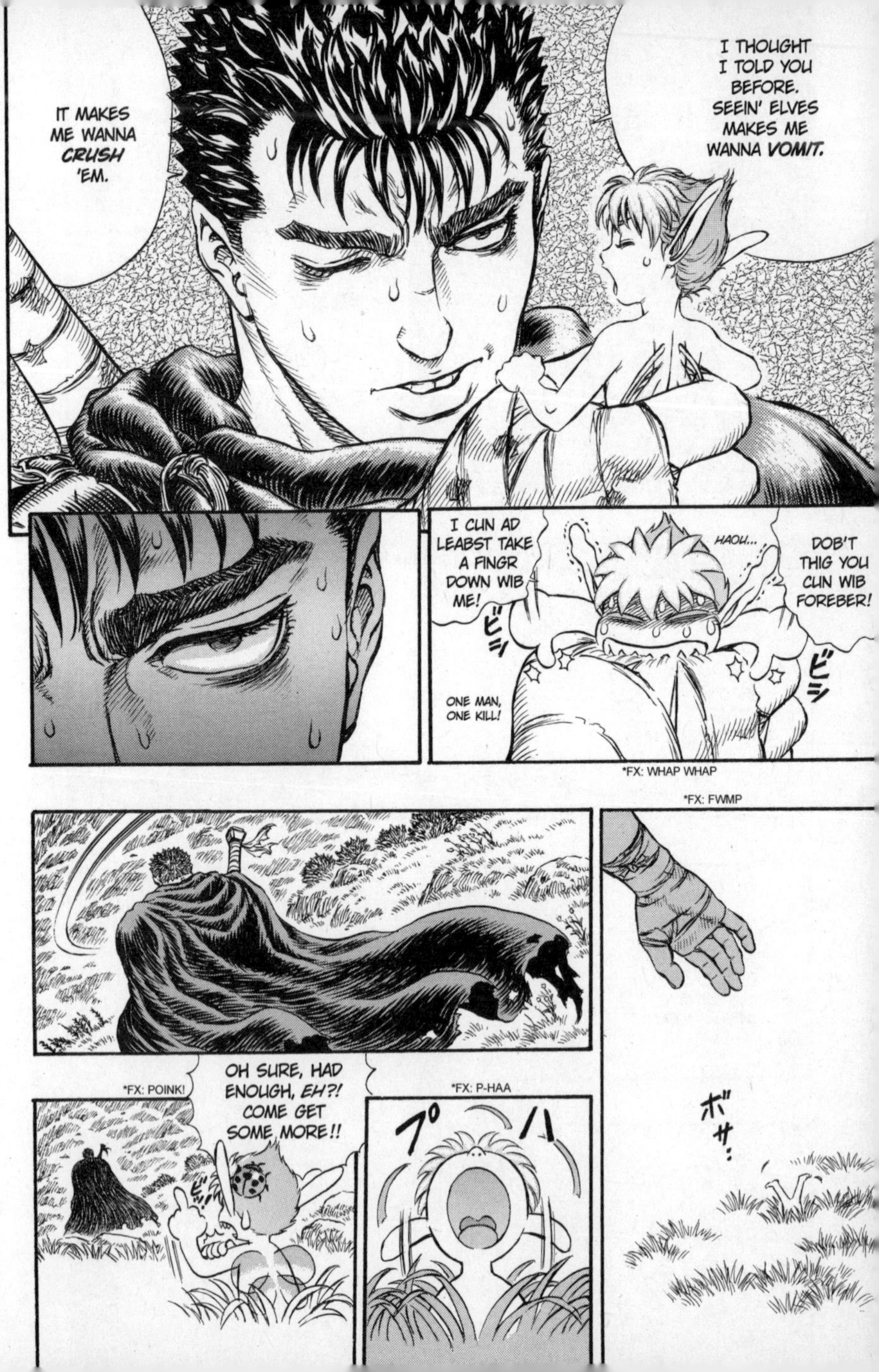

I THOUGHT I TOLD YOU BEFORE. SEEIN' ELVES MAKES ME WANNA *VOMIT.*
IT MAKES ME WANNA *CRUSH* 'EM.
DOB'T THIG YOU CUN WIB FOREBER!
HAOU...
I CUN AD LEABST TAKE A FINGR DOWN WIB ME!
ONE MAN, ONE KILL!
ビシ
ビシ
*FX: WHAP WHAP
*FX: FWMP
ボサ
*FX: P-HAA
プハ
OH SURE, HAD ENOUGH, *EH?!* COME GET SOME MORE!!
*FX: POINK!

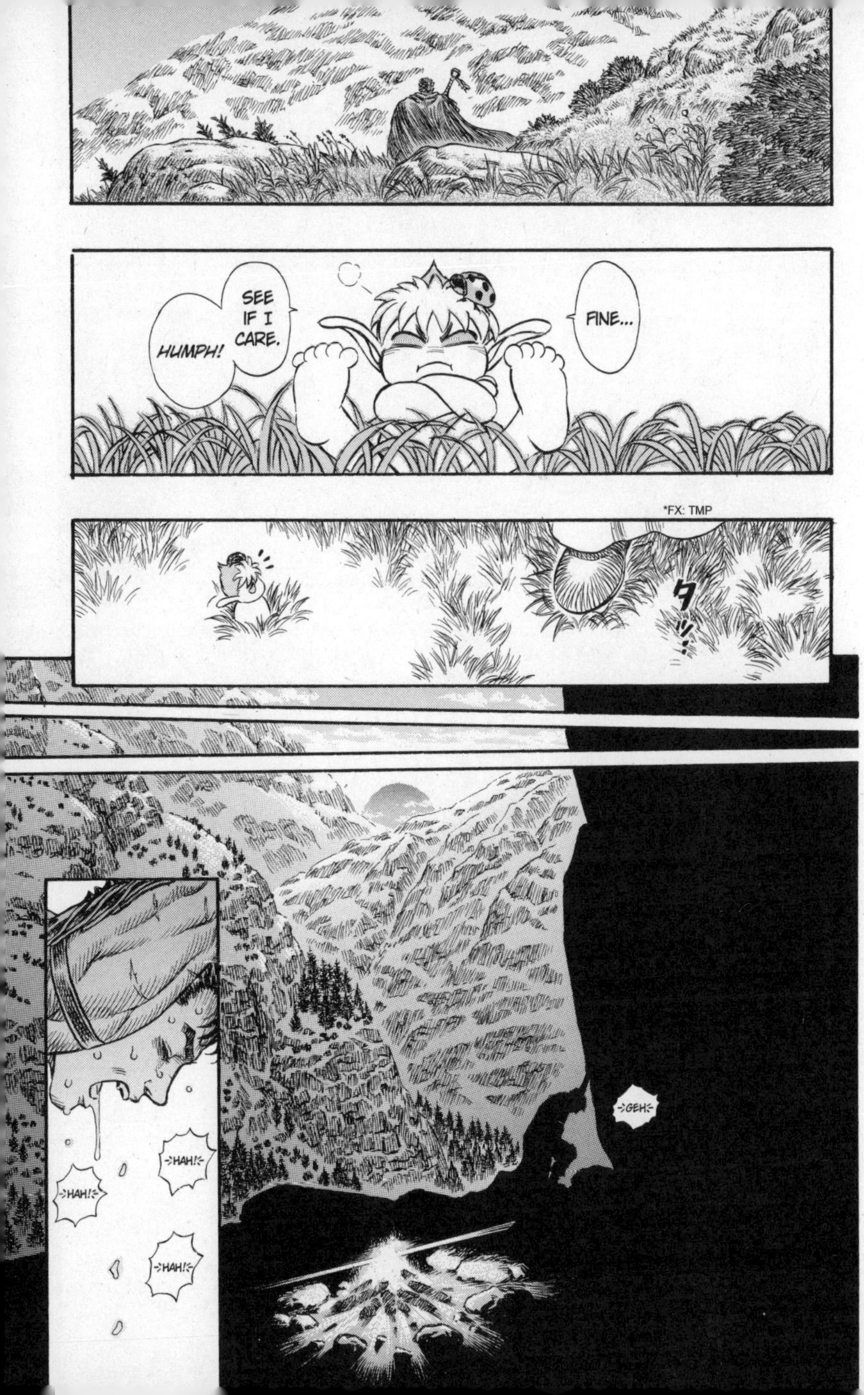
FINE...
SEE IF I CARE.
HUMPH!
*FX: TMP
タッ
GEH
HAH!
HAH!
HAH!

*FX: SHRRRIP

*FX: VP

*FX: TUG

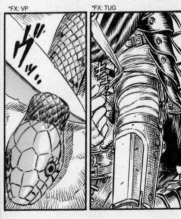

*FX: GLUNK GLUNK

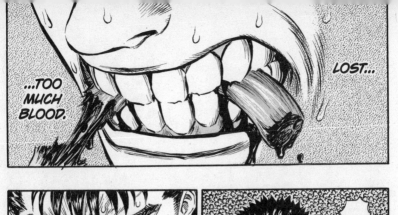

...TOO MUCH BLOOD.

LOST...

LIGH
...

...
...

GULP

*HAHH HAHH

*CHMP

COCA LEAVES

...POISON AND WEARINESS.

ON TOP OF THAT...

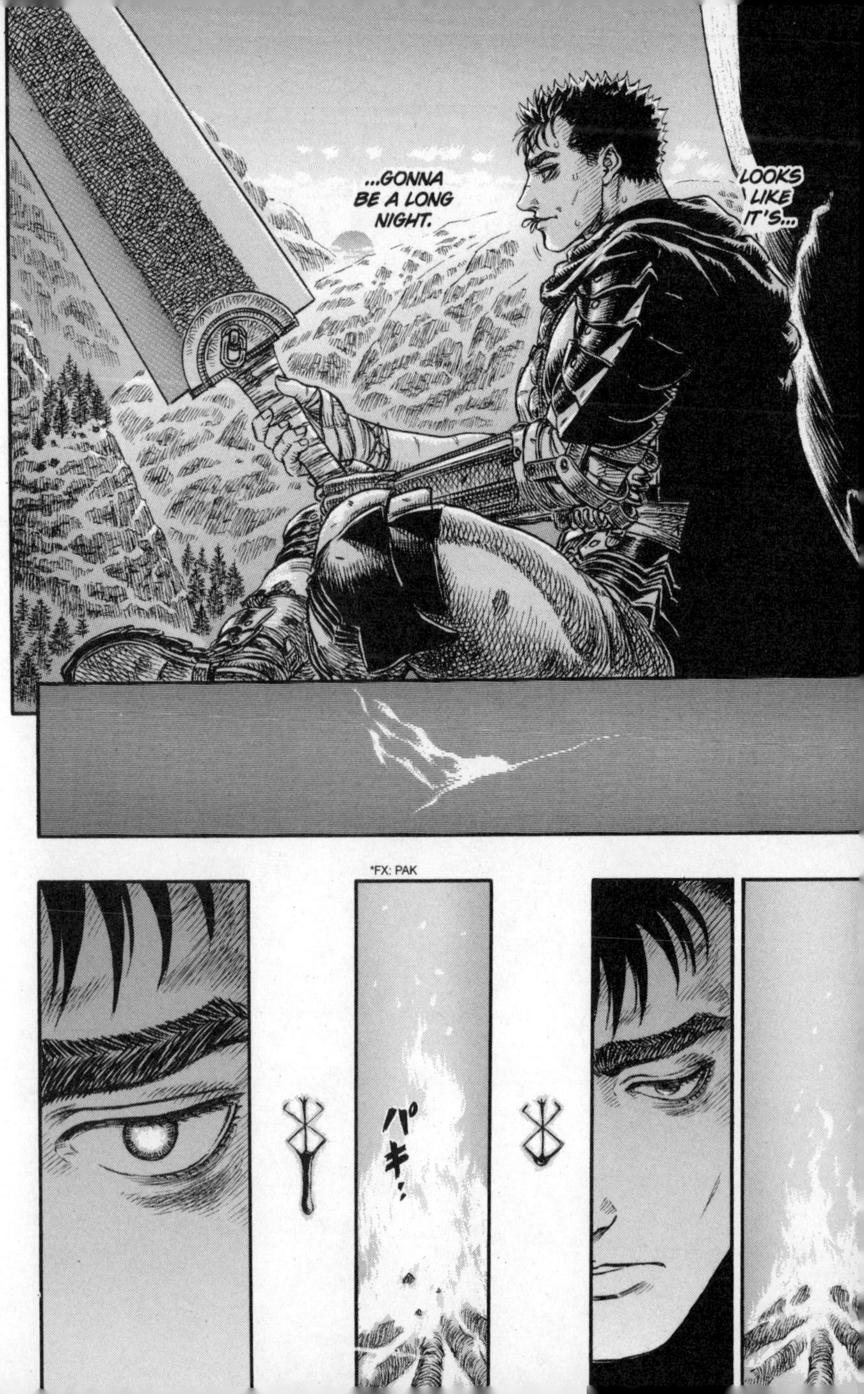
LOOKS LIKE IT'S...
...GONNA BE A LONG NIGHT.
*FX: PAK

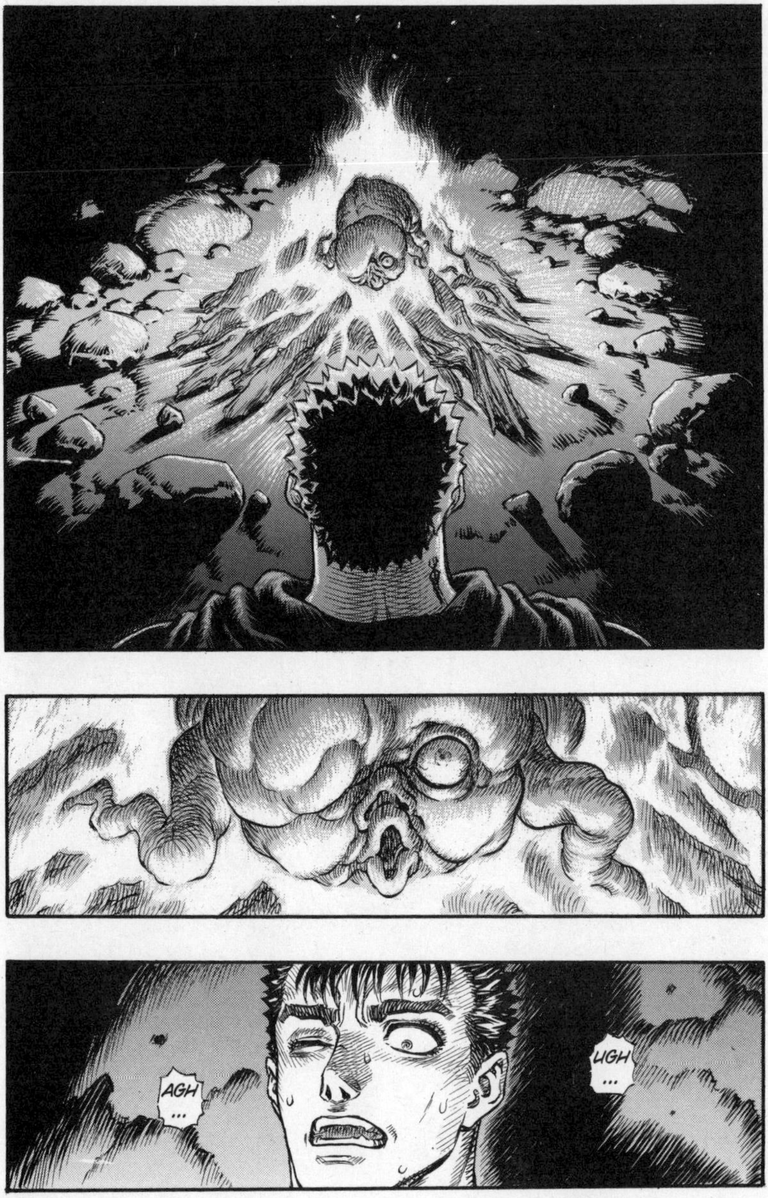
UGH ...
AGH ...

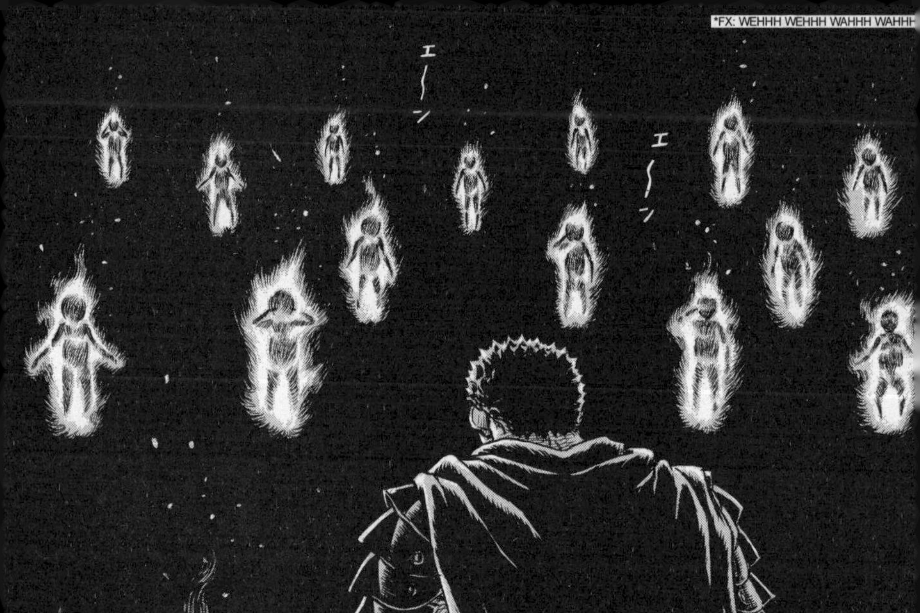
*FX: WEHHH WEHHH WAHHH WAHHH
エーン
エーン
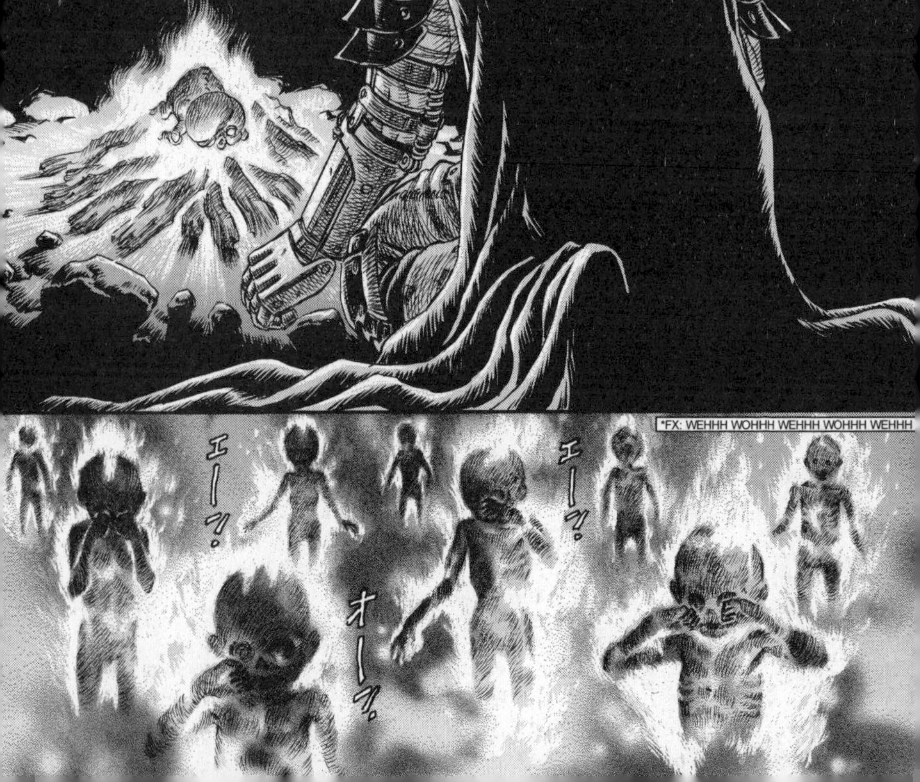
*FX: WEHHH WOHHH WEHHH WOHHH WEHHH
エーッ
エーッ
オーッ

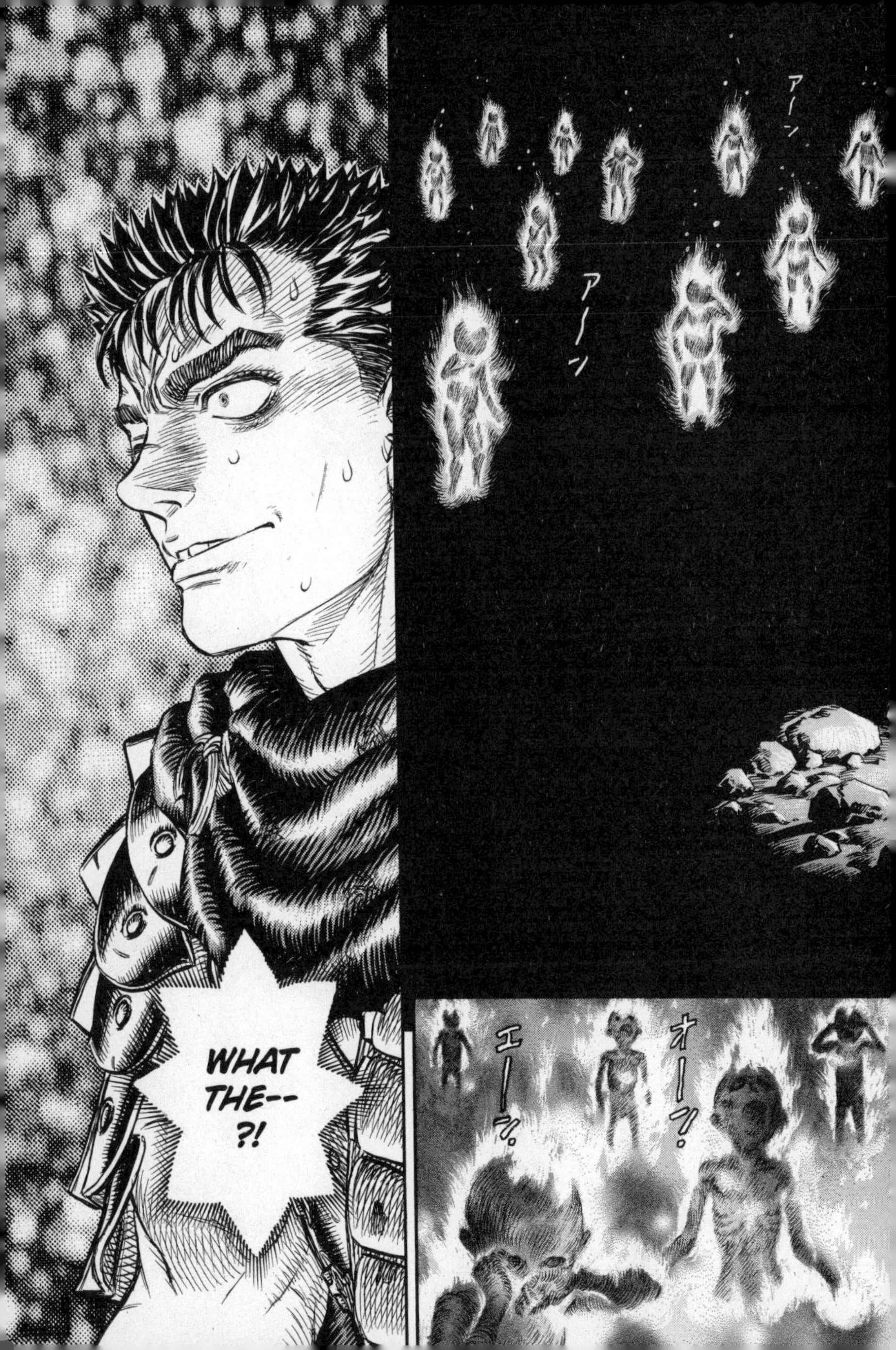

アーン
アーン
オーッ!
エーッ!
WHAT THE--?!

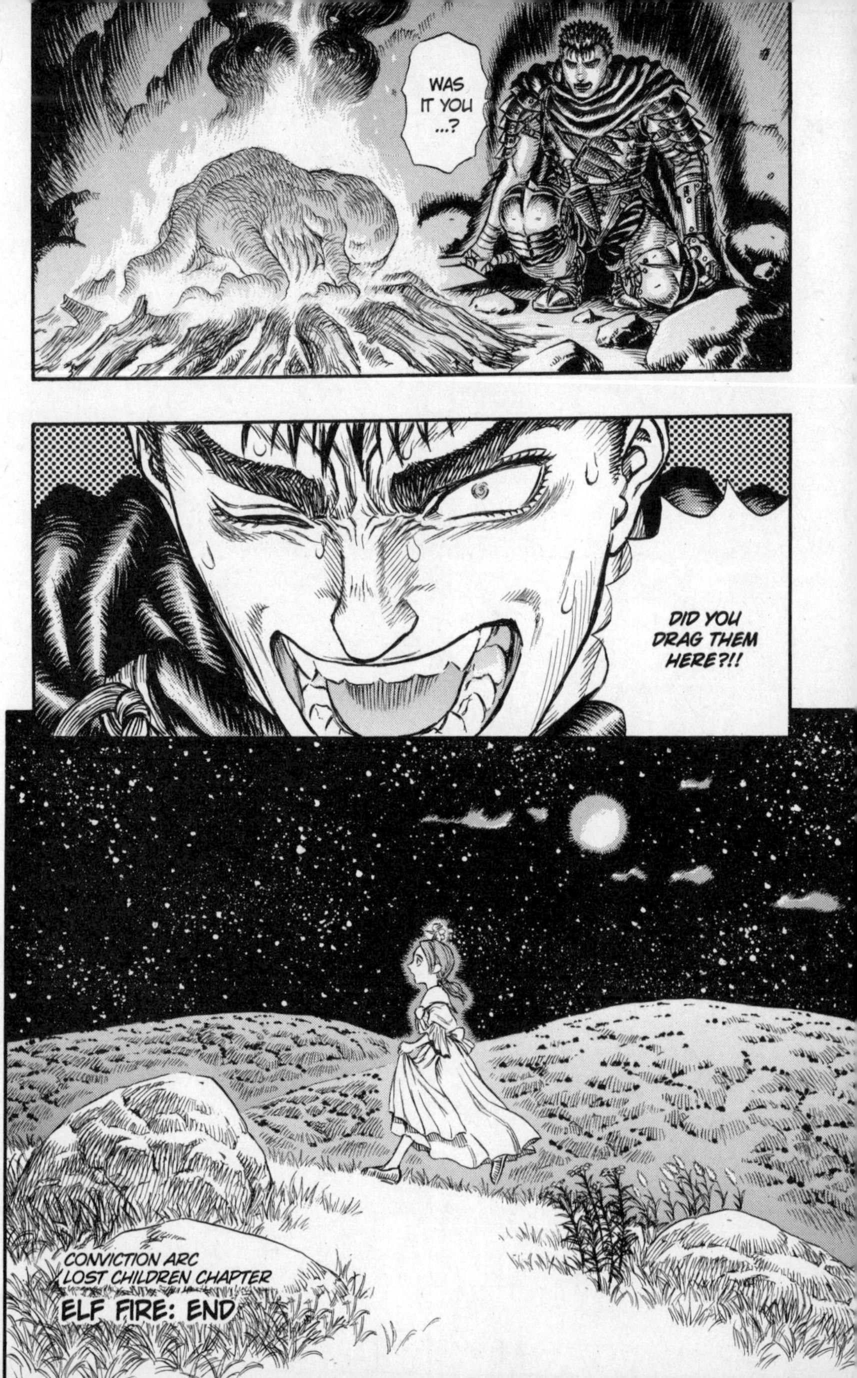
WAS IT YOU ...?
DID YOU DRAG THEM HERE?!!
CONVICTION ARC
LOST CHILDREN CHAPTER
ELF FIRE: END

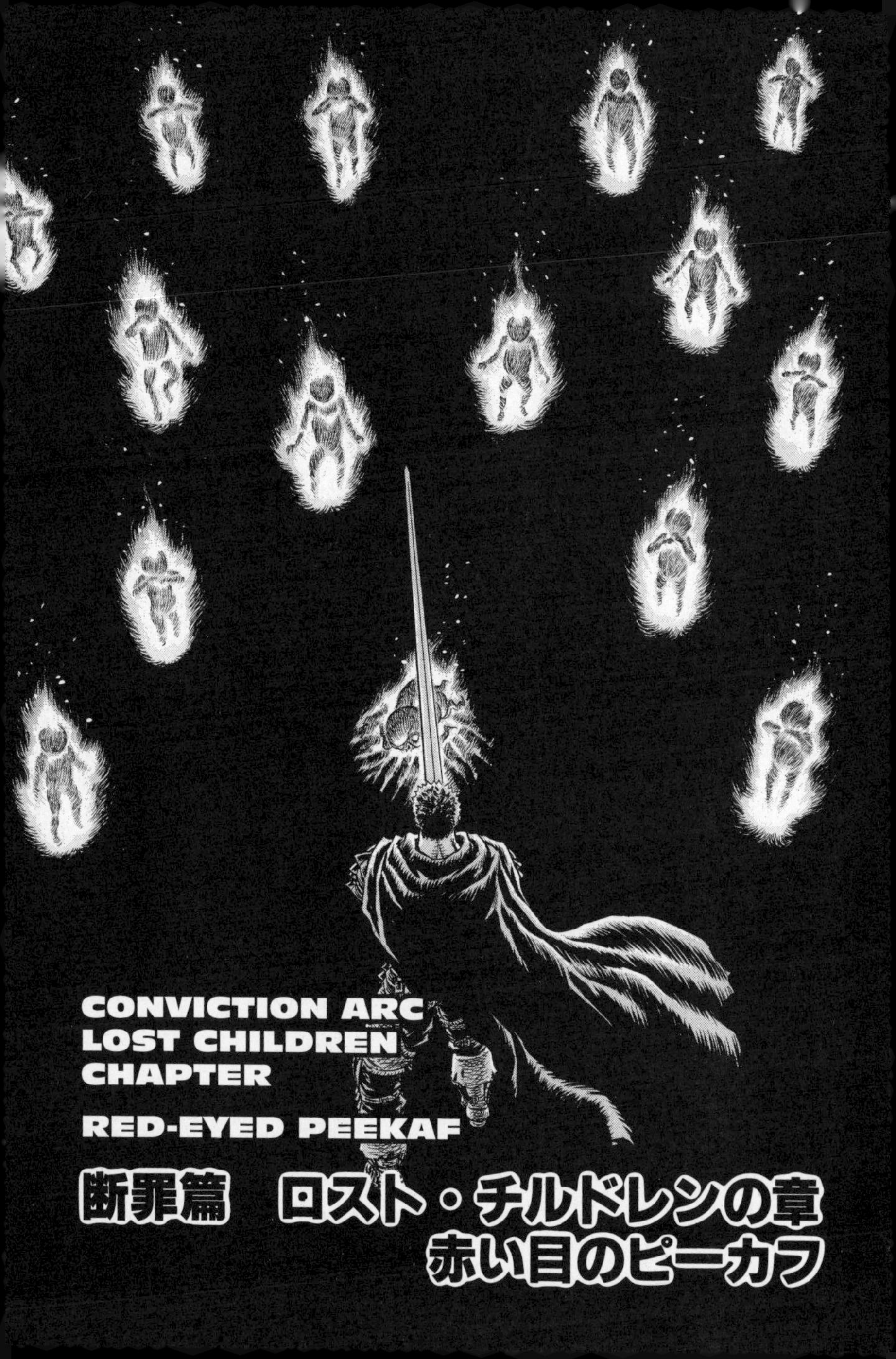
CONVICTION ARC
LOST CHILDREN
CHAPTER
RED-EYED PEEKAF
断罪篇　ロスト・チルドレンの章
赤い目のピーカフ

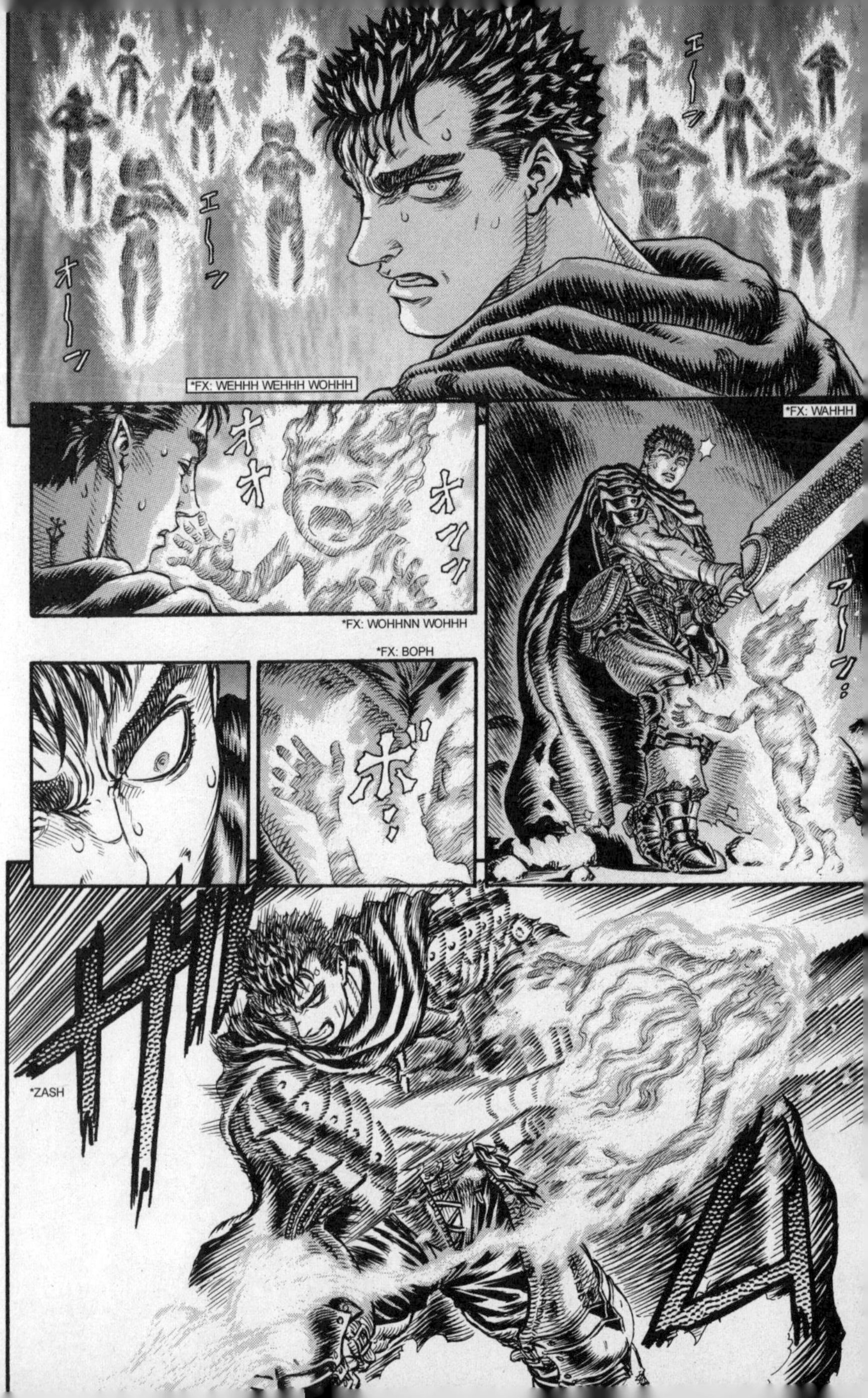

*FX: WEHHH WEHHH WOHHH
*FX: WAHHH
*FX: WOHHNN WOHHH
*FX: BOPH
*ZASH

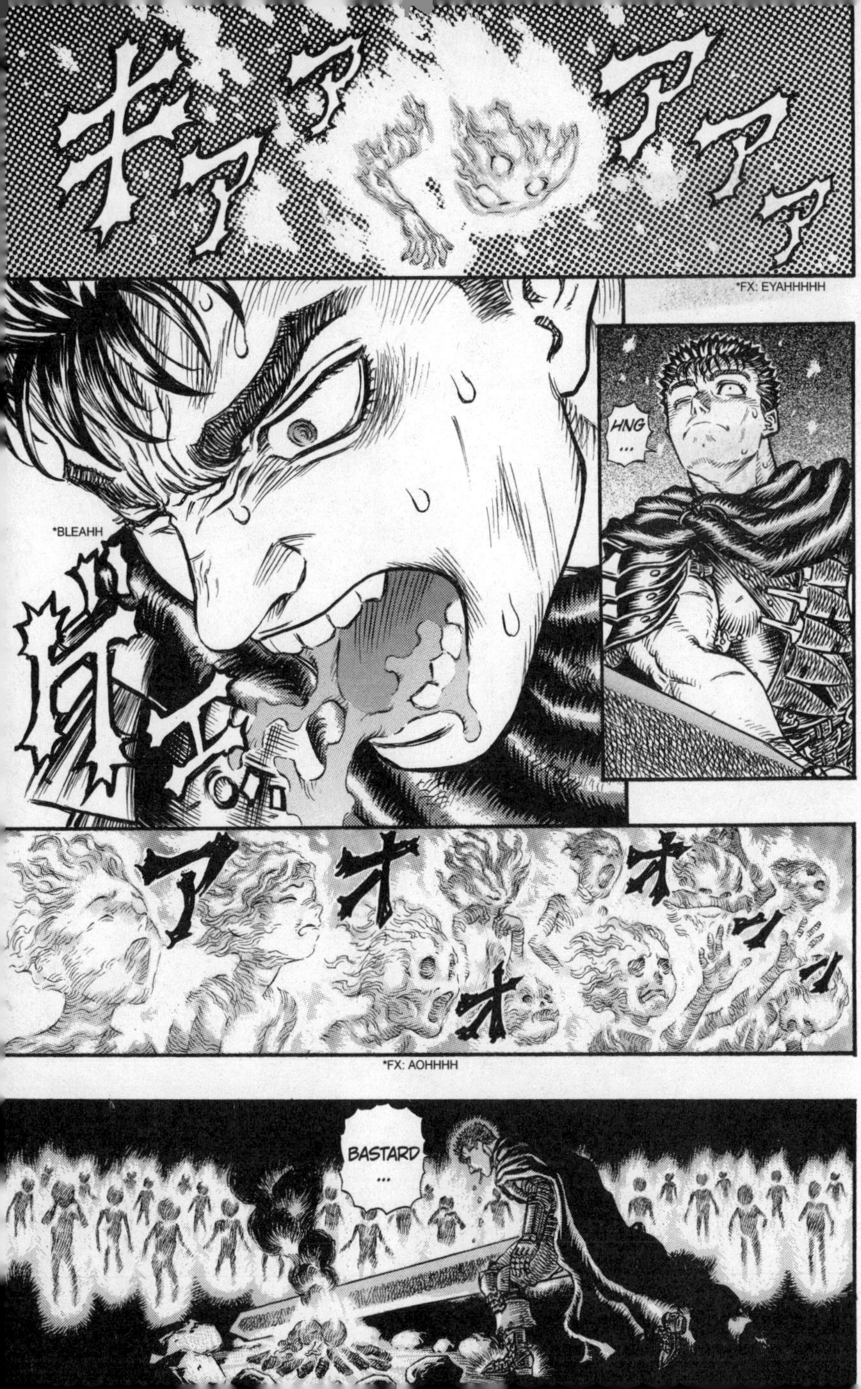
*FX: EYAHHHHH
HNG ...
*BLEAHH
*FX: AOHHHH
BASTARD ...

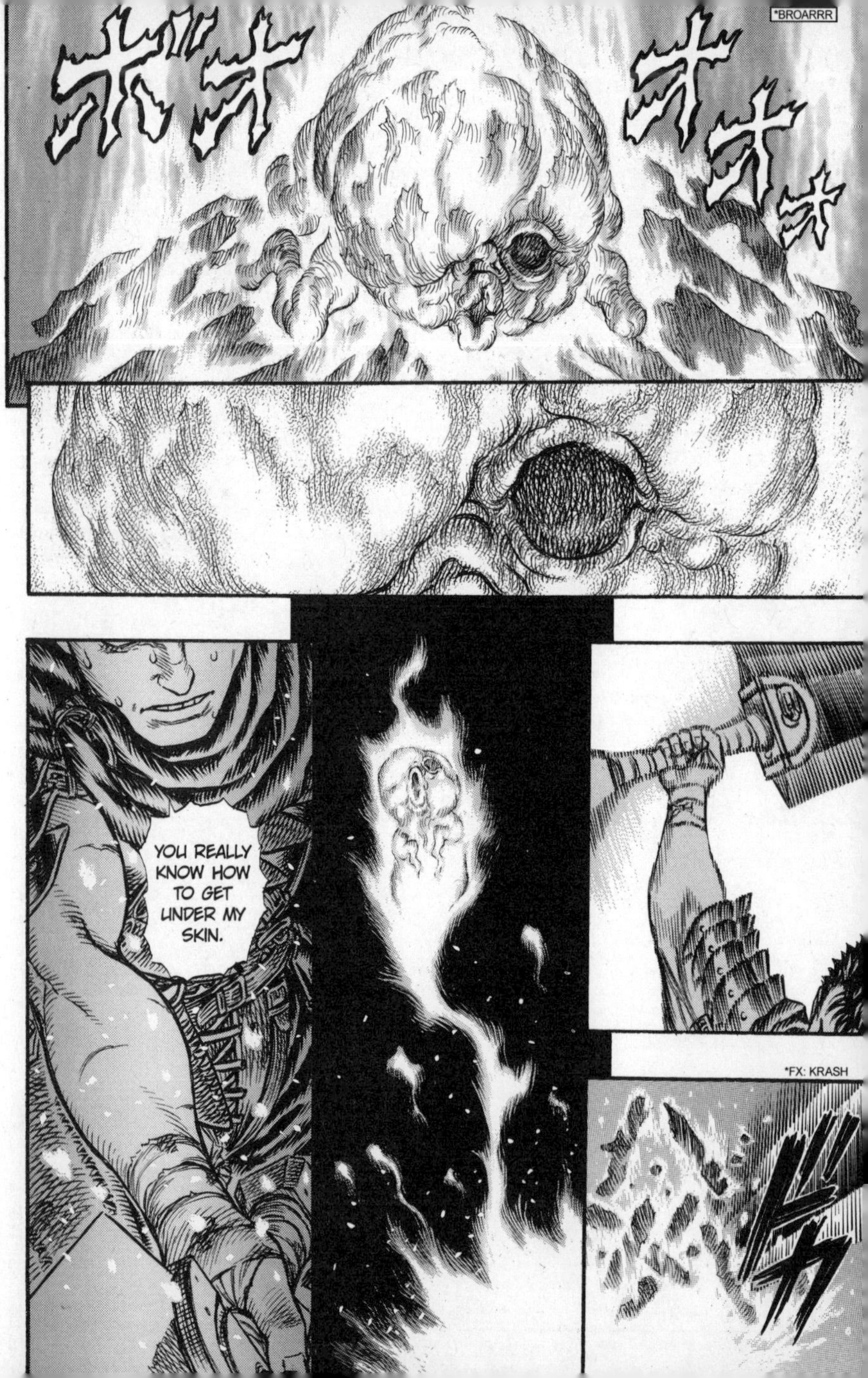
*BROARRR
*FX: KRASH
YOU REALLY KNOW HOW TO GET UNDER MY SKIN.

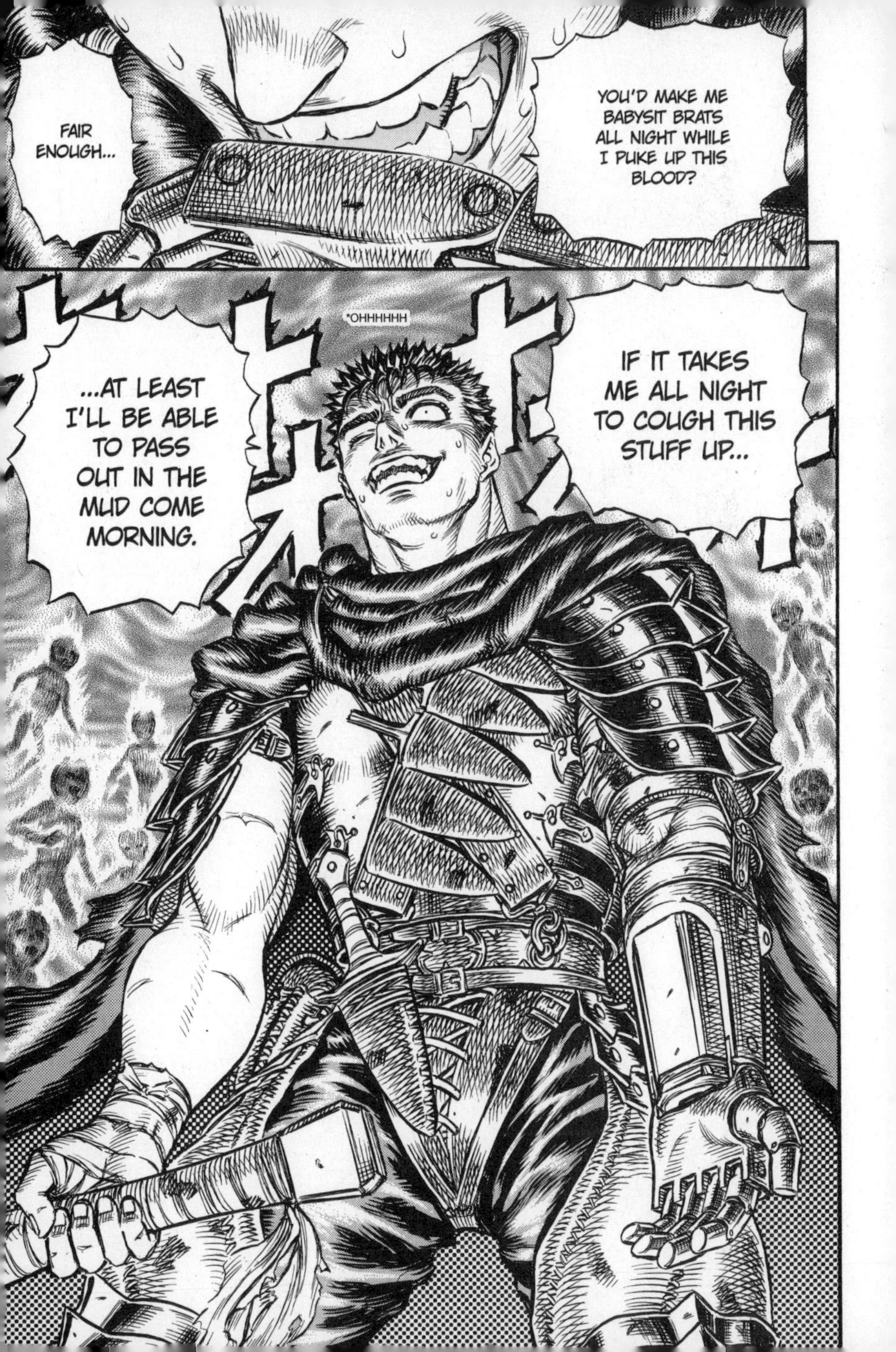
YOU'D MAKE ME BABYSIT BRATS ALL NIGHT WHILE I PUKE UP THIS BLOOD?
FAIR ENOUGH...
*OHHHHHH
IF IT TAKES ME ALL NIGHT TO COUGH THIS STUFF UP...
...AT LEAST I'LL BE ABLE TO PASS OUT IN THE MUD COME MORNING.

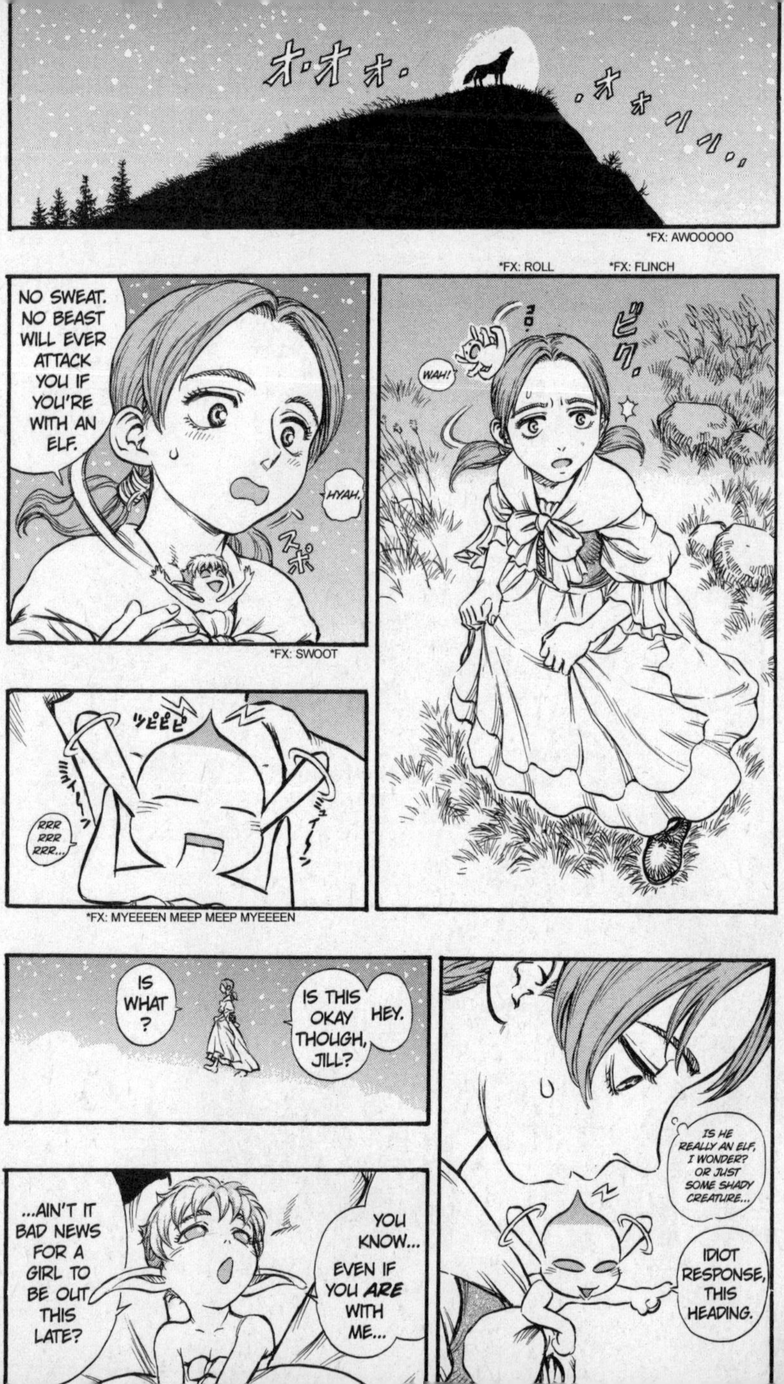

*FX: AWOOOOO
*FX: FLINCH
ビク。
*FX: ROLL
コロ
WAH!
NO SWEAT. NO BEAST WILL EVER ATTACK YOU IF YOU'RE WITH AN ELF.
HYAH.
スポ
*FX: SWOOT
ツピピピ
RRR RRR RRR...
*FX: MYEEEEN MEEP MEEP MYEEEEN
IS HE REALLY AN ELF, I WONDER? OR JUST SOME SHADY CREATURE...
IDIOT RESPONSE, THIS HEADING.
HEY.
IS THIS OKAY THOUGH, JILL?
IS WHAT?
YOU KNOW... EVEN IF YOU ***ARE*** WITH ME...
...AIN'T IT BAD NEWS FOR A GIRL TO BE OUT THIS LATE?

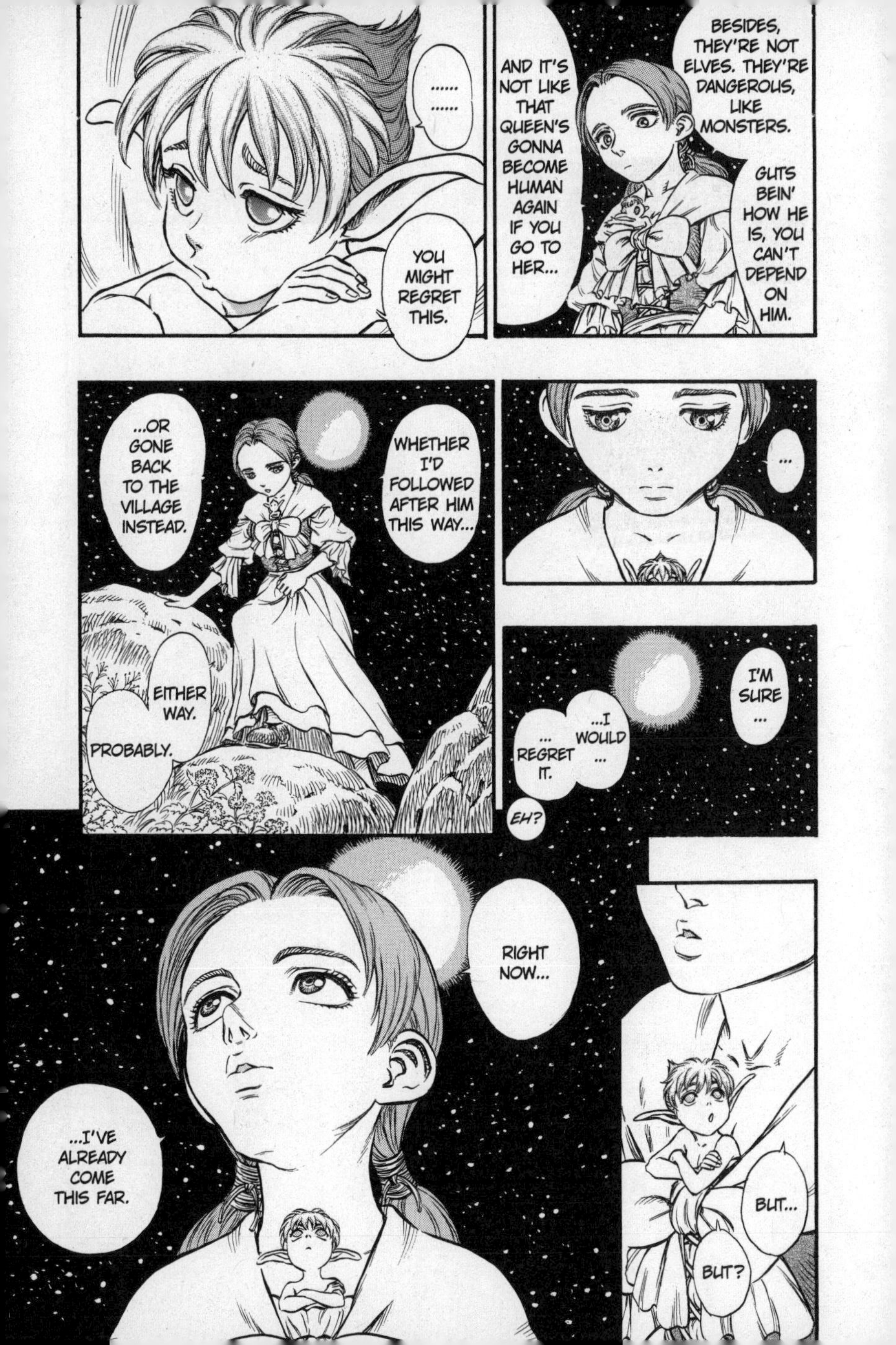
BESIDES, THEY'RE NOT ELVES. THEY'RE DANGEROUS, LIKE MONSTERS.
GUTS BEIN' HOW HE IS, YOU CAN'T DEPEND ON HIM.
AND IT'S NOT LIKE THAT QUEEN'S GONNA BECOME HUMAN AGAIN IF YOU GO TO HER...
....
YOU MIGHT REGRET THIS.
...
WHETHER I'D FOLLOWED AFTER HIM THIS WAY...
...OR GONE BACK TO THE VILLAGE INSTEAD.
EITHER WAY.
PROBABLY.
I'M SURE ...
...I WOULD ...
... REGRET IT.
EH?
RIGHT NOW...
...I'VE ALREADY COME THIS FAR.
BUT...
BUT?

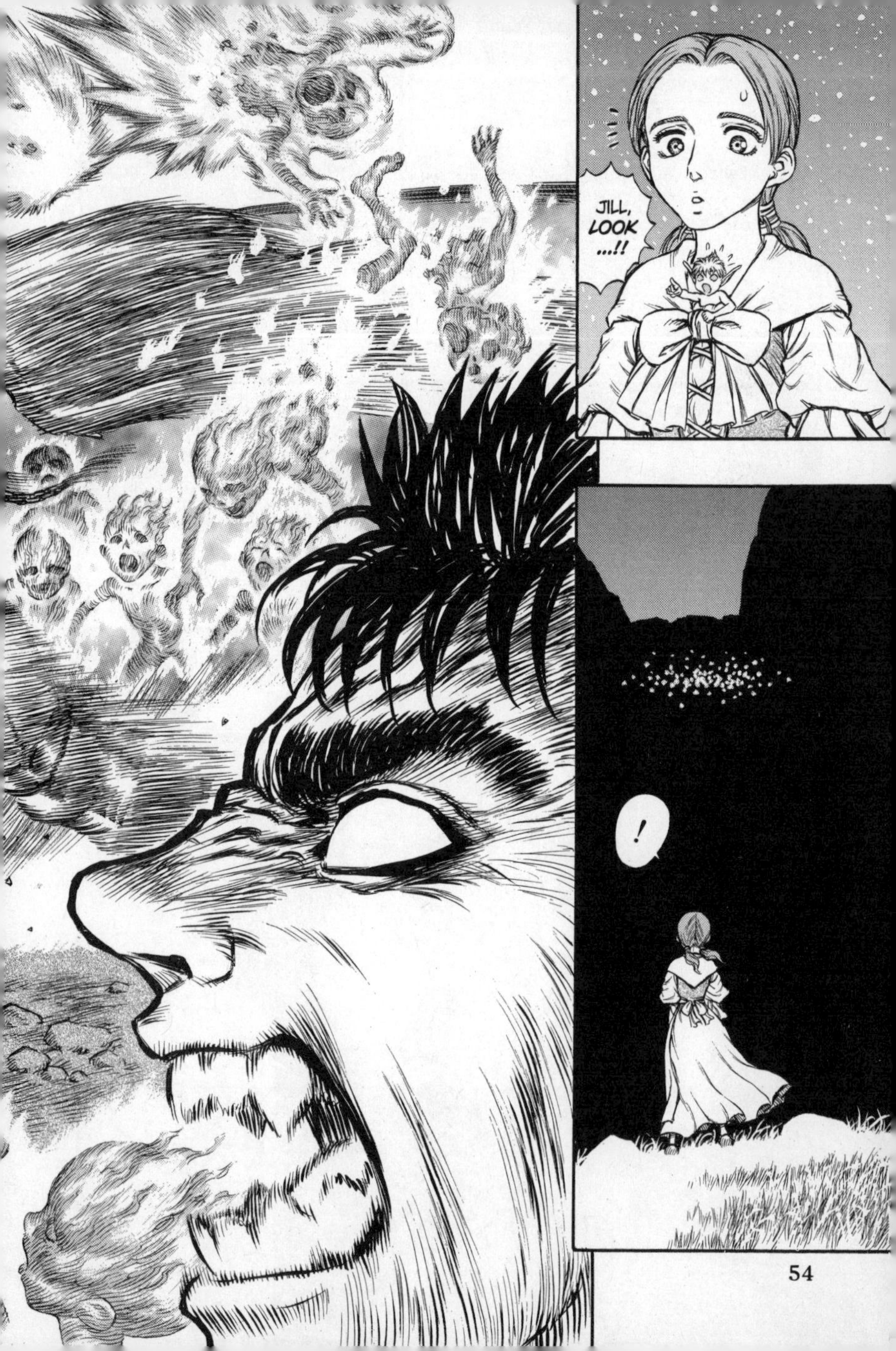
JILL, LOOK ...!!
!

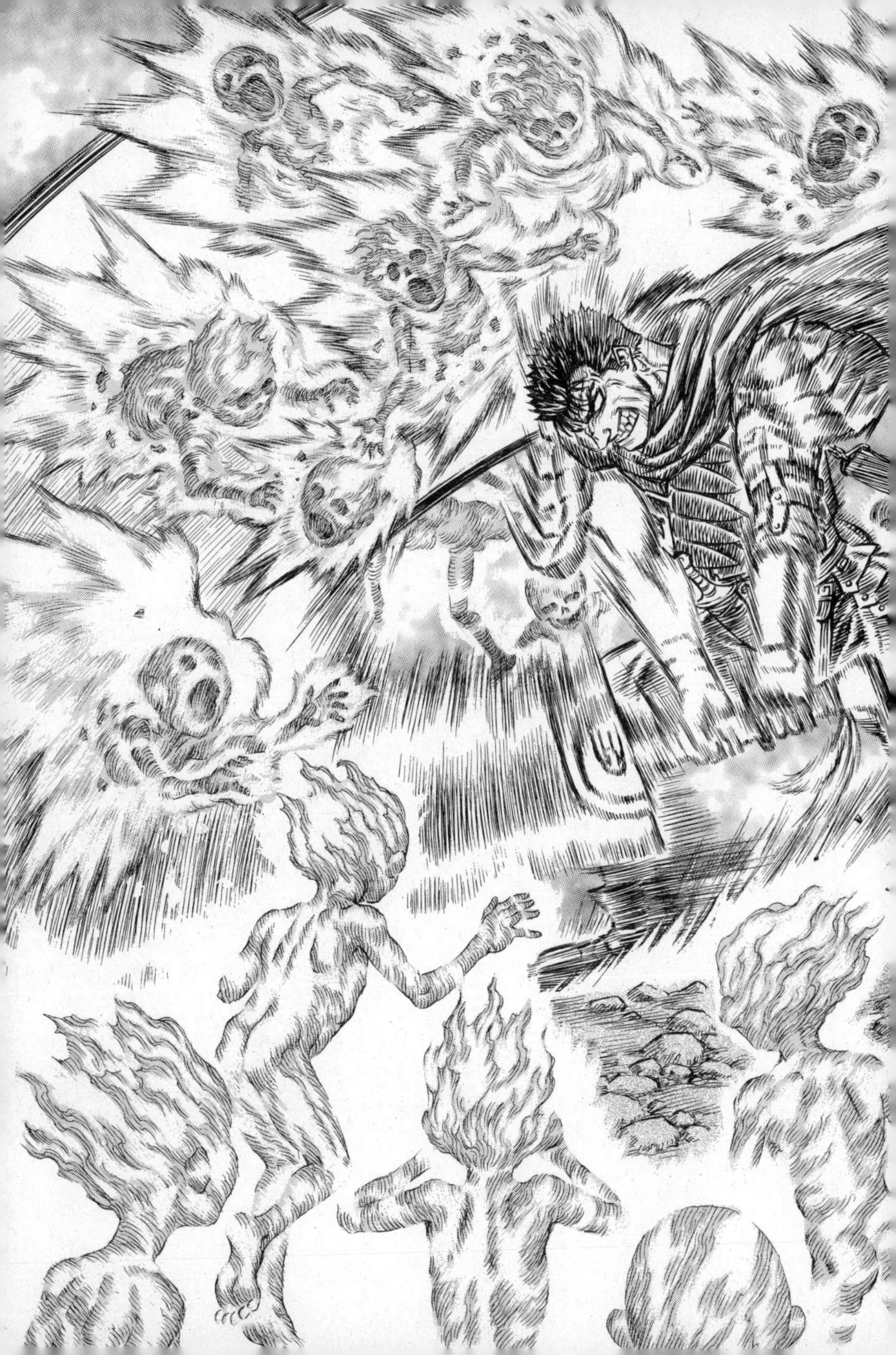

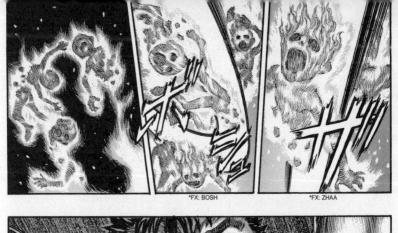

*FX: BOSH

*FX: ZHAA

*SHNK

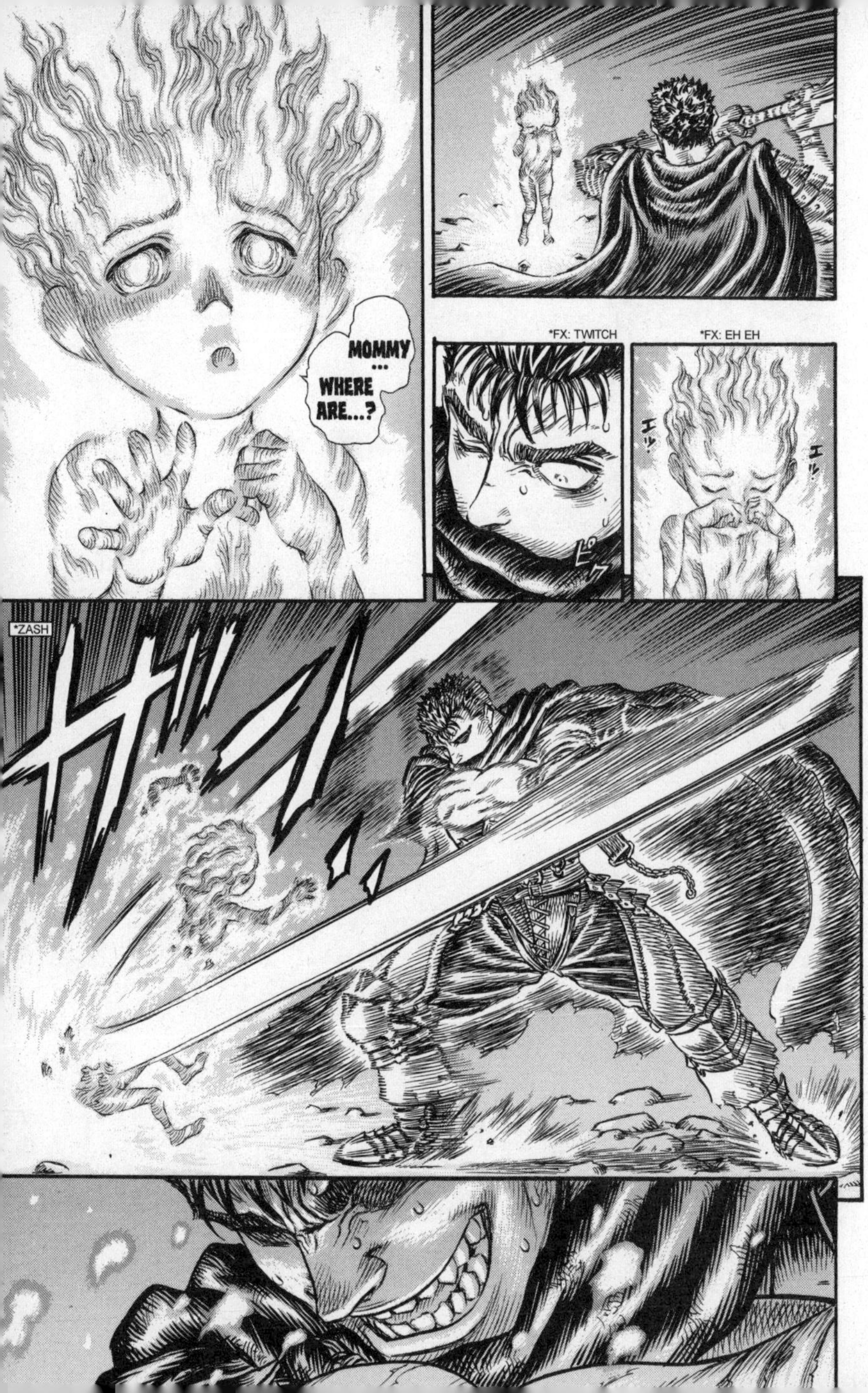
*FX: EH EH
エッ
エッ
*FX: TWITCH
MOMMY ... WHERE ARE...?
*ZASH

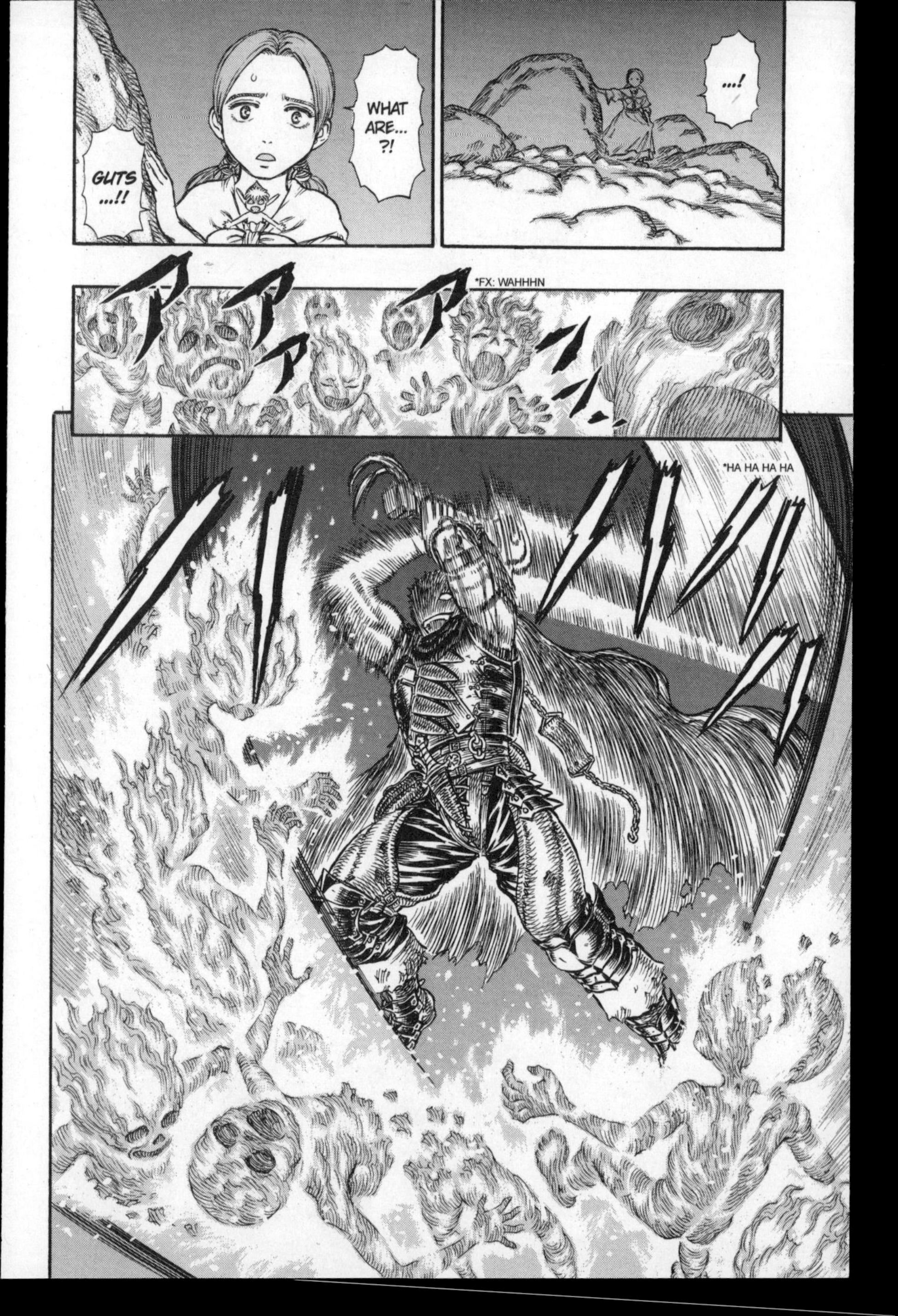
...!
WHAT ARE... ?!
GUTS ...!!
*FX: WAHHHN
*HA HA HA HA

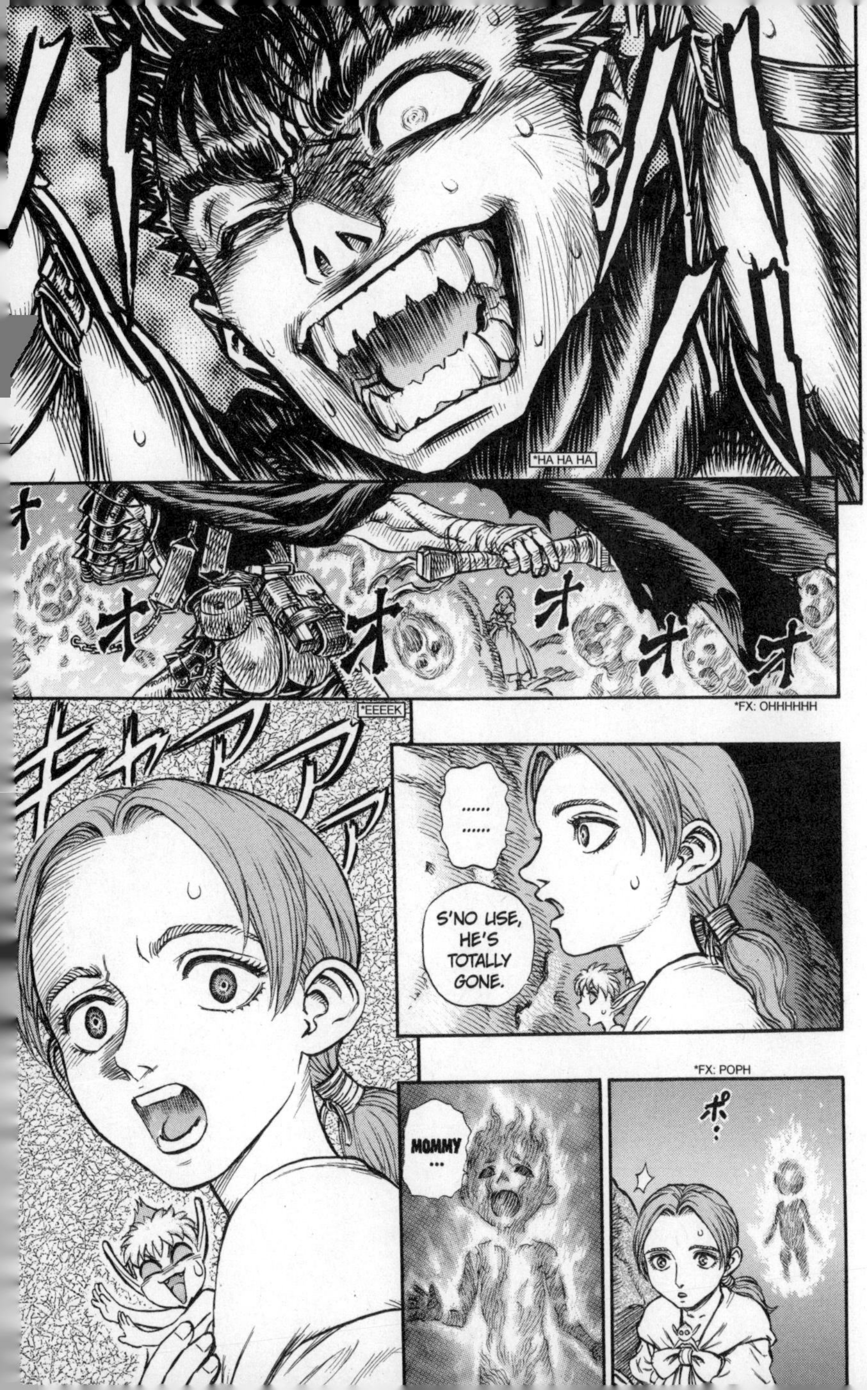
*HA HA HA
オ オ オ オ オ オ
*FX: OHHHHHH
......
......
S'NO USE, HE'S TOTALLY GONE.
*FX: POPH
ポ
MOMMY ...
キャアアア
*EEEEK

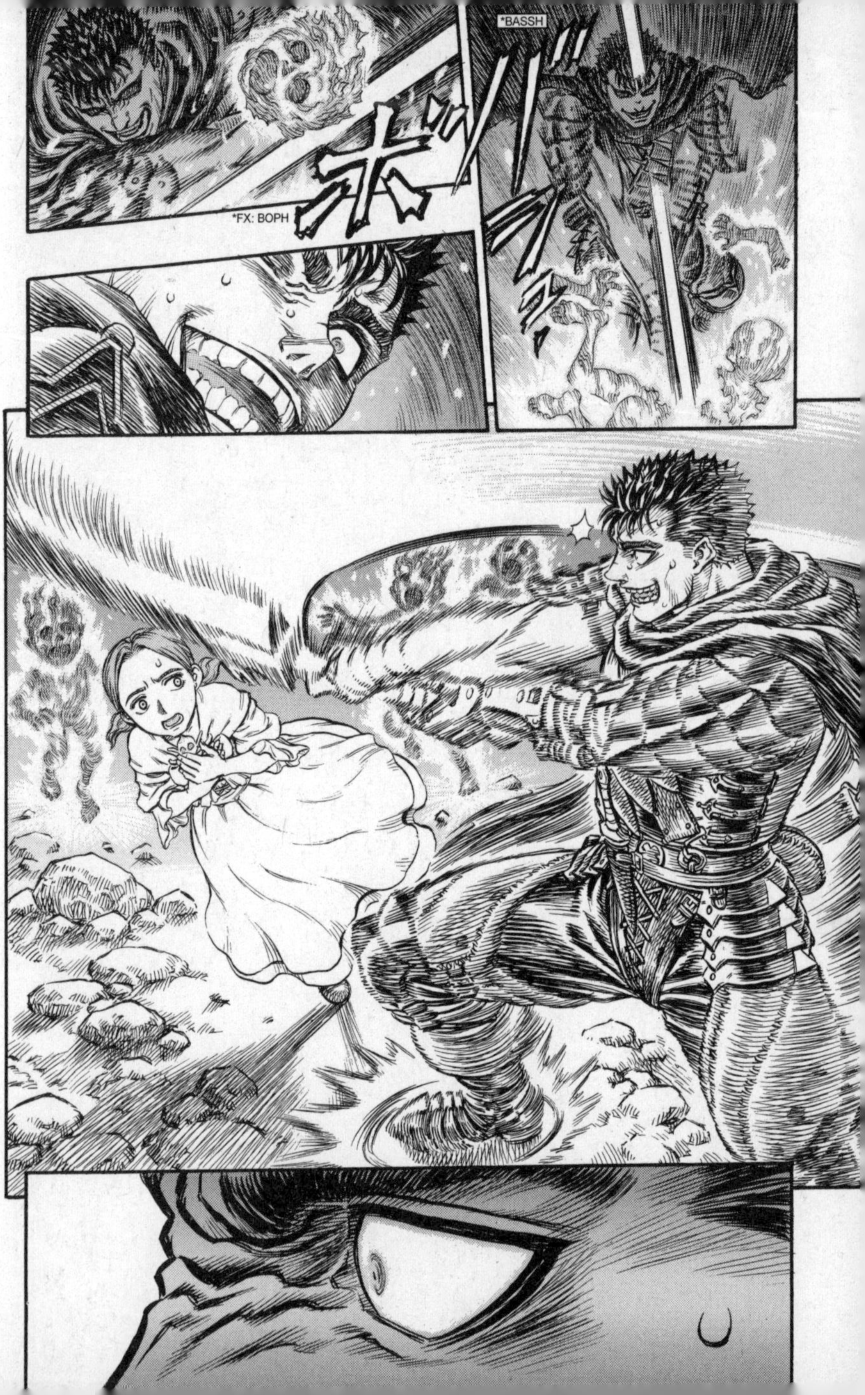
*BASSH
*FX: BOPH

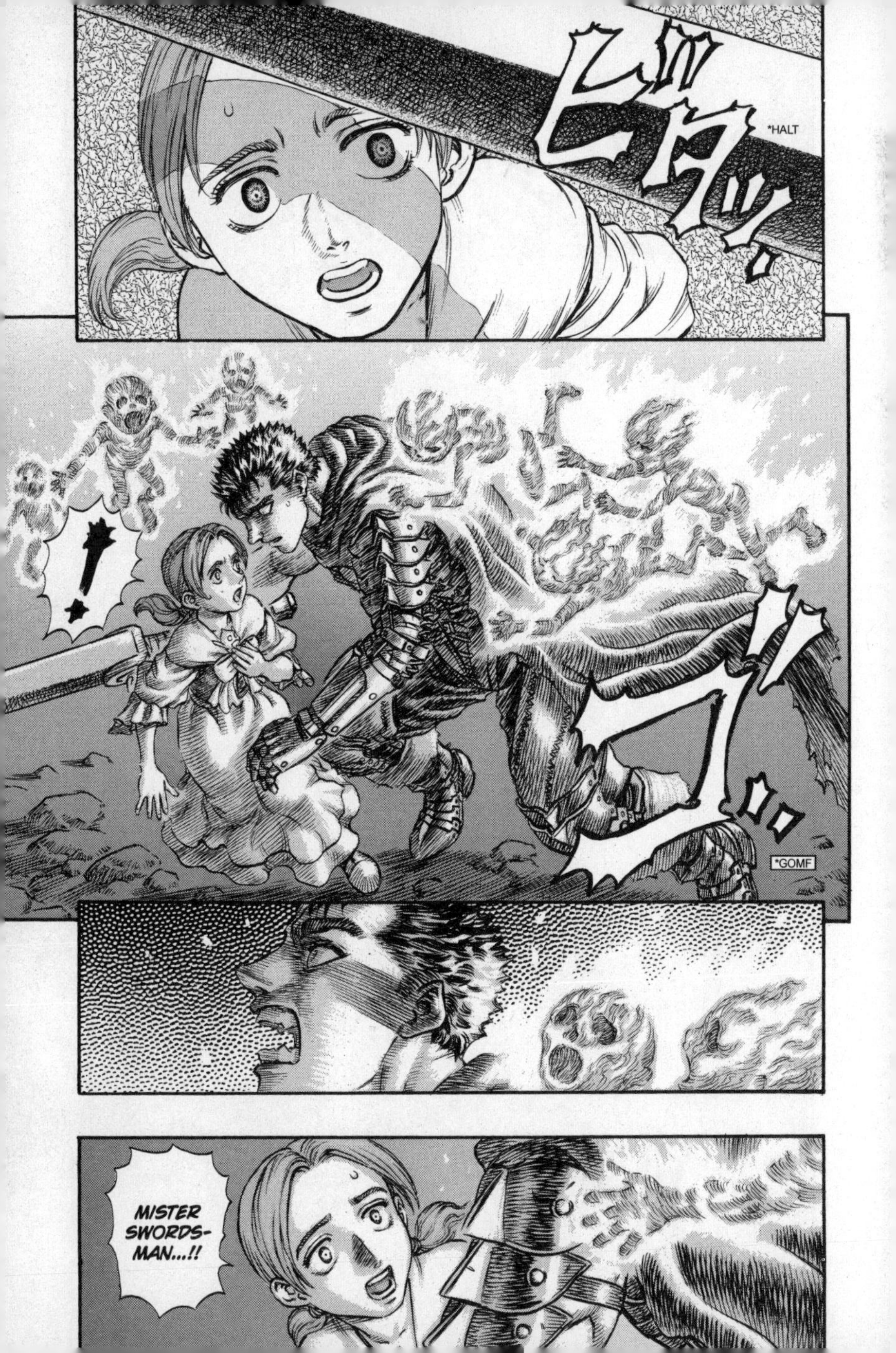
ヒタッ!
*HALT
!
*GOMF
MISTER SWORDS-MAN...!!

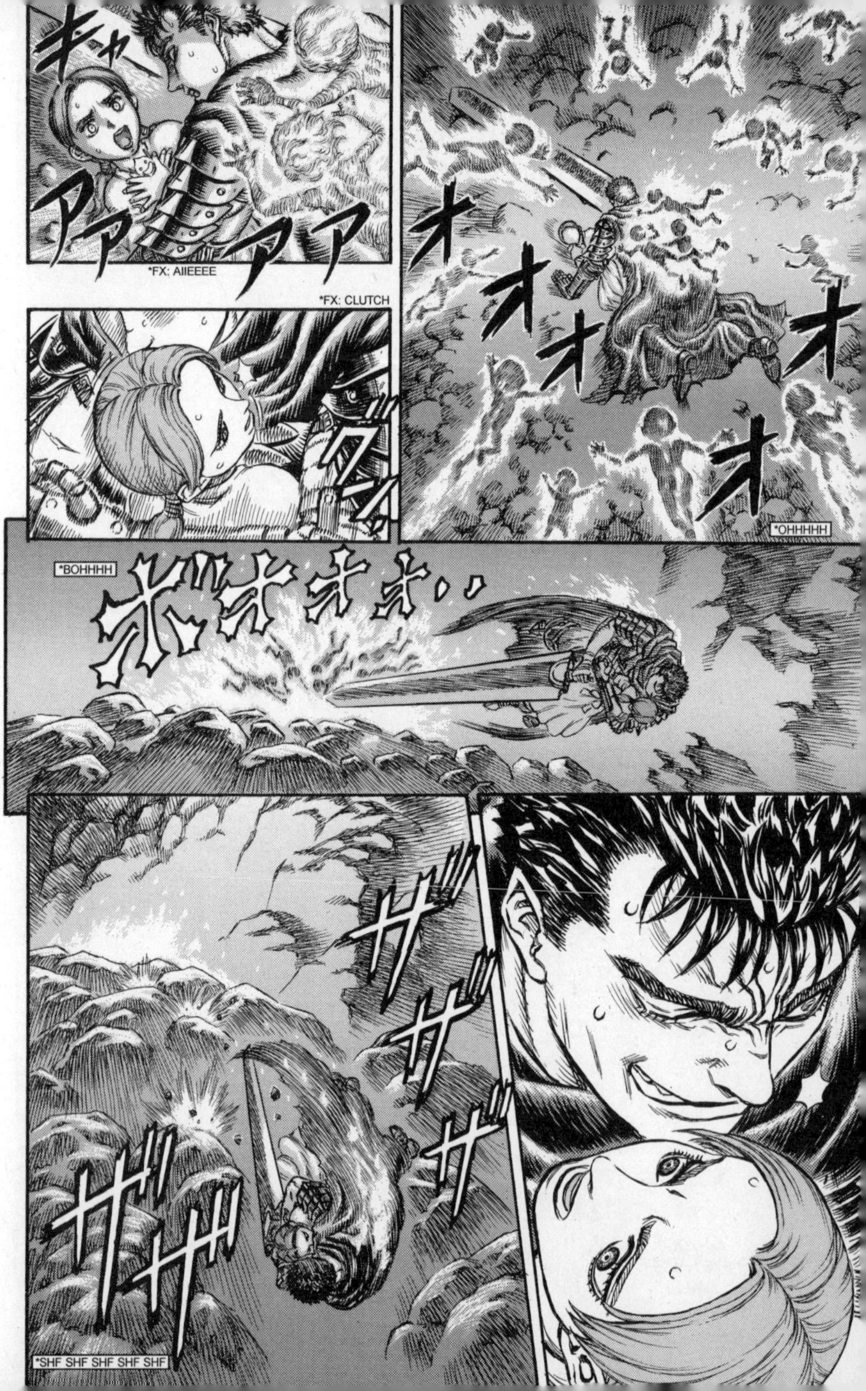
オオオオオ
*OHHHHH
ギャーアアアアア
*FX: AIIEEEE
*FX: CLUTCH
ボオオオ…
*BOHHHH
*SHF SHF SHF SHF SHF

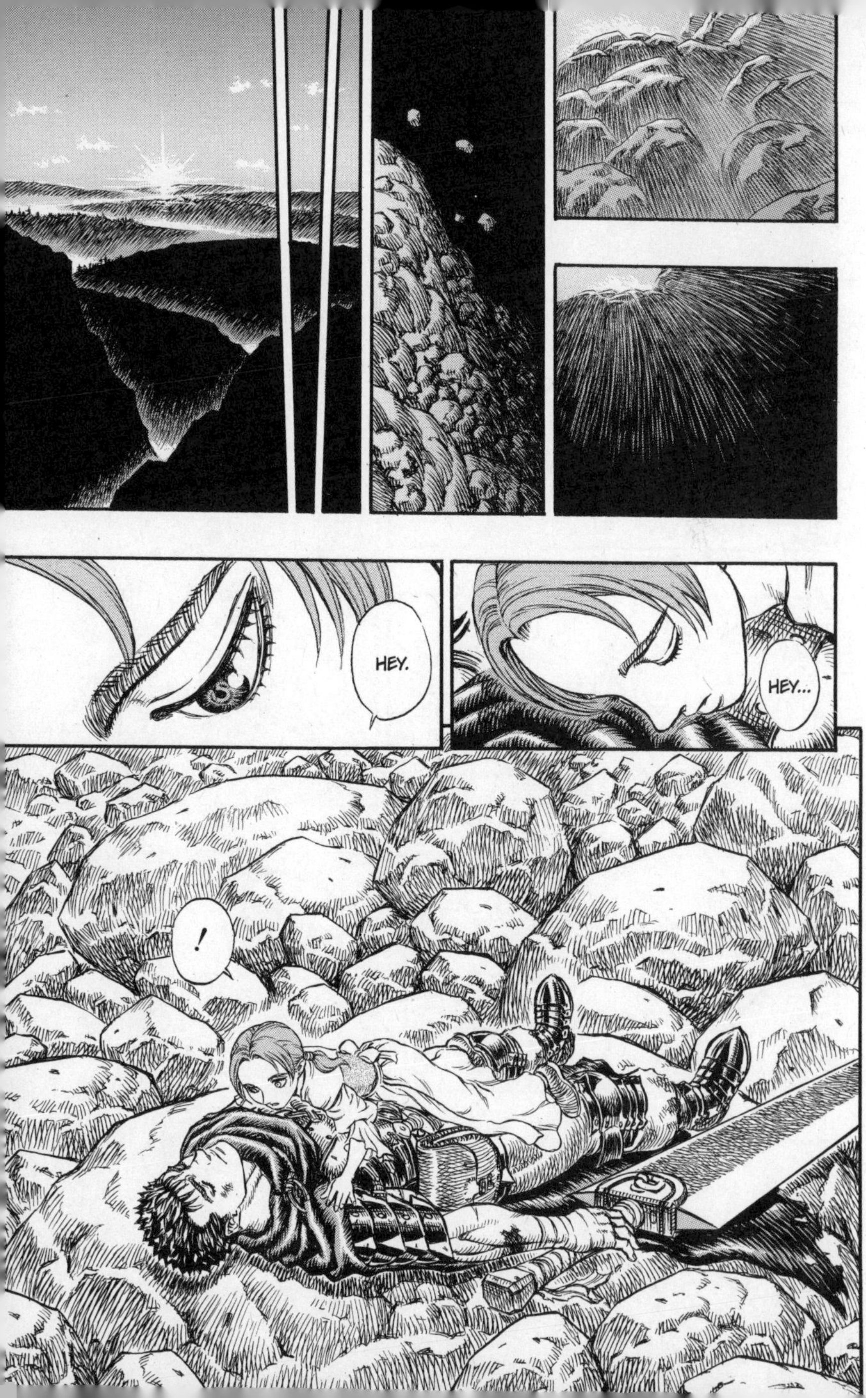
HEY...
HEY.
!

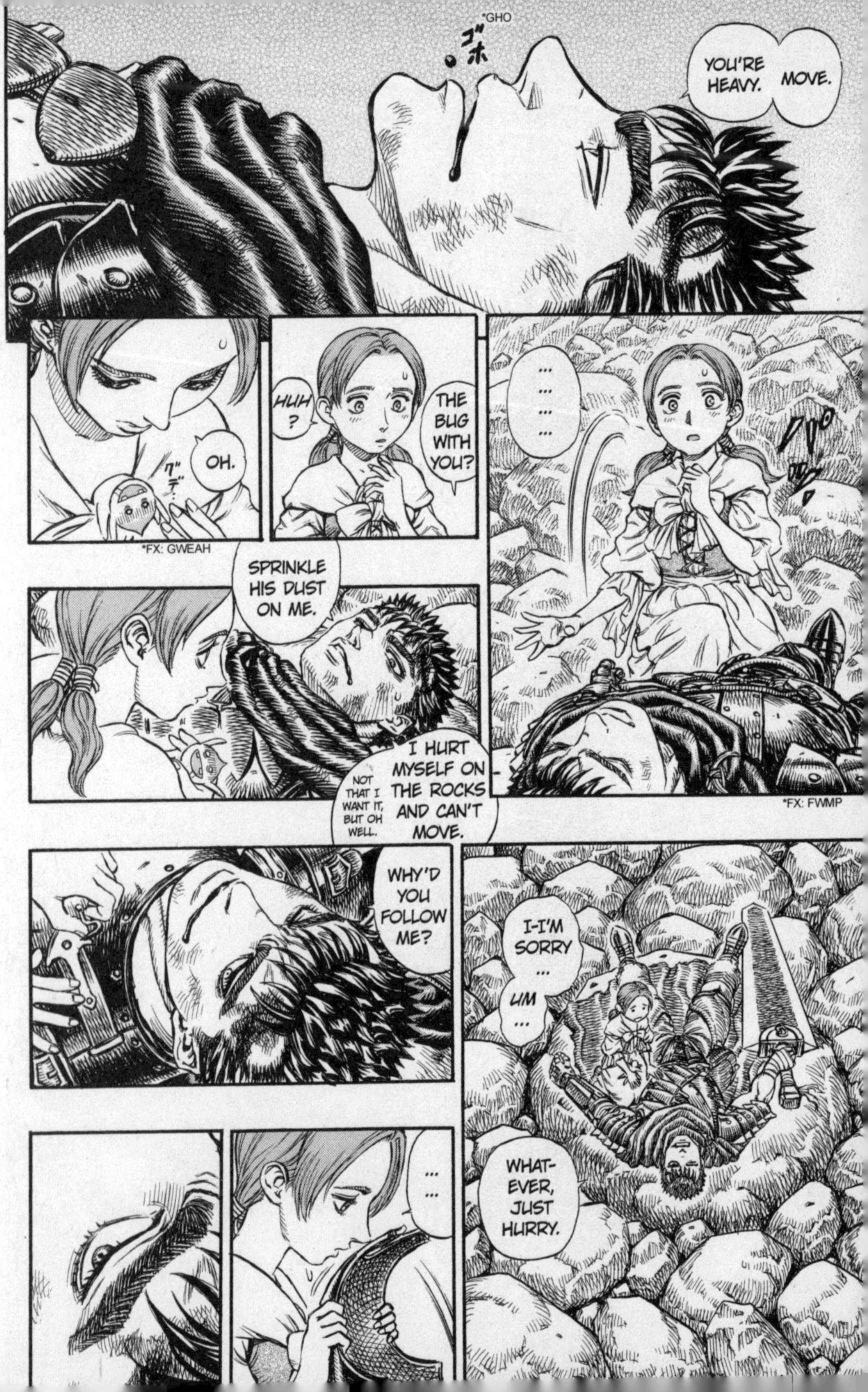
*GHO
YOU'RE HEAVY.
MOVE.
......
*FX: FWMP
THE BUG WITH YOU?
HUH?
OH.
*FX: GWEAH
SPRINKLE HIS DUST ON ME.
I HURT MYSELF ON THE ROCKS AND CAN'T MOVE.
NOT THAT I WANT IT, BUT OH WELL.
I-I'M SORRY... UM...
WHAT-EVER, JUST HURRY.
WHY'D YOU FOLLOW ME?
......

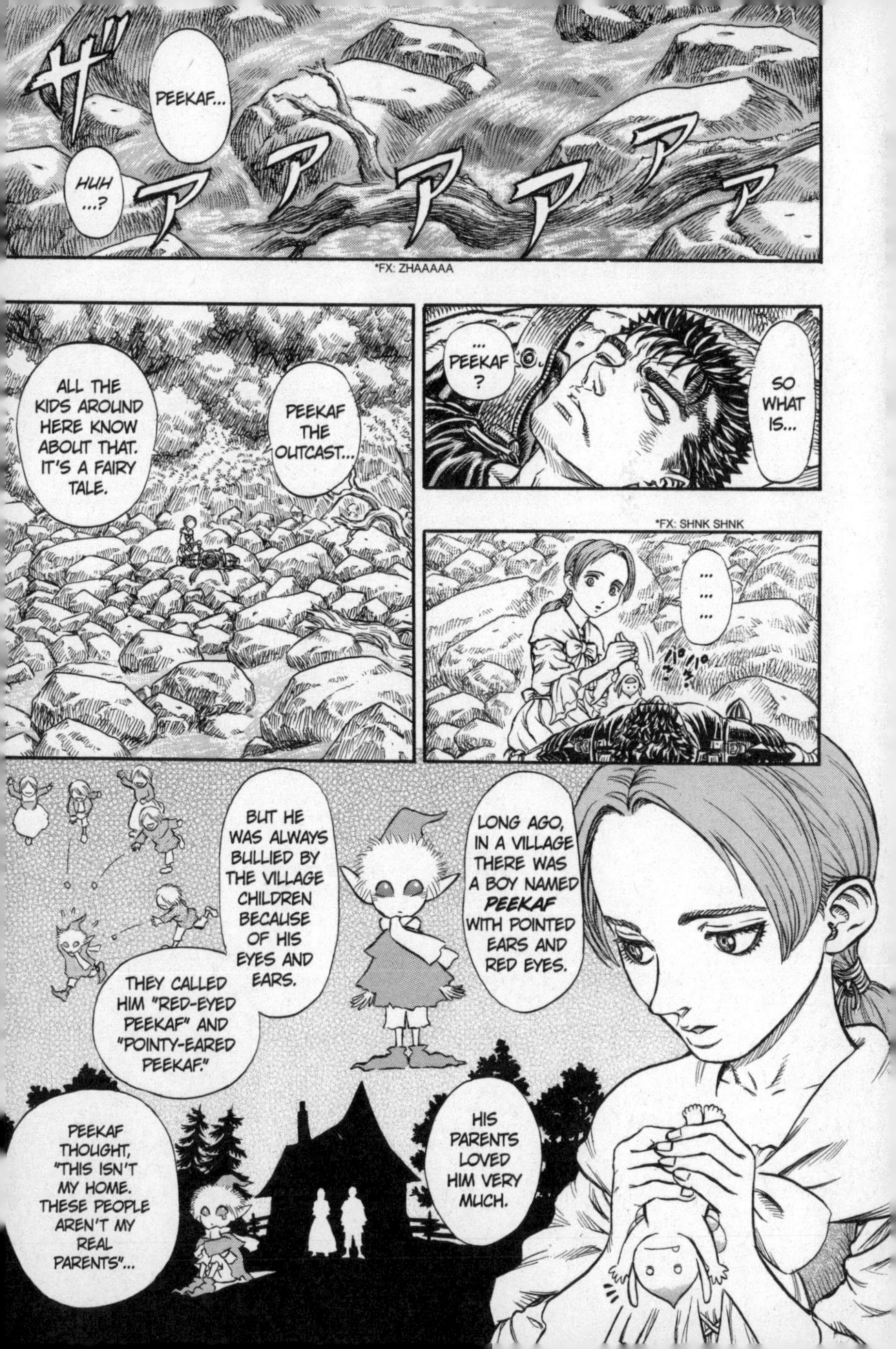
PEEKAF...
HUH ...?
*FX: ZHAAAAA
SO WHAT IS...
... PEEKAF ?
*FX: SHNK SHNK
... ...
PEEKAF THE OUTCAST...
ALL THE KIDS AROUND HERE KNOW ABOUT THAT. IT'S A FAIRY TALE.
LONG AGO, IN A VILLAGE THERE WAS A BOY NAMED **PEEKAF** WITH POINTED EARS AND RED EYES.
BUT HE WAS ALWAYS BULLIED BY THE VILLAGE CHILDREN BECAUSE OF HIS EYES AND EARS.
THEY CALLED HIM "RED-EYED PEEKAF" AND "POINTY-EARED PEEKAF."
HIS PARENTS LOVED HIM VERY MUCH.
PEEKAF THOUGHT, "THIS ISN'T MY HOME. THESE PEOPLE AREN'T MY REAL PARENTS"...

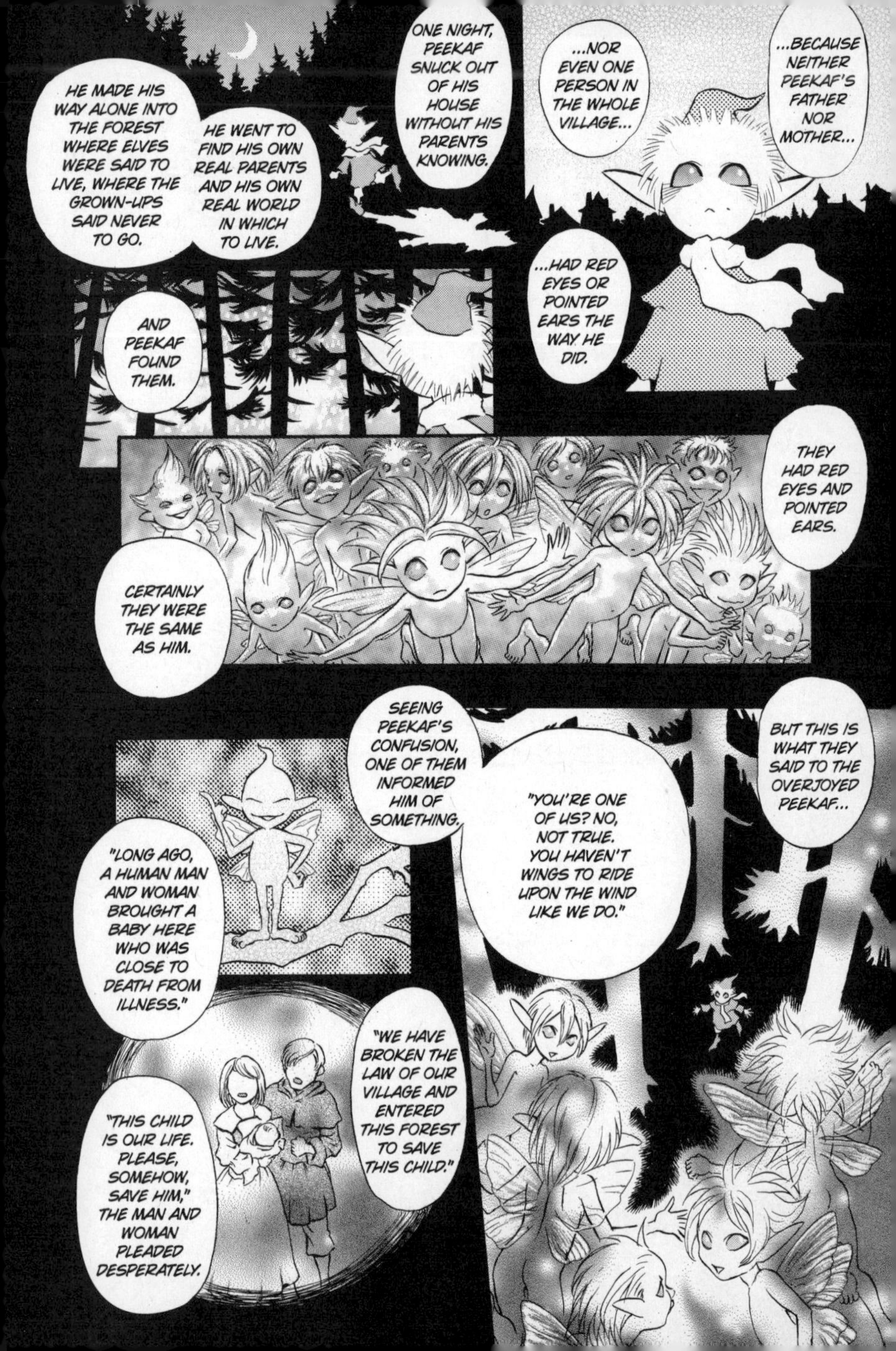

...BECAUSE NEITHER PEEKAF'S FATHER NOR MOTHER...
...NOR EVEN ONE PERSON IN THE WHOLE VILLAGE...
...HAD RED EYES OR POINTED EARS THE WAY HE DID.
ONE NIGHT, PEEKAF SNUCK OUT OF HIS HOUSE WITHOUT HIS PARENTS KNOWING.
HE WENT TO FIND HIS OWN REAL PARENTS AND HIS OWN REAL WORLD IN WHICH TO LIVE.
HE MADE HIS WAY ALONE INTO THE FOREST WHERE ELVES WERE SAID TO LIVE, WHERE THE GROWN-UPS SAID NEVER TO GO.
AND PEEKAF FOUND THEM.
THEY HAD RED EYES AND POINTED EARS.
CERTAINLY THEY WERE THE SAME AS HIM.
BUT THIS IS WHAT THEY SAID TO THE OVERJOYED PEEKAF...
"YOU'RE ONE OF US? NO, NOT TRUE. YOU HAVEN'T WINGS TO RIDE UPON THE WIND LIKE WE DO."
SEEING PEEKAF'S CONFUSION, ONE OF THEM INFORMED HIM OF SOMETHING.
"LONG AGO, A HUMAN MAN AND WOMAN BROUGHT A BABY HERE WHO WAS CLOSE TO DEATH FROM ILLNESS."
"WE HAVE BROKEN THE LAW OF OUR VILLAGE AND ENTERED THIS FOREST TO SAVE THIS CHILD."
"THIS CHILD IS OUR LIFE. PLEASE, SOMEHOW, SAVE HIM," THE MAN AND WOMAN PLEADED DESPERATELY.

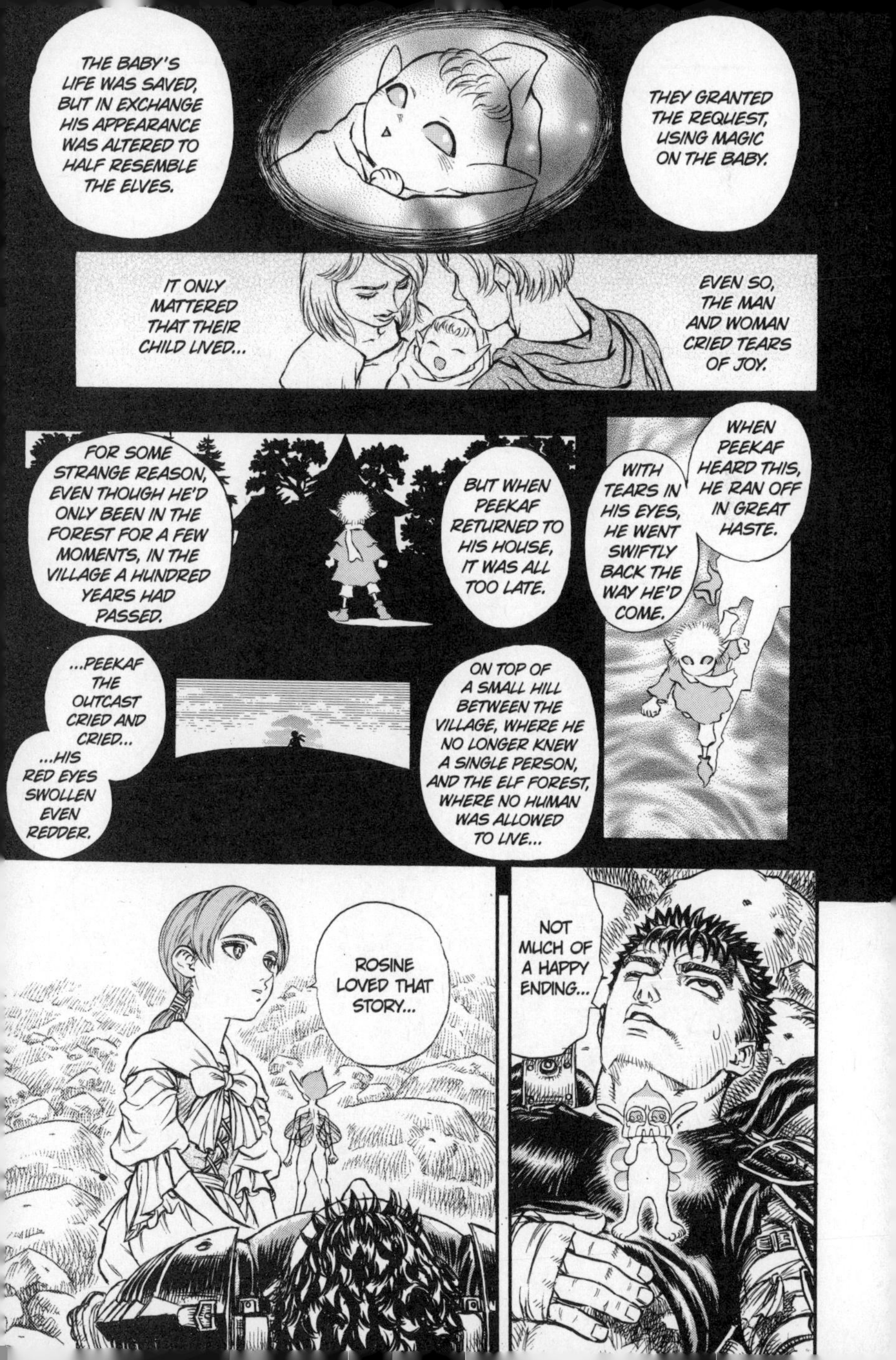
THEY GRANTED THE REQUEST, USING MAGIC ON THE BABY.
THE BABY'S LIFE WAS SAVED, BUT IN EXCHANGE HIS APPEARANCE WAS ALTERED TO HALF RESEMBLE THE ELVES.
EVEN SO, THE MAN AND WOMAN CRIED TEARS OF JOY.
IT ONLY MATTERED THAT THEIR CHILD LIVED...
WHEN PEEKAF HEARD THIS, HE RAN OFF IN GREAT HASTE.
WITH TEARS IN HIS EYES, HE WENT SWIFTLY BACK THE WAY HE'D COME.
BUT WHEN PEEKAF RETURNED TO HIS HOUSE, IT WAS ALL TOO LATE.
FOR SOME STRANGE REASON, EVEN THOUGH HE'D ONLY BEEN IN THE FOREST FOR A FEW MOMENTS, IN THE VILLAGE A HUNDRED YEARS HAD PASSED.
ON TOP OF A SMALL HILL BETWEEN THE VILLAGE, WHERE HE NO LONGER KNEW A SINGLE PERSON, AND THE ELF FOREST, WHERE NO HUMAN WAS ALLOWED TO LIVE...
...PEEKAF THE OUTCAST CRIED AND CRIED...
...HIS RED EYES SWOLLEN EVEN REDDER.
NOT MUCH OF A HAPPY ENDING...
ROSINE LOVED THAT STORY...

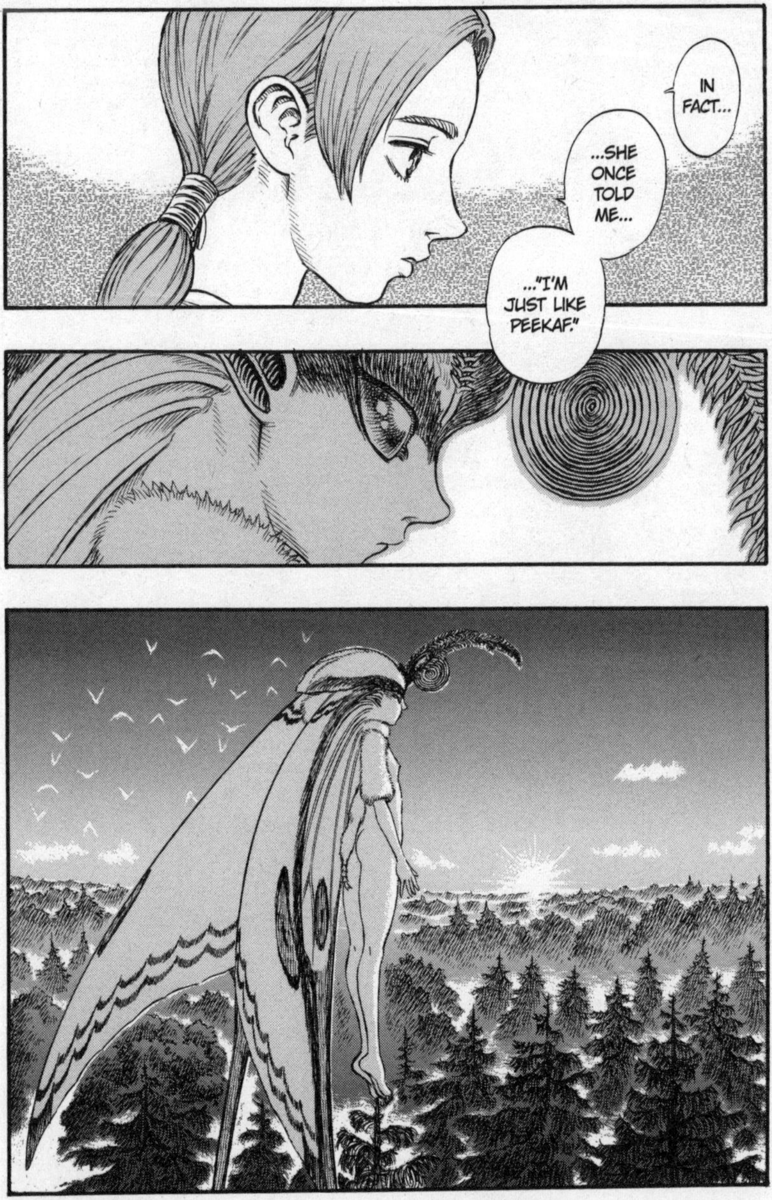
IN FACT...
...SHE ONCE TOLD ME...
..."I'M JUST LIKE PEEKAF."

CONVICTION ARC
LOST CHILDREN CHAPTER

RED-EYED PEEKAF: END

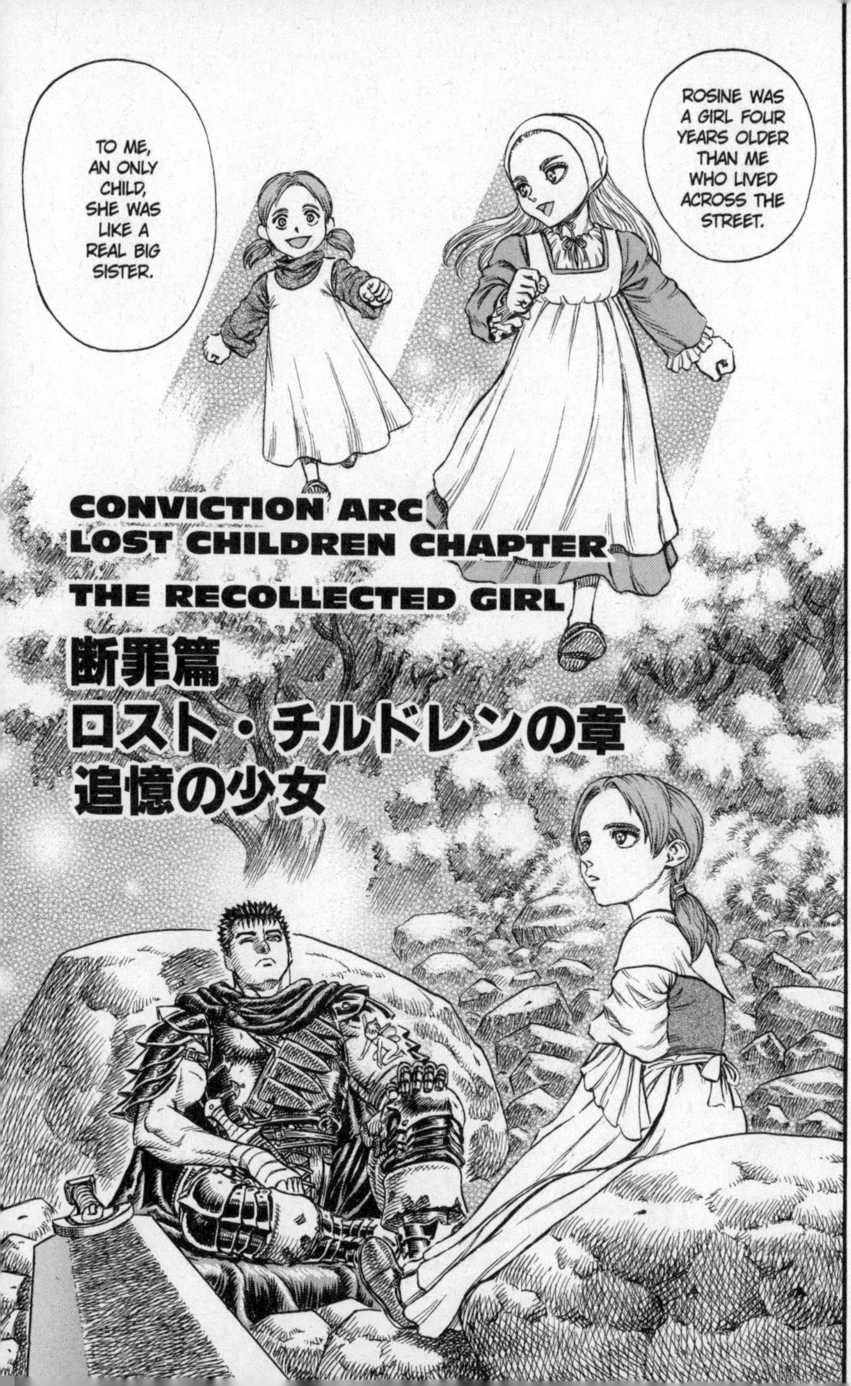
ROSINE WAS A GIRL FOUR YEARS OLDER THAN ME WHO LIVED ACROSS THE STREET.
TO ME, AN ONLY CHILD, SHE WAS LIKE A REAL BIG SISTER.
CONVICTION ARC
LOST CHILDREN CHAPTER
THE RECOLLECTED GIRL
断罪篇
ロスト・チルドレンの章
追憶の少女

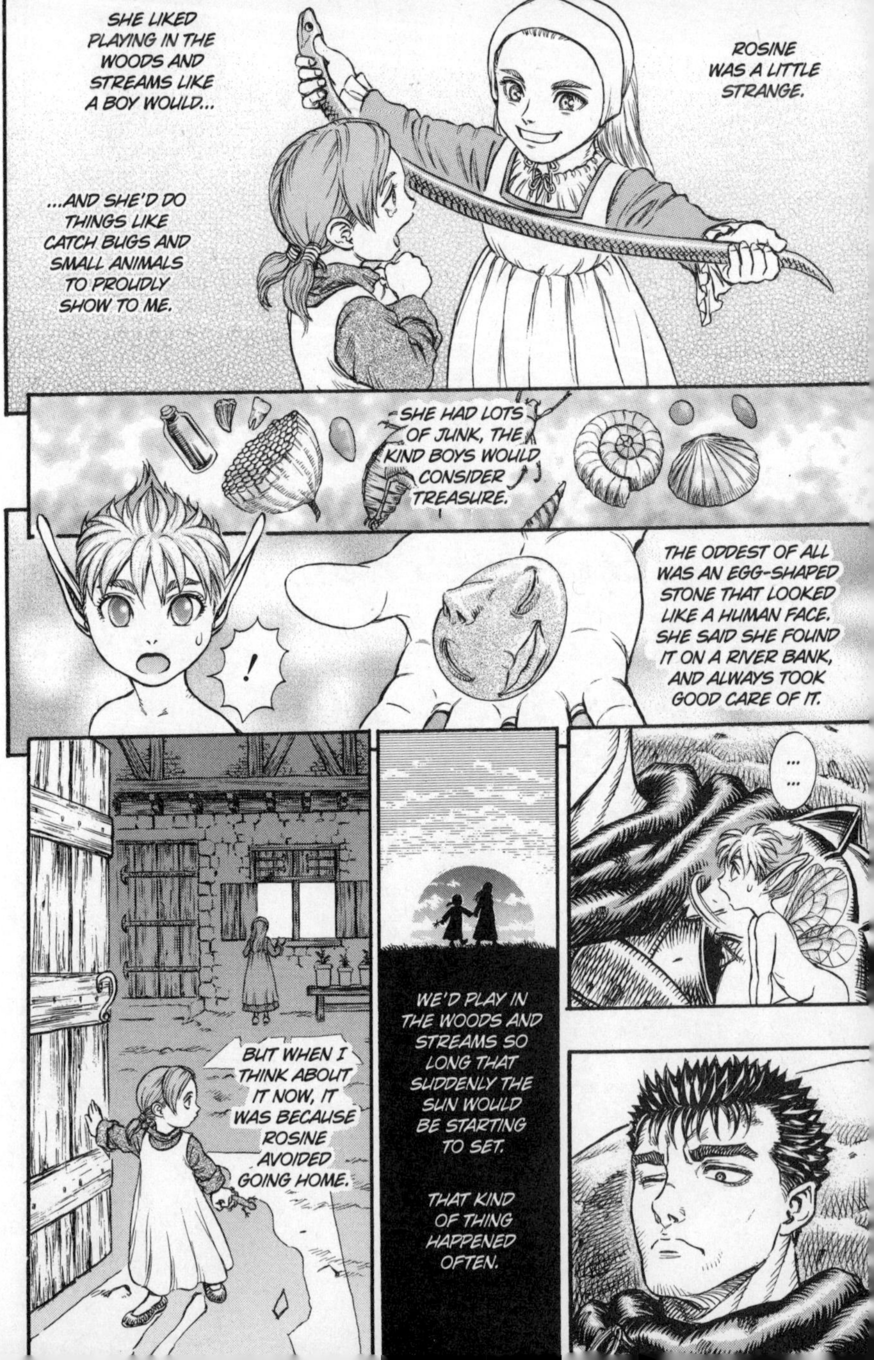
ROSINE WAS A LITTLE STRANGE.
SHE LIKED PLAYING IN THE WOODS AND STREAMS LIKE A BOY WOULD...
...AND SHE'D DO THINGS LIKE CATCH BUGS AND SMALL ANIMALS TO PROUDLY SHOW TO ME.
SHE HAD LOTS OF JUNK, THE KIND BOYS WOULD CONSIDER TREASURE.
THE ODDEST OF ALL WAS AN EGG-SHAPED STONE THAT LOOKED LIKE A HUMAN FACE. SHE SAID SHE FOUND IT ON A RIVER BANK, AND ALWAYS TOOK GOOD CARE OF IT.
!
... ...
WE'D PLAY IN THE WOODS AND STREAMS SO LONG THAT SUDDENLY THE SUN WOULD BE STARTING TO SET.
THAT KIND OF THING HAPPENED OFTEN.
BUT WHEN I THINK ABOUT IT NOW, IT WAS BECAUSE ROSINE AVOIDED GOING HOME.

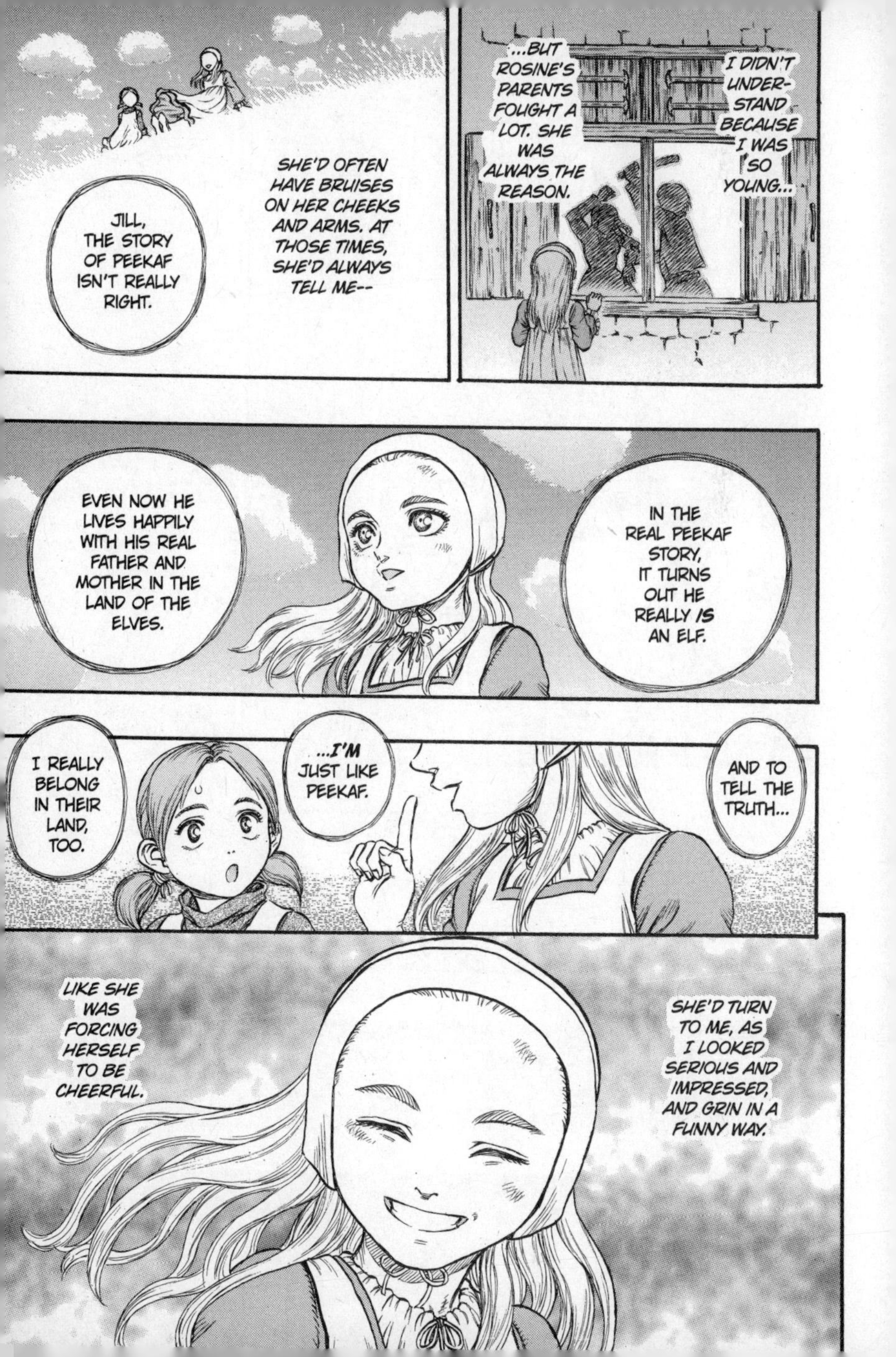
I DIDN'T UNDERSTAND BECAUSE I WAS SO YOUNG...
...BUT ROSINE'S PARENTS FOUGHT A LOT. SHE WAS ALWAYS THE REASON.
SHE'D OFTEN HAVE BRUISES ON HER CHEEKS AND ARMS. AT THOSE TIMES, SHE'D ALWAYS TELL ME--
JILL, THE STORY OF PEEKAF ISN'T REALLY RIGHT.
IN THE REAL PEEKAF STORY, IT TURNS OUT HE REALLY *IS* AN ELF.
EVEN NOW HE LIVES HAPPILY WITH HIS REAL FATHER AND MOTHER IN THE LAND OF THE ELVES.
AND TO TELL THE TRUTH...
...I'M JUST LIKE PEEKAF.
I REALLY BELONG IN THEIR LAND, TOO.
SHE'D TURN TO ME, AS I LOOKED SERIOUS AND IMPRESSED, AND GRIN IN A FUNNY WAY.
LIKE SHE WAS FORCING HERSELF TO BE CHEERFUL.

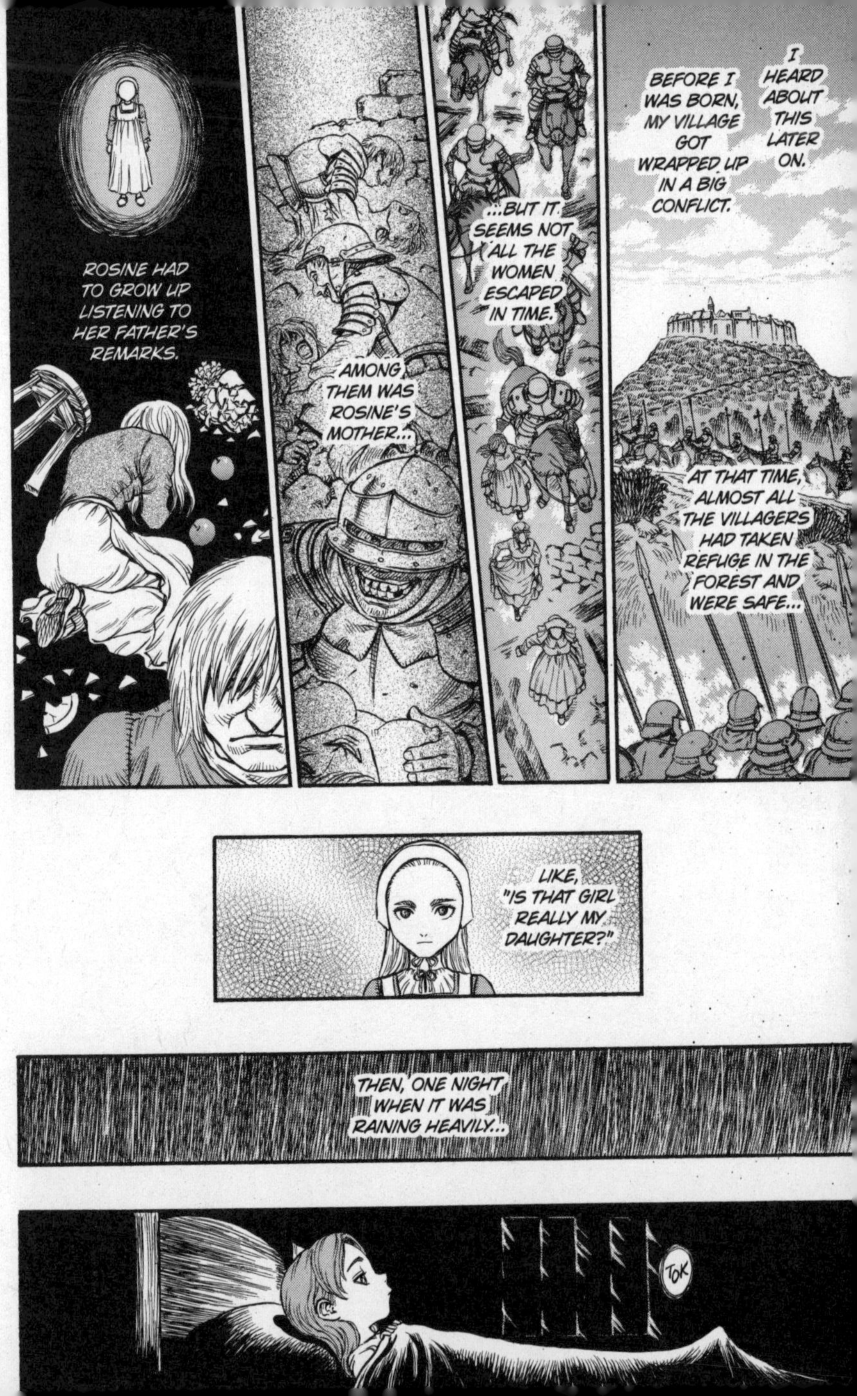
I HEARD ABOUT THIS LATER ON.
BEFORE I WAS BORN, MY VILLAGE GOT WRAPPED UP IN A BIG CONFLICT.
AT THAT TIME, ALMOST ALL THE VILLAGERS HAD TAKEN REFUGE IN THE FOREST AND WERE SAFE...
...BUT IT SEEMS NOT ALL THE WOMEN ESCAPED IN TIME.
AMONG THEM WAS ROSINE'S MOTHER...
ROSINE HAD TO GROW UP LISTENING TO HER FATHER'S REMARKS.
LIKE, "IS THAT GIRL REALLY MY DAUGHTER?"
THEN, ONE NIGHT WHEN IT WAS RAINING HEAVILY...
TOK

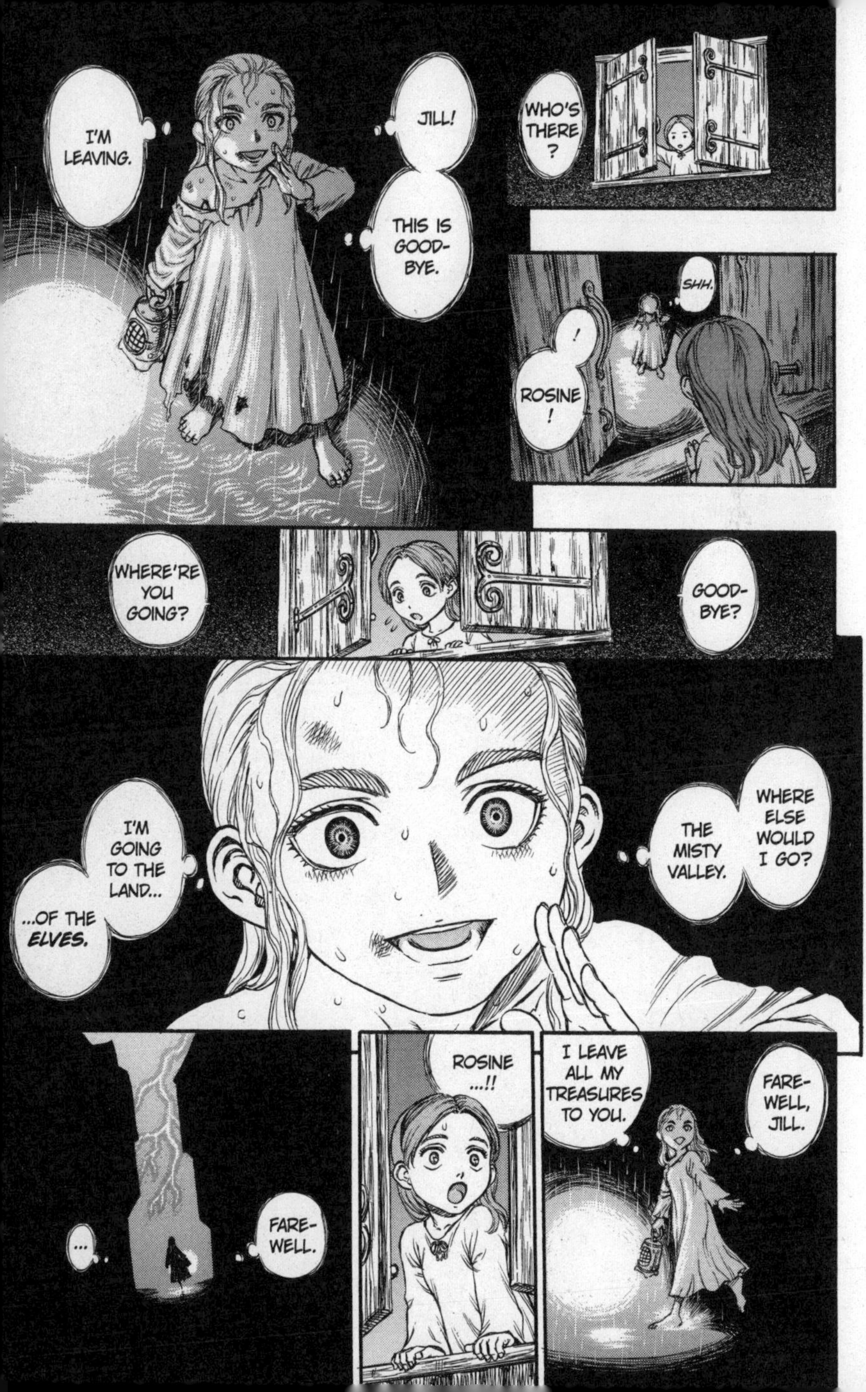
WHO'S THERE?
SHH.
!
ROSINE!
JILL!
THIS IS GOOD-BYE.
I'M LEAVING.
GOOD-BYE?
WHERE'RE YOU GOING?
WHERE ELSE WOULD I GO?
THE MISTY VALLEY.
I'M GOING TO THE LAND...
...OF THE *ELVES.*
FARE-WELL, JILL.
I LEAVE ALL MY TREASURES TO YOU.
ROSINE ...!!
FARE-WELL.
...

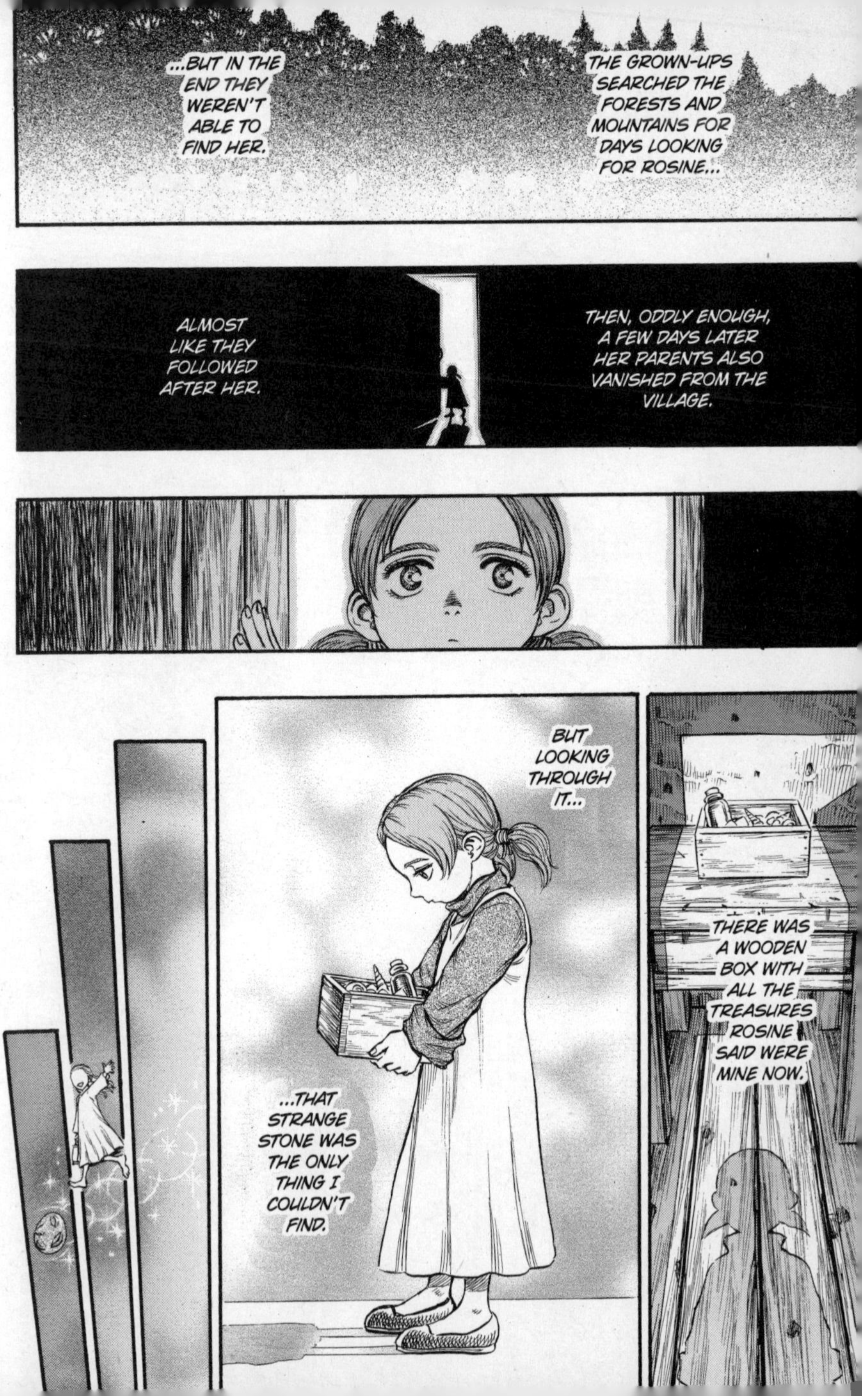
THE GROWN-UPS SEARCHED THE FORESTS AND MOUNTAINS FOR DAYS LOOKING FOR ROSINE...
...BUT IN THE END THEY WEREN'T ABLE TO FIND HER.
THEN, ODDLY ENOUGH, A FEW DAYS LATER HER PARENTS ALSO VANISHED FROM THE VILLAGE.
ALMOST LIKE THEY FOLLOWED AFTER HER.
THERE WAS A WOODEN BOX WITH ALL THE TREASURES ROSINE SAID WERE MINE NOW.
BUT LOOKING THROUGH IT...
...THAT STRANGE STONE WAS THE ONLY THING I COULDN'T FIND.

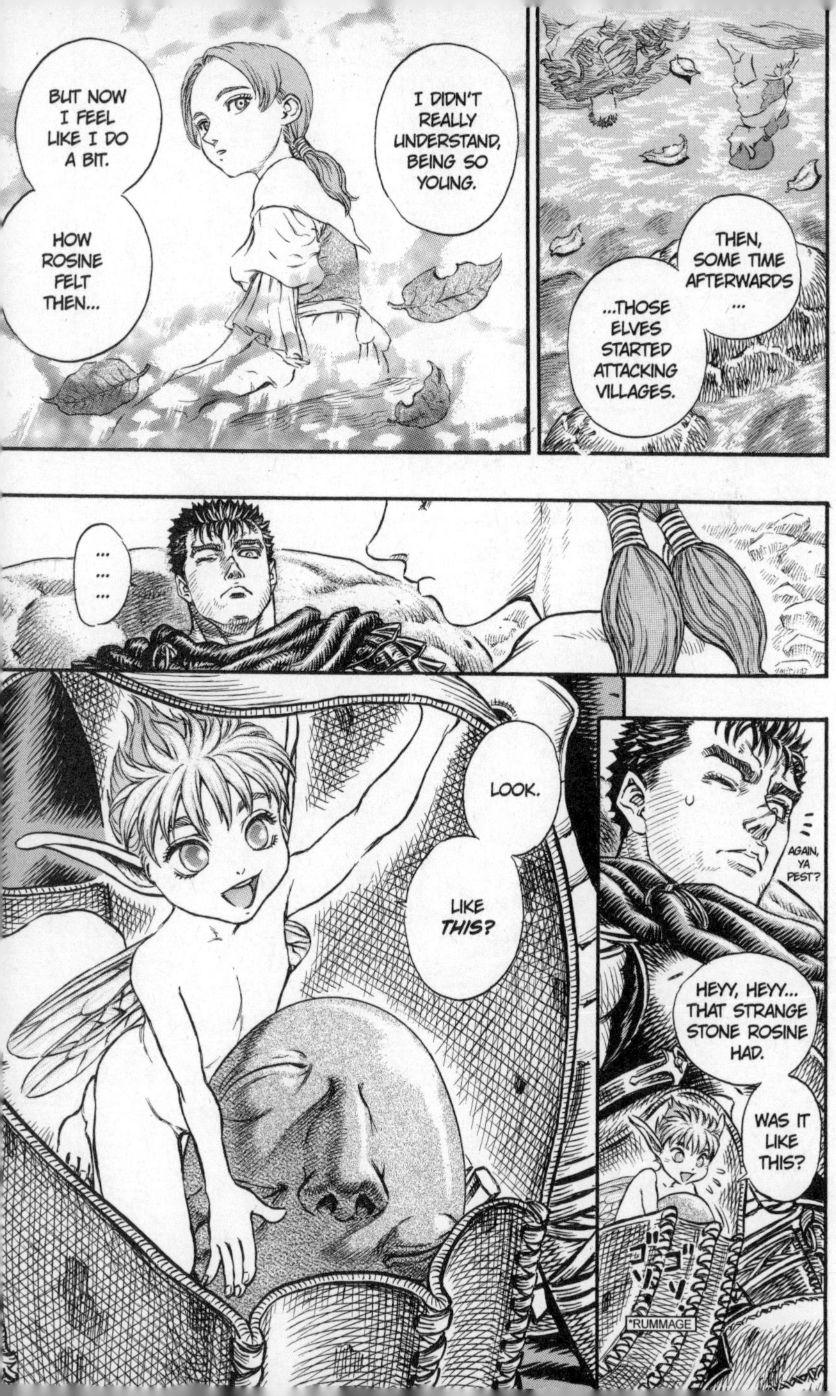
THEN, SOME TIME AFTERWARDS ...
...THOSE ELVES STARTED ATTACKING VILLAGES.
I DIDN'T REALLY UNDERSTAND, BEING SO YOUNG.
BUT NOW I FEEL LIKE I DO A BIT.
HOW ROSINE FELT THEN...
... ...
AGAIN, YA PEST?
HEYY, HEYY... THAT STRANGE STONE ROSINE HAD.
WAS IT LIKE THIS?
*RUMMAGE
LOOK.
LIKE *THIS?*

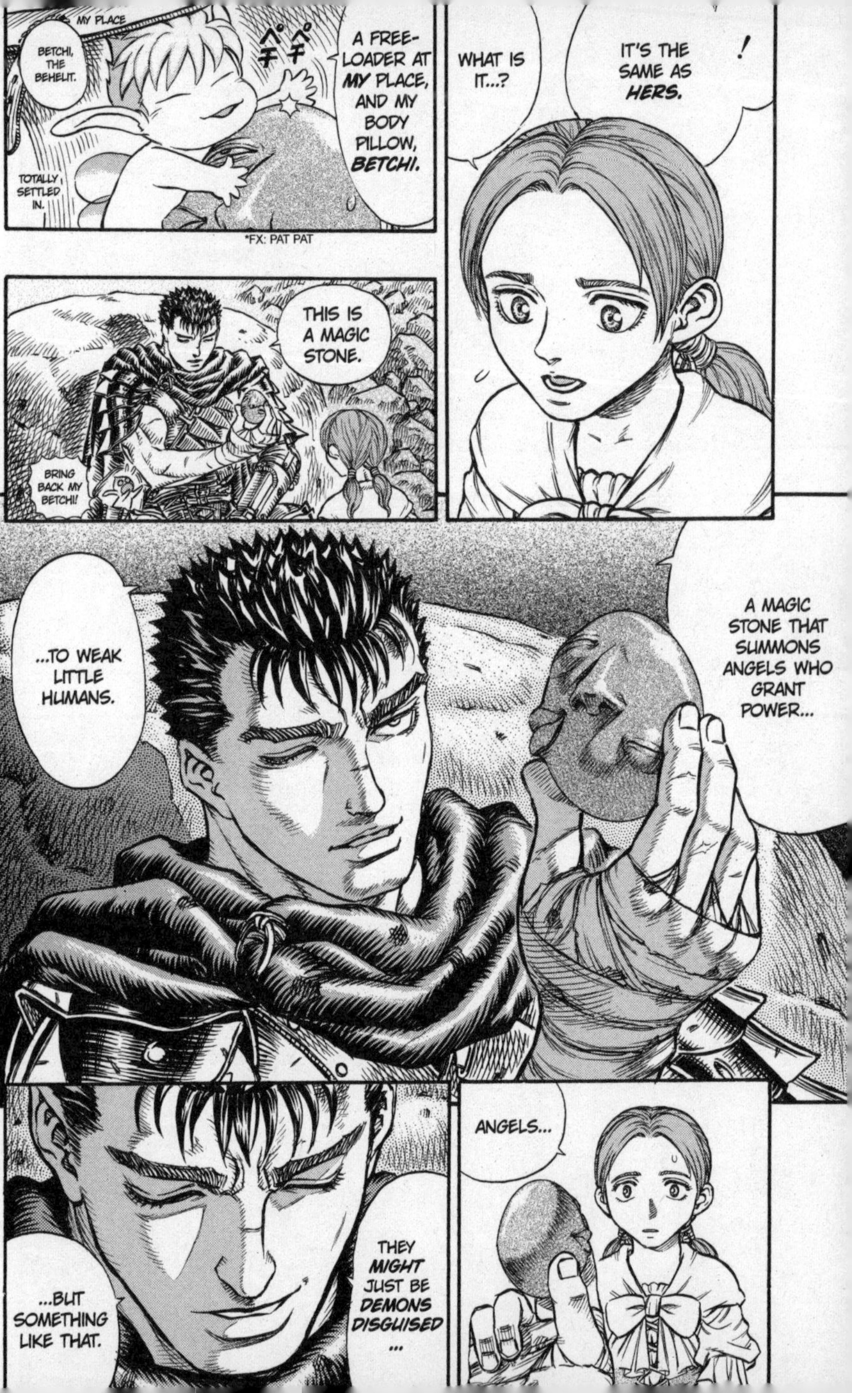

!
IT'S THE SAME AS **HERS.**
WHAT IS IT...?
A FREE-LOADER AT **MY** PLACE, AND MY BODY PILLOW, **BETCHI.**
ペチ ペチ
BETCHI, THE BEHELIT.
MY PLACE
TOTALLY SETTLED IN.
*FX: PAT PAT
THIS IS A MAGIC STONE.
BRING BACK MY BETCHI!
A MAGIC STONE THAT SUMMONS ANGELS WHO GRANT POWER...
...TO WEAK LITTLE HUMANS.
ANGELS...
THEY **MIGHT** JUST BE **DEMONS DISGUISED** ...
...BUT SOMETHING LIKE THAT.

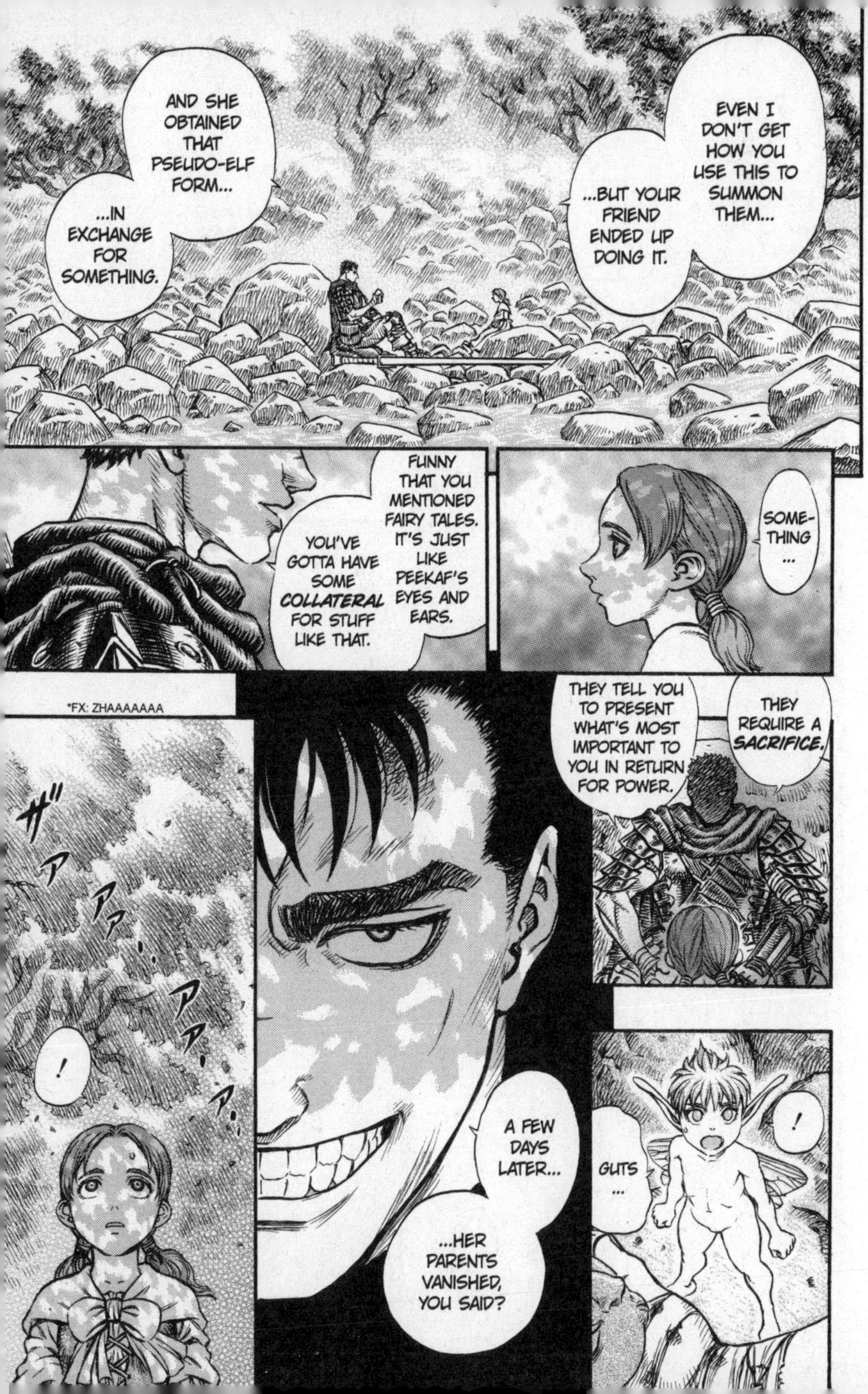
EVEN I DON'T GET HOW YOU USE THIS TO SUMMON THEM...
...BUT YOUR FRIEND ENDED UP DOING IT.
AND SHE OBTAINED THAT PSEUDO-ELF FORM...
...IN EXCHANGE FOR SOMETHING.
SOME-THING ...
FUNNY THAT YOU MENTIONED FAIRY TALES. IT'S JUST LIKE PEEKAF'S EYES AND EARS.
YOU'VE GOTTA HAVE SOME **COLLATERAL** FOR STUFF LIKE THAT.
THEY REQUIRE A ***SACRIFICE.***
THEY TELL YOU TO PRESENT WHAT'S MOST IMPORTANT TO YOU IN RETURN FOR POWER.
!
GUTS ...
A FEW DAYS LATER...
...HER PARENTS VANISHED, YOU SAID?
ザァァ...
!
*FX: ZHAAAAAAA

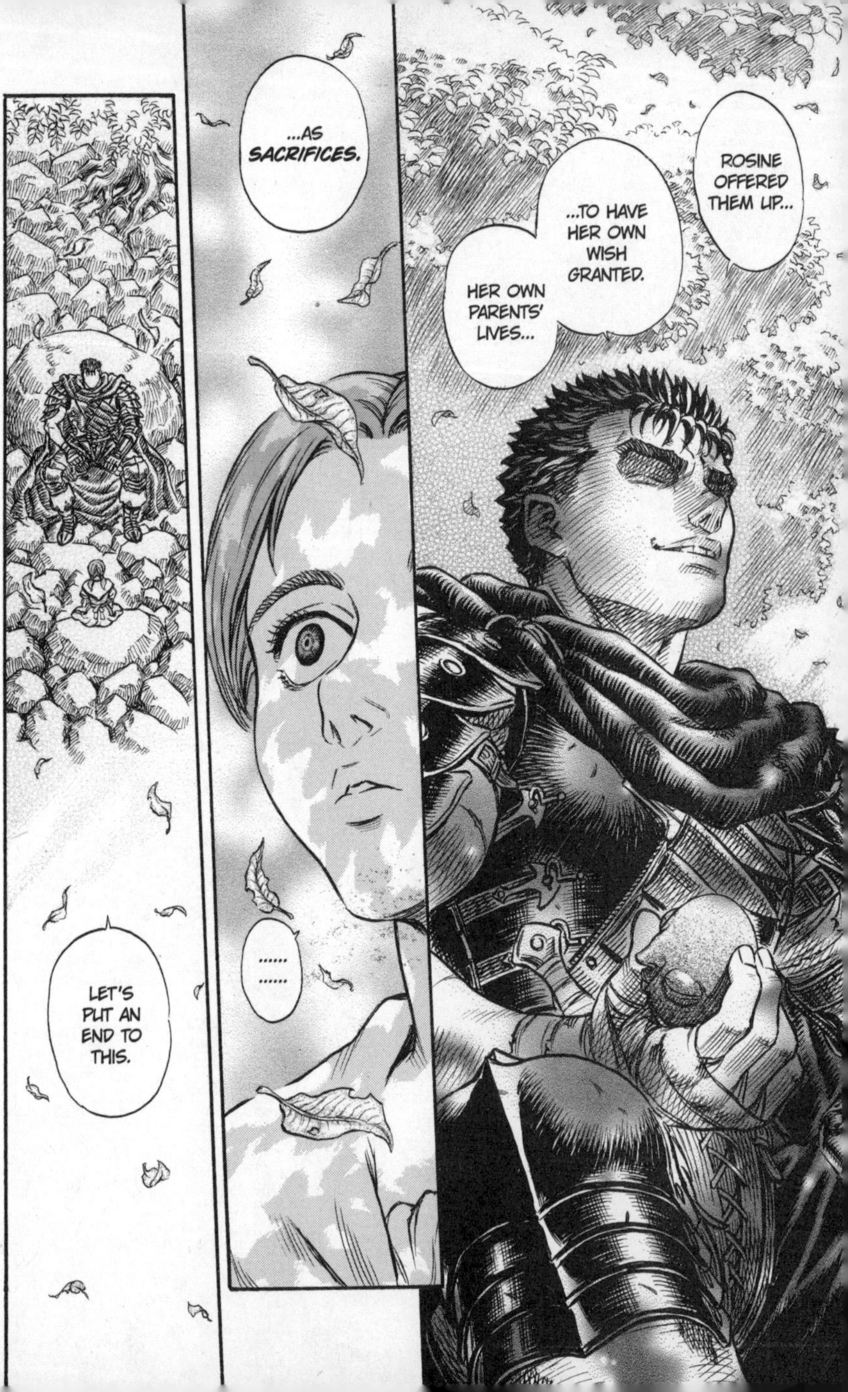
ROSINE OFFERED THEM UP...
...TO HAVE HER OWN WISH GRANTED.
HER OWN PARENTS' LIVES...
...AS SACRIFICES.
......
......
LET'S PUT AN END TO THIS.

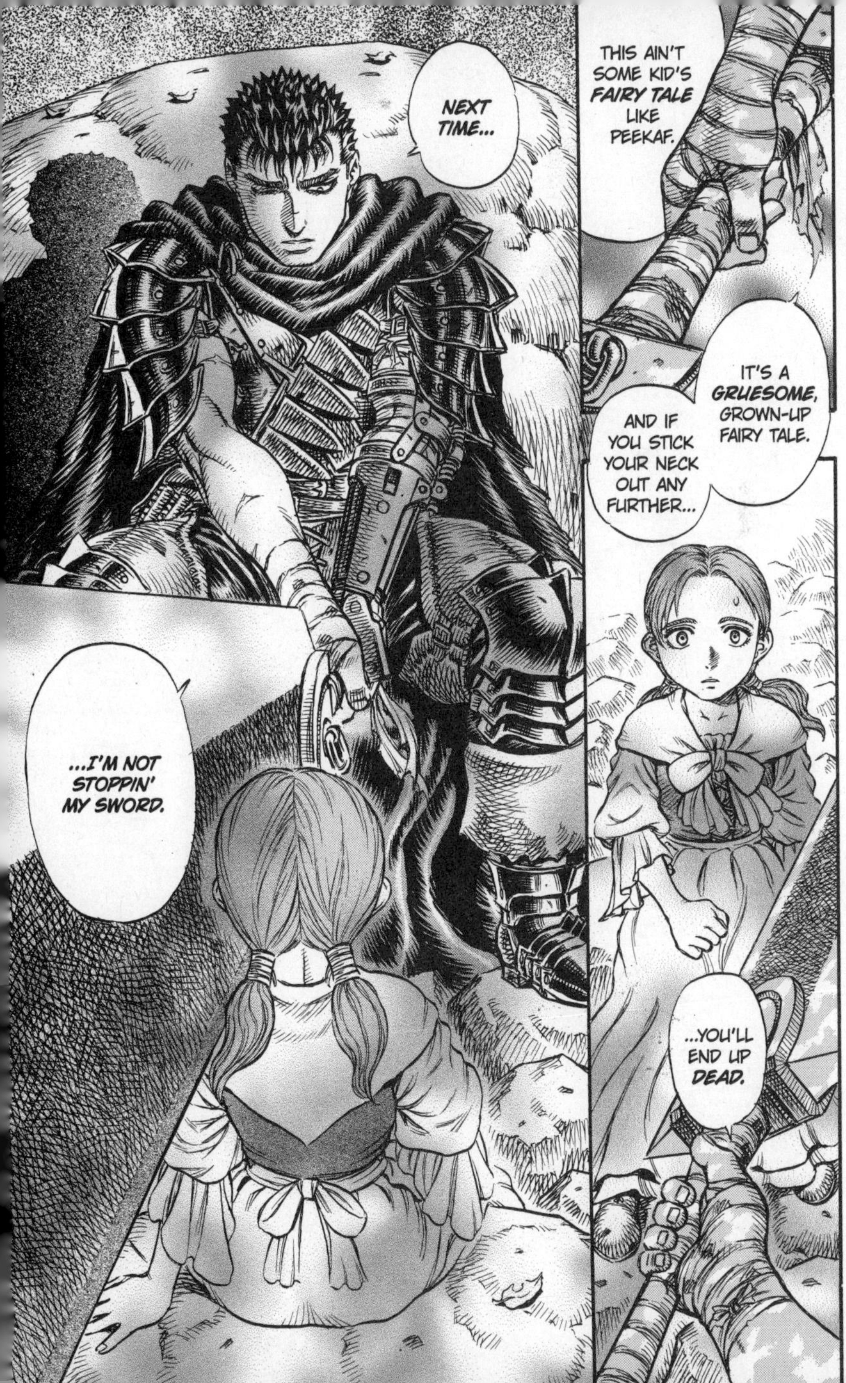
THIS AIN'T SOME KID'S FAIRY TALE LIKE PEEKAF.
IT'S A GRUESOME, GROWN-UP FAIRY TALE.
AND IF YOU STICK YOUR NECK OUT ANY FURTHER...
...YOU'LL END UP DEAD.
NEXT TIME...
...I'M NOT STOPPIN' MY SWORD.

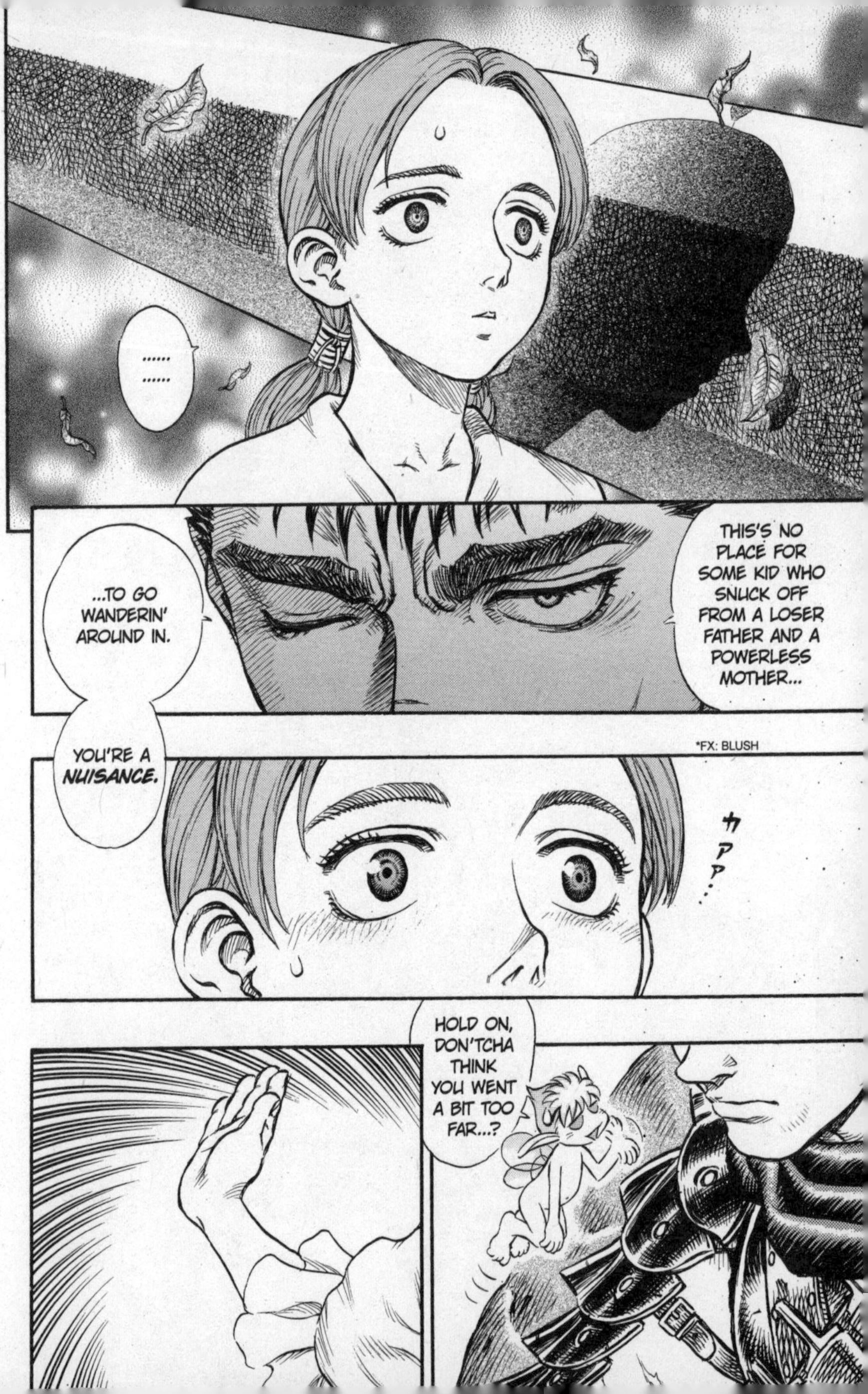

……
……
THIS'S NO PLACE FOR SOME KID WHO SNUCK OFF FROM A LOSER FATHER AND A POWERLESS MOTHER...
...TO GO WANDERIN' AROUND IN.
YOU'RE A ***NUISANCE.***
*FX: BLUSH
カァァ…
HOLD ON, DON'TCHA THINK YOU WENT A BIT TOO FAR...?

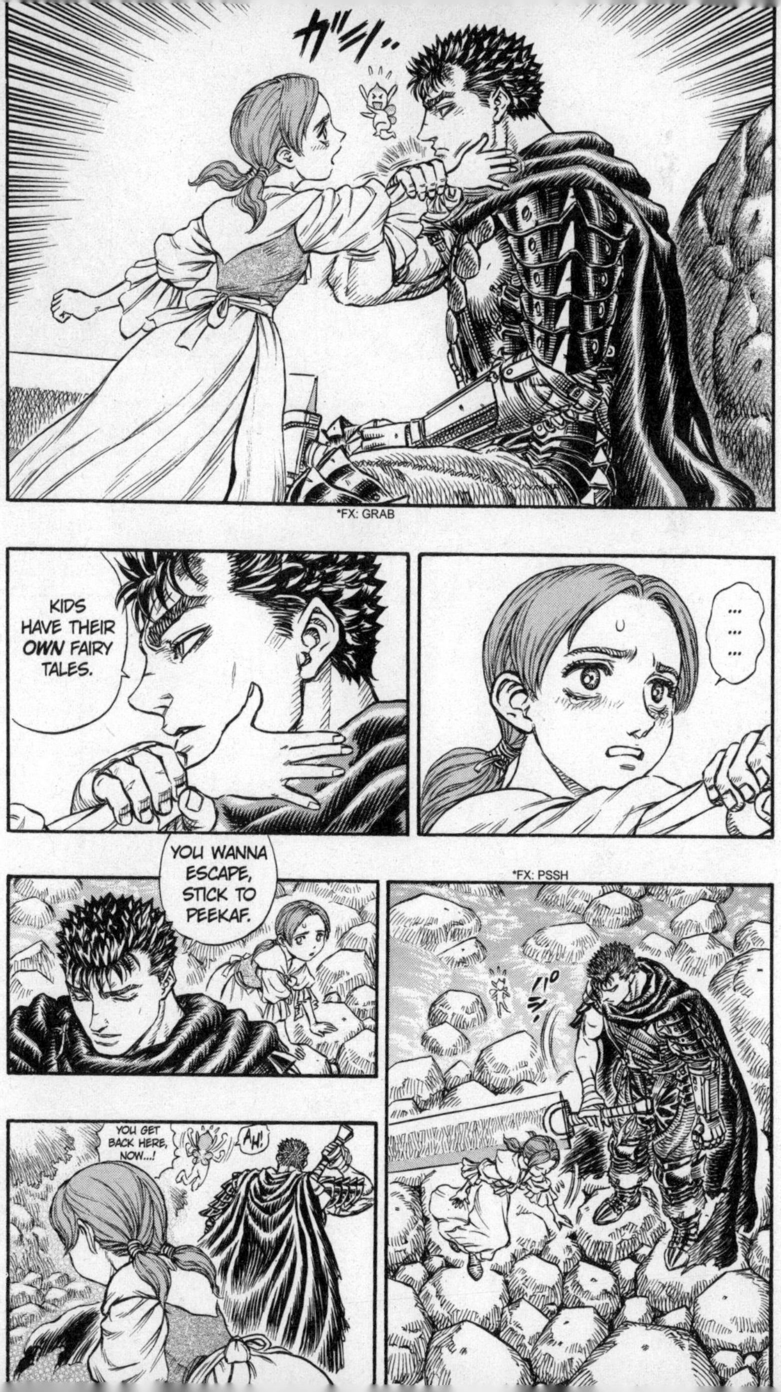
*FX: GRAB
...
...
...
KIDS HAVE THEIR OWN FAIRY TALES.
*FX: PSSH
YOU WANNA ESCAPE, STICK TO PEEKAF.
AH!
YOU GET BACK HERE, NOW...!

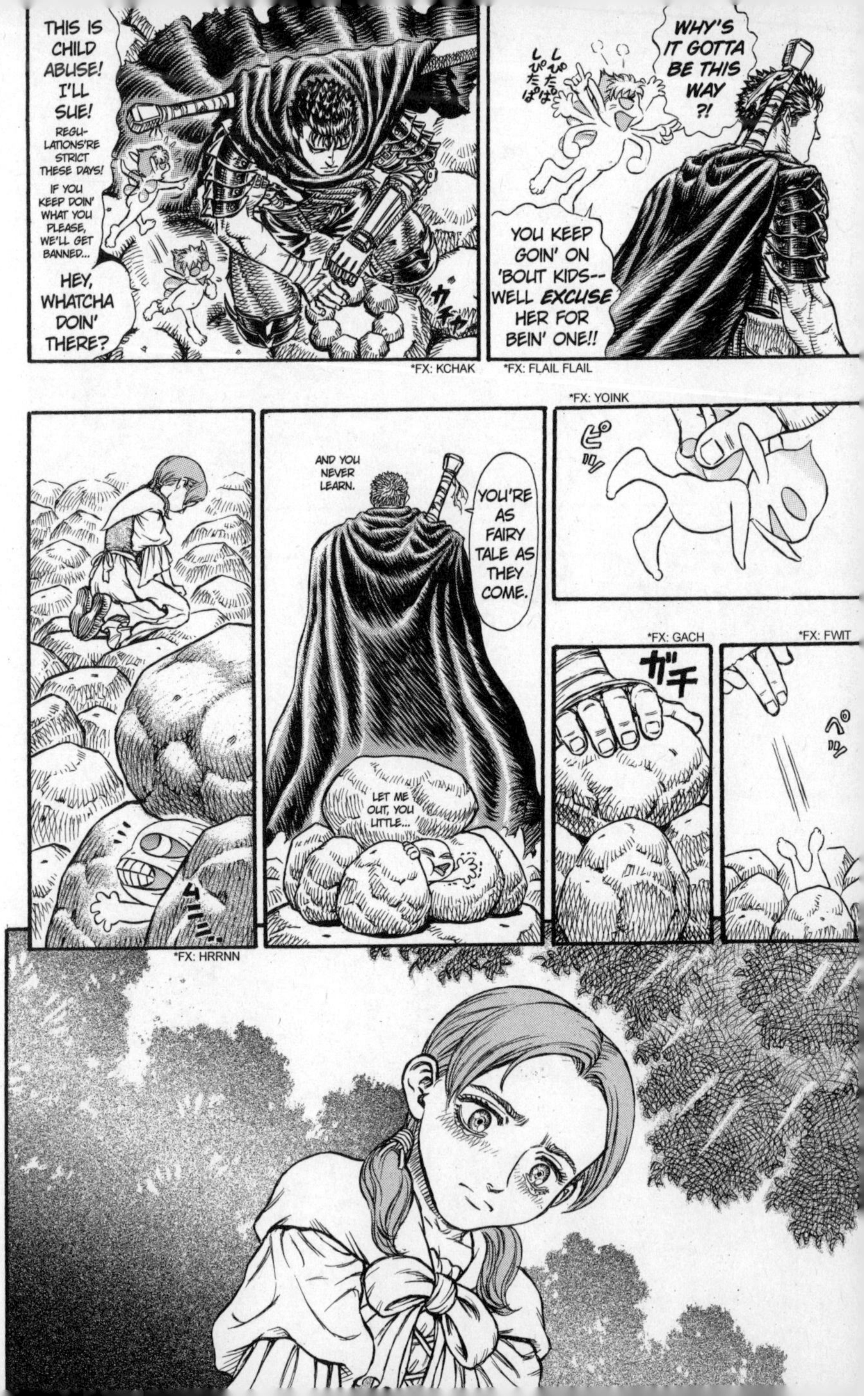
WHY'S IT GOTTA BE THIS WAY?!
YOU KEEP GOIN' ON 'BOUT KIDS-- WELL EXCUSE HER FOR BEIN' ONE!!
*FX: FLAIL FLAIL
THIS IS CHILD ABUSE! I'LL SUE!
REGULATIONS'RE STRICT THESE DAYS!
IF YOU KEEP DOIN' WHAT YOU PLEASE, WE'LL GET BANNED...
HEY, WHATCHA DOIN' THERE?
*FX: KCHAK
*FX: YOINK
*FX: FWIT
*FX: GACH
YOU'RE AS FAIRY TALE AS THEY COME.
AND YOU NEVER LEARN.
LET ME OUT, YOU LITTLE...
*FX: HRRNN

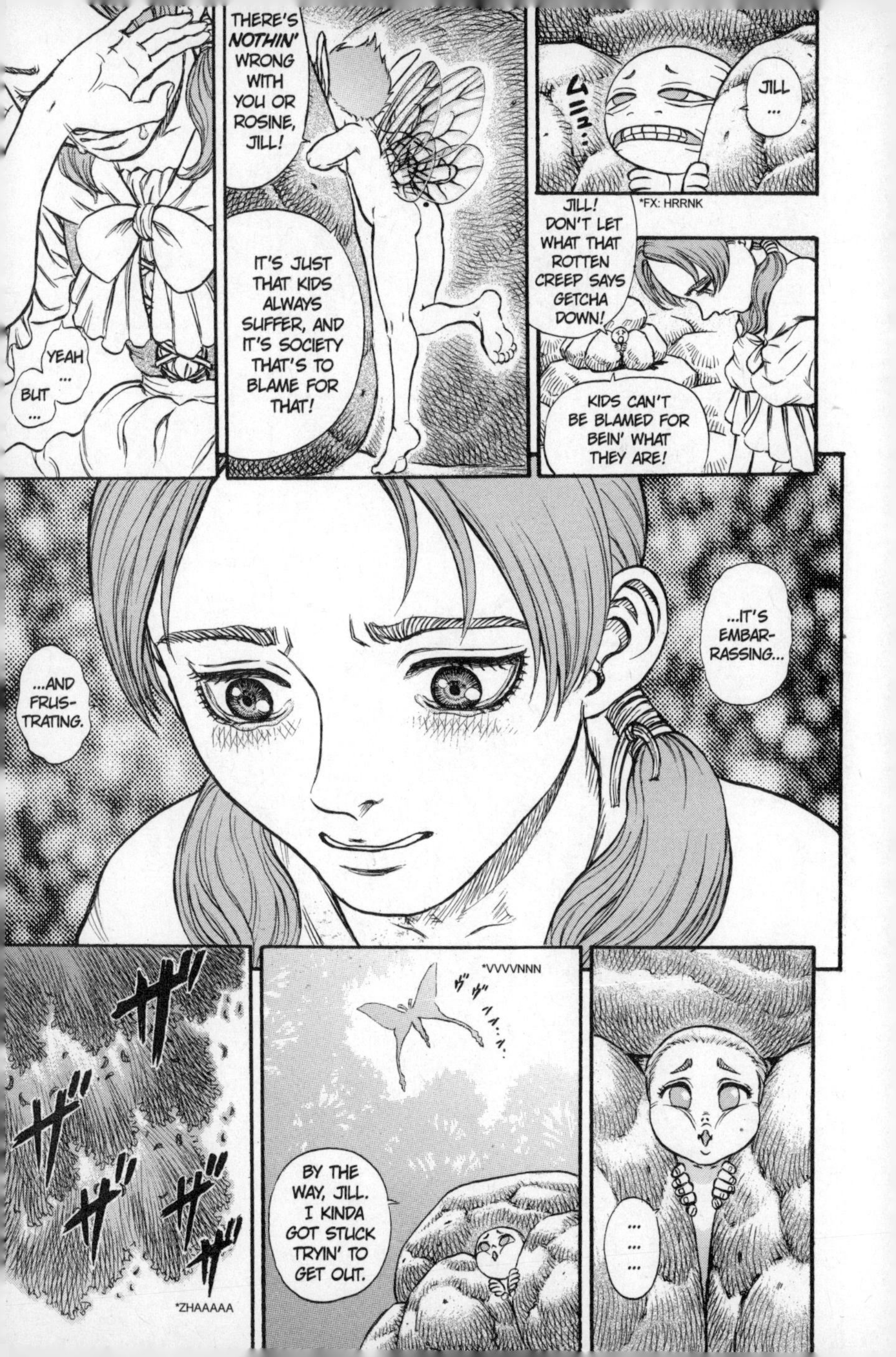
JILL ...
*FX: HRRNK
JILL! DON'T LET WHAT THAT ROTTEN CREEP SAYS GETCHA DOWN!
KIDS CAN'T BE BLAMED FOR BEIN' WHAT THEY ARE!
THERE'S *NOTHIN'* WRONG WITH YOU OR ROSINE, JILL!
IT'S JUST THAT KIDS ALWAYS SUFFER, AND IT'S SOCIETY THAT'S TO BLAME FOR THAT!
YEAH ... BUT ...
...IT'S EMBAR-RASSING...
...AND FRUS-TRATING.
... ...
*VVVVNNN
BY THE WAY, JILL. I KINDA GOT STUCK TRYIN' TO GET OUT.
*ZHAAAAA

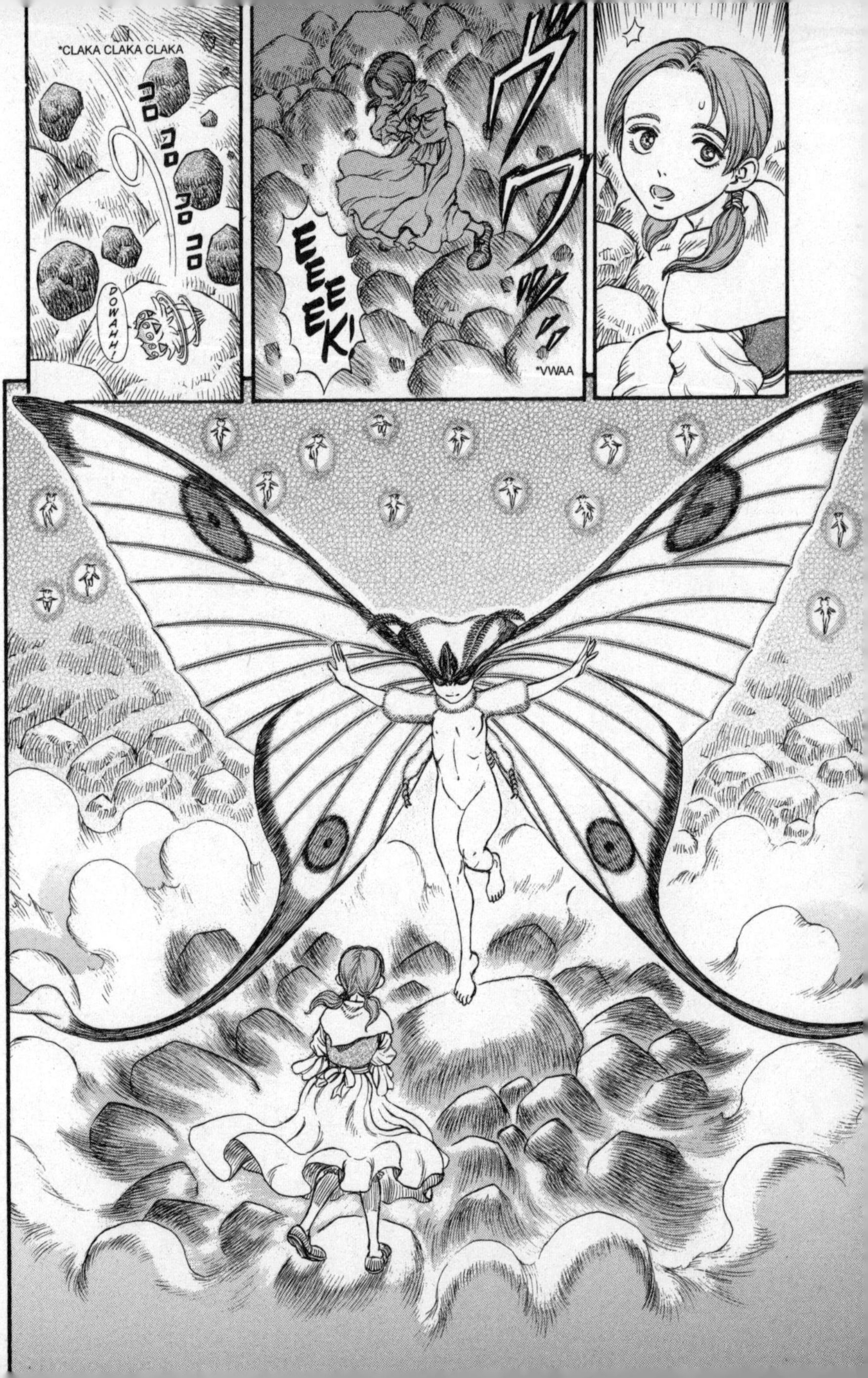
EEEEK!
*VWAA
*CLAKA CLAKA CLAKA
コロ コロ コロ コロ
DOWAHH!

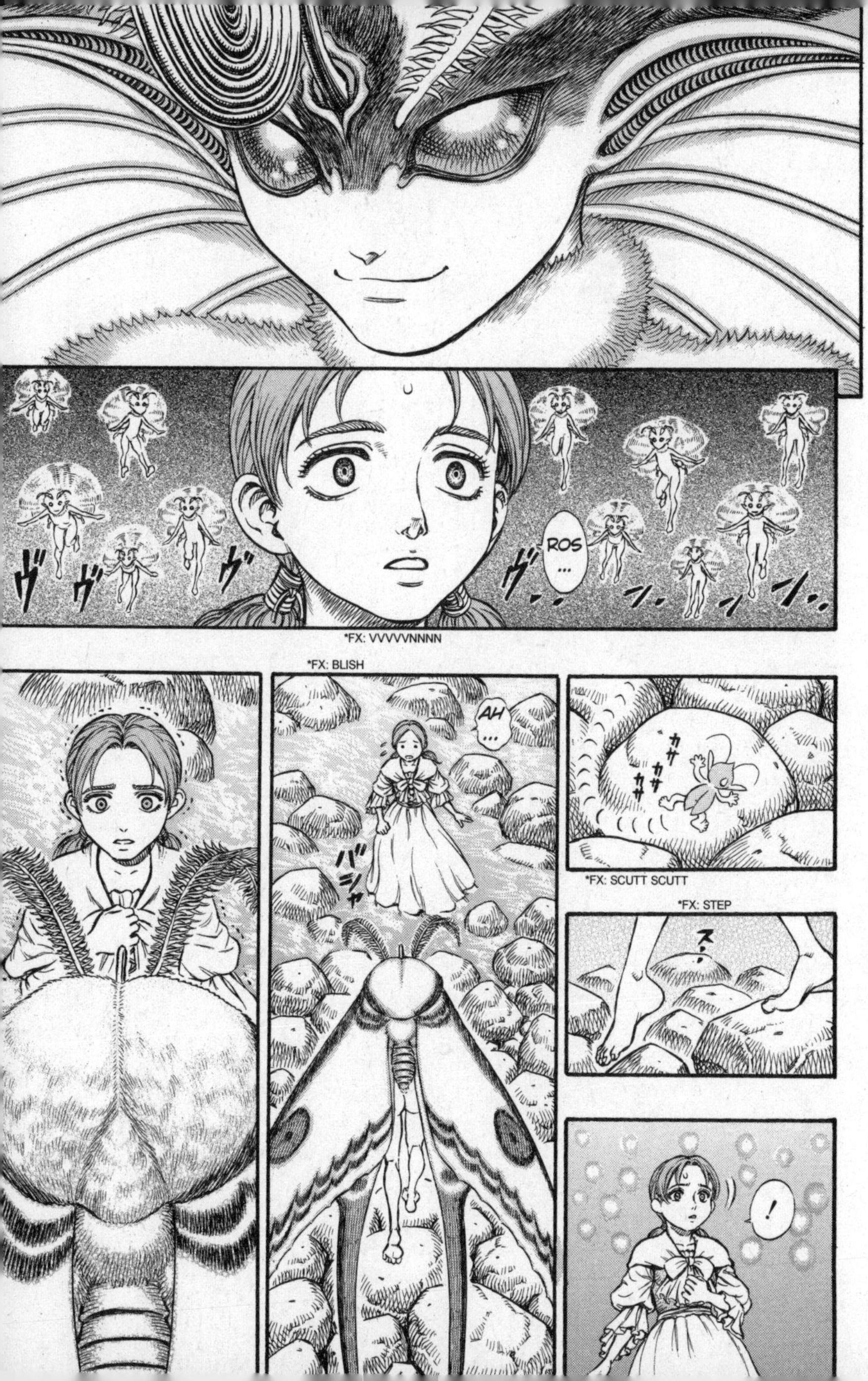
ROS ...
*FX: VVVVVNNNN
*FX: SCUTT SCUTT
*FX: STEP
!
*FX: BLISH
AH ...

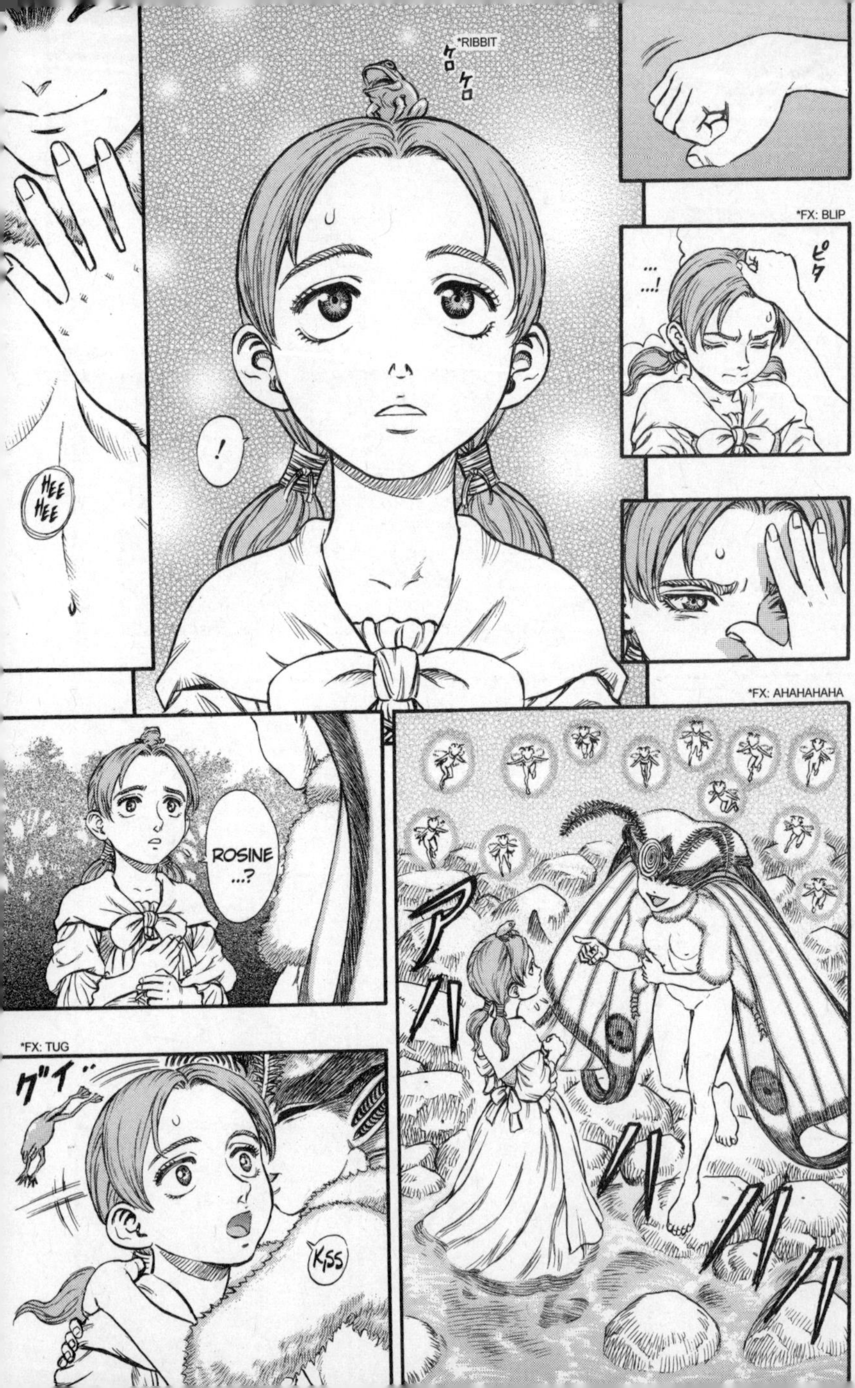

*FX: BLIP
ピタ
...
...!
*RIBBIT
ケロ ケロ
!
HEE HEE
*FX: AHAHAHAHA
ROSINE ...?
*FX: TUG
グイ
KISS

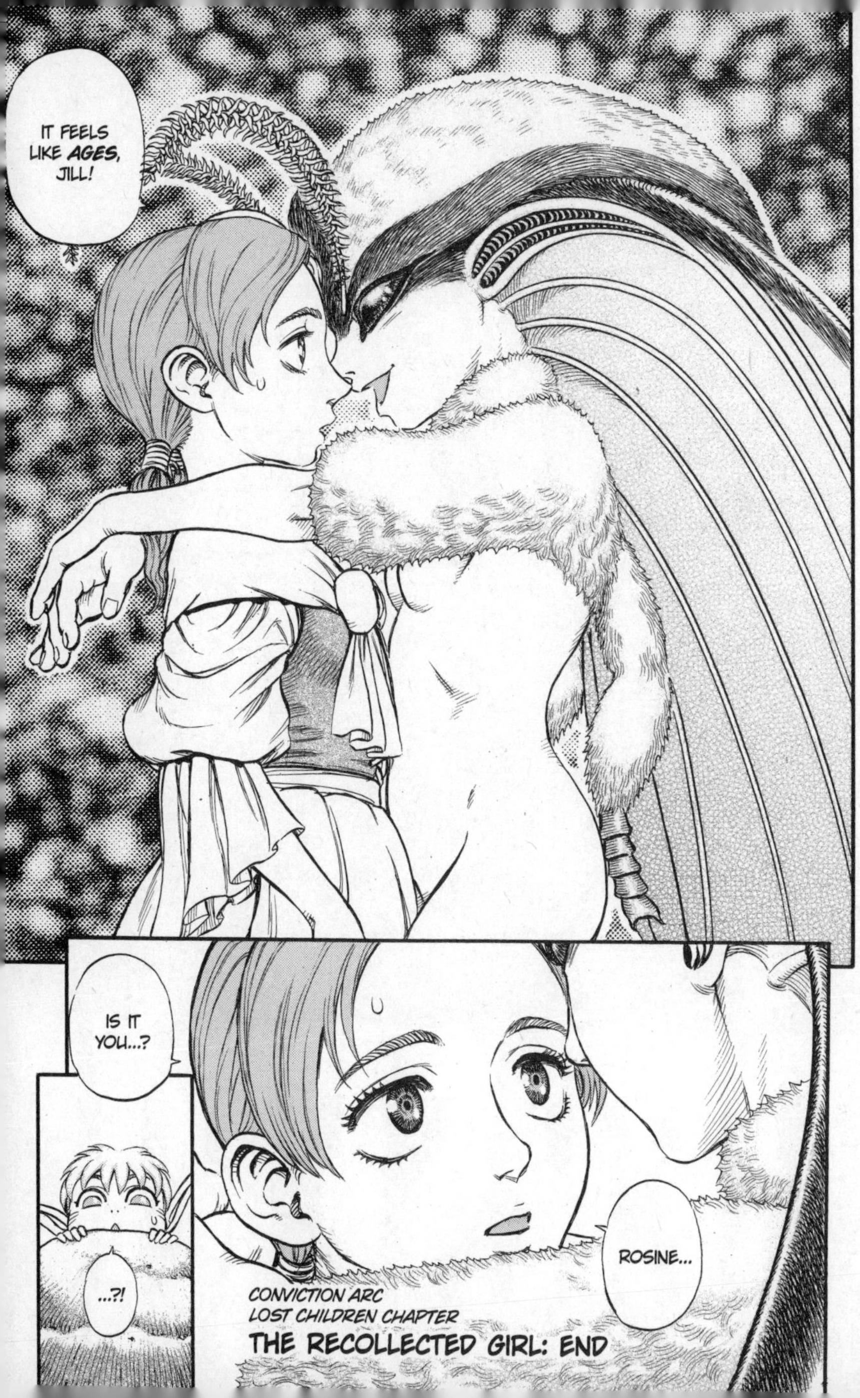
IT FEELS LIKE AGES, JILL!
IS IT YOU...?
ROSINE...
CONVICTION ARC
LOST CHILDREN CHAPTER
THE RECOLLECTED GIRL: END
...?!

BERSERK

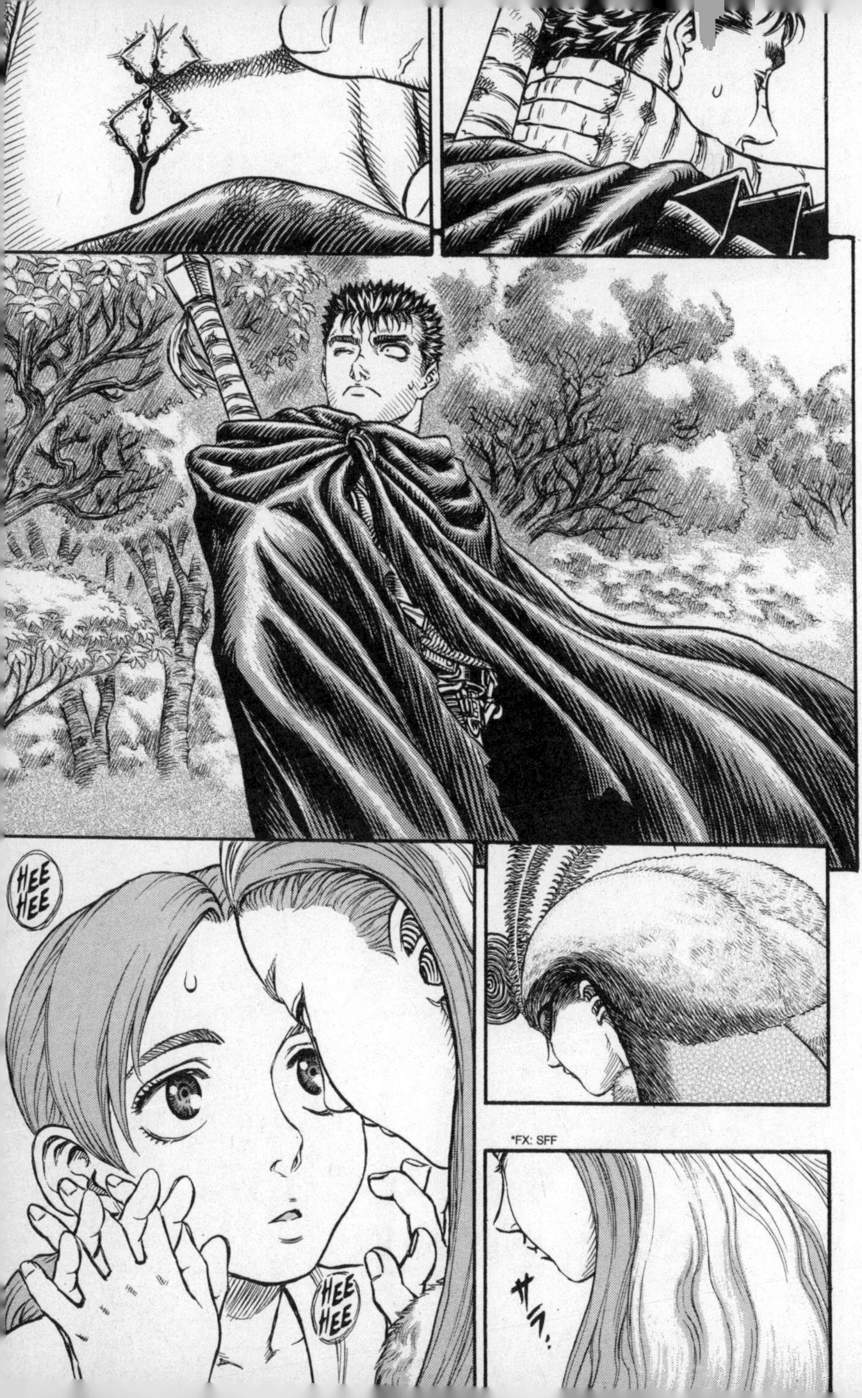
*FX: SFF
HEE HEE
HEE HEE

CONVICTION ARC
LOST CHILDREN CHAPTER
THE WORLD OF WINGED THINGS

断罪篇
ロスト・チルドレンの章
羽あるものの世界

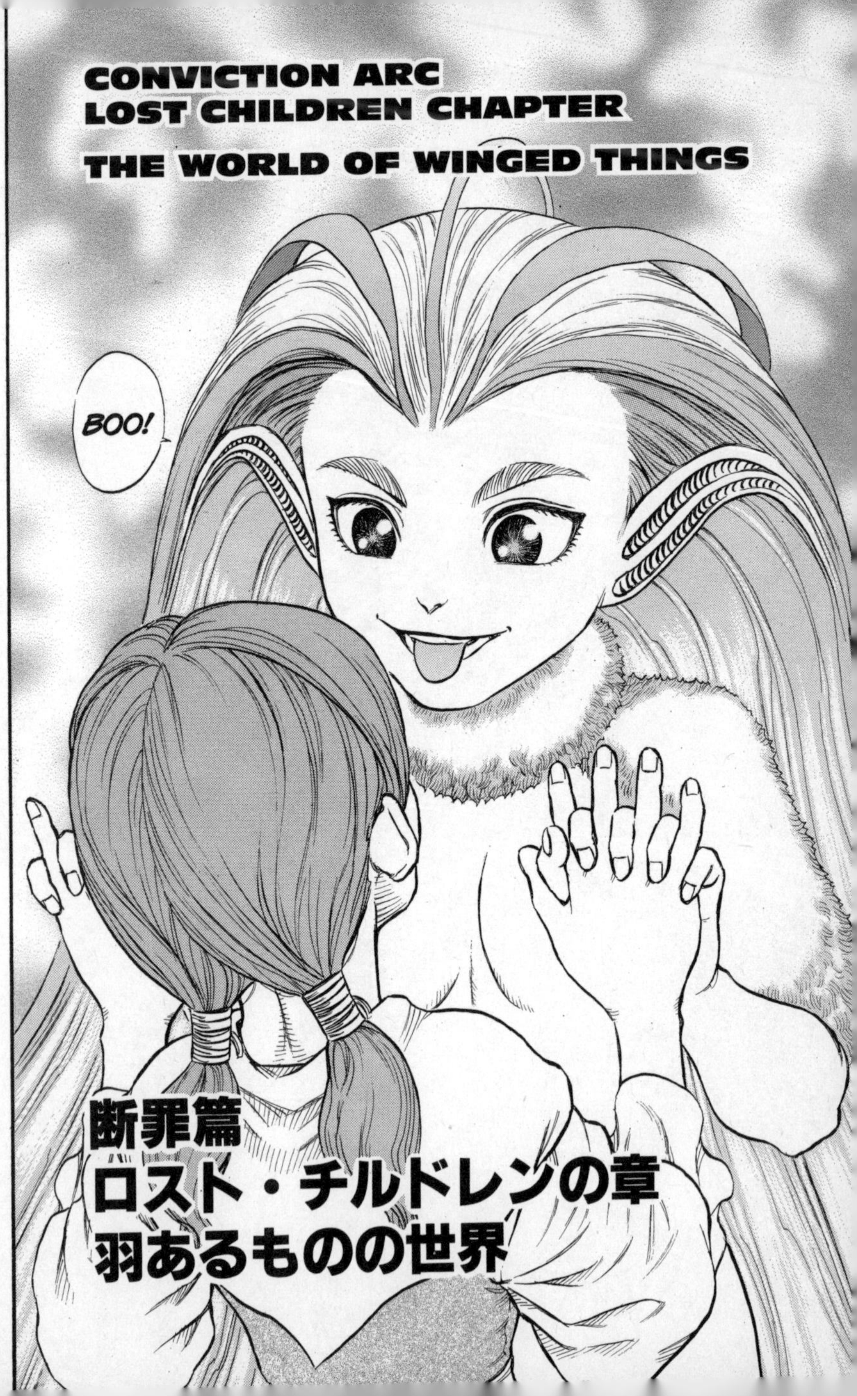
BOO!

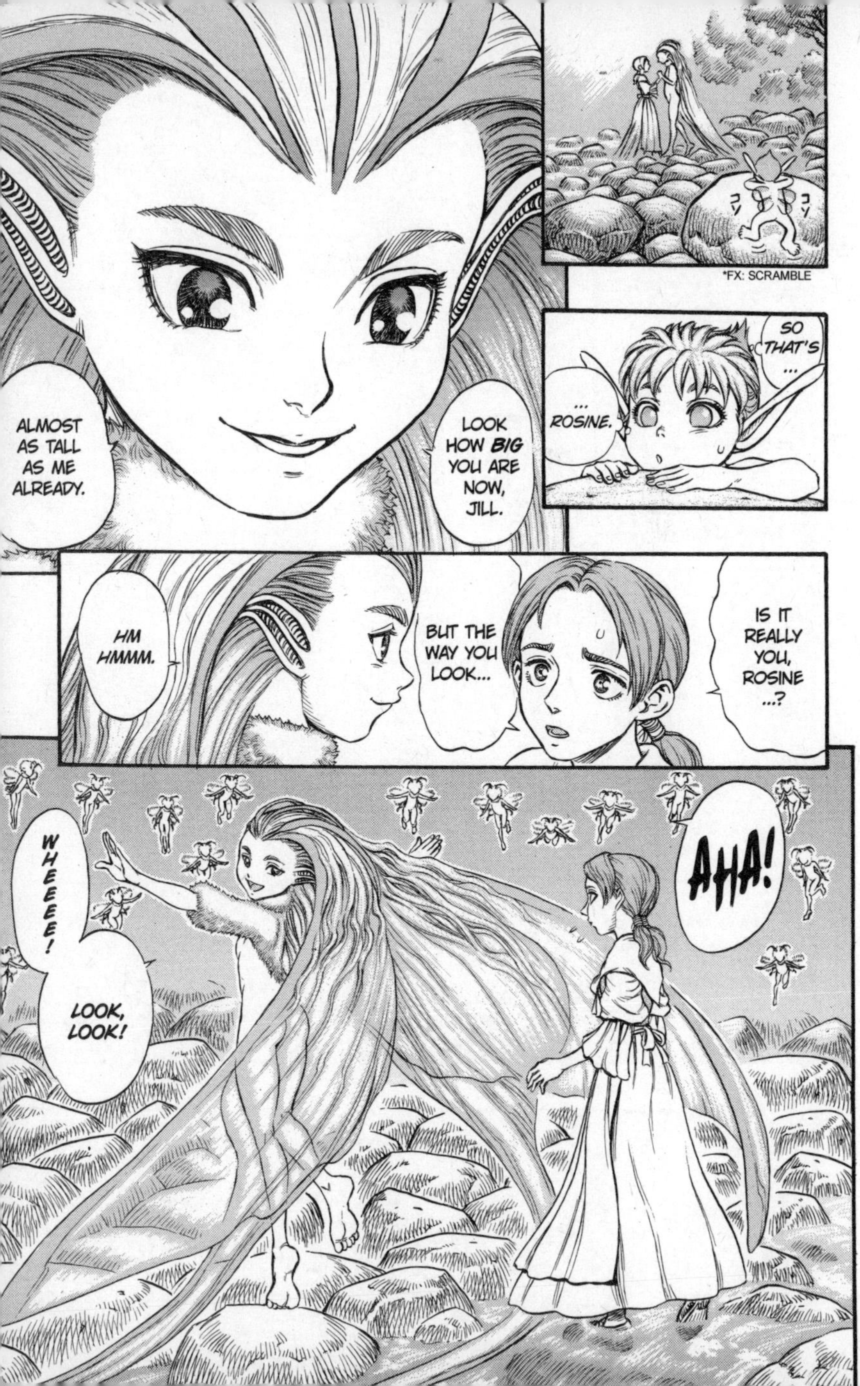
*FX: SCRAMBLE
SO THAT'S ...
... ROSINE.
LOOK HOW *BIG* YOU ARE NOW, JILL.
ALMOST AS TALL AS ME ALREADY.
IS IT REALLY YOU, ROSINE ...?
BUT THE WAY YOU LOOK...
HM HMMM.
AHA!
WHEEEEE!
LOOK, LOOK!

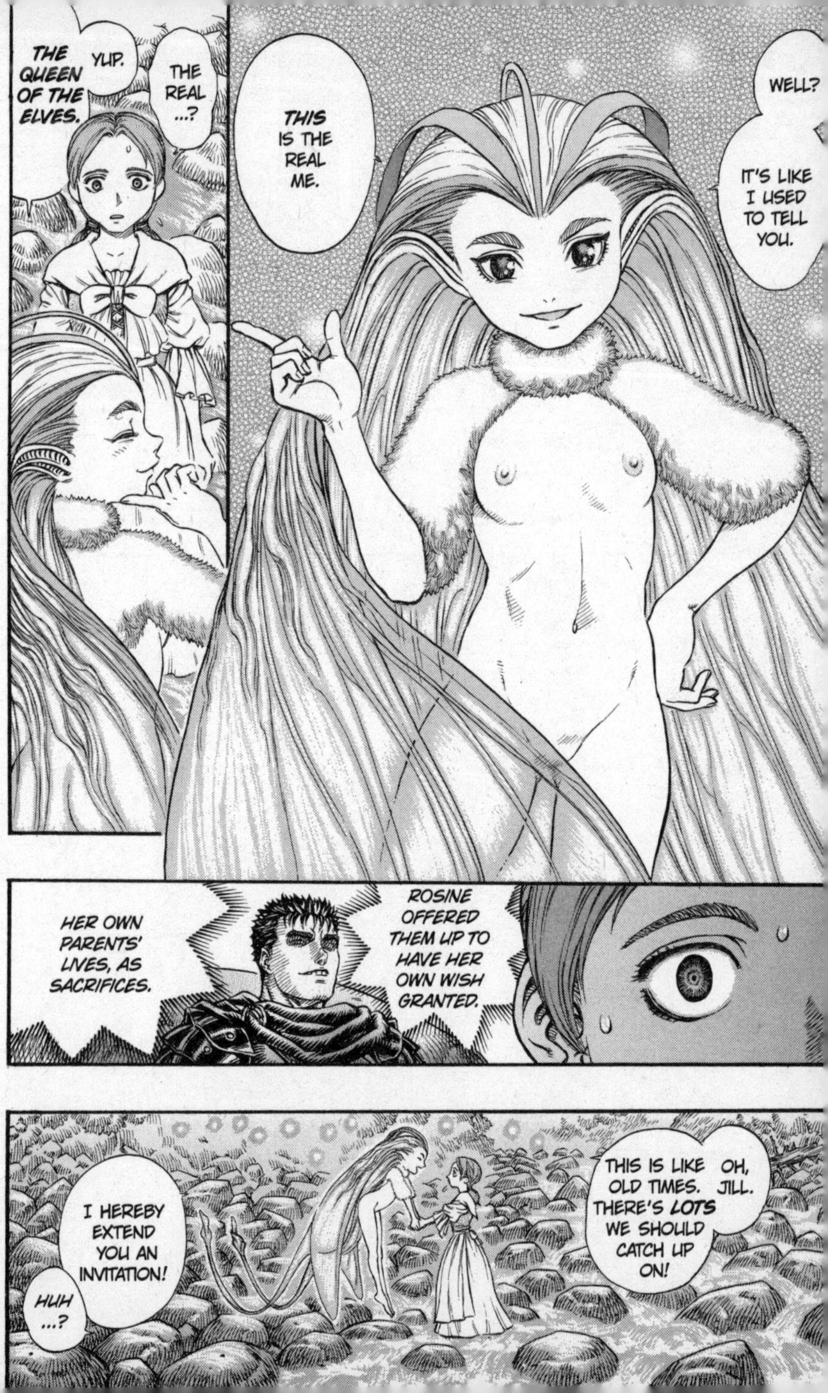
WELL?
IT'S LIKE I USED TO TELL YOU.
THIS IS THE REAL ME.
THE REAL ...?
YUP.
THE QUEEN OF THE ELVES.
ROSINE OFFERED THEM UP TO HAVE HER OWN WISH GRANTED.
HER OWN PARENTS' LIVES, AS SACRIFICES.
OH, JILL.
THIS IS LIKE OLD TIMES. THERE'S LOTS WE SHOULD CATCH UP ON!
I HEREBY EXTEND YOU AN INVITATION!
HUH ...?

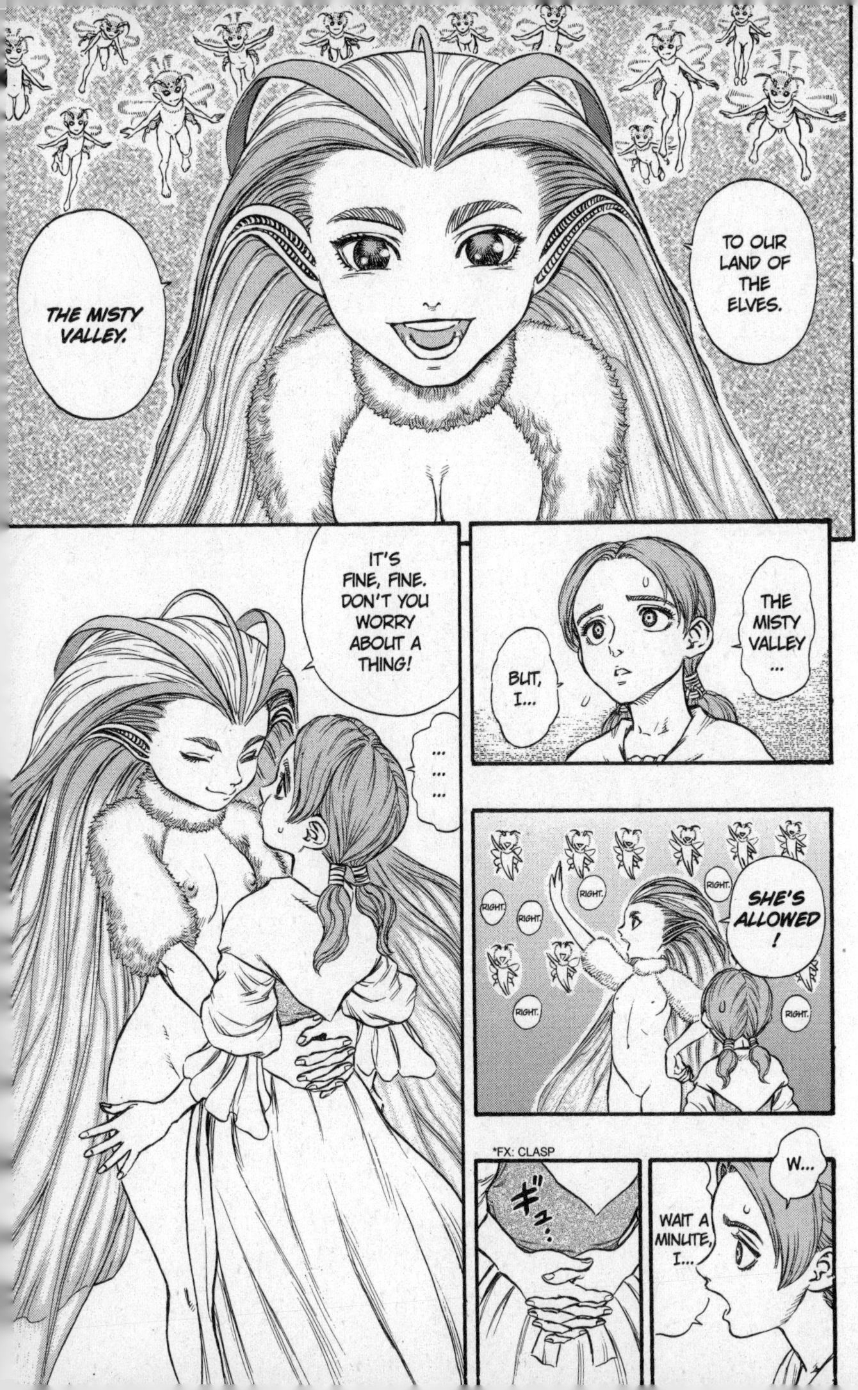
TO OUR LAND OF THE ELVES.
THE MISTY VALLEY.
THE MISTY VALLEY ...
BUT, I...
SHE'S ALLOWED!
RIGHT.
RIGHT.
RIGHT.
RIGHT.
RIGHT.
RIGHT.
W...
WAIT A MINUTE, I...
*FX: CLASP
ギュ..
IT'S FINE, FINE. DON'T YOU WORRY ABOUT A THING!
... ...

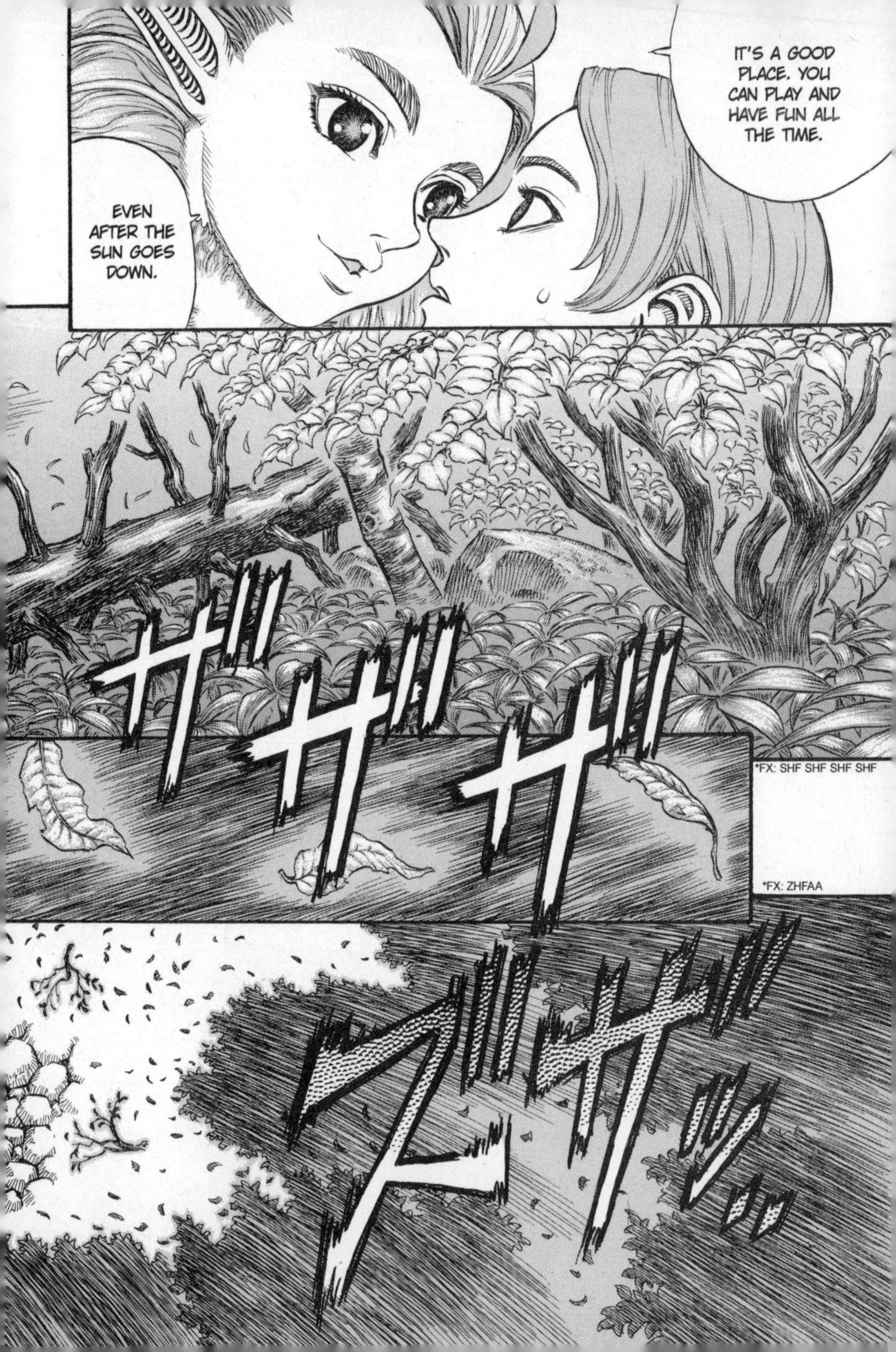
IT'S A GOOD PLACE. YOU CAN PLAY AND HAVE FUN ALL THE TIME.
EVEN AFTER THE SUN GOES DOWN.
*FX: SHF SHF SHF SHF
*FX: ZHFAA

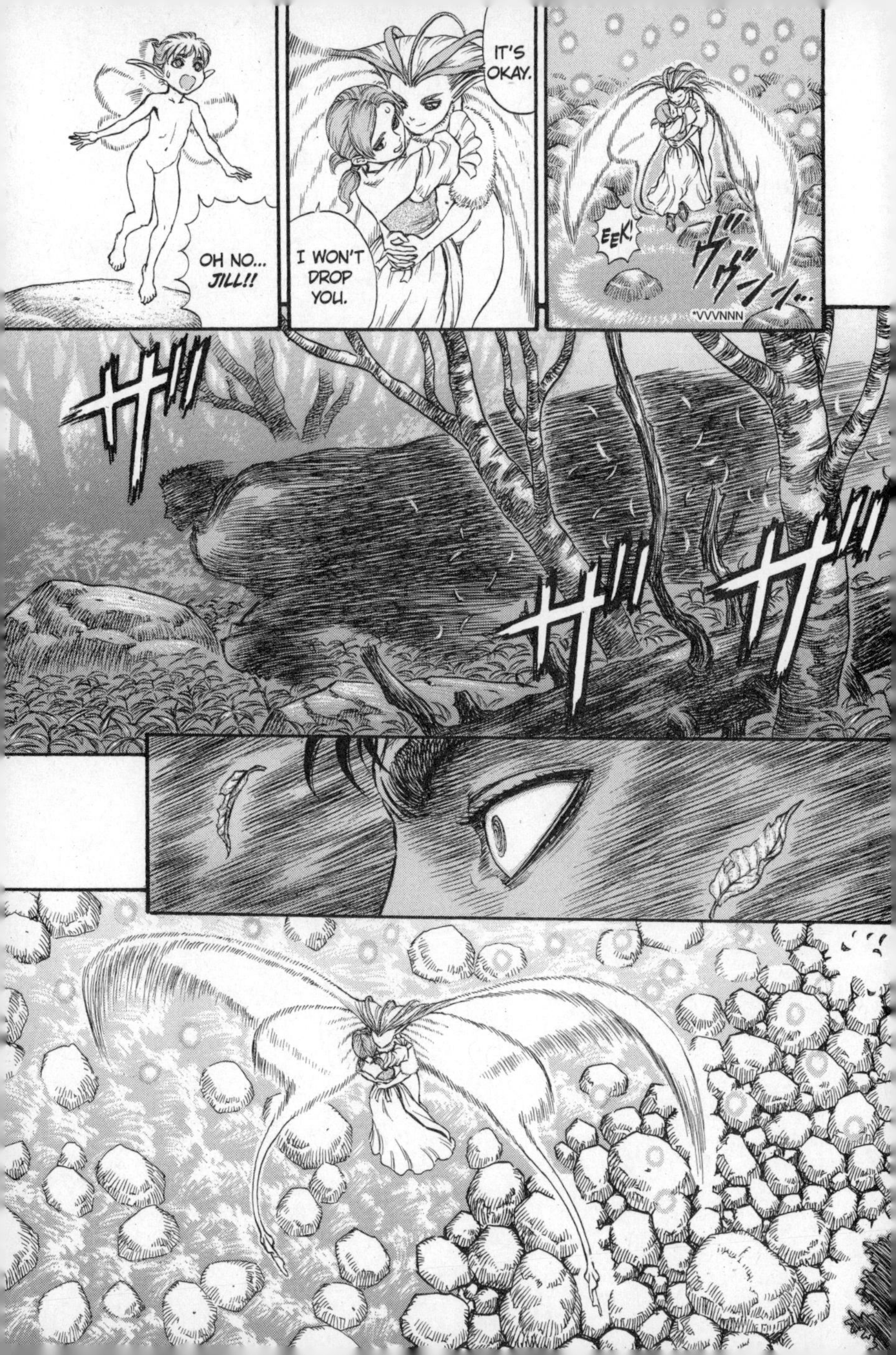
EEK!
*VVVNNN
IT'S OKAY.
I WON'T DROP YOU.
OH NO... JILL!!

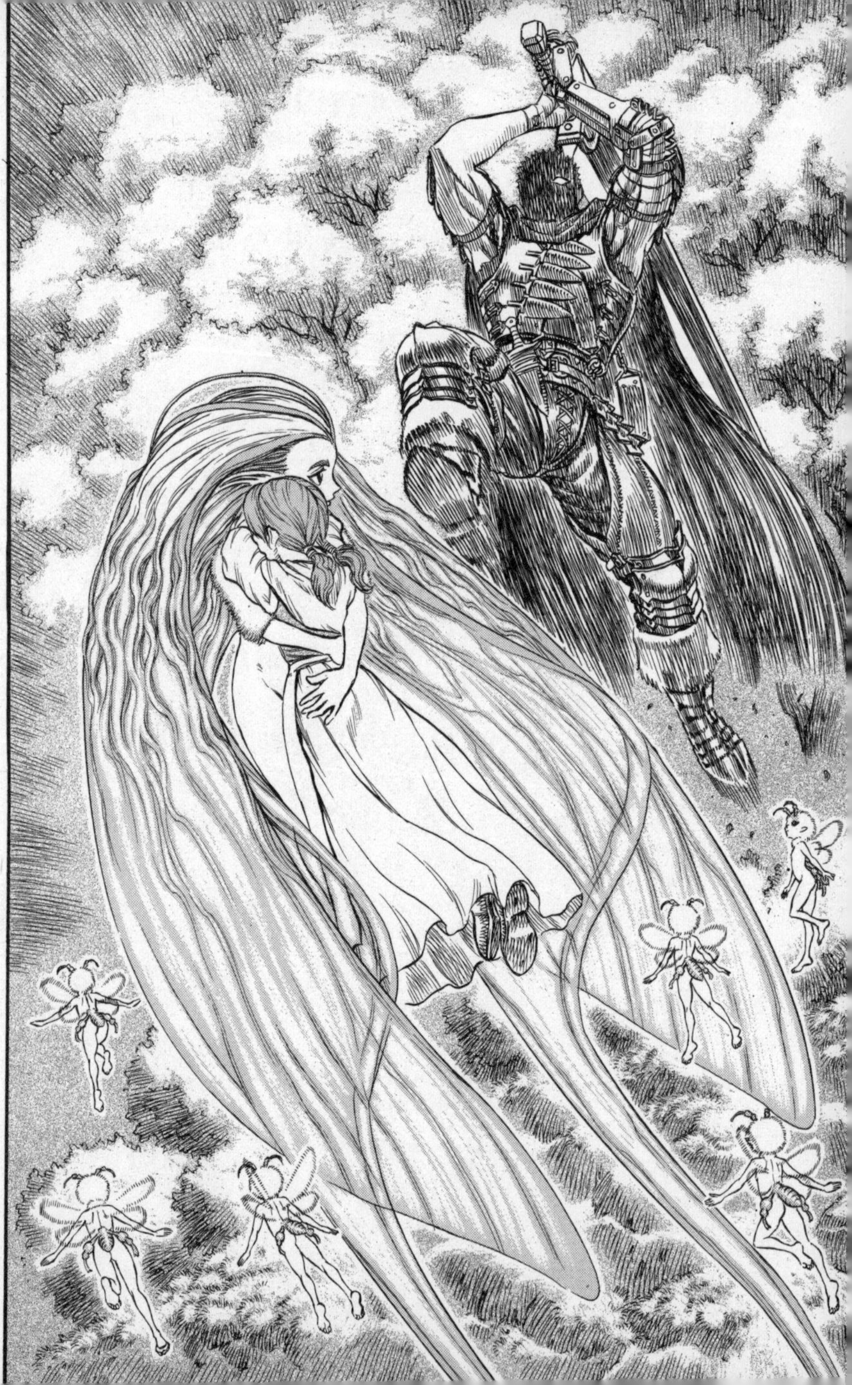

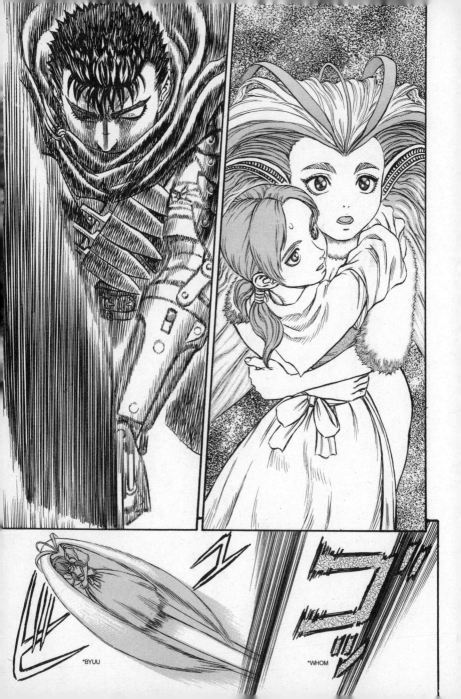

*BYUU

*WHOM

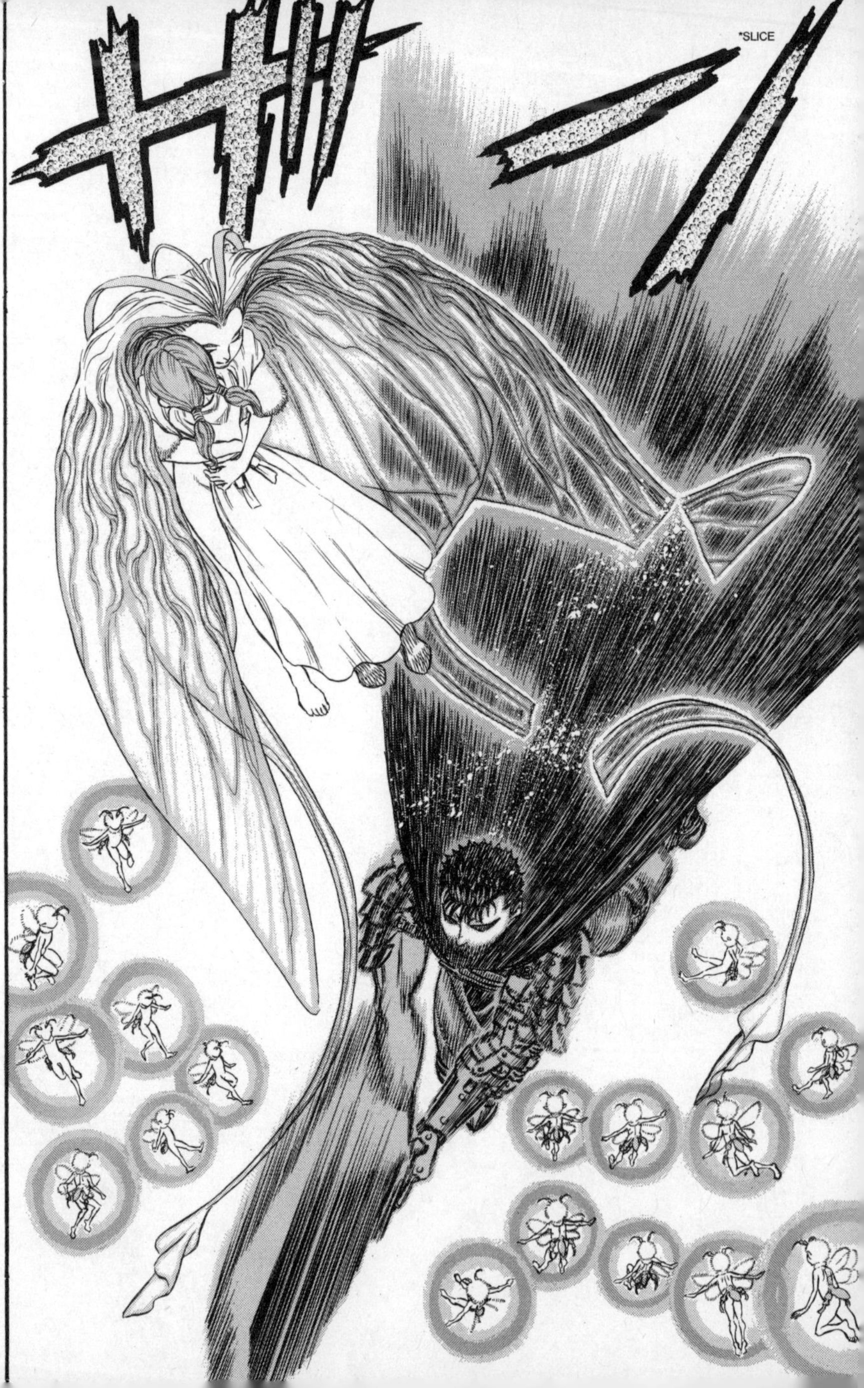
*SLICE

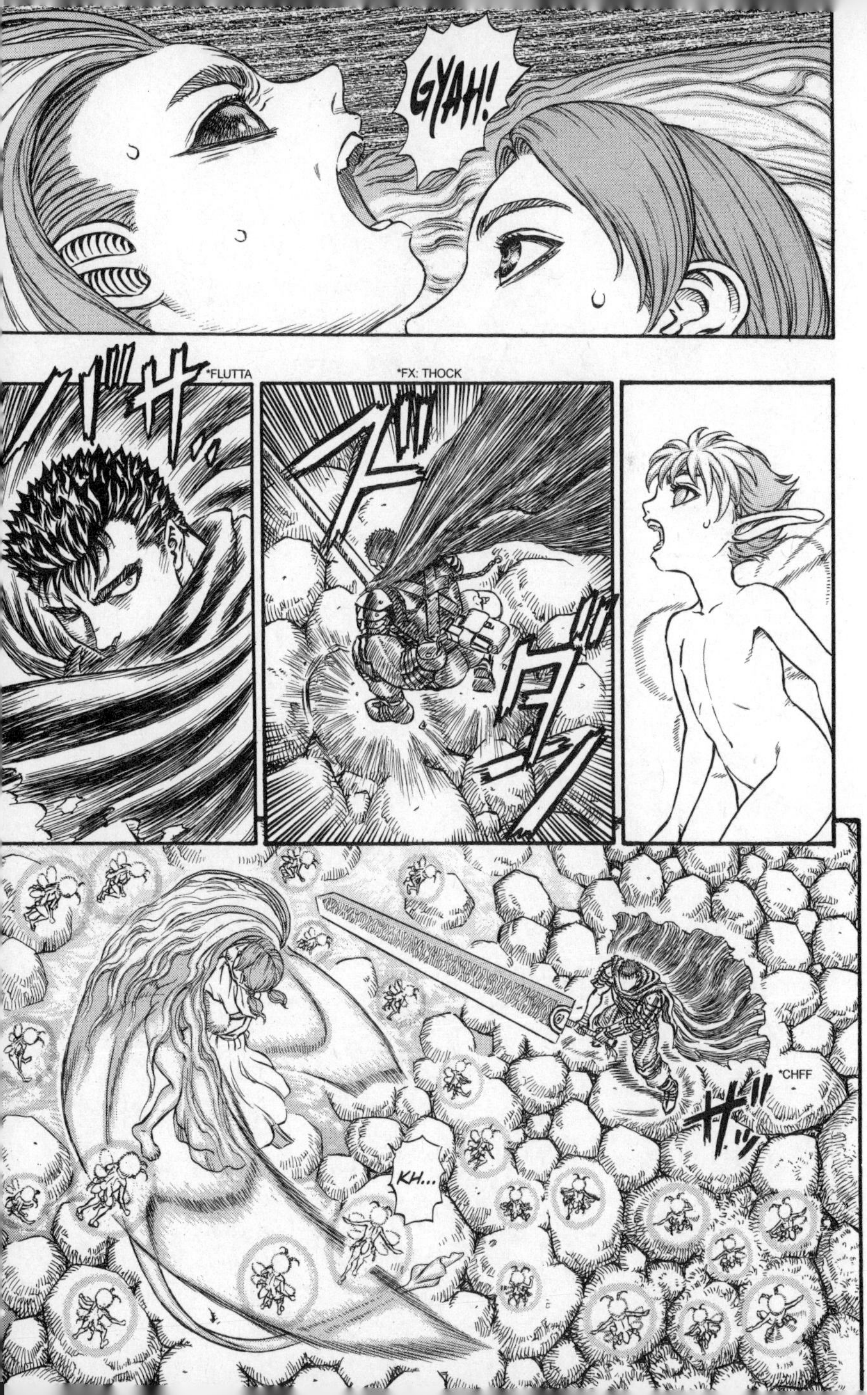
GYAH!
*FX: THOCK
*FLUTTA
*CHFF
KH...

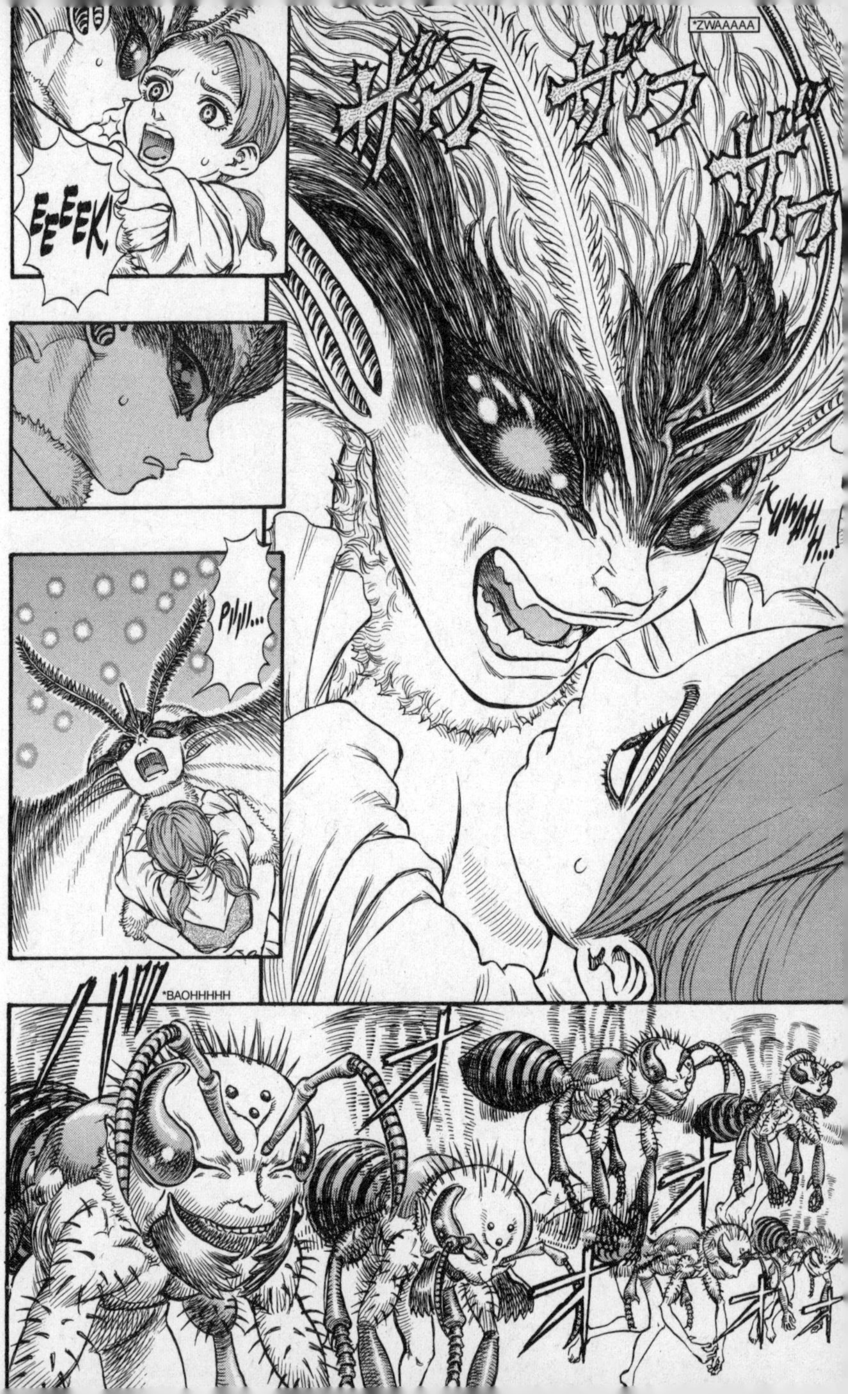
*ZWAAAAA
ザワ ザワ ザワ ザワ
KUWAHH...
EEEEEK!
PYIII...
*BAOHHHHH

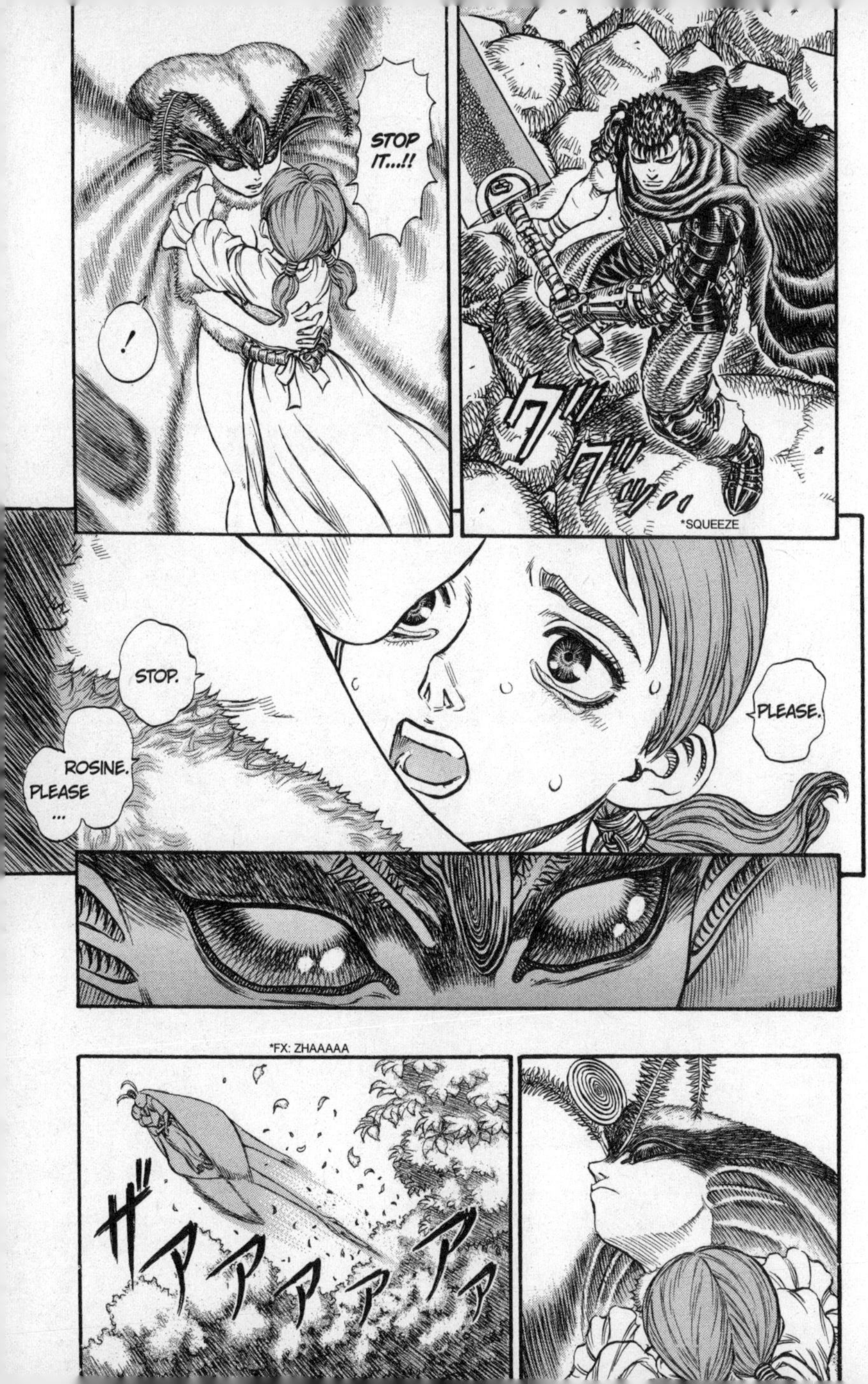
*SQUEEZE
STOP IT...!!
!
PLEASE.
STOP.
ROSINE. PLEASE ...
*FX: ZHAAAAA

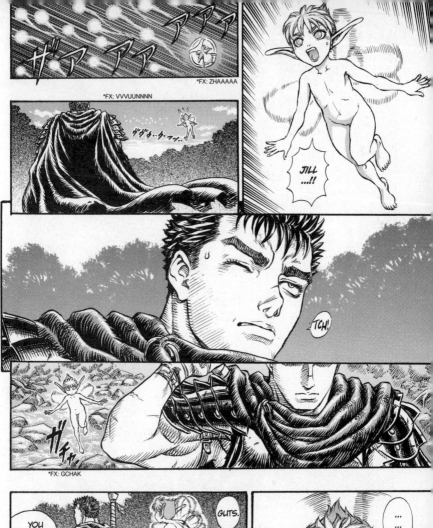

*FX: ZHAAAAA

*FX: VVVUUNNNN

JILL
...!!

TCH!

*FX: GCHAK

YOU SEEMED ABOUT TO KILL JILL, TOO...

GUTS.

*FX: GCHAK GCHAK

...
...

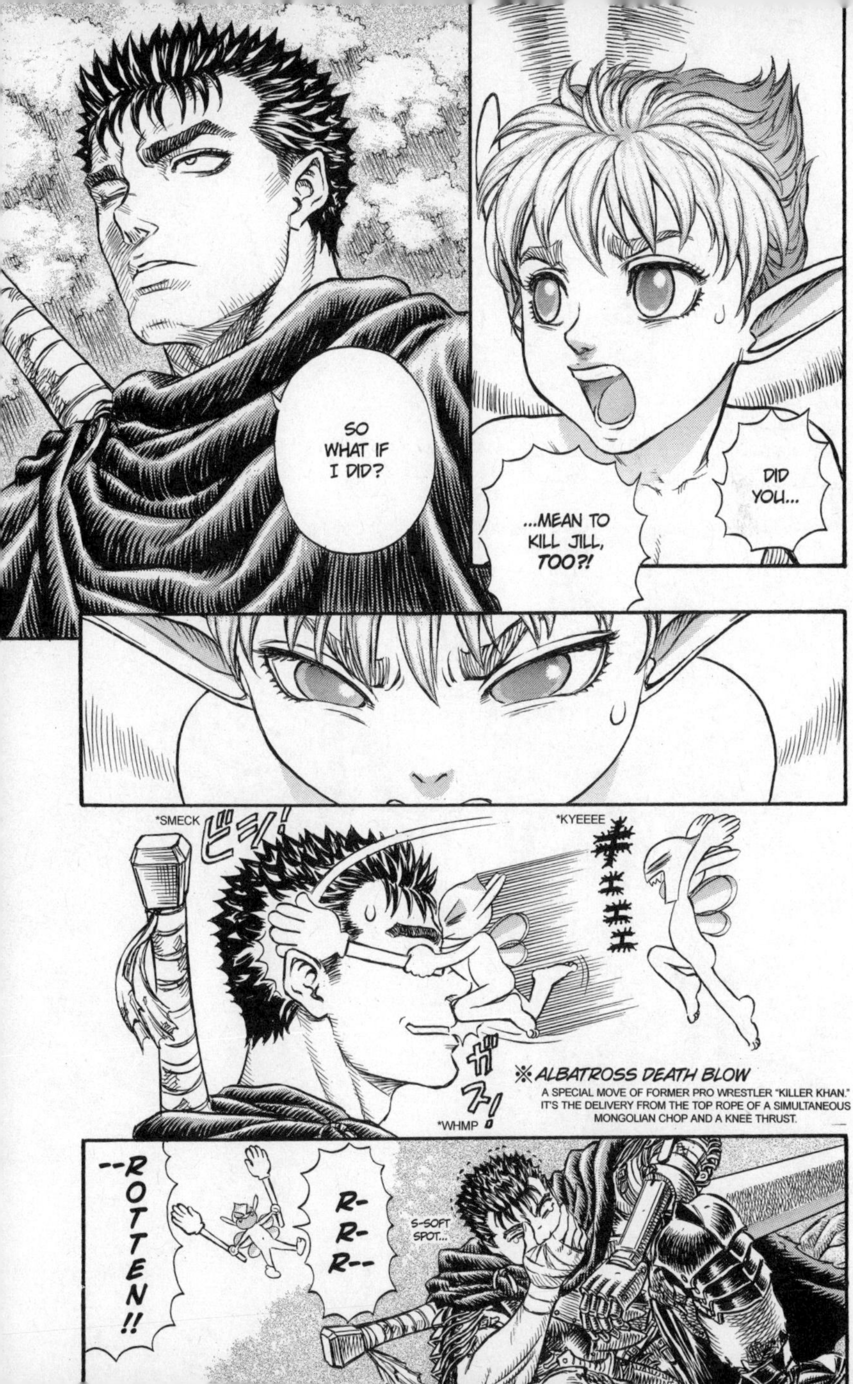
DID YOU...
...MEAN TO KILL JILL, TOO?!
SO WHAT IF I DID?
*KYEEEE
*SMECK
※ALBATROSS DEATH BLOW
A SPECIAL MOVE OF FORMER PRO WRESTLER "KILLER KHAN." IT'S THE DELIVERY FROM THE TOP ROPE OF A SIMULTANEOUS MONGOLIAN CHOP AND A KNEE THRUST.
*WHMP
S-SOFT SPOT...
R-R-R--
--ROTTEN!!

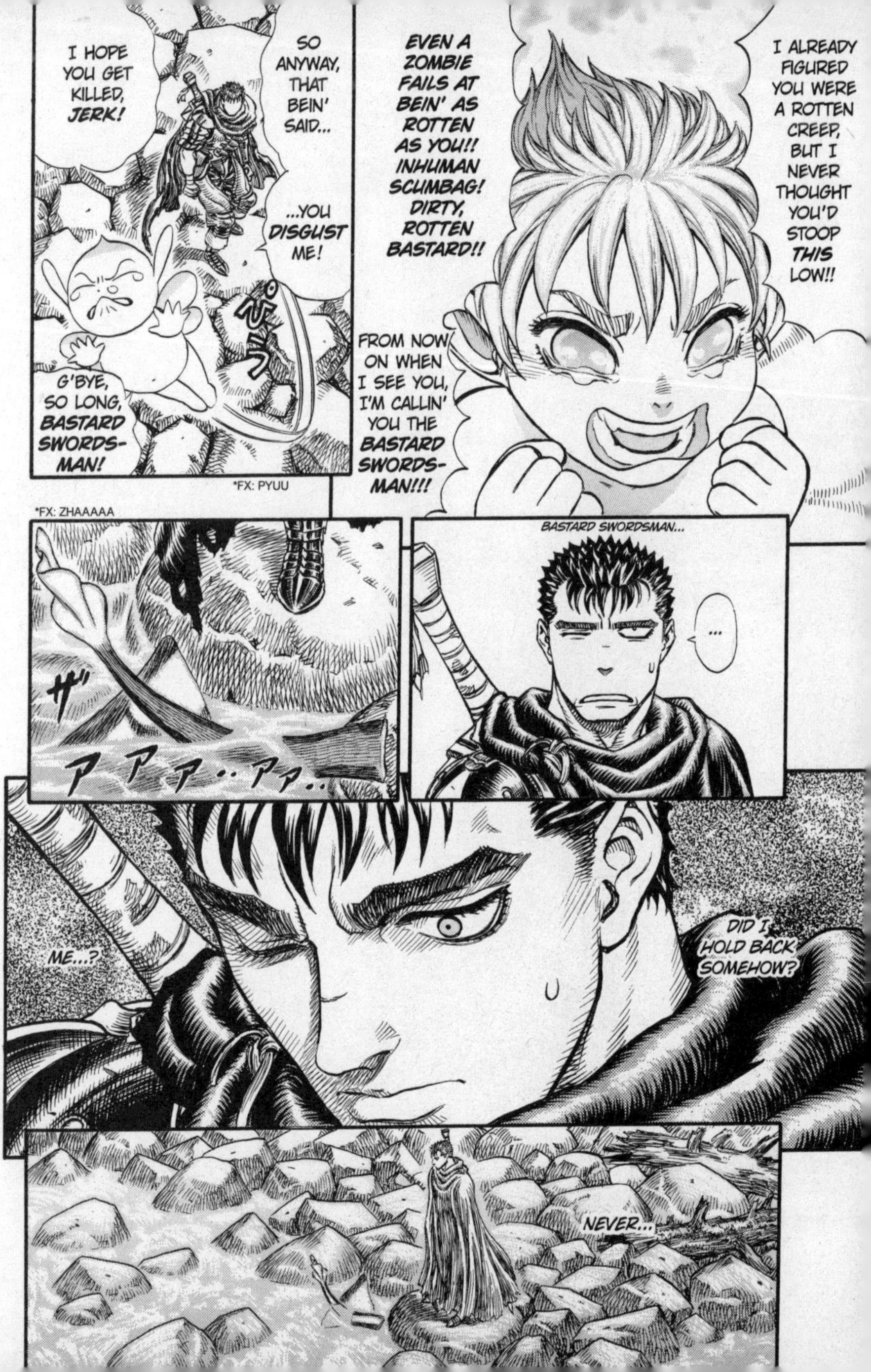
I ALREADY FIGURED YOU WERE A ROTTEN CREEP, BUT I NEVER THOUGHT YOU'D STOOP THIS LOW!!
EVEN A ZOMBIE FAILS AT BEIN' AS ROTTEN AS YOU!! INHUMAN SCUMBAG! DIRTY, ROTTEN BASTARD!!
FROM NOW ON WHEN I SEE YOU, I'M CALLIN' YOU THE BASTARD SWORDSMAN!!!
SO ANYWAY, THAT BEIN' SAID...
I HOPE YOU GET KILLED, JERK!
...YOU DISGUST ME!
G'BYE, SO LONG, BASTARD SWORDSMAN!
*FX: PYUU
BASTARD SWORDSMAN...
...
*FX: ZHAAAAA
DID I HOLD BACK SOMEHOW?
ME...?
NEVER...

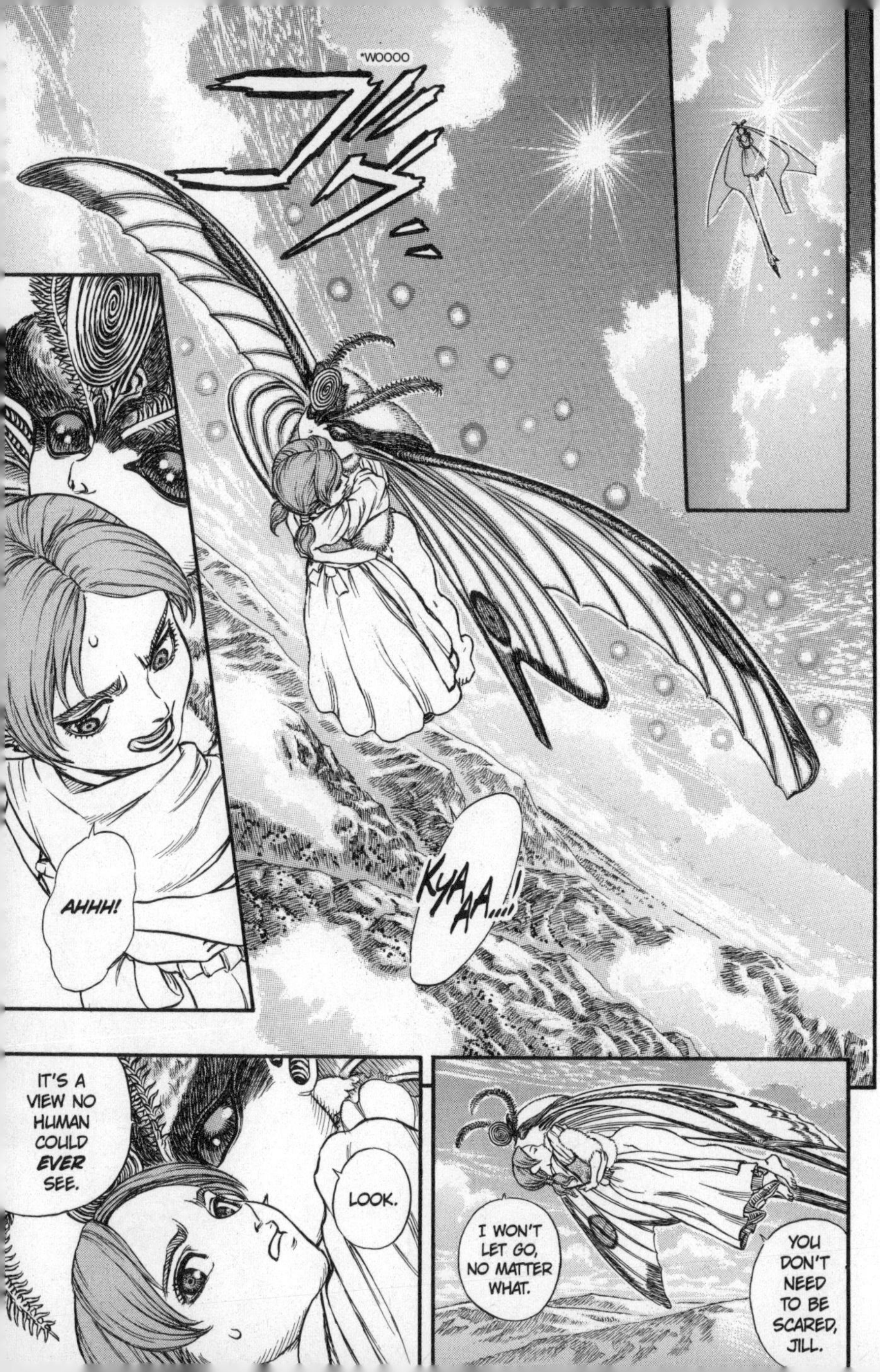
*WOOOO
KYAAA...!
AHHH!
YOU DON'T NEED TO BE SCARED, JILL.
I WON'T LET GO, NO MATTER WHAT.
LOOK.
IT'S A VIEW NO HUMAN COULD EVER SEE.

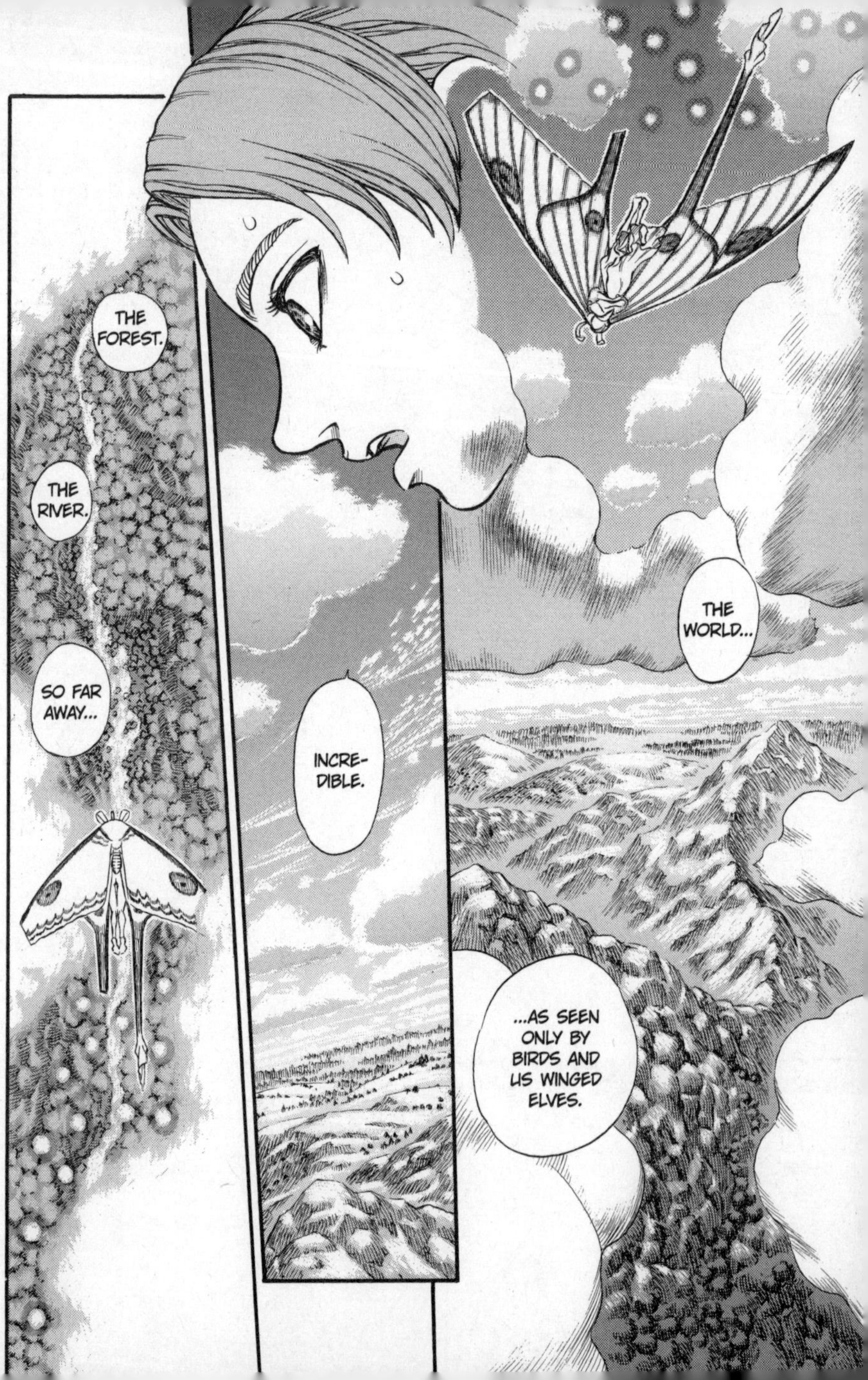
THE WORLD...
...AS SEEN ONLY BY BIRDS AND US WINGED ELVES.
INCREDIBLE.
THE FOREST.
THE RIVER.
SO FAR AWAY...

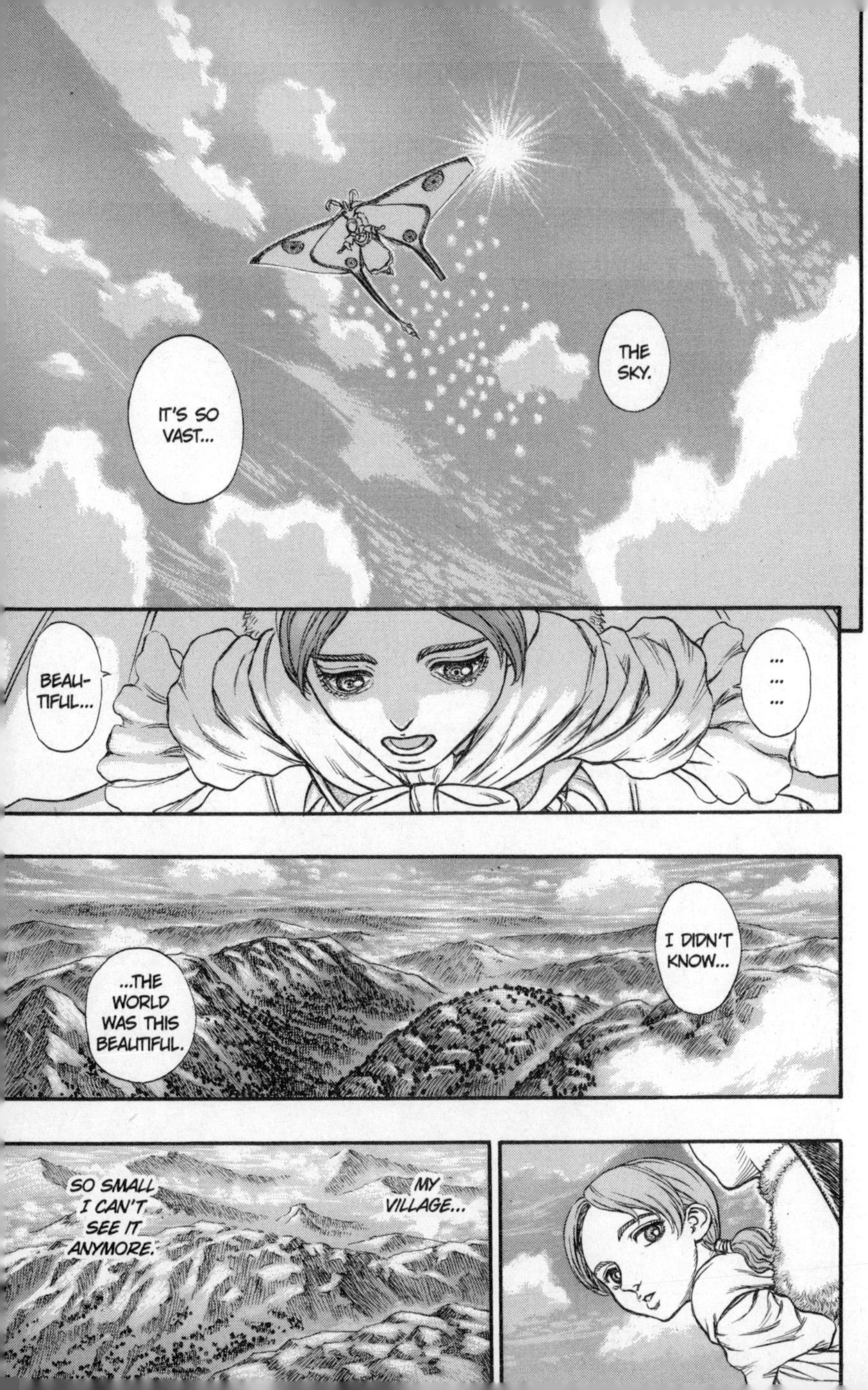
THE SKY.
IT'S SO VAST...
... ...
BEAUTIFUL...
I DIDN'T KNOW...
...THE WORLD WAS THIS BEAUTIFUL.
MY VILLAGE...
SO SMALL I CAN'T SEE IT ANYMORE.

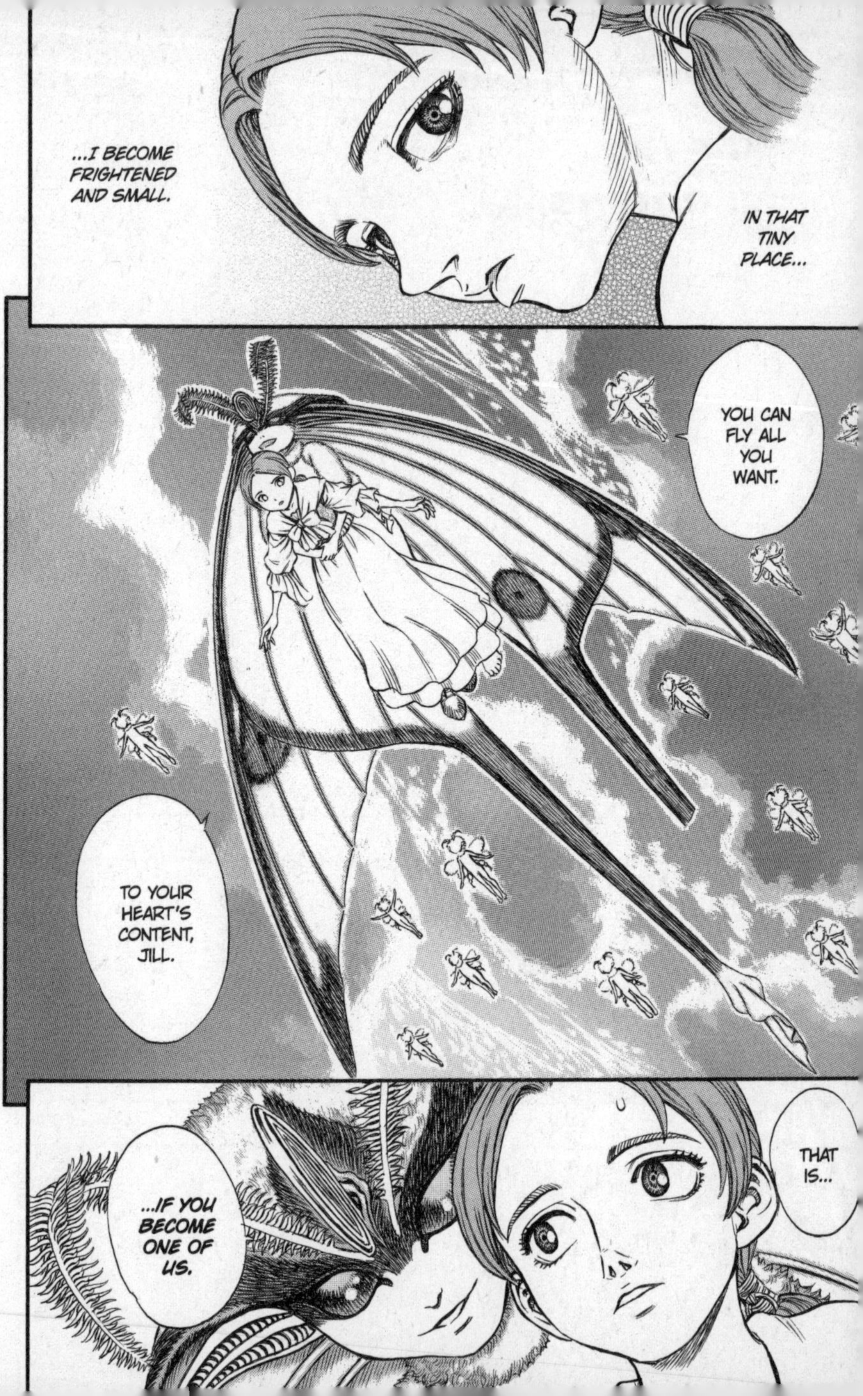
IN THAT TINY PLACE...
...I BECOME FRIGHTENED AND SMALL.
YOU CAN FLY ALL YOU WANT.
TO YOUR HEART'S CONTENT, JILL.
THAT IS...
...IF YOU BECOME ONE OF US.

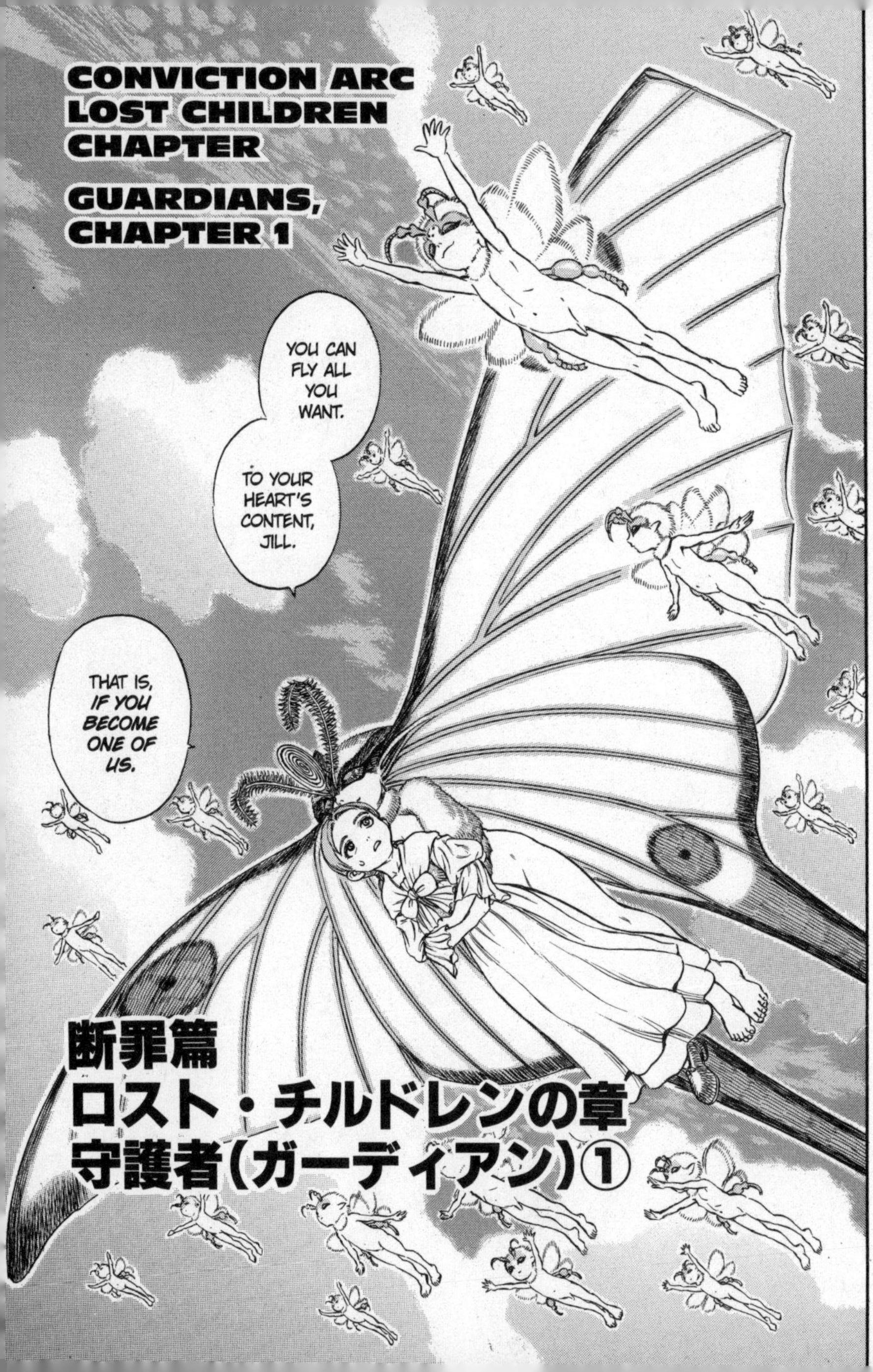
CONVICTION ARC
LOST CHILDREN
CHAPTER
GUARDIANS,
CHAPTER 1
YOU CAN FLY ALL YOU WANT.
TO YOUR HEART'S CONTENT, JILL.
THAT IS, IF YOU BECOME ONE OF US.
断罪篇
ロスト・チルドレンの章
守護者(ガーディアン)①

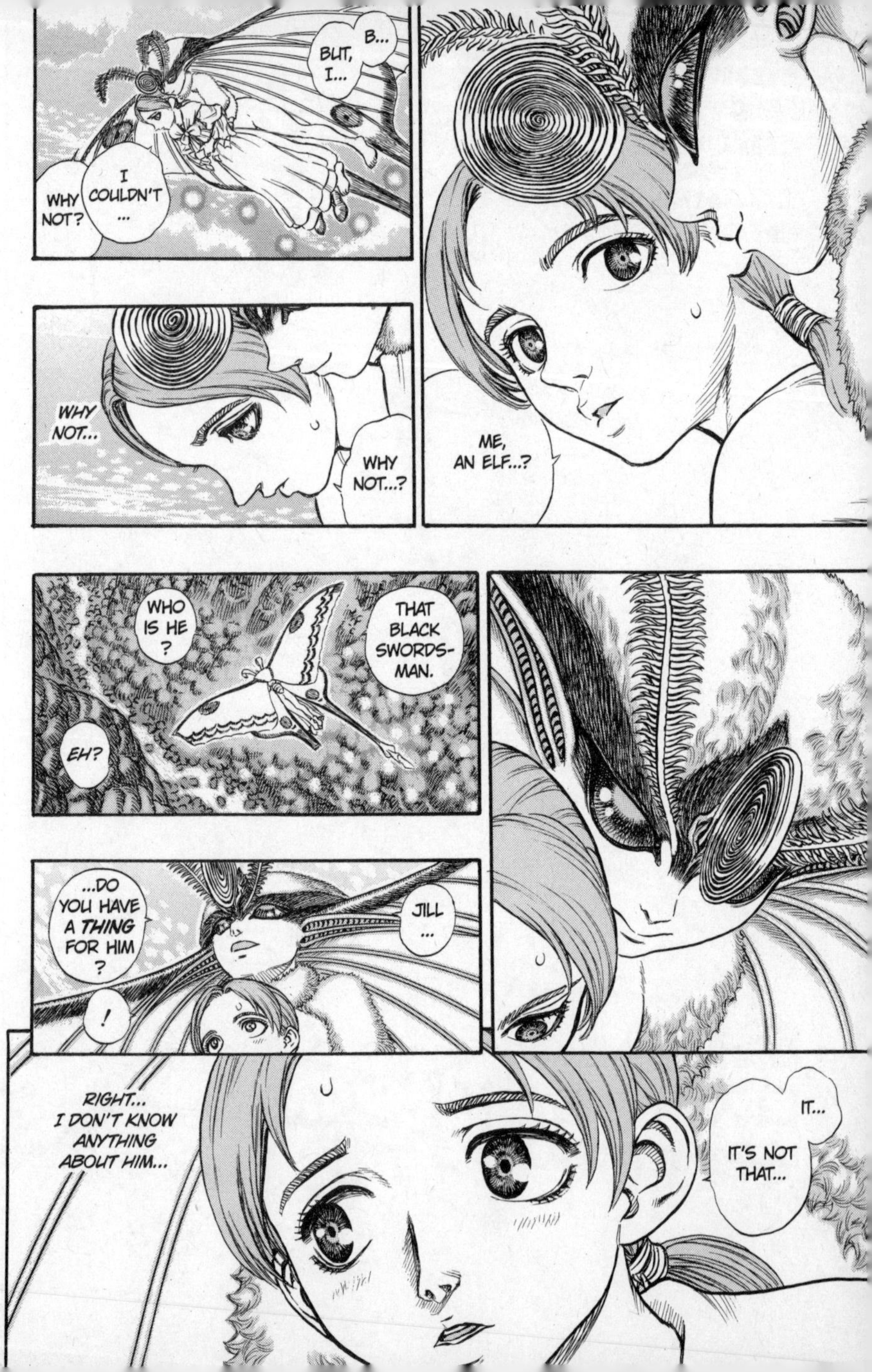
ME, AN ELF...?
B...
BUT, I...
I COULDN'T ...
WHY NOT?
WHY NOT...?
WHY NOT...
THAT BLACK SWORDS-MAN.
WHO IS HE ?
EH?
JILL ...
...DO YOU HAVE A *THING* FOR HIM ?
!
IT...
IT'S NOT THAT...
RIGHT... I DON'T KNOW ANYTHING ABOUT HIM...

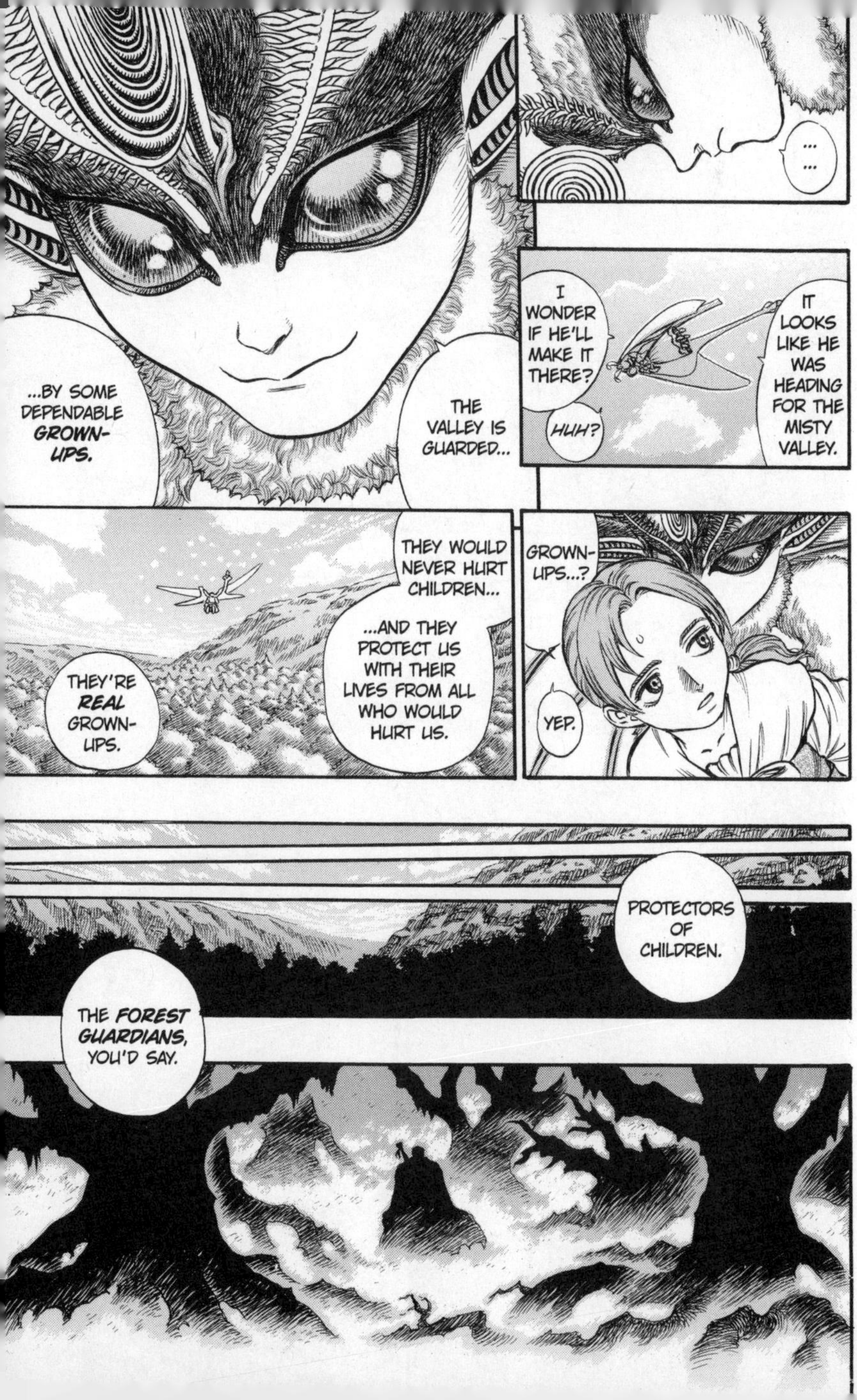

... ...
IT LOOKS LIKE HE WAS HEADING FOR THE MISTY VALLEY.
HUH?
I WONDER IF HE'LL MAKE IT THERE?
THE VALLEY IS GUARDED...
...BY SOME DEPENDABLE GROWN-UPS.
GROWN-UPS...?
YEP.
THEY WOULD NEVER HURT CHILDREN...
...AND THEY PROTECT US WITH THEIR LIVES FROM ALL WHO WOULD HURT US.
THEY'RE REAL GROWN-UPS.
PROTECTORS OF CHILDREN.
THE FOREST GUARDIANS, YOU'D SAY.

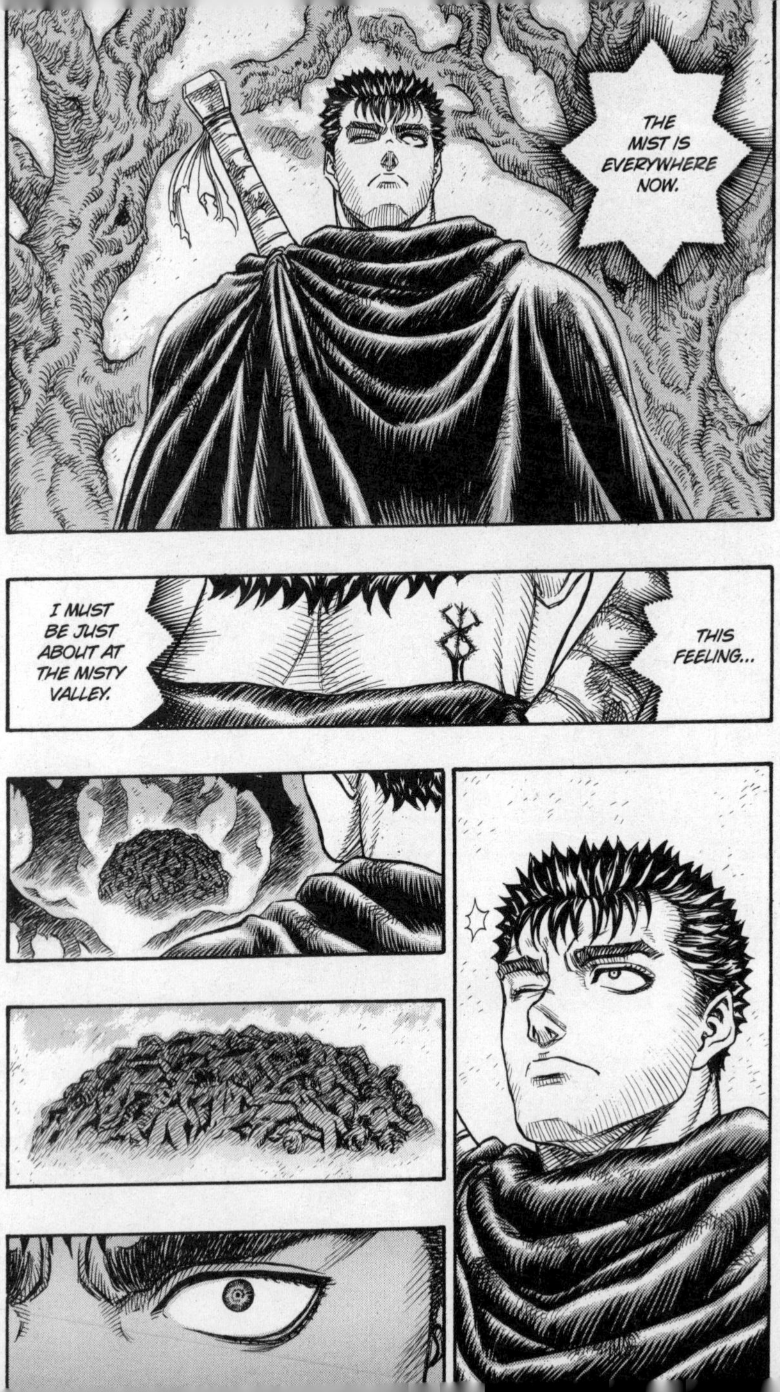
THE MIST IS EVERYWHERE NOW.
THIS FEELING...
I MUST BE JUST ABOUT AT THE MISTY VALLEY.

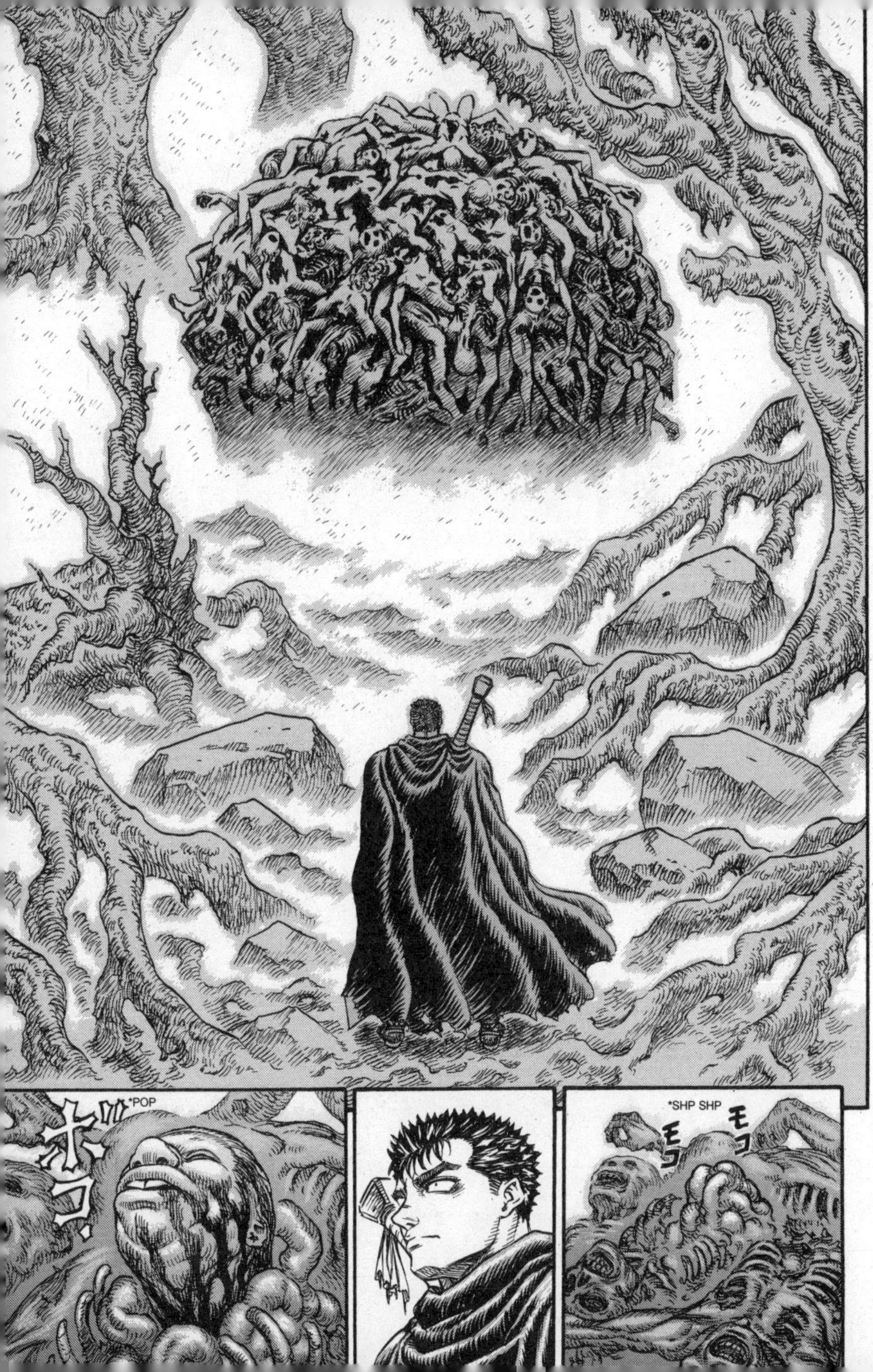
*SHP SHP
モコ
モコ
*POP
ボコッ

WE
...
...MEET
AGAIN.
HEE
HEE
...

KEHEE

KEHEE

...YOU
FORGOT
ABOUT
US.

DON'T
SAY...

*FX: BOP

*FX: SHLLP

*FX: MCH MCH

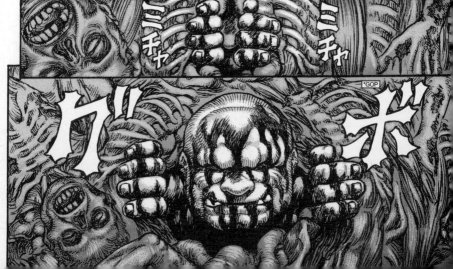

*GOP

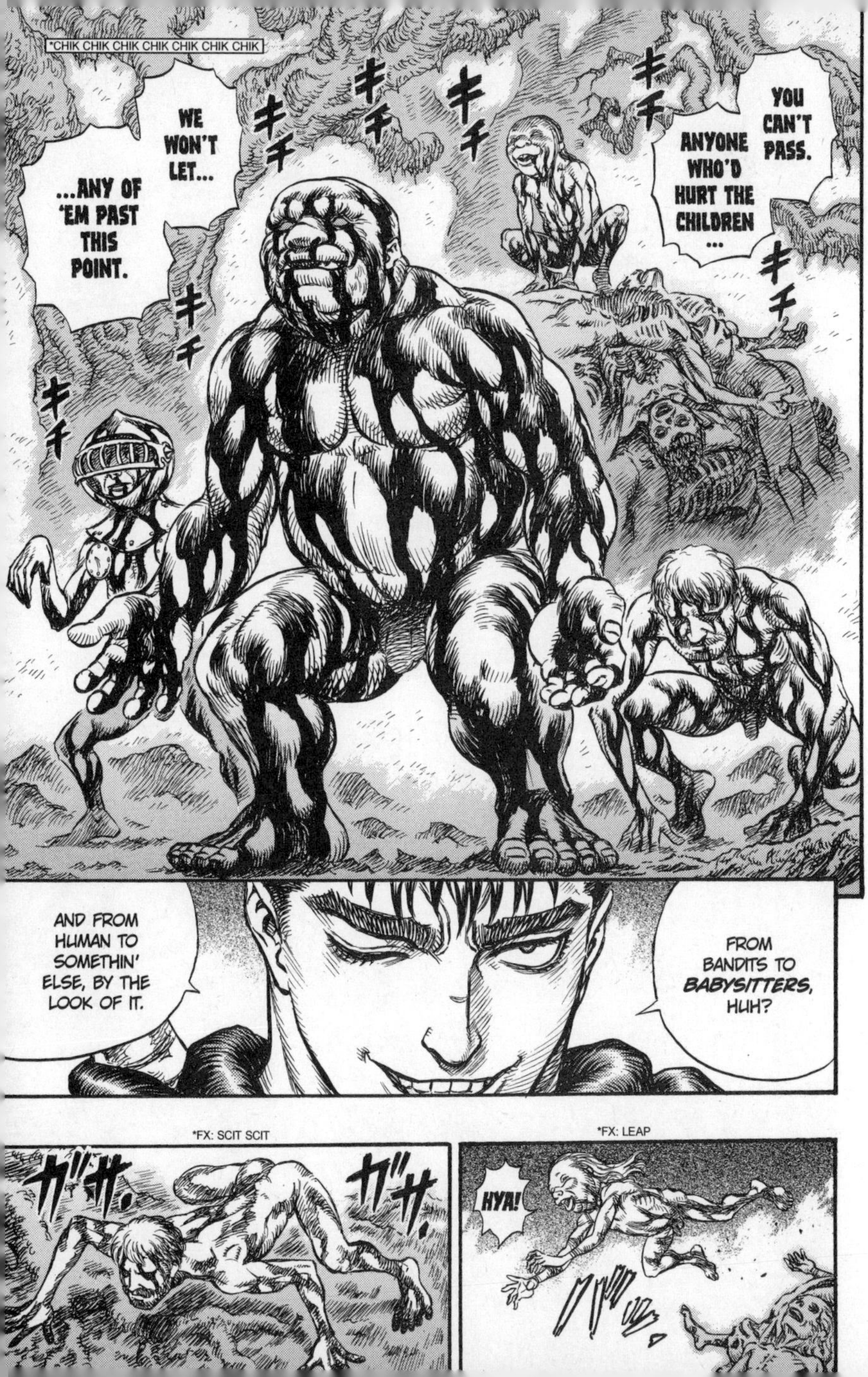
*CHIK CHIK CHIK CHIK CHIK CHIK CHIK
YOU CAN'T PASS.
ANYONE WHO'D HURT THE CHILDREN ...
WE WON'T LET...
...ANY OF 'EM PAST THIS POINT.
FROM BANDITS TO *BABYSITTERS*, HUH?
AND FROM HUMAN TO SOMETHIN' ELSE, BY THE LOOK OF IT.
*FX: LEAP
HYA!
*FX: SCIT SCIT

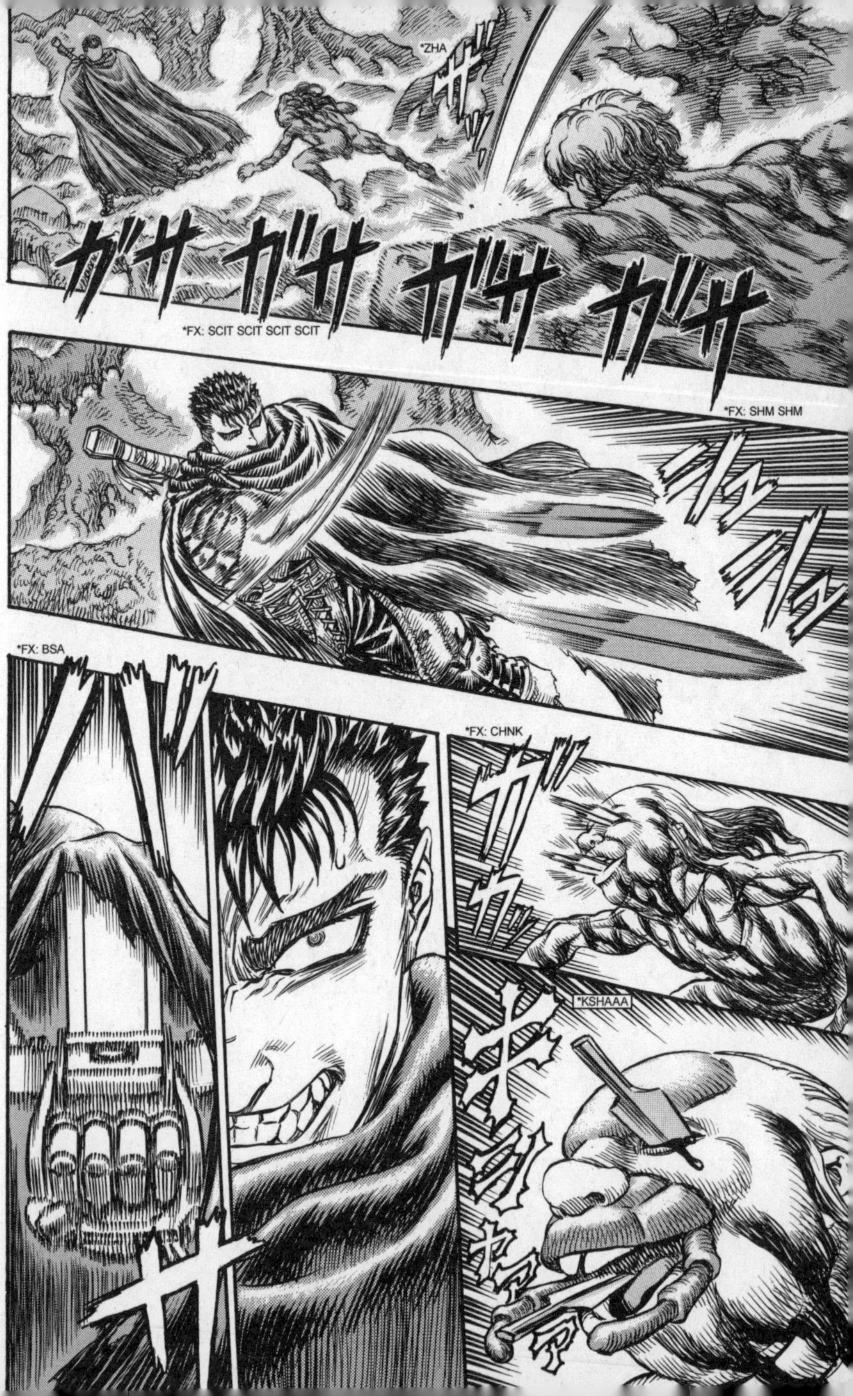
*ZHA
*FX: SCIT SCIT SCIT SCIT
*FX: SHM SHM
*FX: CHNK
*KSHAAA
*FX: BSA

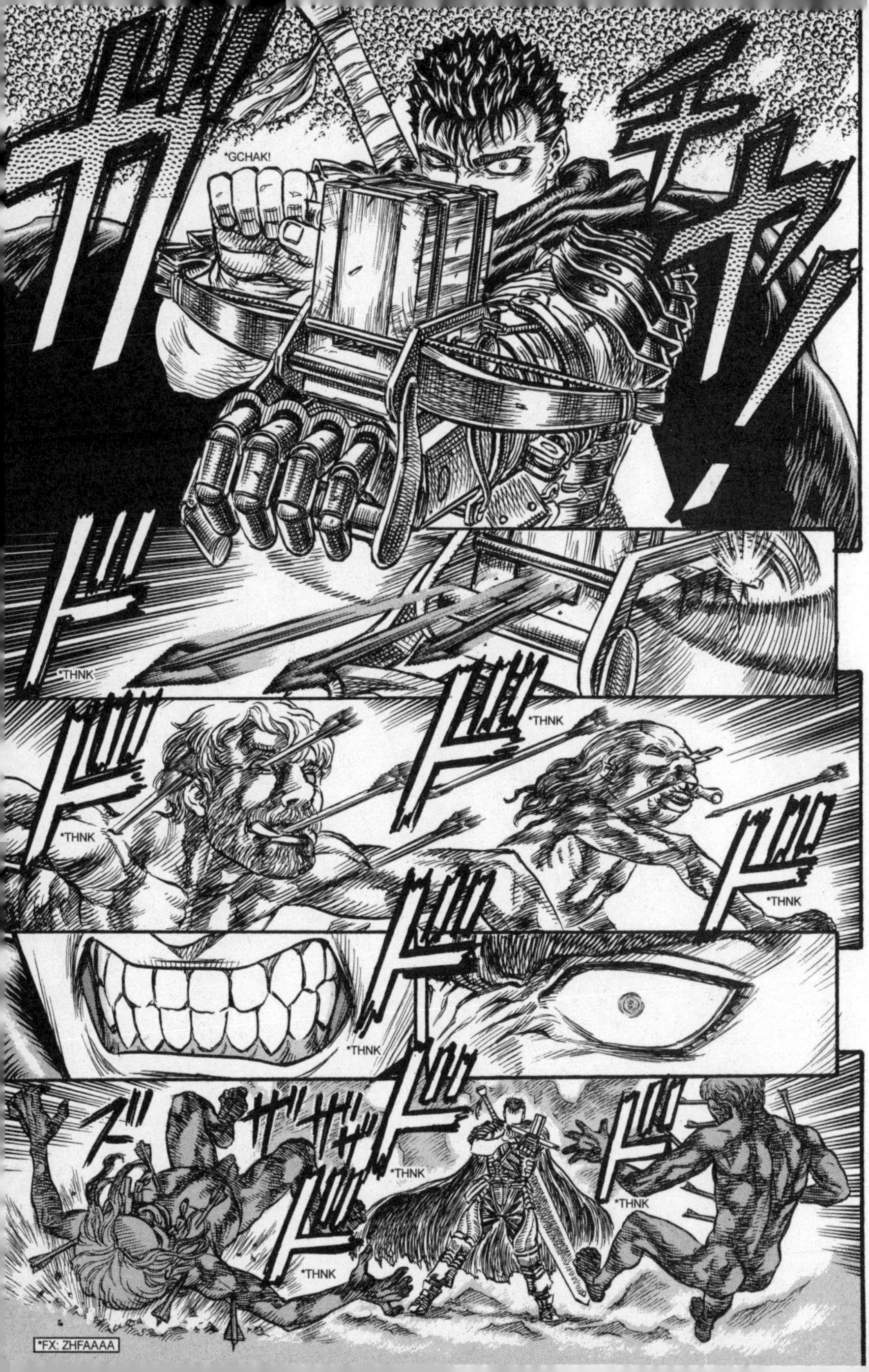
*GCHAK!
*THNK
*THNK
*THNK
*THNK
*THNK
*THNK
*THNK
*THNK
*FX: ZHFAAAA

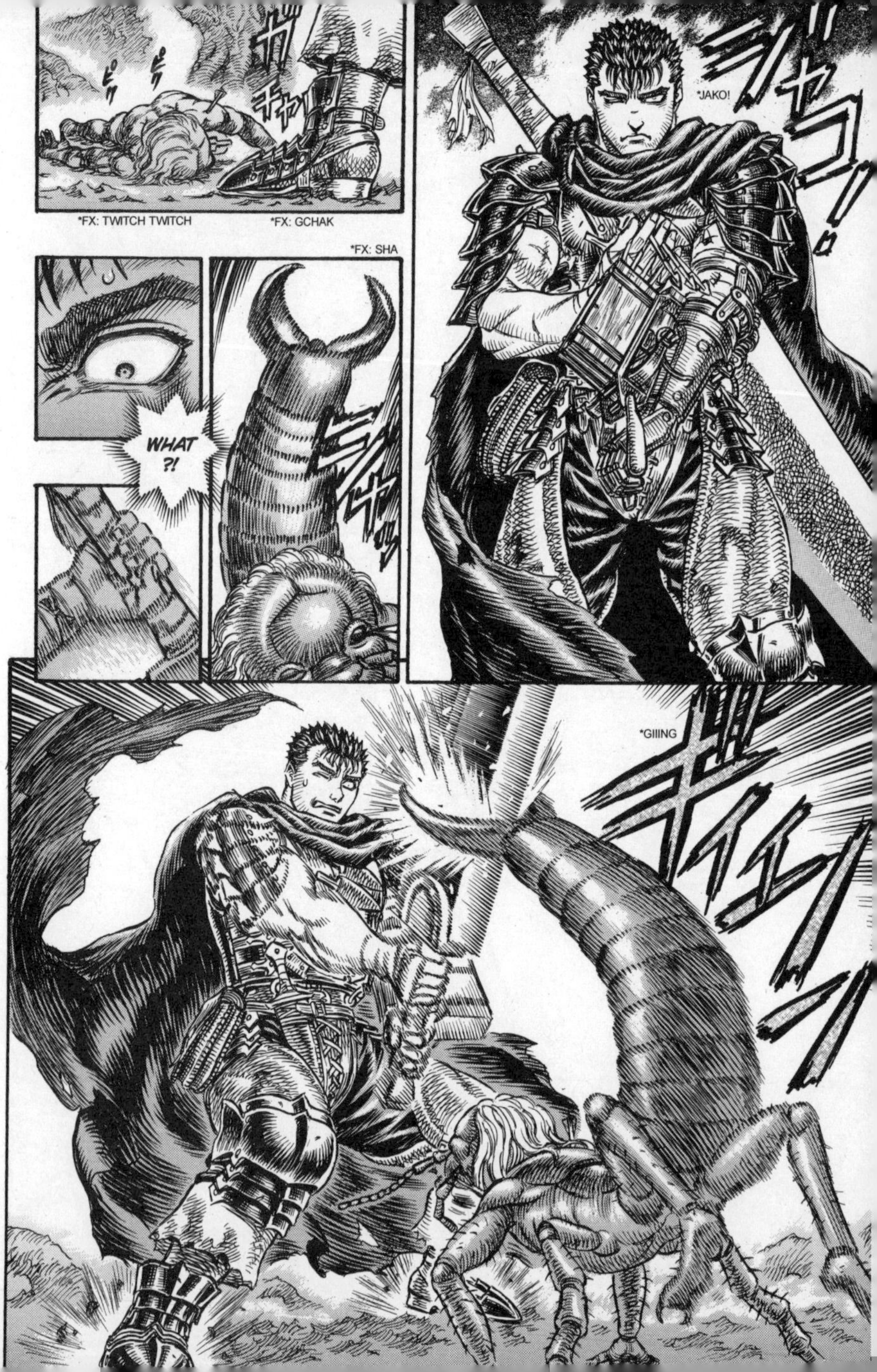

*JAKO!
*FX: TWITCH TWITCH
*FX: GCHAK
*FX: SHA
WHAT ?!
*GIIING

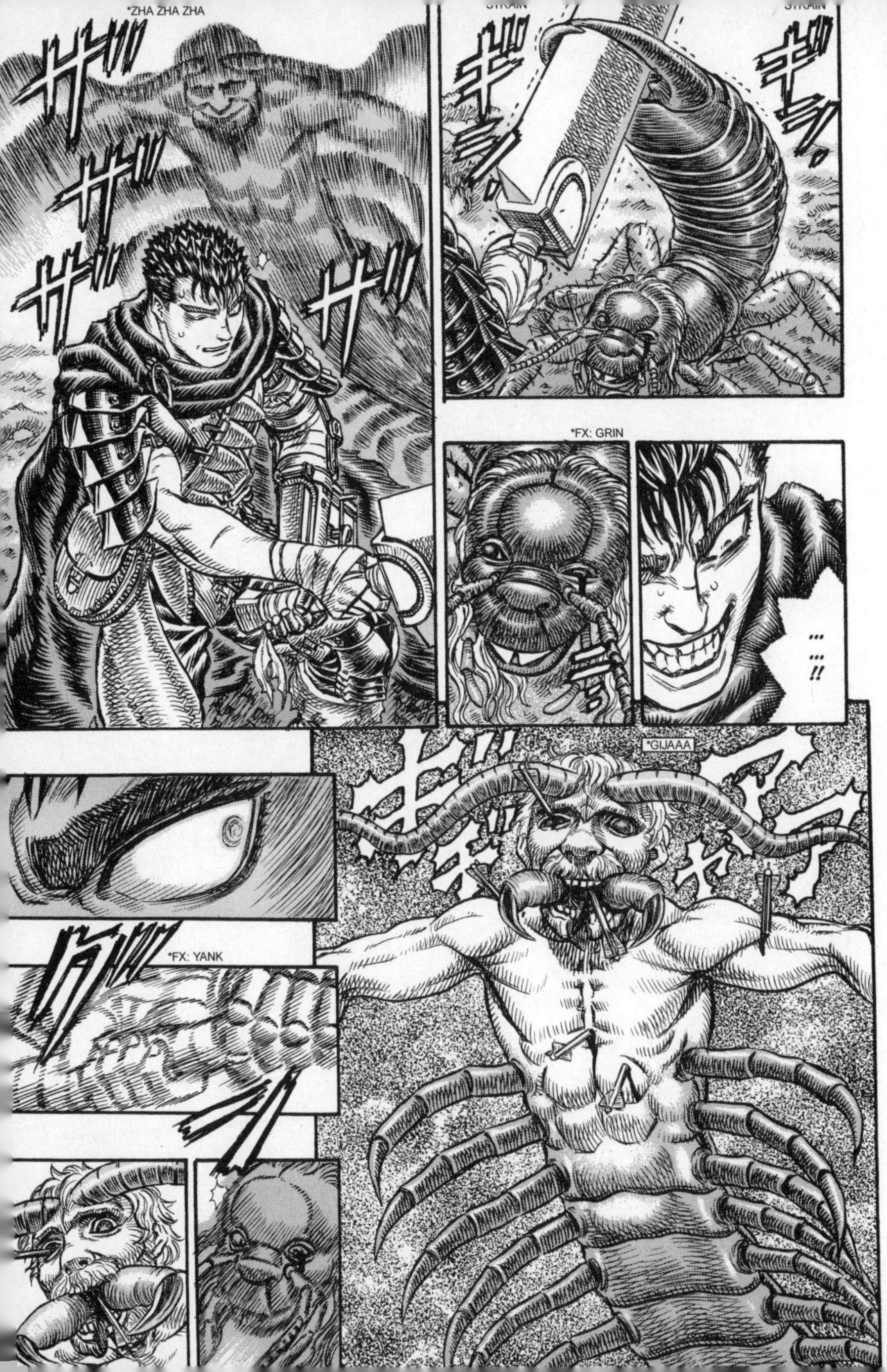
STRAIN
STRAIN
*ZHA ZHA ZHA
*FX: GRIN
...
...
!!
*GIJAAA
*FX: YANK

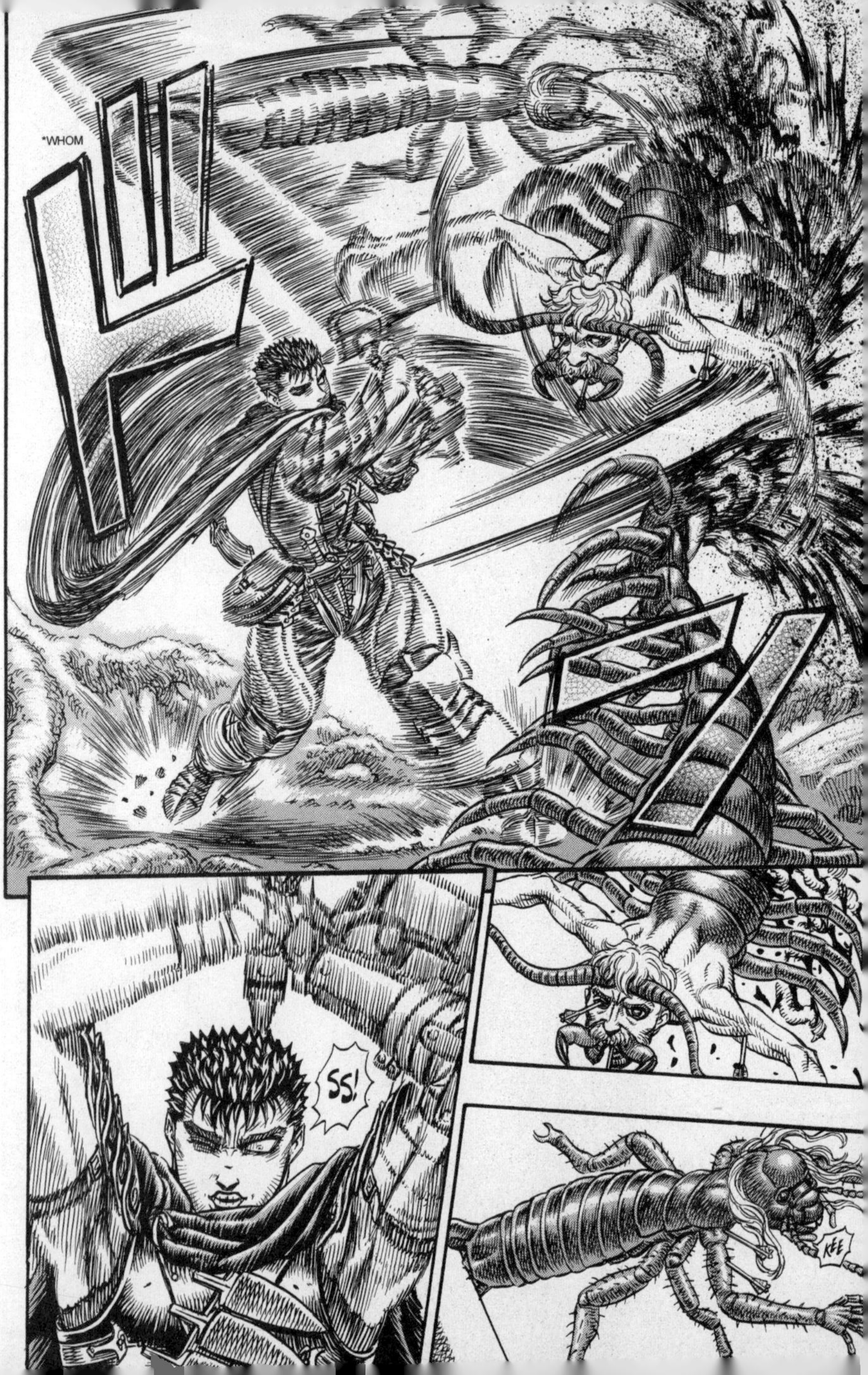
*WHOM
KEE
SS!

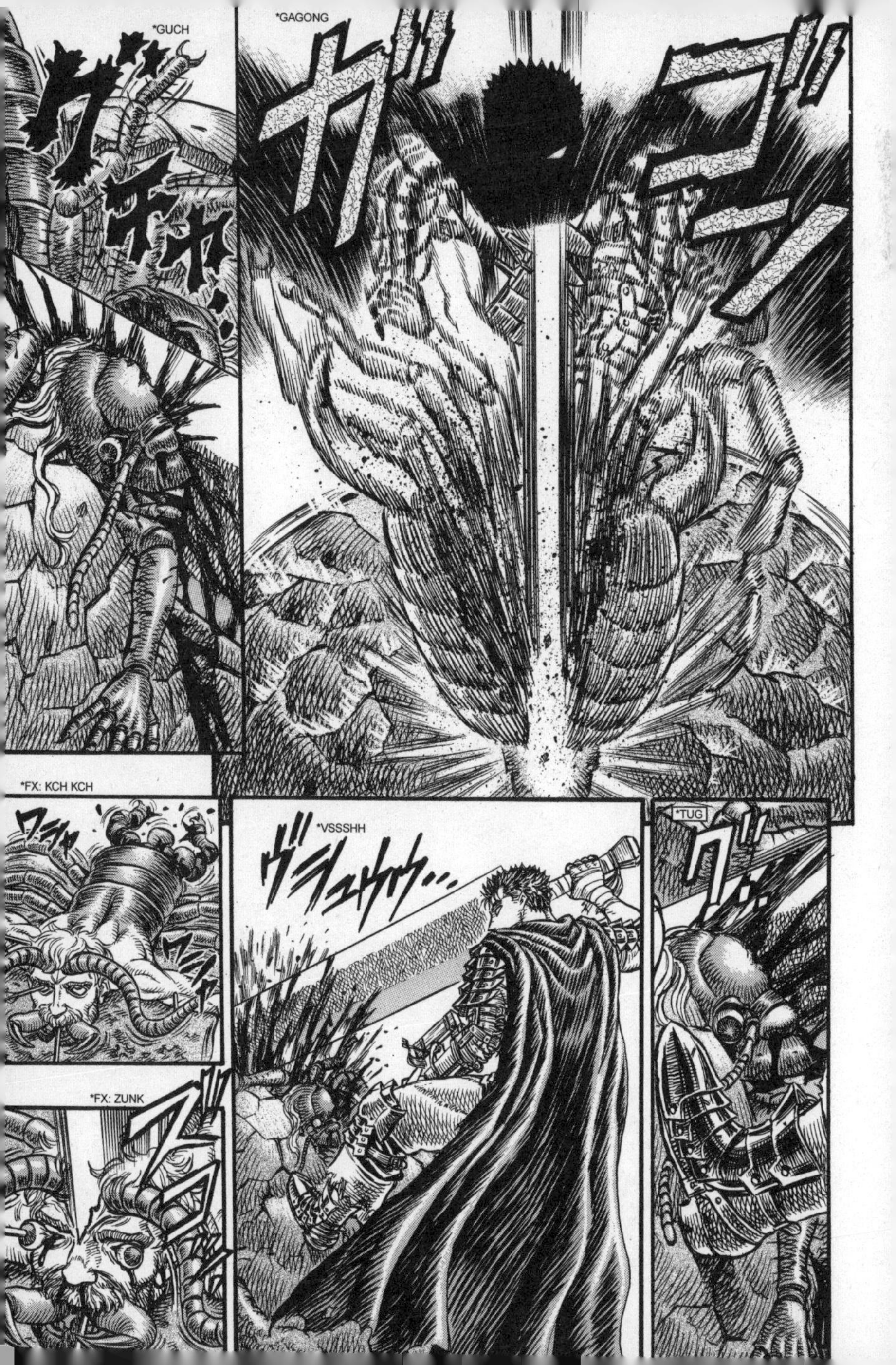
*GAGONG
*GUCH
*TUG
*VSSSHH
*FX: KCH KCH
*FX: ZUNK

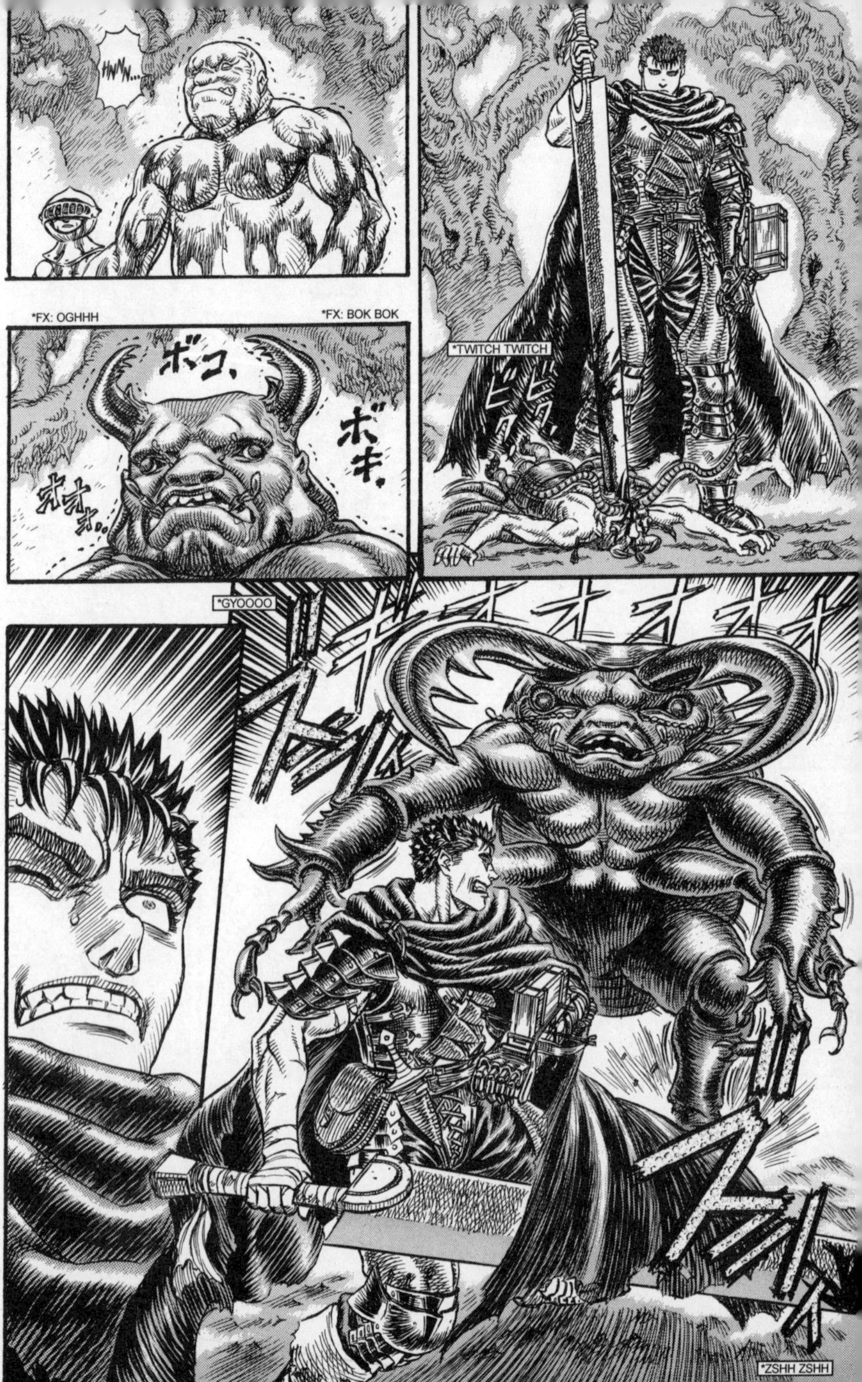
*TWITCH TWITCH
HNNN...
*FX: BOK BOK
ボコ、
ボキ、
*FX: OGHHH
*GYOOOO
*ZSHH ZSHH

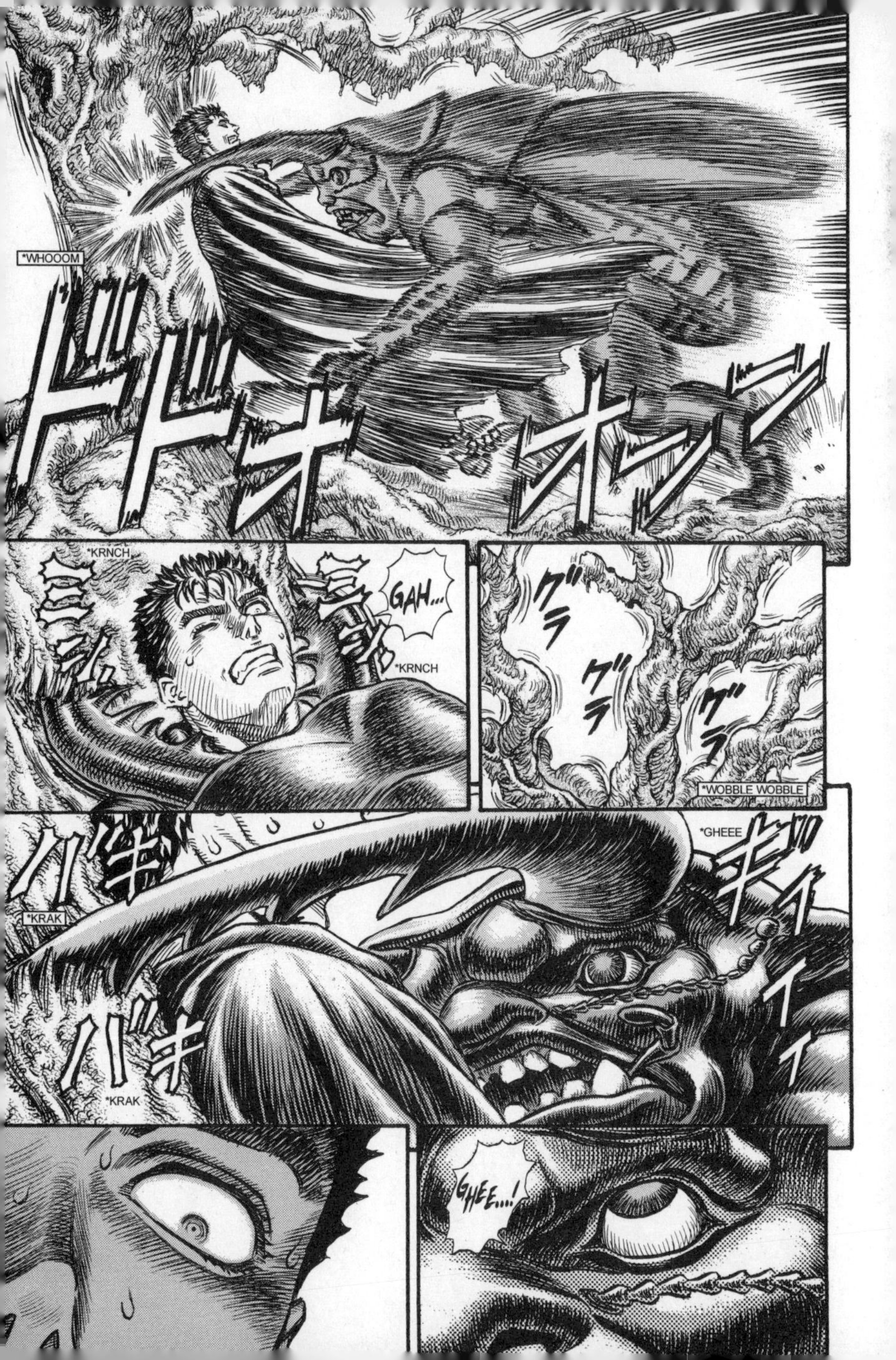
*WHOOOM
*WOBBLE WOBBLE
GAH...
*KRNCH
*KRNCH
*GHEEE
*KRAK
*KRAK
GHEE...!

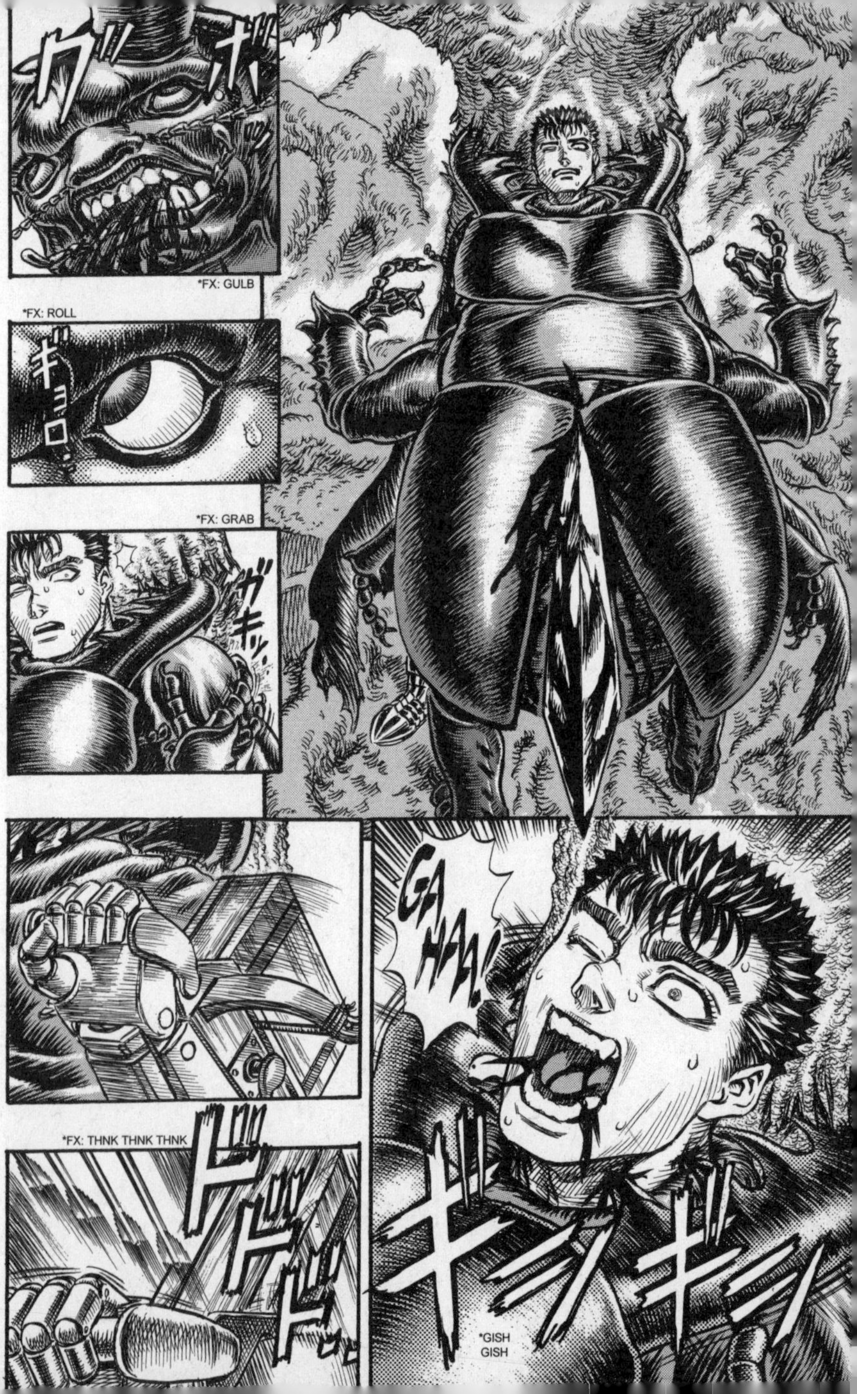
*FX: GULB
*FX: ROLL
*FX: GRAB
GAHAAA!
*GISH GISH
*FX: THNK THNK THNK

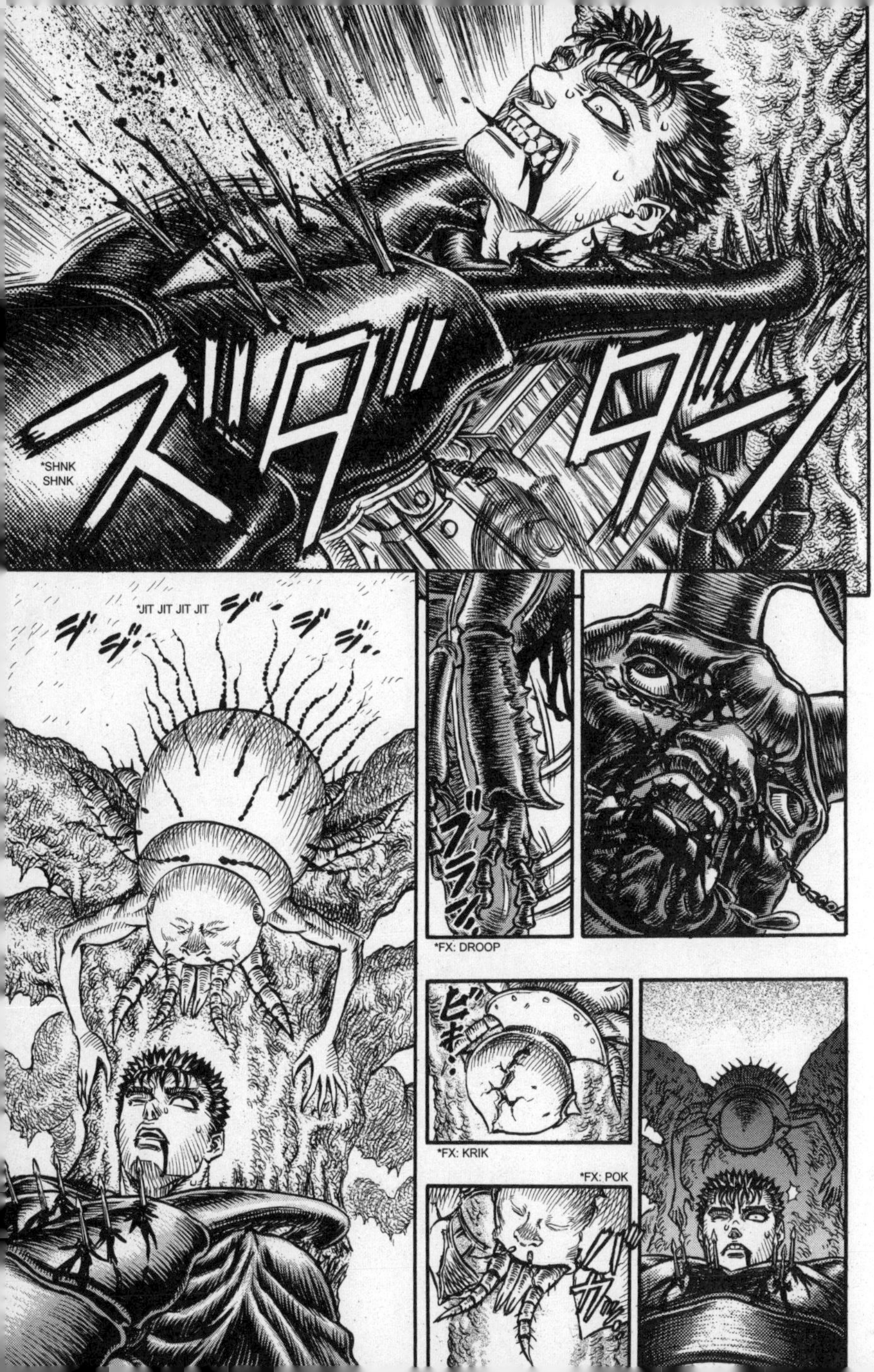
ズダダン
*SHNK SHNK
*FX: DROOP
*FX: KRIK
*FX: POK
*JIT JIT JIT JIT

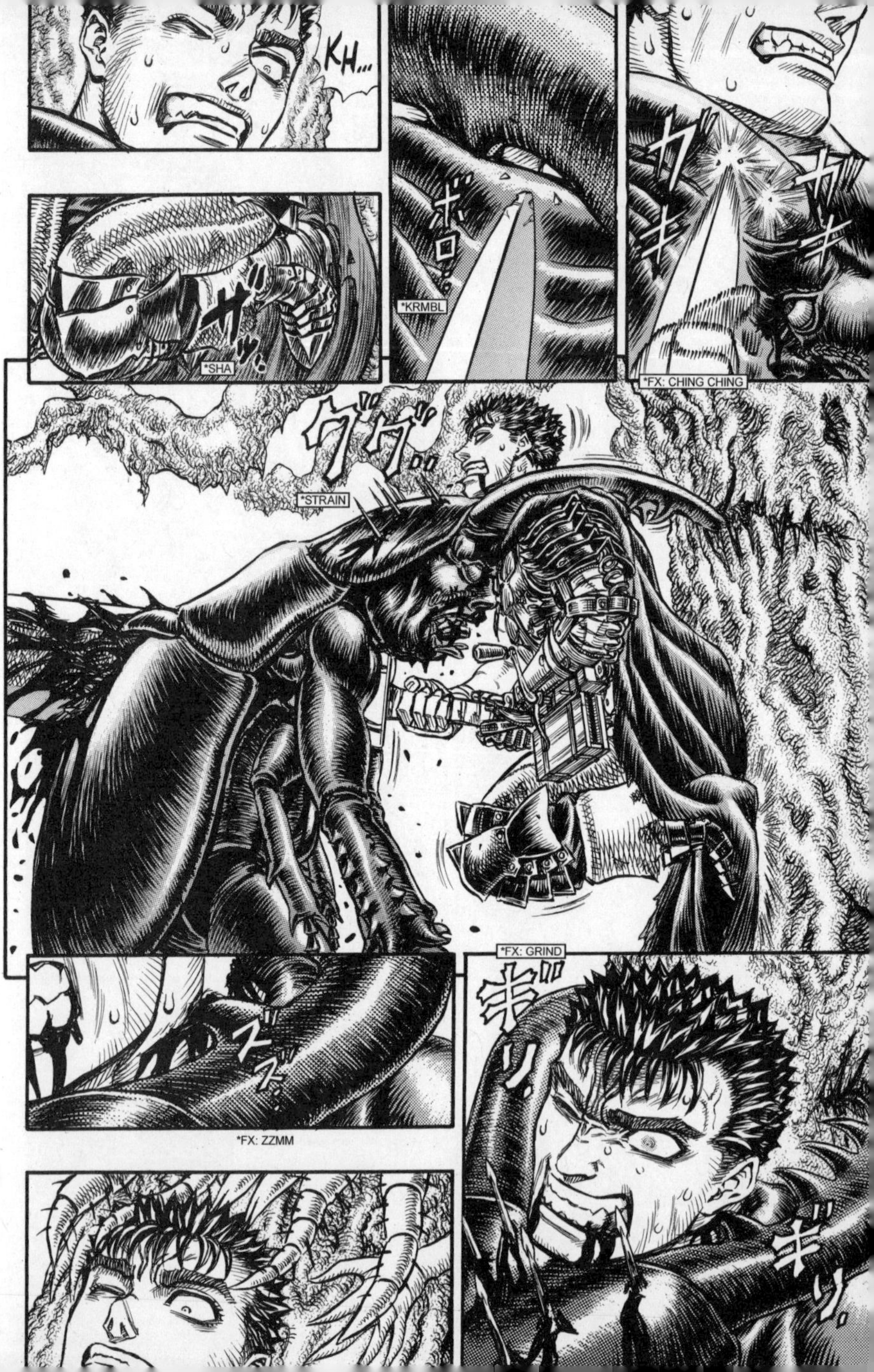
*FX: CHING CHING
*KRMBL
KH...
*SHA
*STRAIN
*FX: GRIND
*FX: ZZMM

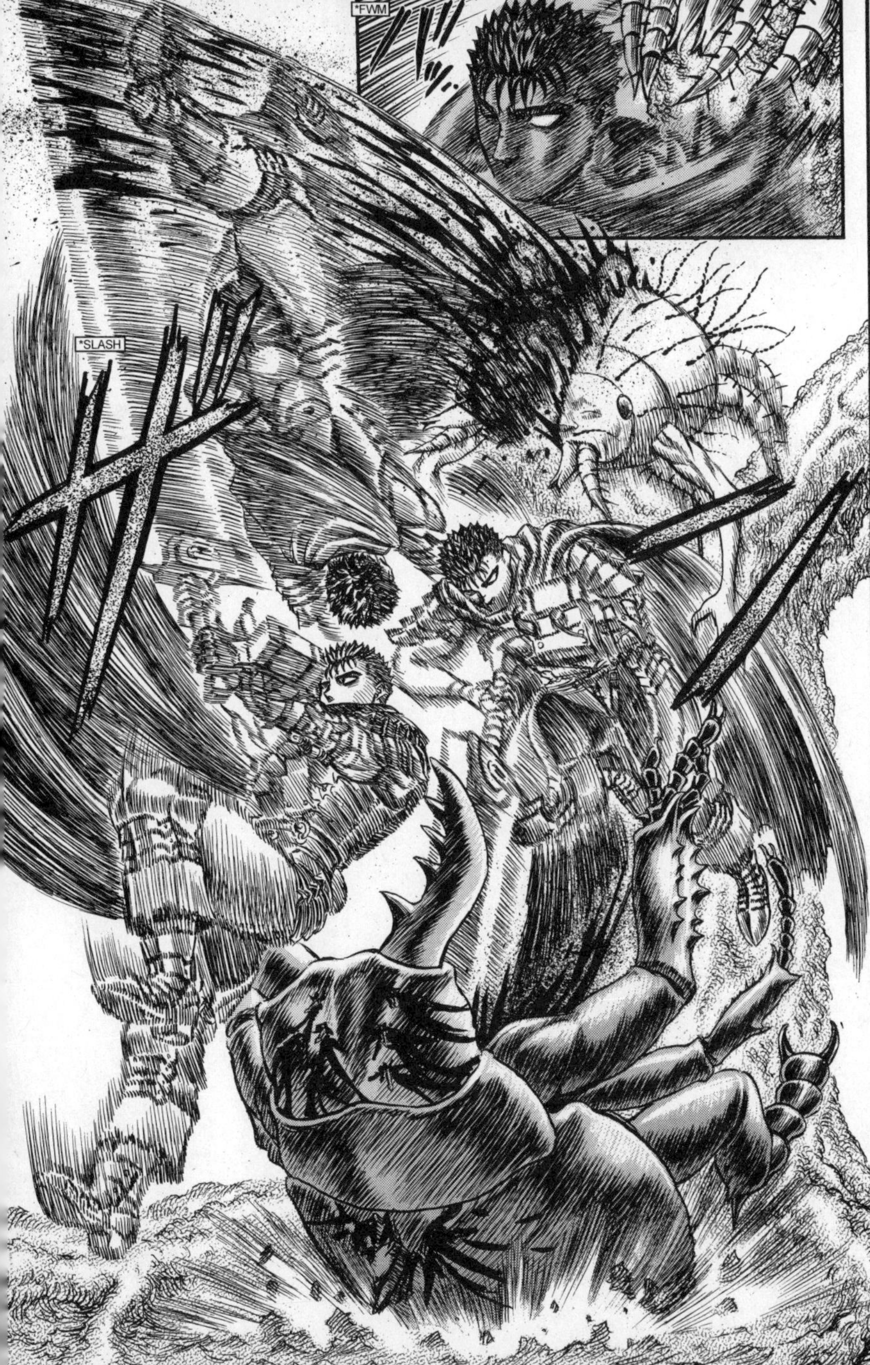
*FWM
*SLASH

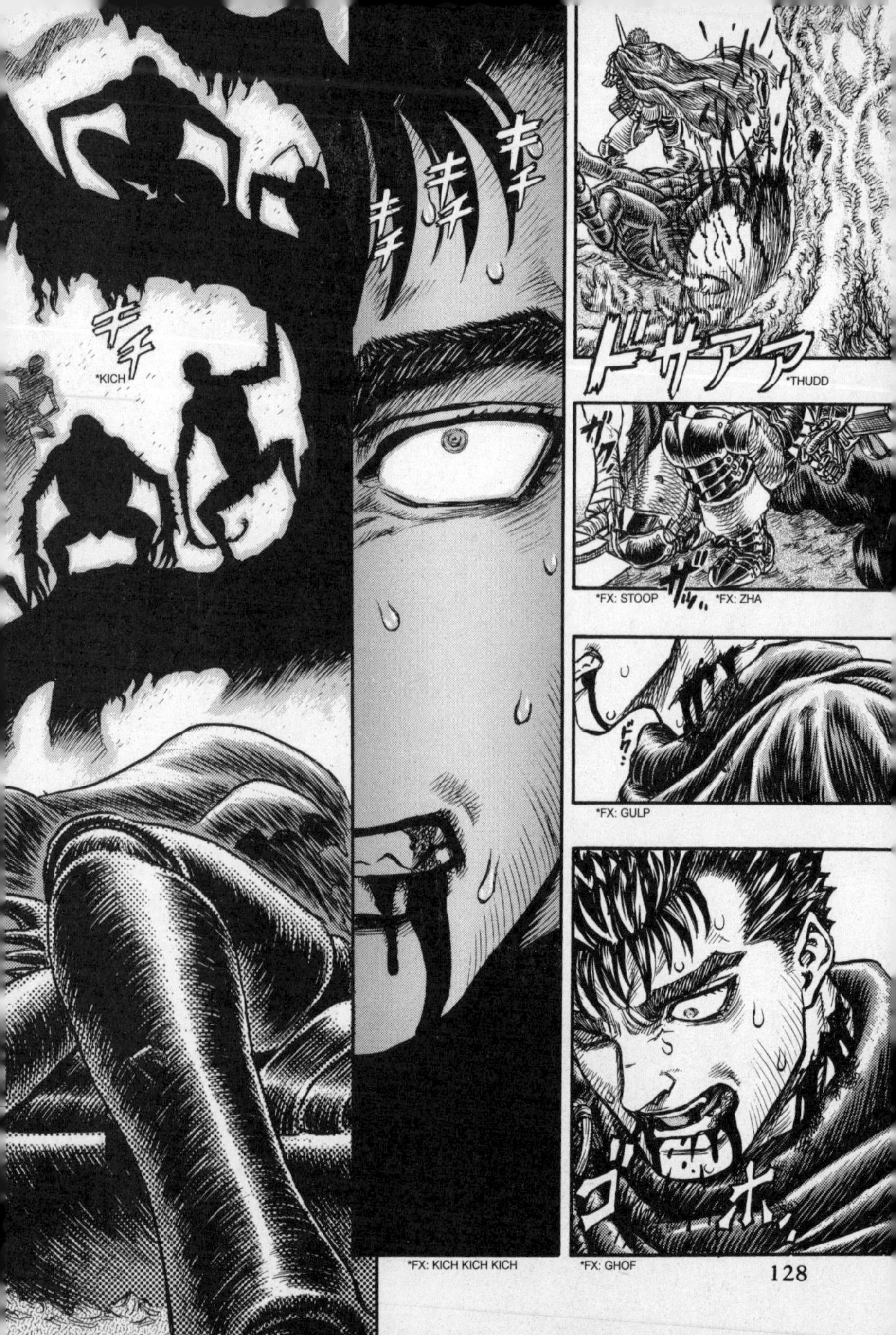
*THUDD
*FX: ZHA
*FX: STOOP
*FX: GULP
*FX: GHOF
*FX: KICH KICH KICH
*KICH

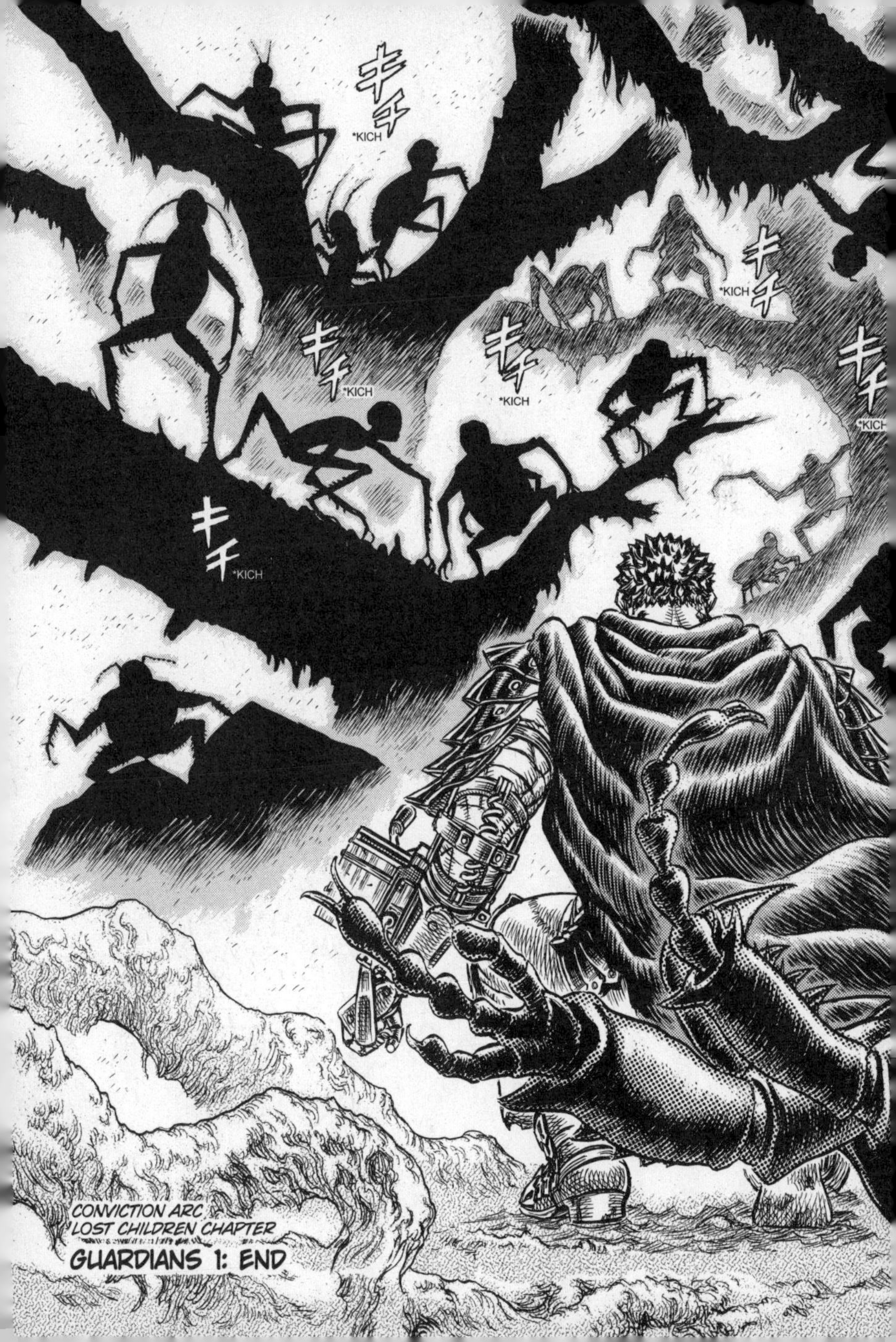

キチ
*KICH
キチ
*KICH
キチ
*KICH
キチ
*KICH
キチ
*KICH
キチ
*KICH
CONVICTION ARC
LOST CHILDREN CHAPTER
GUARDIANS 1: END

BERSERK

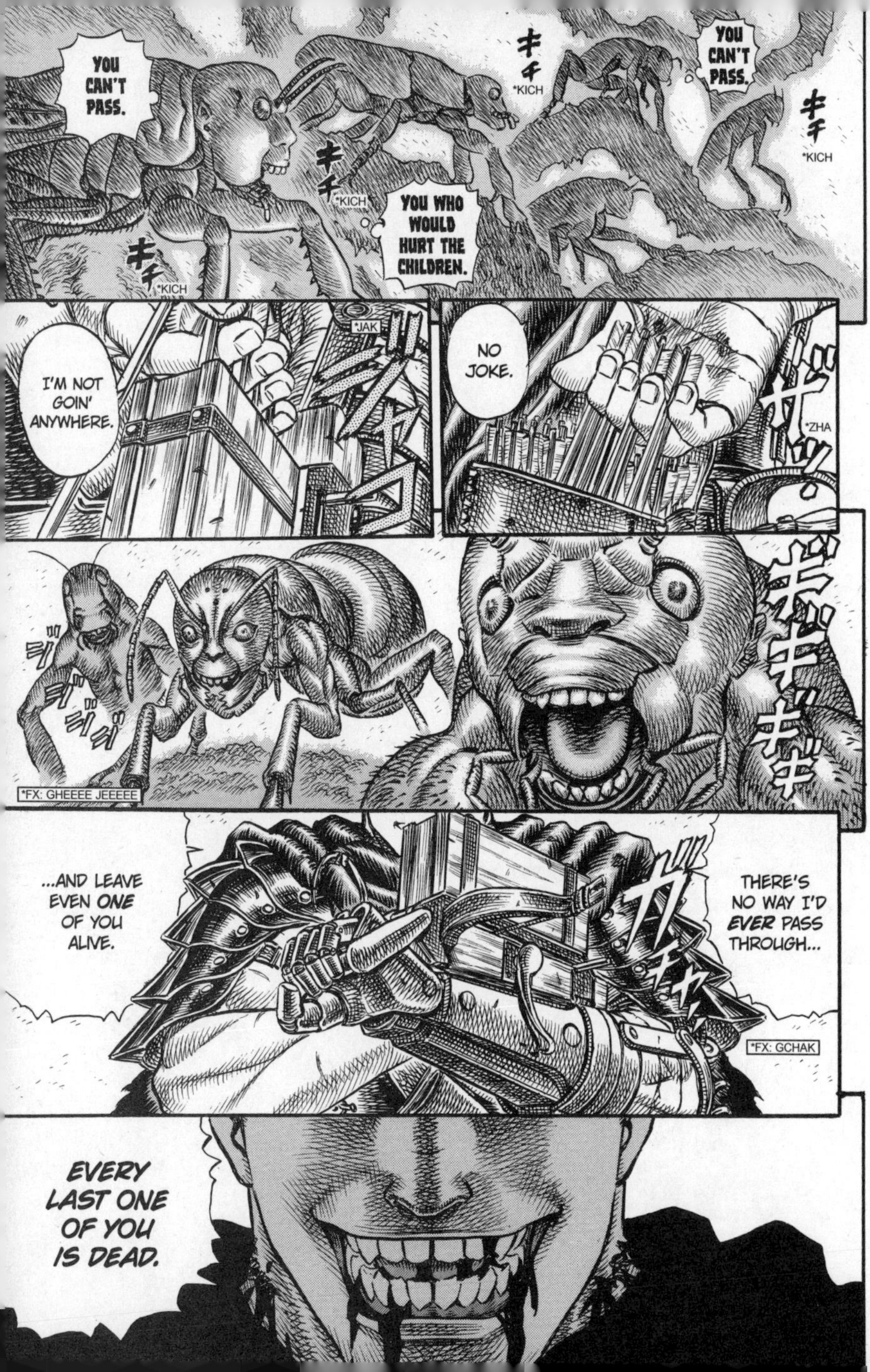
YOU CAN'T PASS.
*KICH
*KICH
YOU CAN'T PASS.
*KICH
YOU WHO WOULD HURT THE CHILDREN.
*KICH
*ZHA
NO JOKE.
*JAK
I'M NOT GOIN' ANYWHERE.
*FX: GHEEEE JEEEEE
THERE'S NO WAY I'D EVER PASS THROUGH...
*FX: GCHAK
...AND LEAVE EVEN ONE OF YOU ALIVE.
EVERY LAST ONE OF YOU IS DEAD.

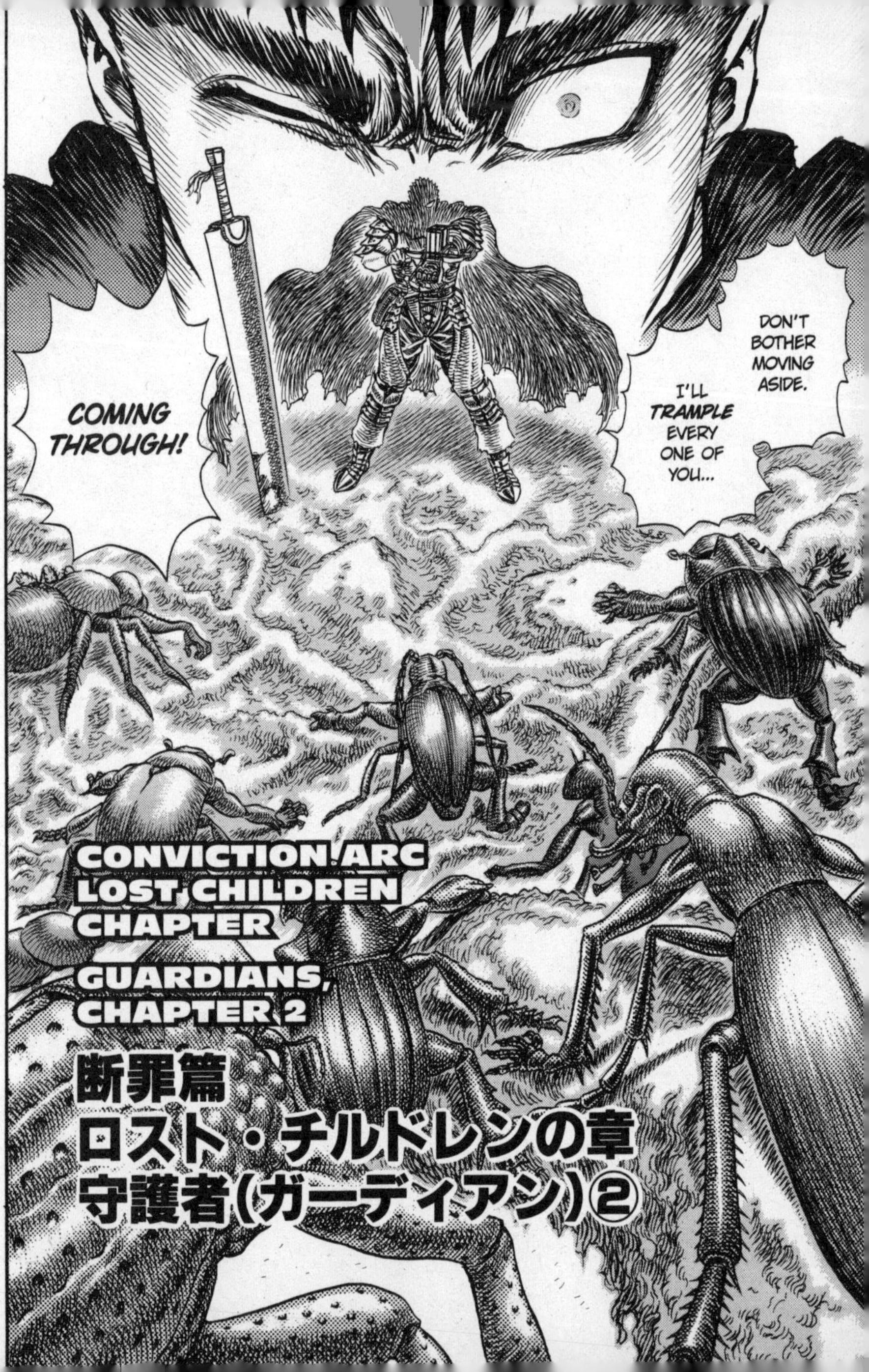
DON'T BOTHER MOVING ASIDE.
I'LL TRAMPLE EVERY ONE OF YOU...
COMING THROUGH!
CONVICTION ARC LOST CHILDREN CHAPTER
GUARDIANS, CHAPTER 2
断罪篇
ロスト・チルドレンの章
守護者(ガーディアン)②

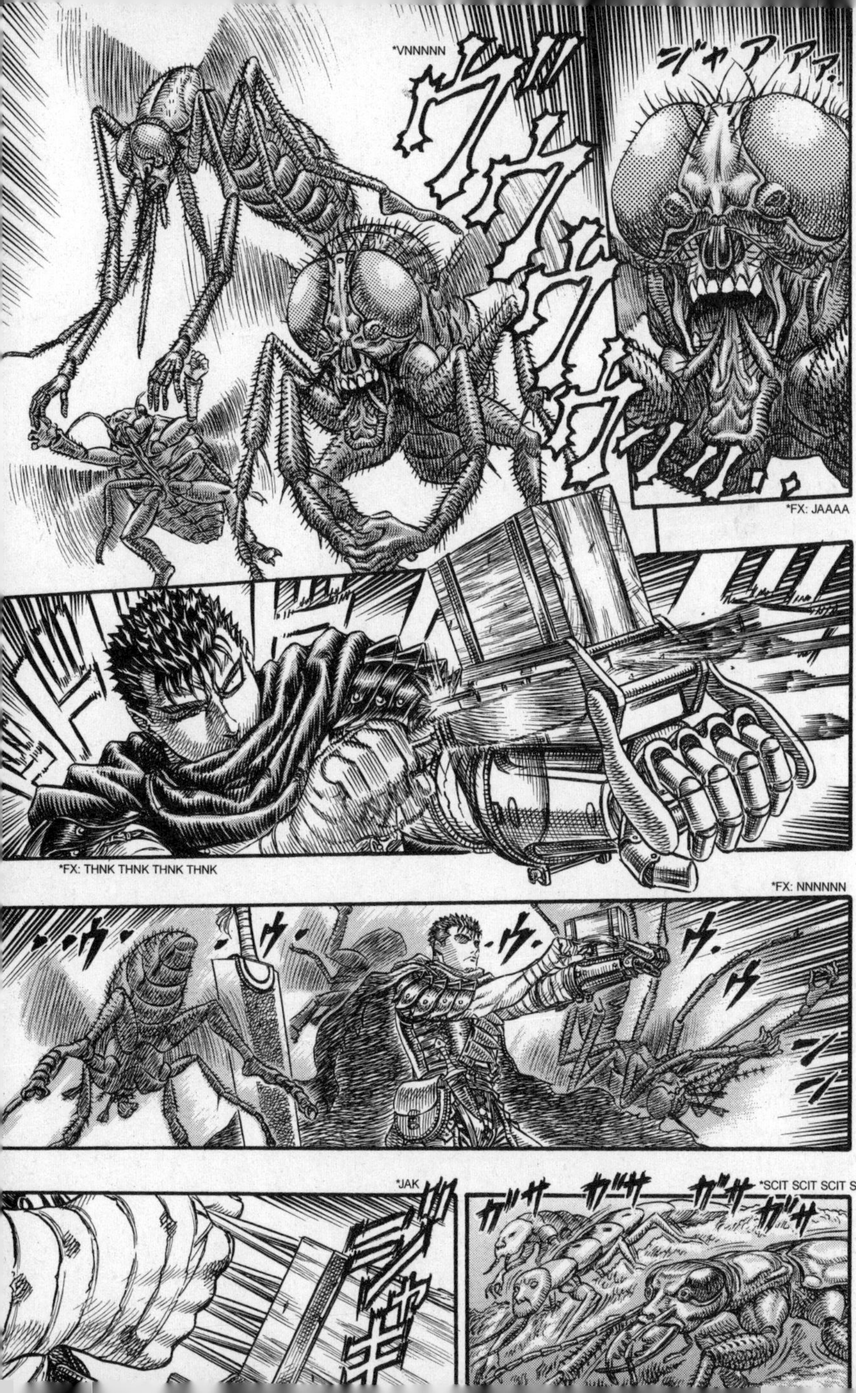

*FX: JAAAA
*VNNNNN
*FX: THNK THNK THNK THNK
*FX: NNNNNN
*SCIT SCIT SCIT SCIT
*JAK

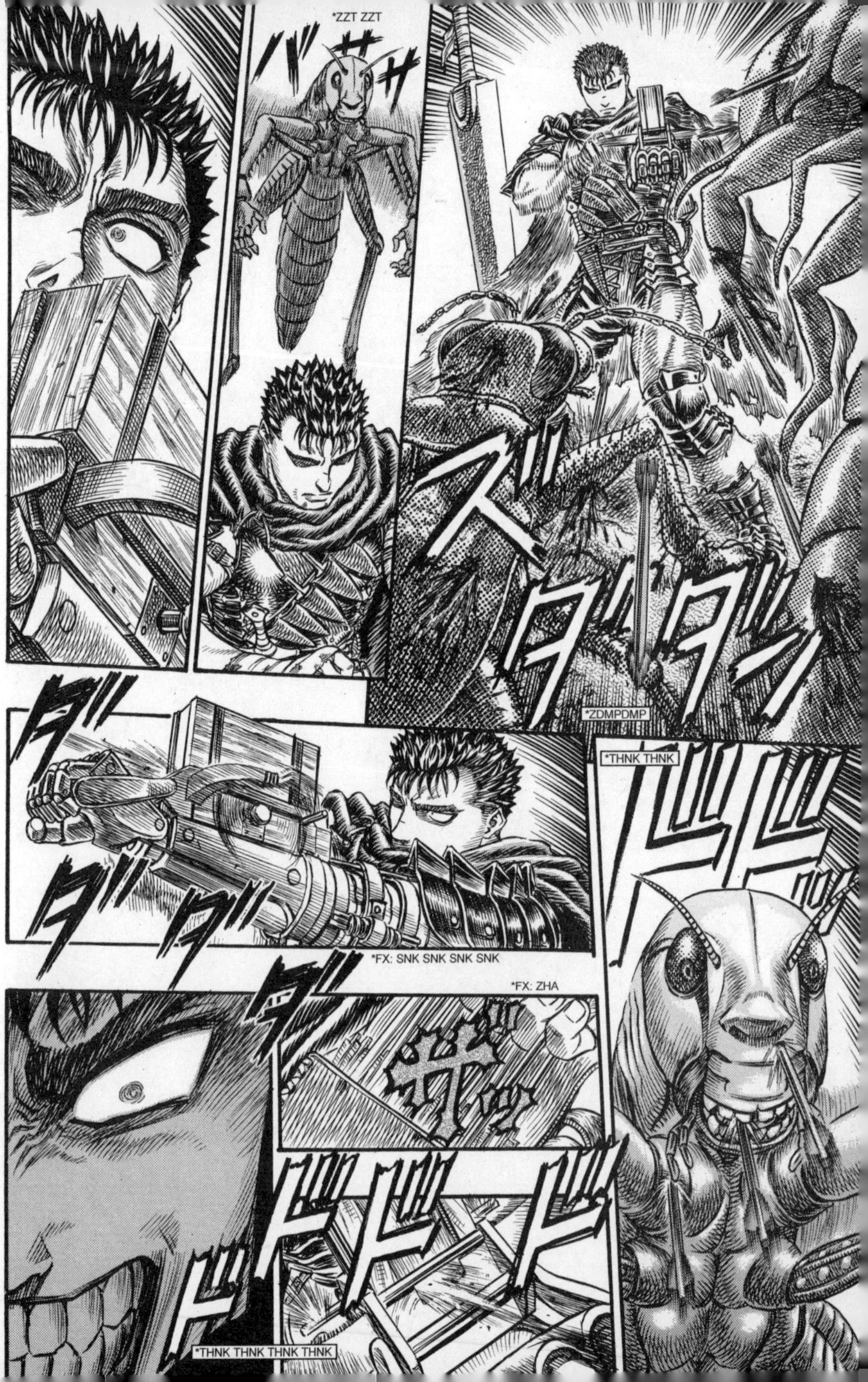
*ZDMPDMP
*ZZT ZZT
*THNK THNK
*FX: SNK SNK SNK SNK
*FX: ZHA
*THNK THNK THNK THNK

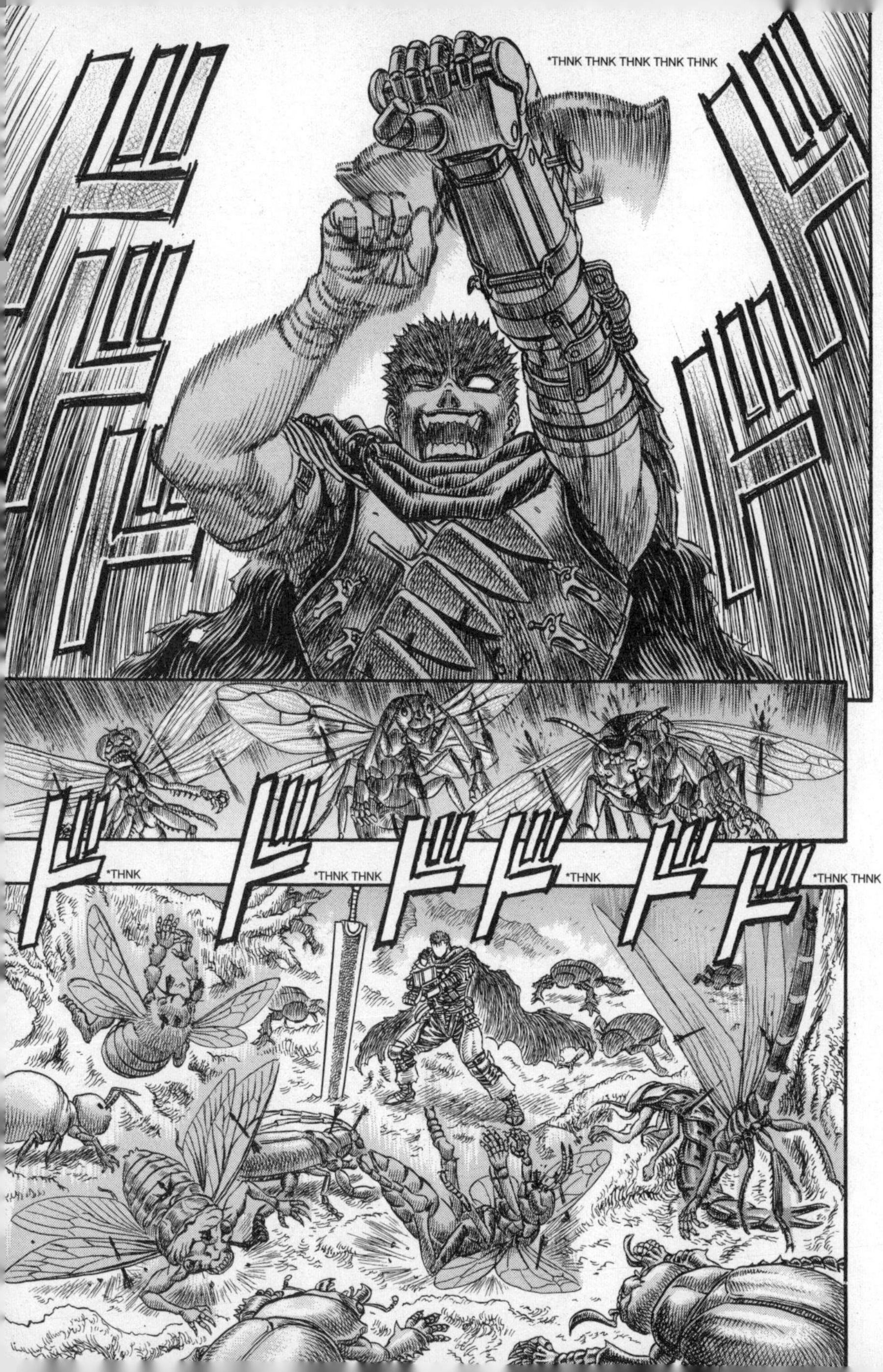

*THNK THNK THNK THNK THNK
*THNK THNK
*THNK
*THNK THNK
*THNK

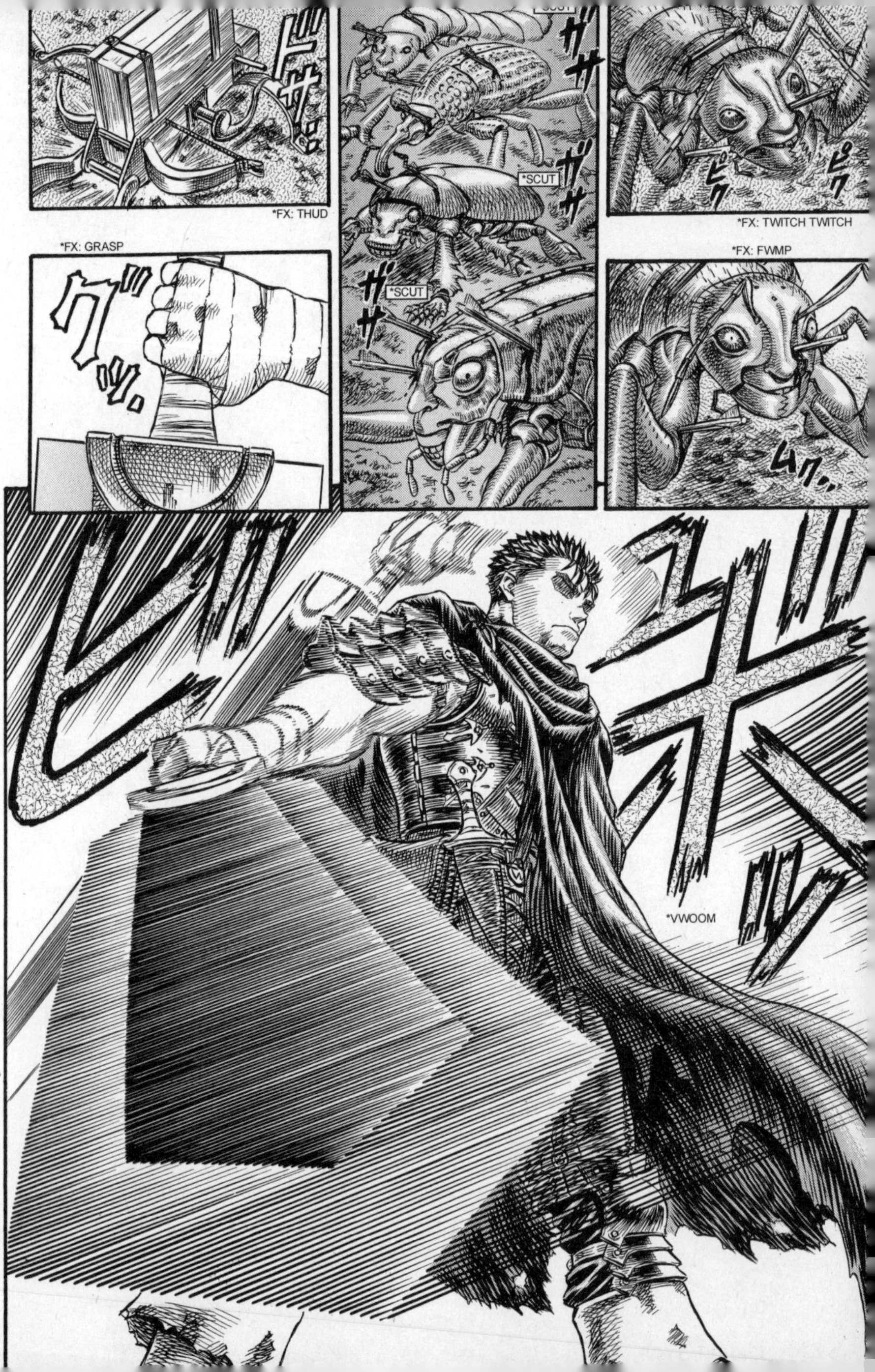
*FX: TWITCH TWITCH
*FX: FWMP
*SCUT
*SCUT
*FX: THUD
*FX: GRASP
*VWOOM

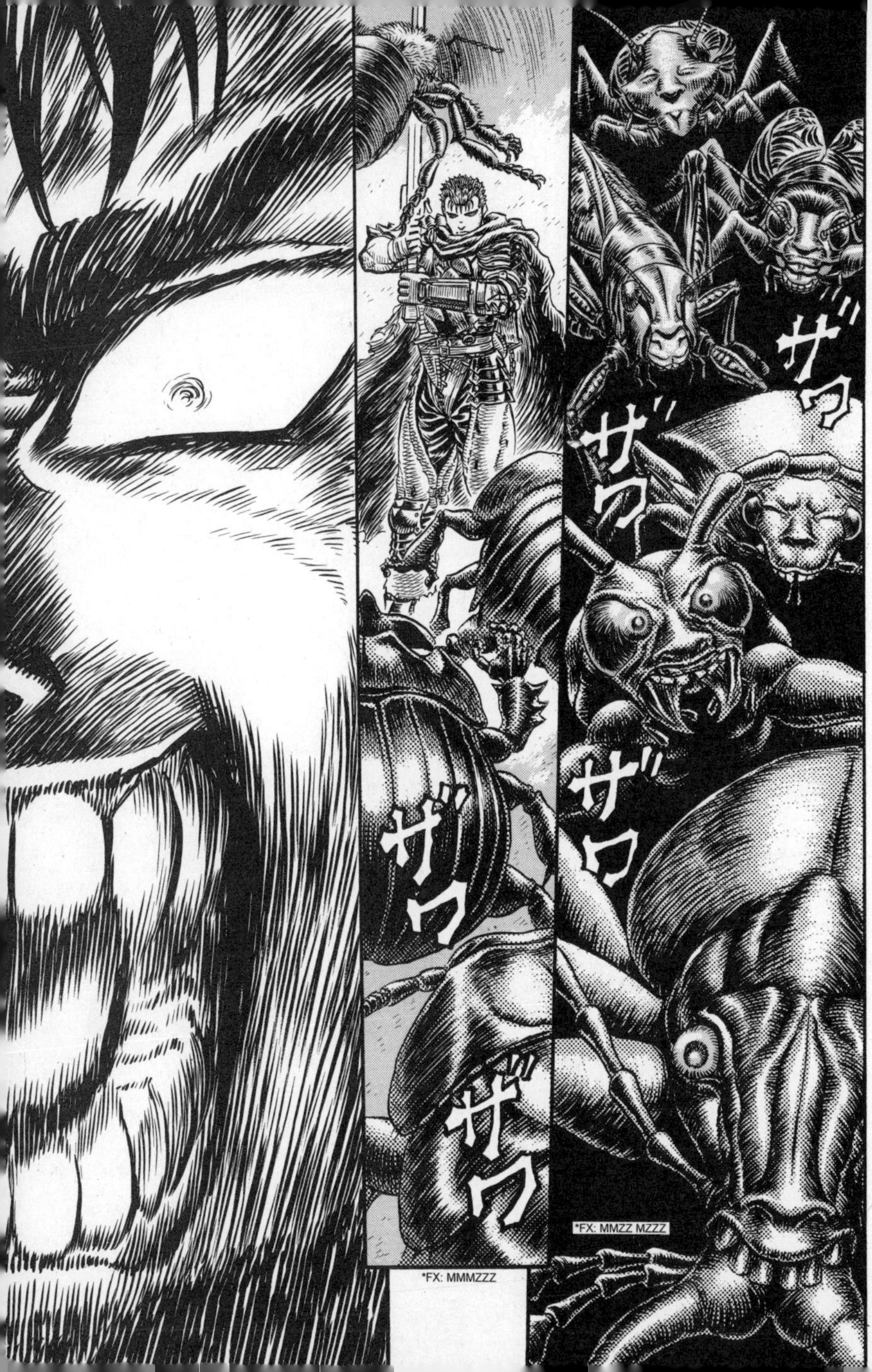
ザワ
ザワ
ザワ
*FX: MMZZ MZZZ
ザワ
ザワ
*FX: MMMZZZ

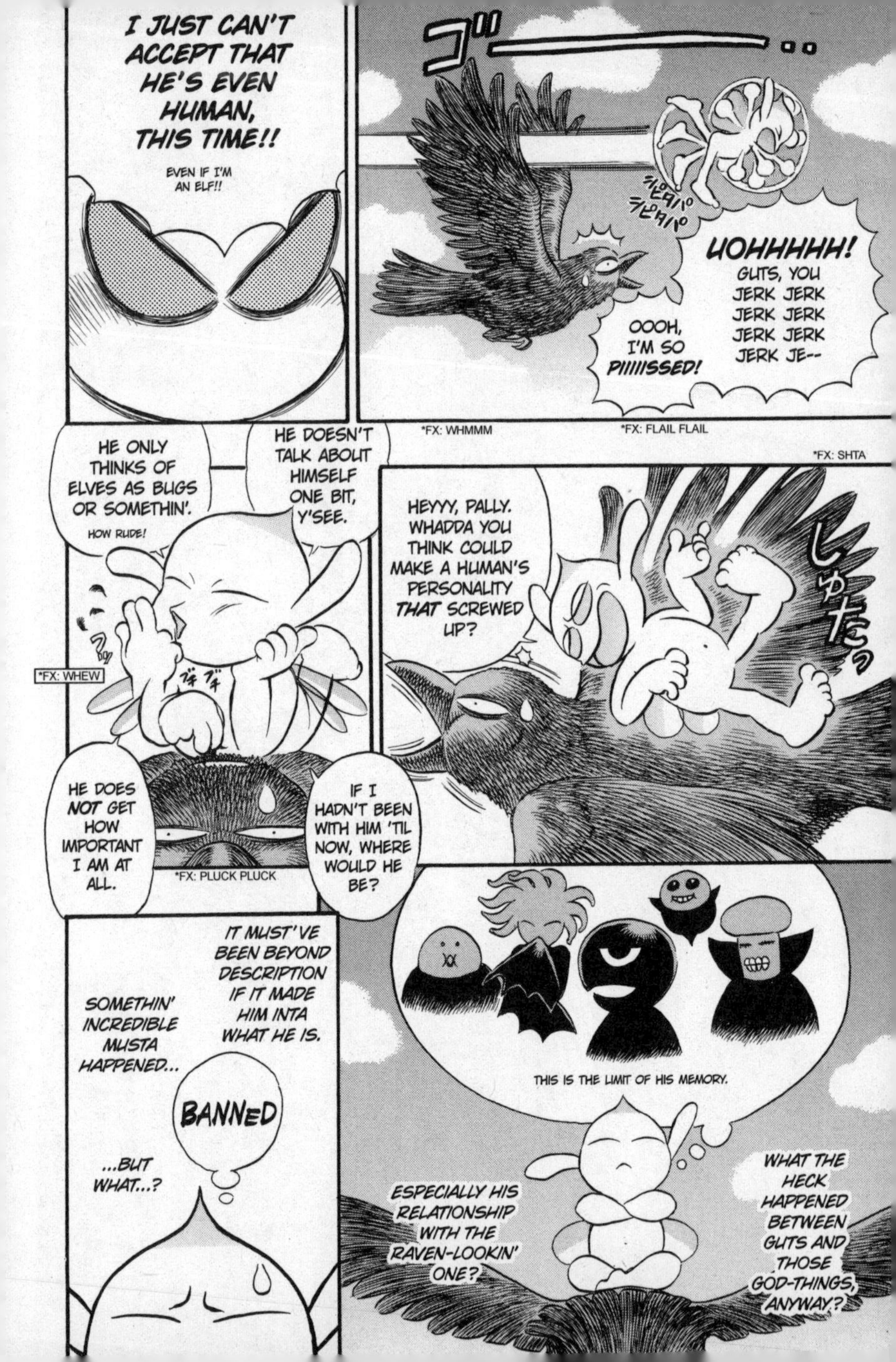
ゴー
UOHHHHH! GUTS, YOU JERK JERK JERK JERK JERK JERK JERK JE--
OOOH, I'M SO PIIIISSED!
*FX: WHMMM
*FX: FLAIL FLAIL
I JUST CAN'T ACCEPT THAT HE'S EVEN HUMAN, THIS TIME!!
EVEN IF I'M AN ELF!!
*FX: SHTA
しゅたっ
HEYYY, PALLY. WHADDA YOU THINK COULD MAKE A HUMAN'S PERSONALITY THAT SCREWED UP?
HE DOESN'T TALK ABOUT HIMSELF ONE BIT, Y'SEE.
HE ONLY THINKS OF ELVES AS BUGS OR SOMETHIN'.
HOW RUDE!
*FX: WHEW
IF I HADN'T BEEN WITH HIM 'TIL NOW, WHERE WOULD HE BE?
HE DOES NOT GET HOW IMPORTANT I AM AT ALL.
*FX: PLUCK PLUCK
THIS IS THE LIMIT OF HIS MEMORY.
WHAT THE HECK HAPPENED BETWEEN GUTS AND THOSE GOD-THINGS, ANYWAY?
ESPECIALLY HIS RELATIONSHIP WITH THE RAVEN-LOOKIN' ONE?
IT MUST'VE BEEN BEYOND DESCRIPTION IF IT MADE HIM INTA WHAT HE IS.
SOMETHIN' INCREDIBLE MUSTA HAPPENED...
BANNED
...BUT WHAT...?

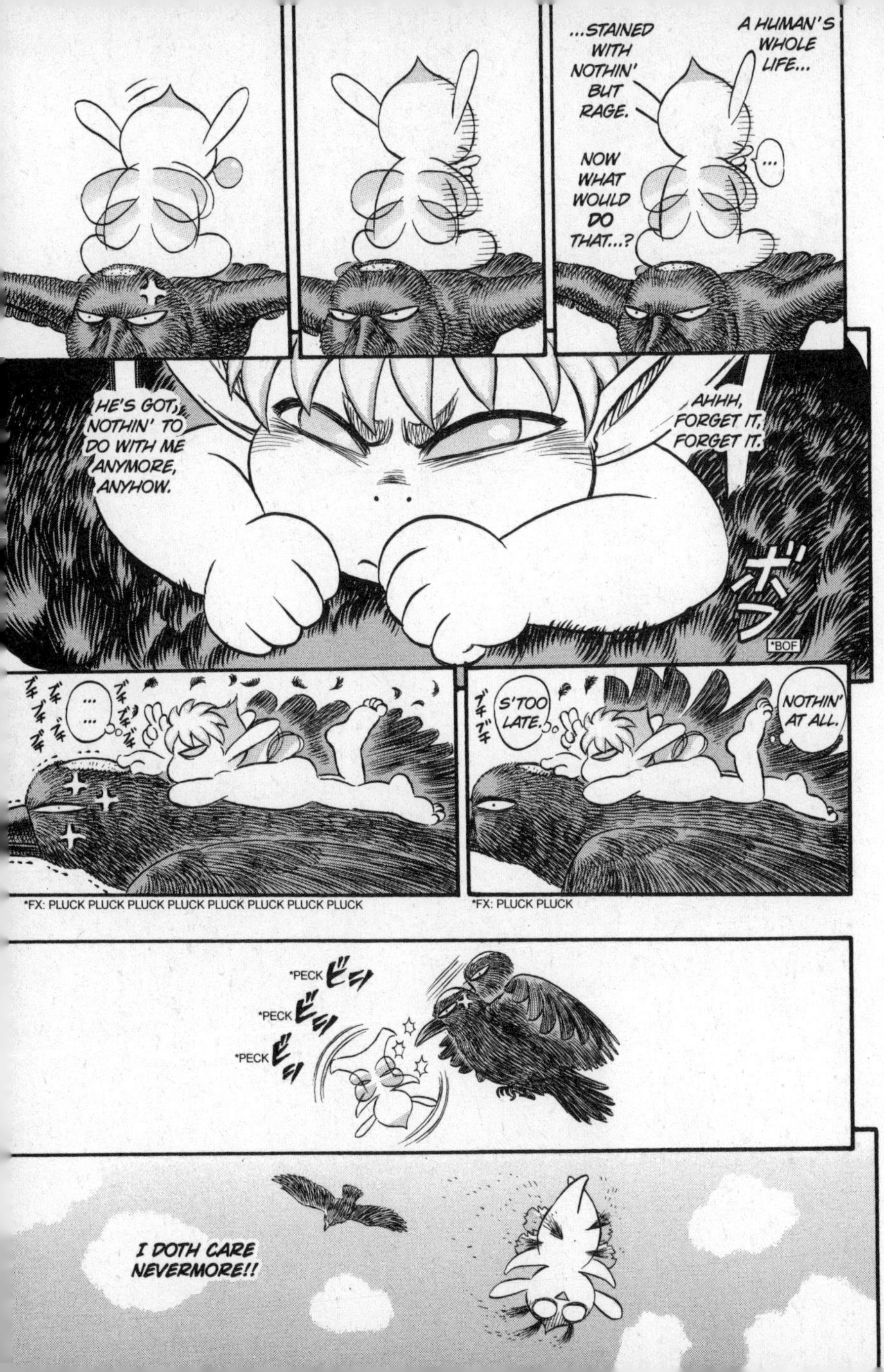
A HUMAN'S WHOLE LIFE...
...STAINED WITH NOTHIN' BUT RAGE.
...
NOW WHAT WOULD DO THAT...?
AHHH, FORGET IT, FORGET IT.
HE'S GOT NOTHIN' TO DO WITH ME ANYMORE, ANYHOW.
ボフ
*BOF
NOTHIN' AT ALL.
S'TOO LATE.
ブチブチ
*FX: PLUCK PLUCK
......
ブチブチブチブチブチブチブチブチ
*FX: PLUCK PLUCK PLUCK PLUCK PLUCK PLUCK PLUCK PLUCK
*PECK ビシ
*PECK ビシ
*PECK ビシ
I DOTH CARE NEVERMORE!!

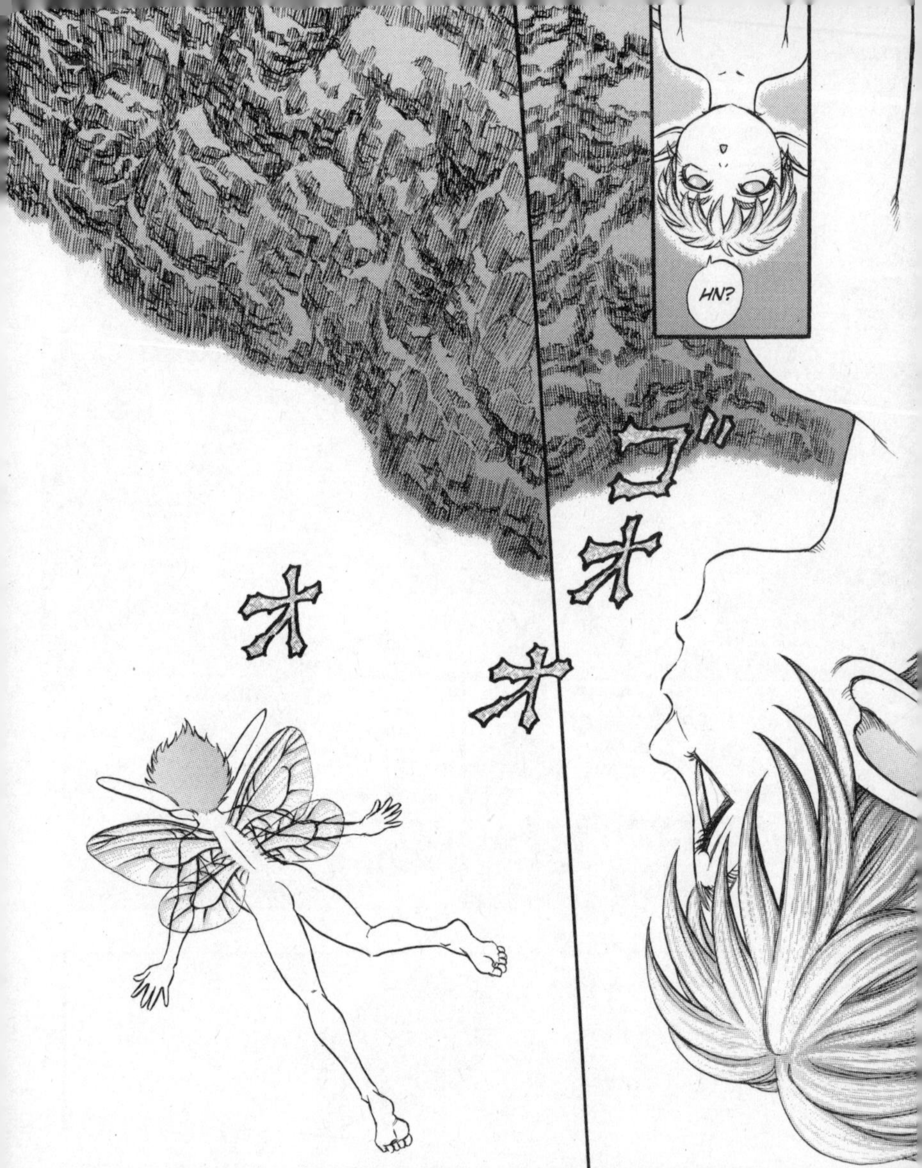
HN?
ゴオオオ

*FX: GOHHHHH

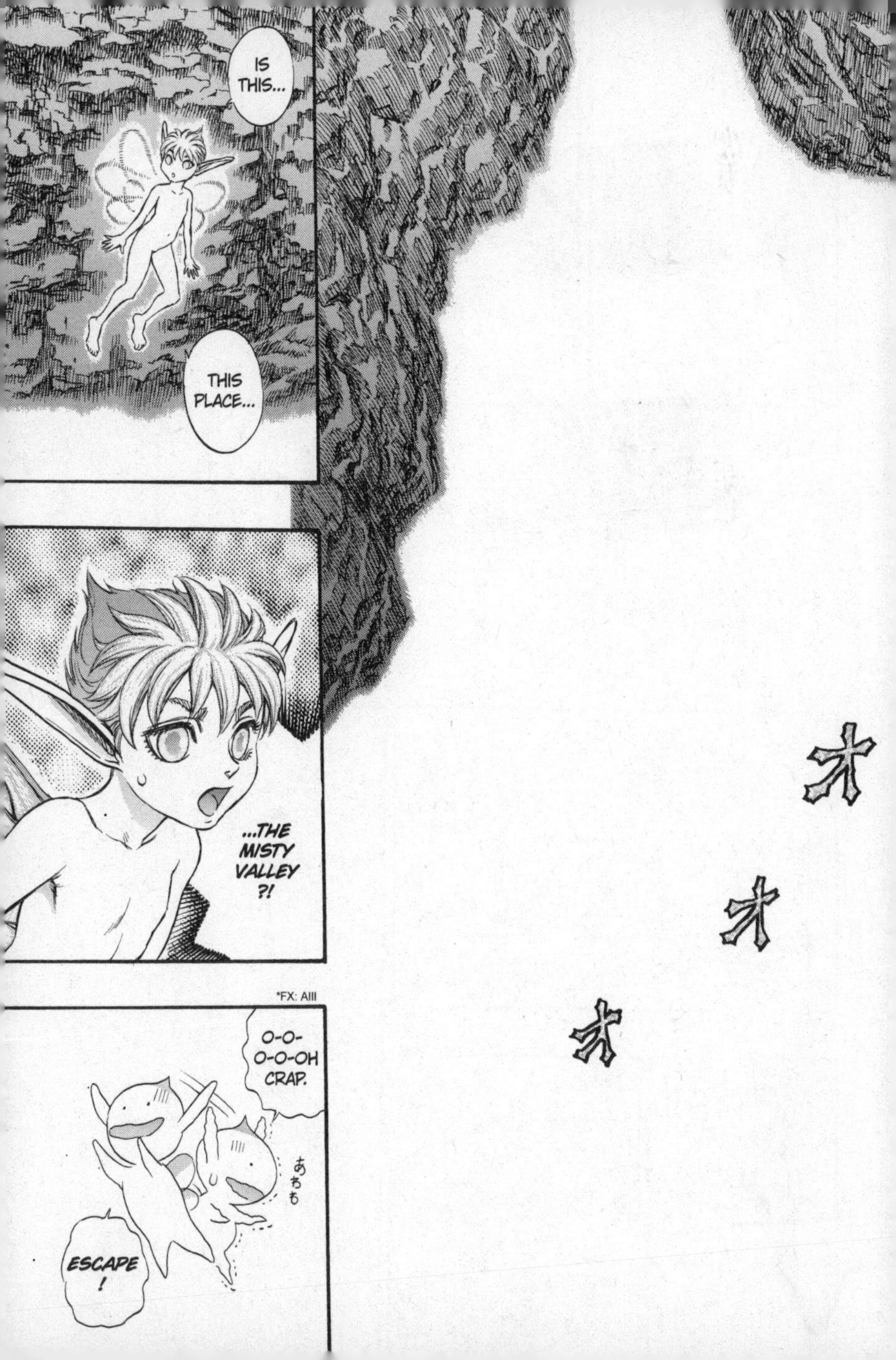
オ
オ
オ
IS THIS...
THIS PLACE...
...THE MISTY VALLEY ?!
*FX: AIII
O-O-O-O-OH CRAP.
ESCAPE !

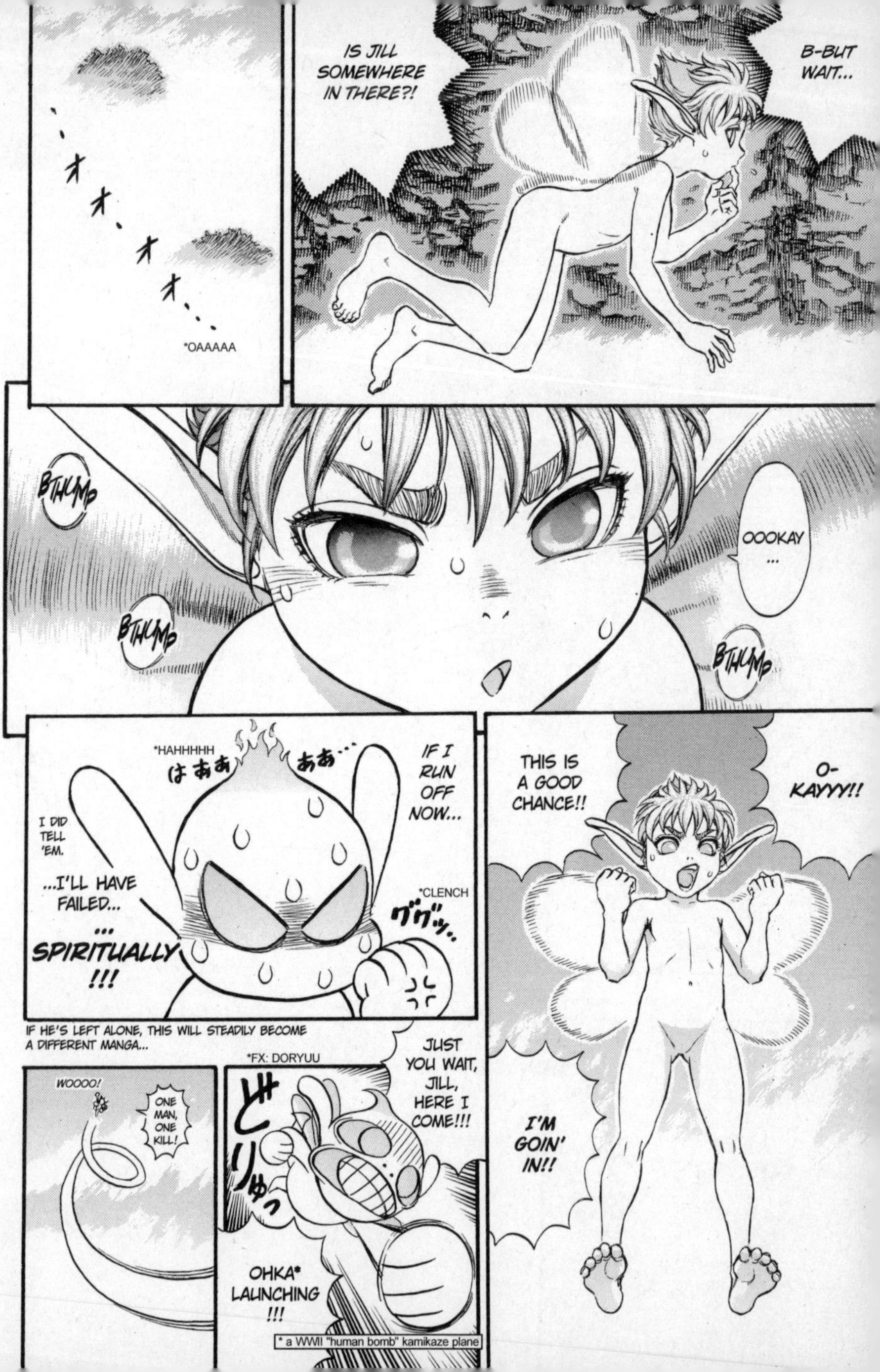
B-BUT WAIT...
IS JILL SOMEWHERE IN THERE?!
オ・オ・オ・オ・・・
*OAAAAA
OOOKAY ...
BTHUMP
BTHUMP
BTHUMP
O-KAYYY!!
THIS IS A GOOD CHANCE!!
I'M GOIN' IN!!
IF I RUN OFF NOW...
*HAHHHHH
はあ あ ああ…
I DID TELL 'EM.
...I'LL HAVE FAILED... ... SPIRITUALLY!!!
*CLENCH
ググッ…
IF HE'S LEFT ALONE, THIS WILL STEADILY BECOME A DIFFERENT MANGA...
JUST YOU WAIT, JILL, HERE I COME!!!
*FX: DORYUU
どりゅっ
OHKA* LAUNCHING!!!
* a WWII "human bomb" kamikaze plane
WOOOO!
ONE MAN, ONE KILL!

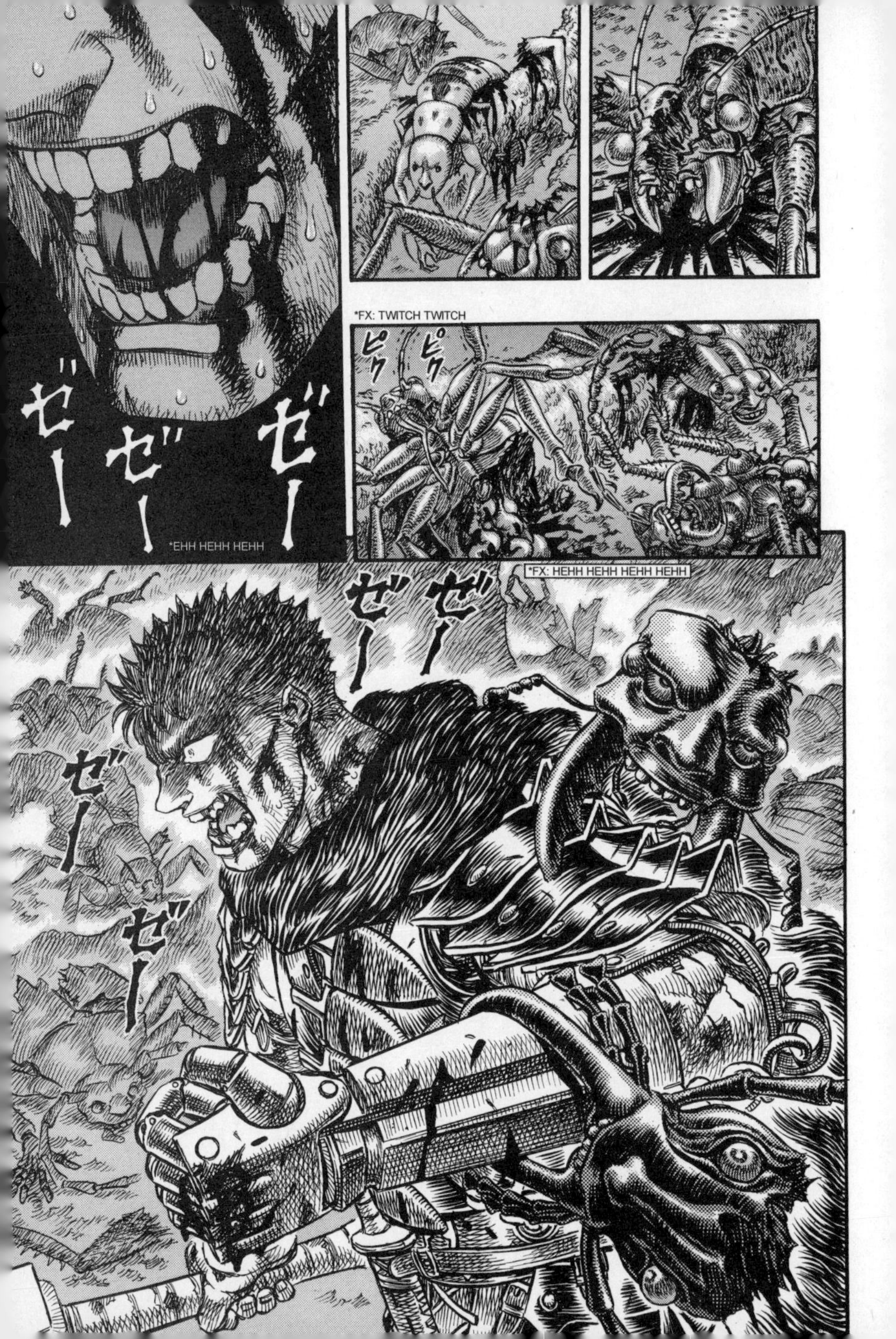

*FX: TWITCH TWITCH
ピク ピク
ゼー ゼー ゼー
*EHH HEHH HEHH
*FX: HEHH HEHH HEHH HEHH
ゼー ゼー ゼー ゼー

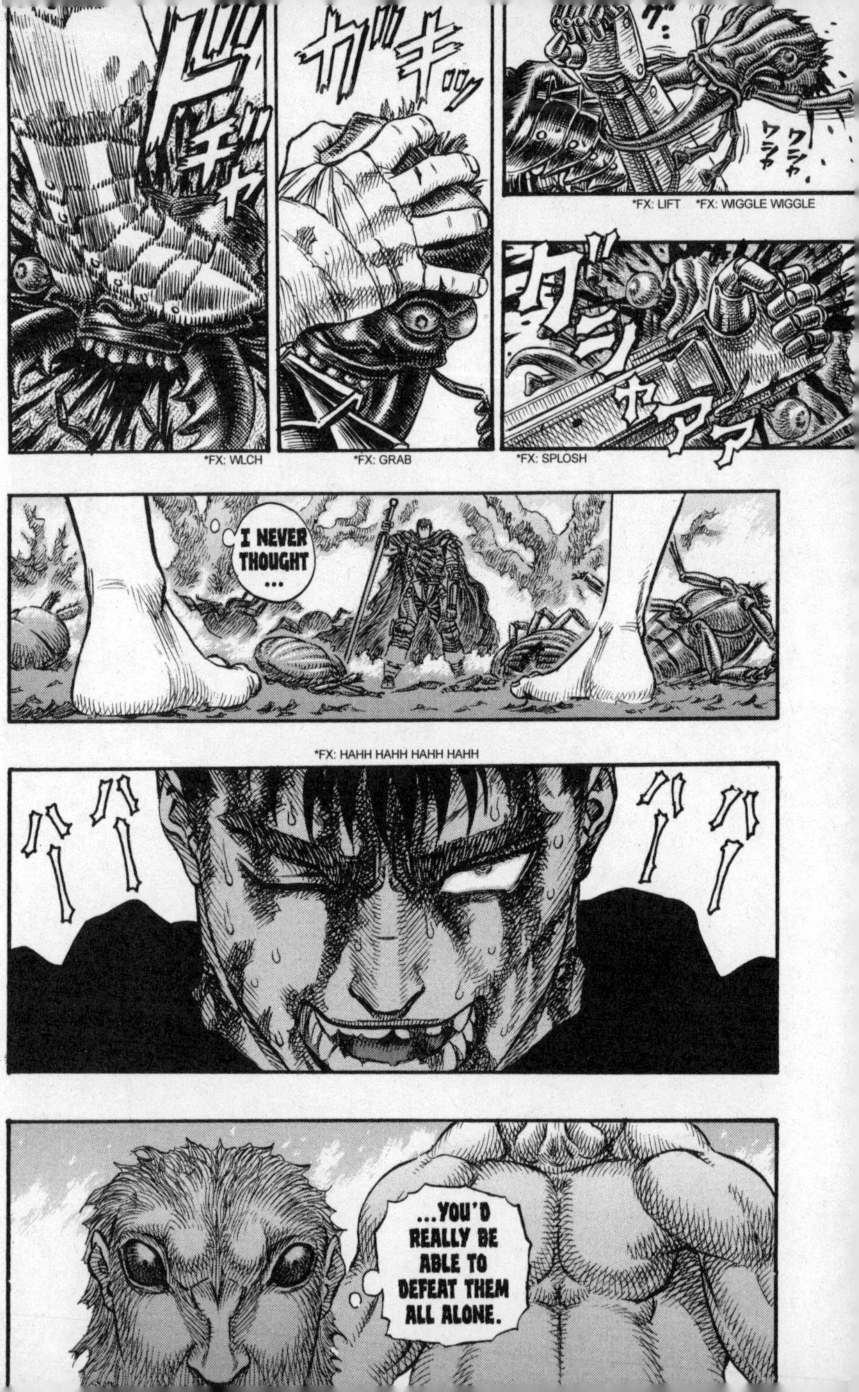
*FX: LIFT
*FX: WIGGLE WIGGLE
*FX: SPLOSH
*FX: GRAB
*FX: WLCH
I NEVER THOUGHT ...
*FX: HAHH HAHH HAHH HAHH
...YOU'D REALLY BE ABLE TO DEFEAT THEM ALL ALONE.

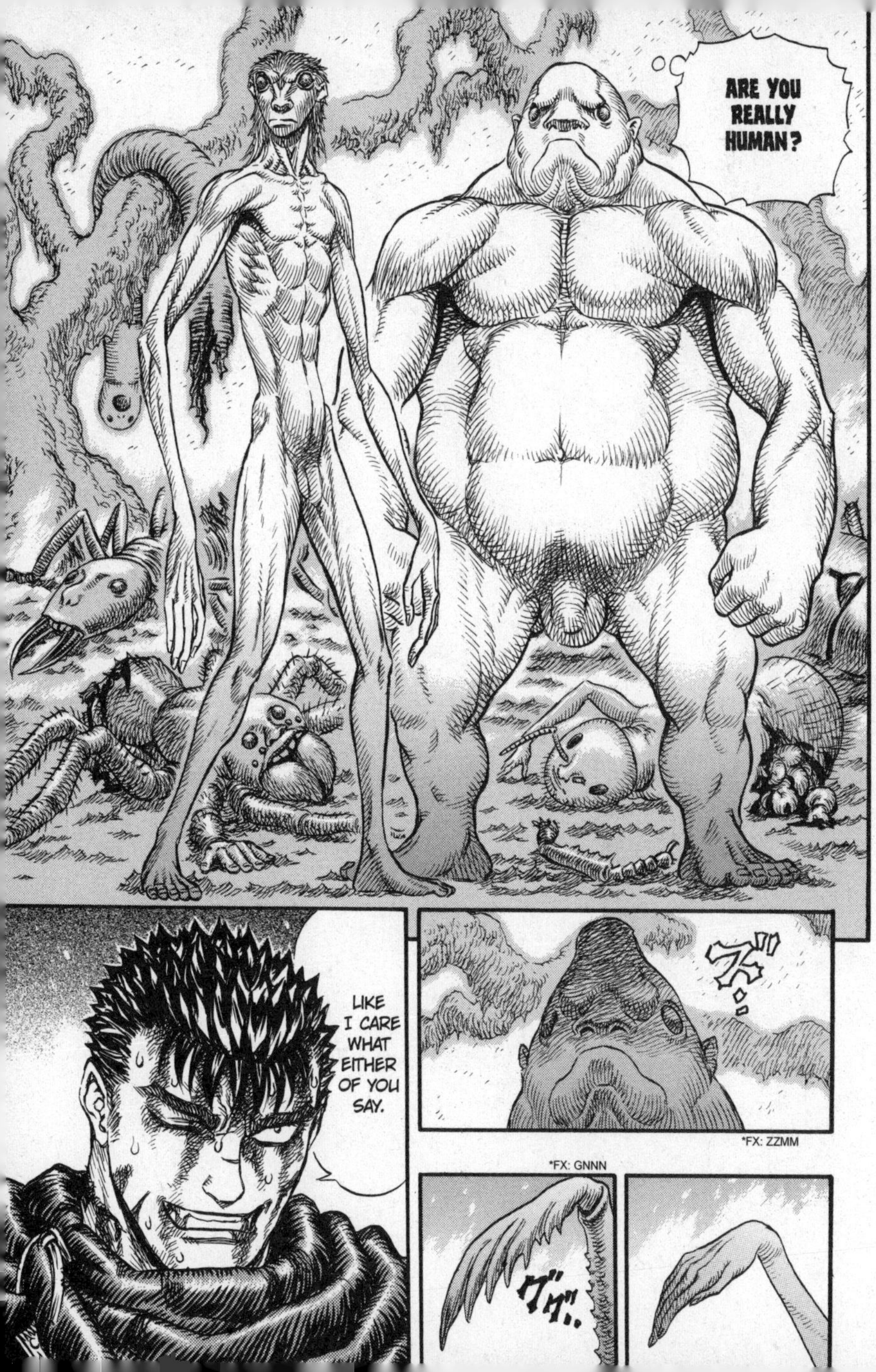
ARE YOU REALLY HUMAN?
*FX: ZZMM
*FX: GNNN
LIKE I CARE WHAT EITHER OF YOU SAY.

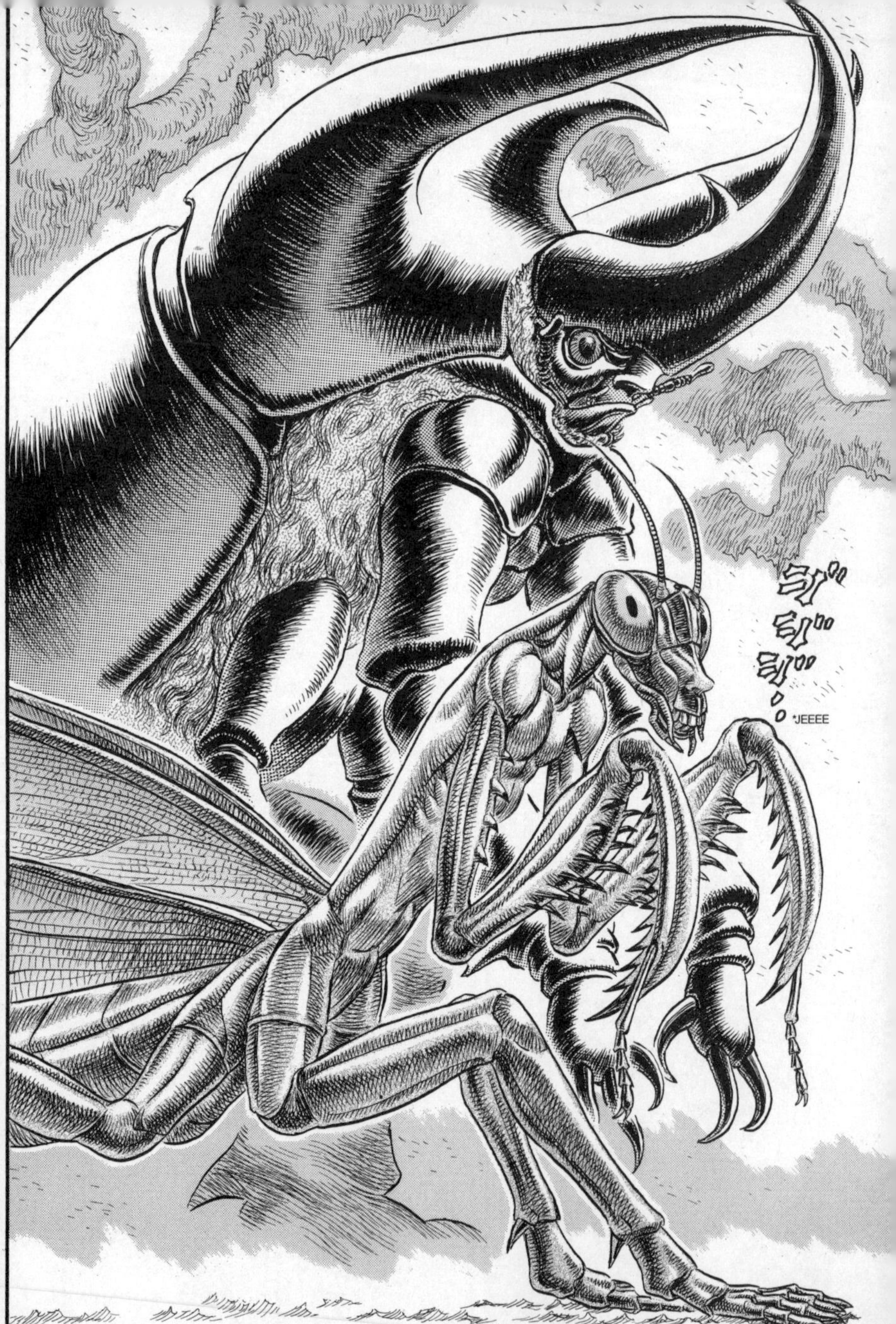
ジジジ゛゛
*JEEEE

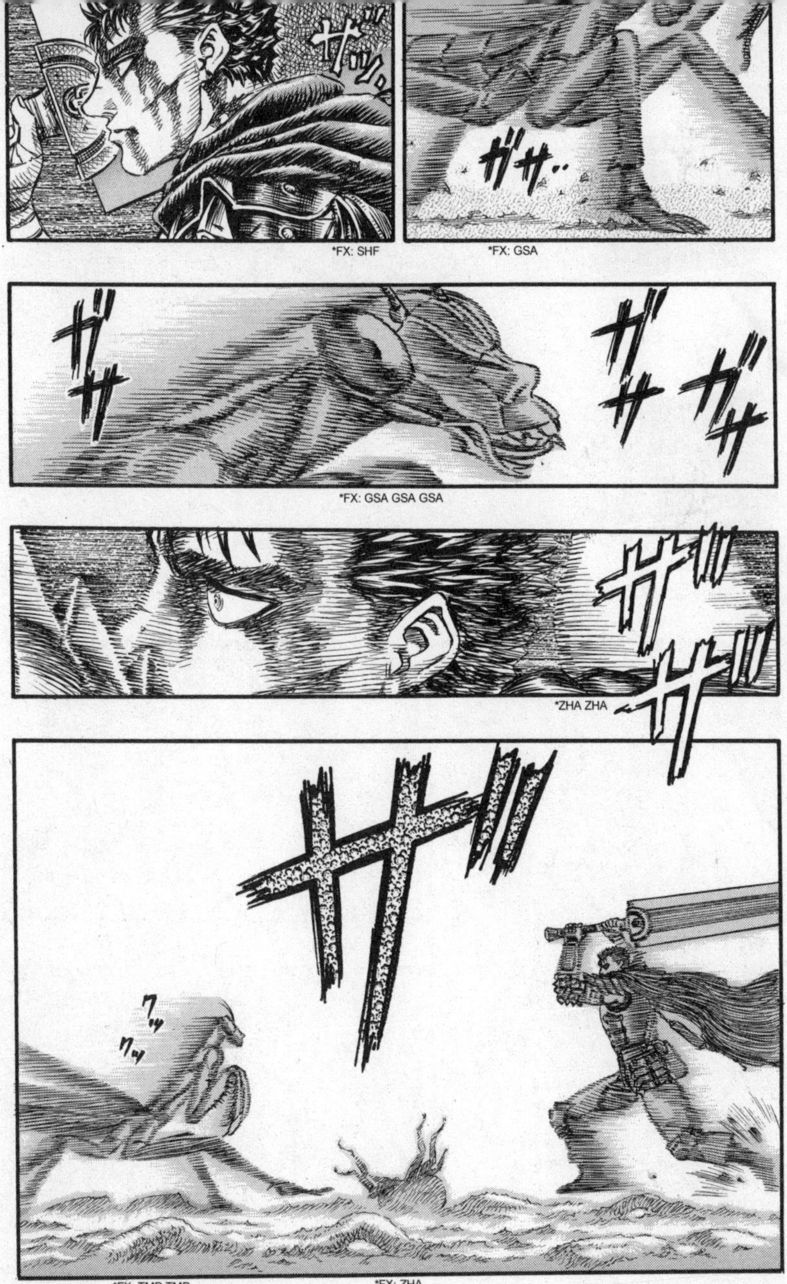

*FX: GSA

*FX: SHF

*FX: GSA GSA GSA

*ZHA ZHA

*FX: ZHA

*FX: TMP TMP

*FX: VISH

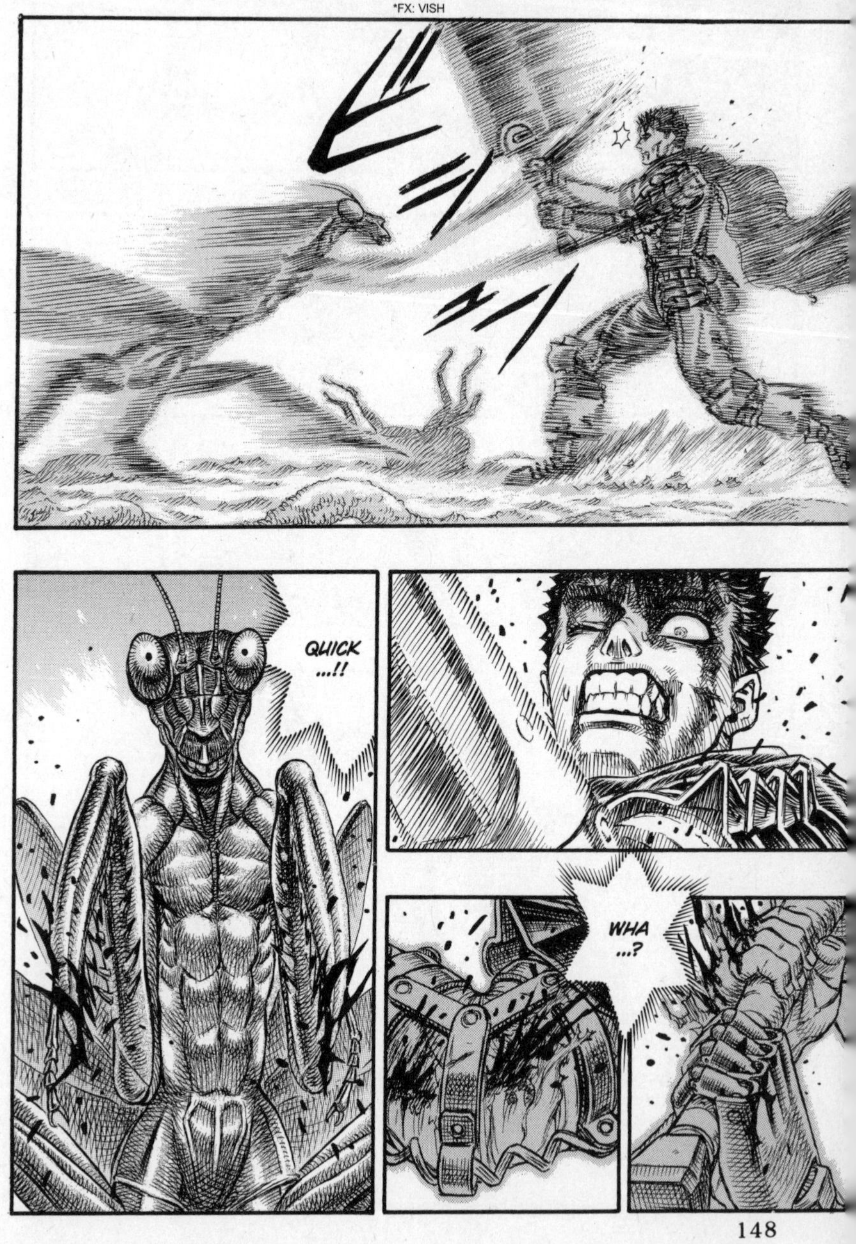
WHA ...?
QUICK ...!!

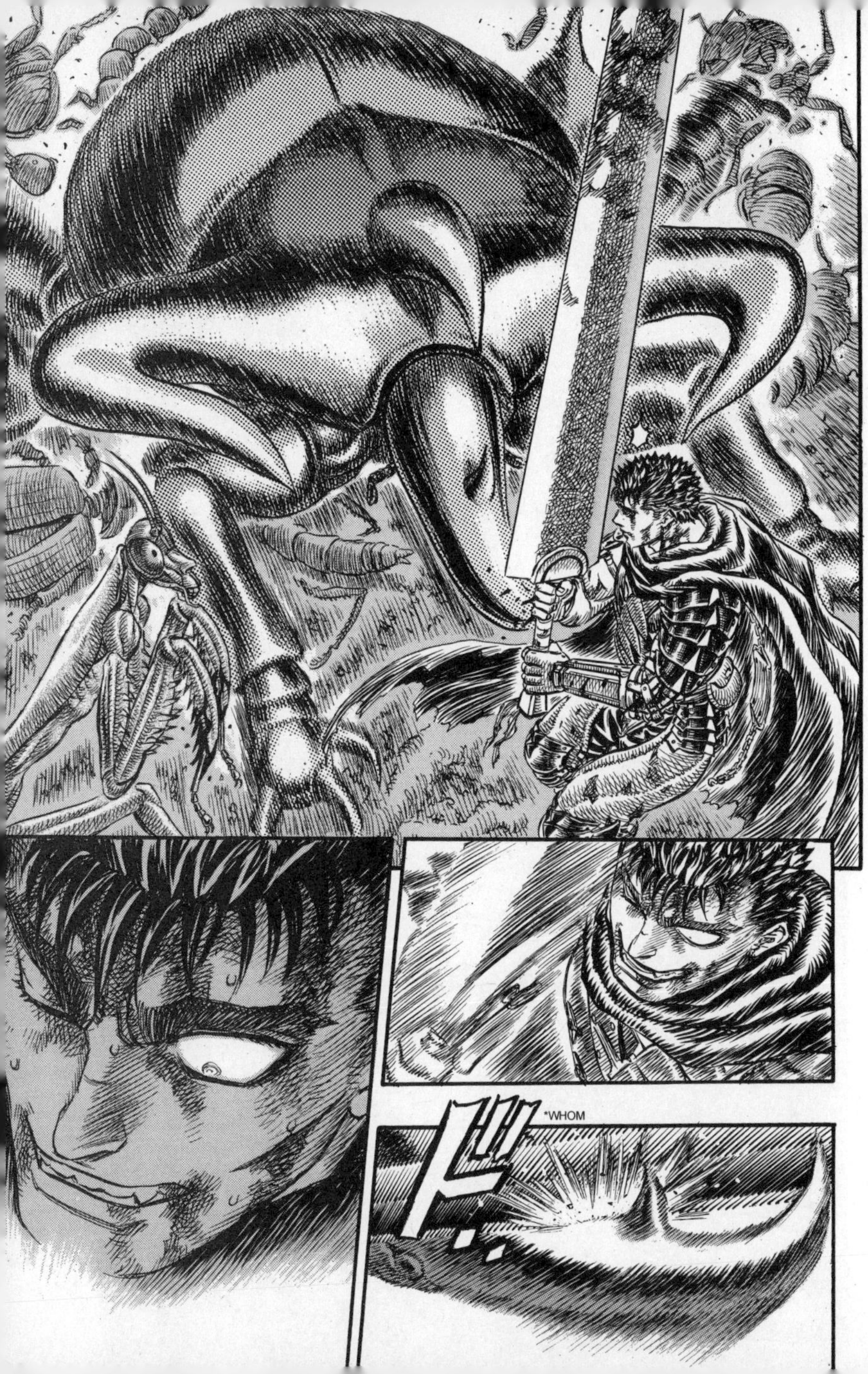
*WHOM

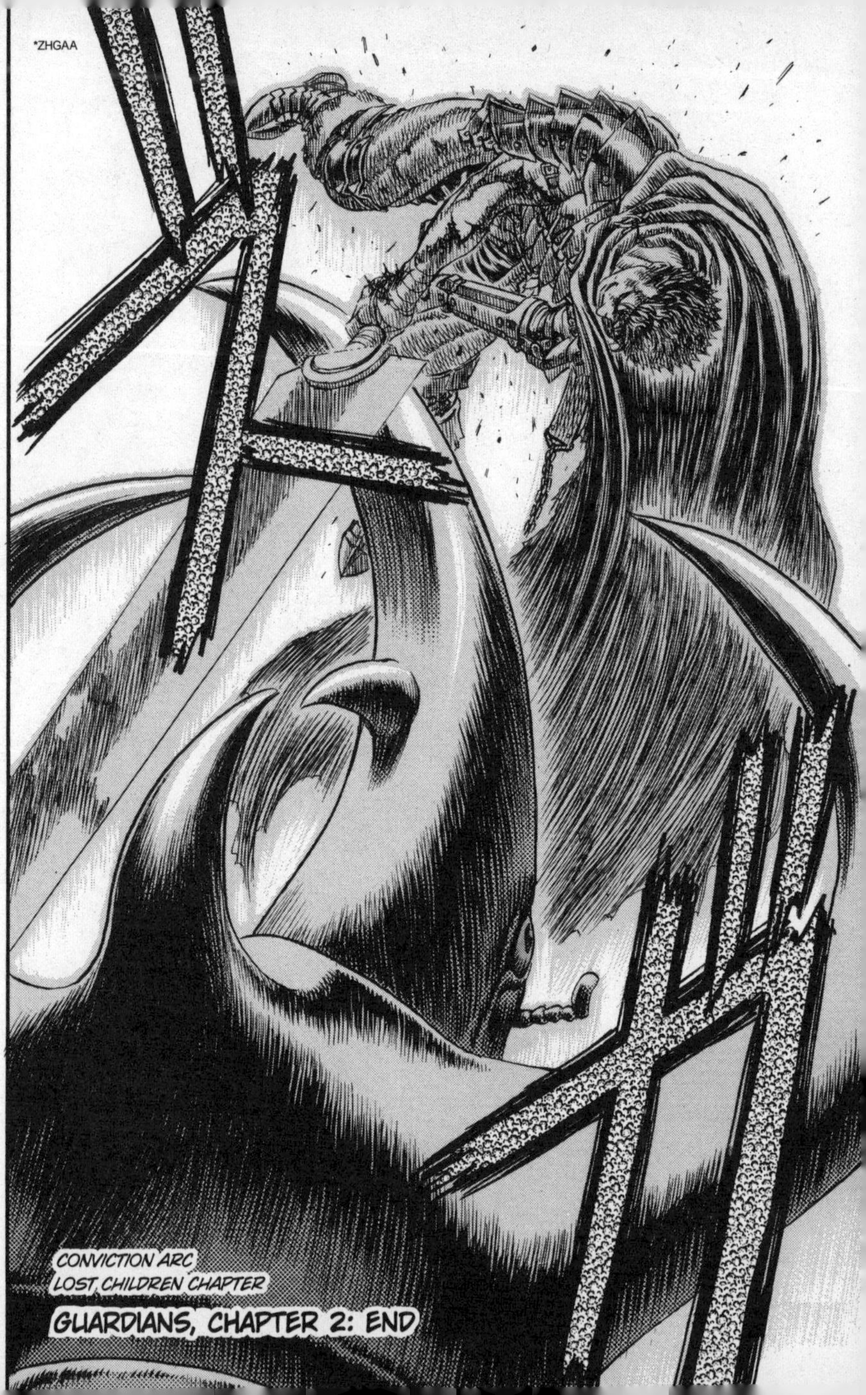
*ZHGAA
CONVICTION ARC
LOST CHILDREN CHAPTER
GUARDIANS, CHAPTER 2: END

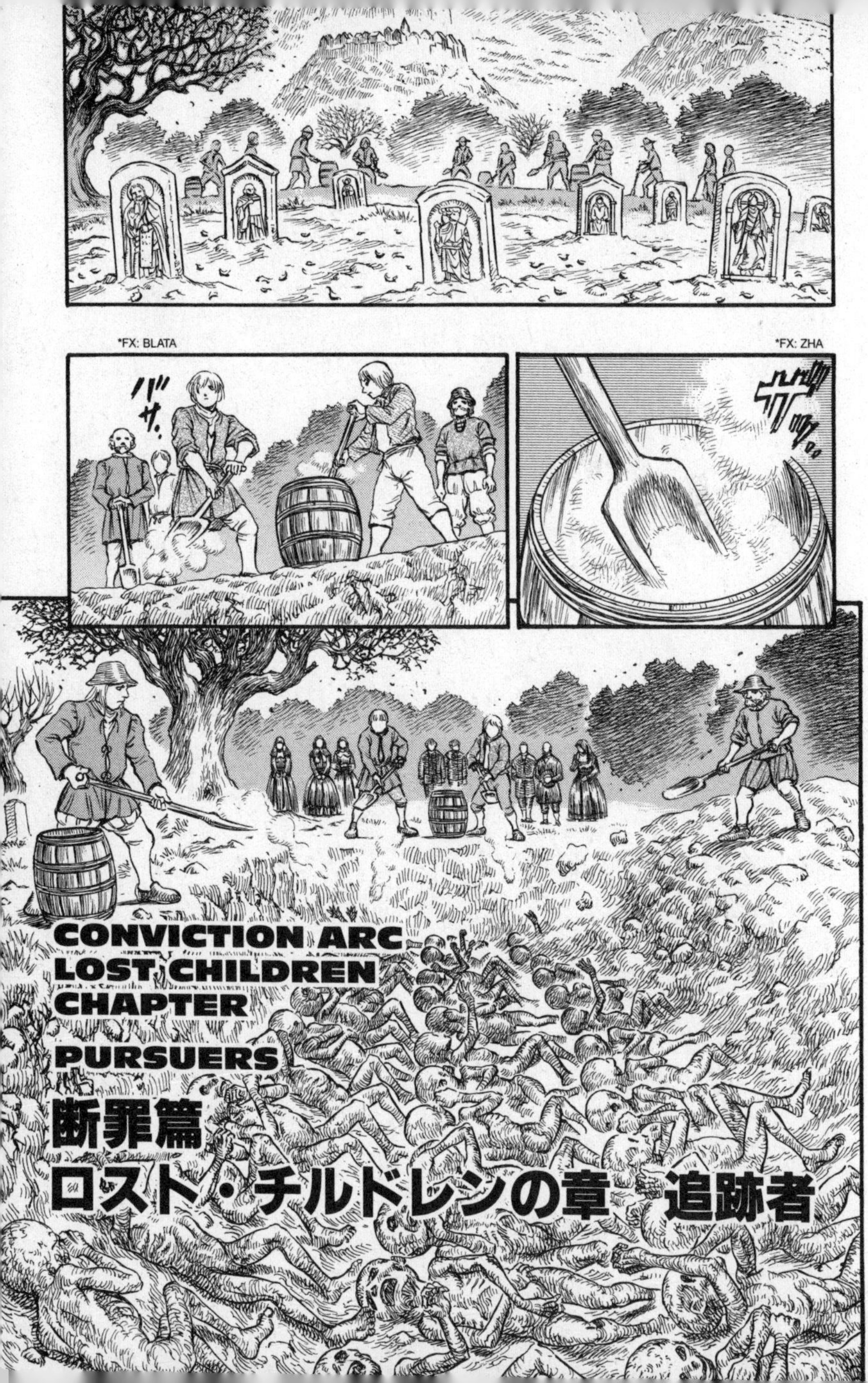

*FX: ZHA
*FX: BLATA
CONVICTION ARC
LOST CHILDREN
CHAPTER
PURSUERS
断罪篇
ロスト・チルドレンの章 追跡者

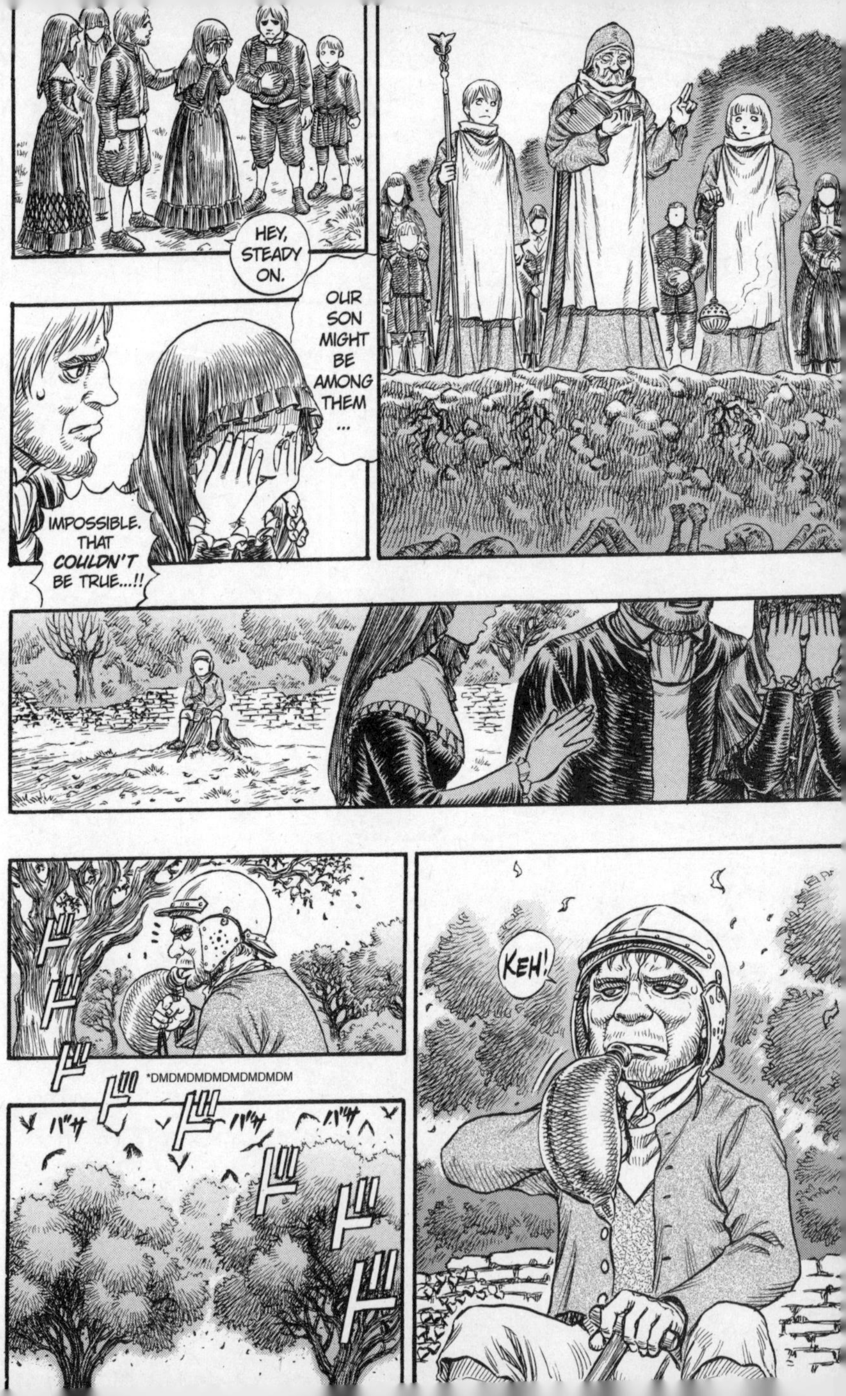
HEY, STEADY ON.
OUR SON MIGHT BE AMONG THEM ...
IMPOSSIBLE. THAT COULDN'T BE TRUE...!!
KEH!
*DMDMDMDMDMDMDMDM

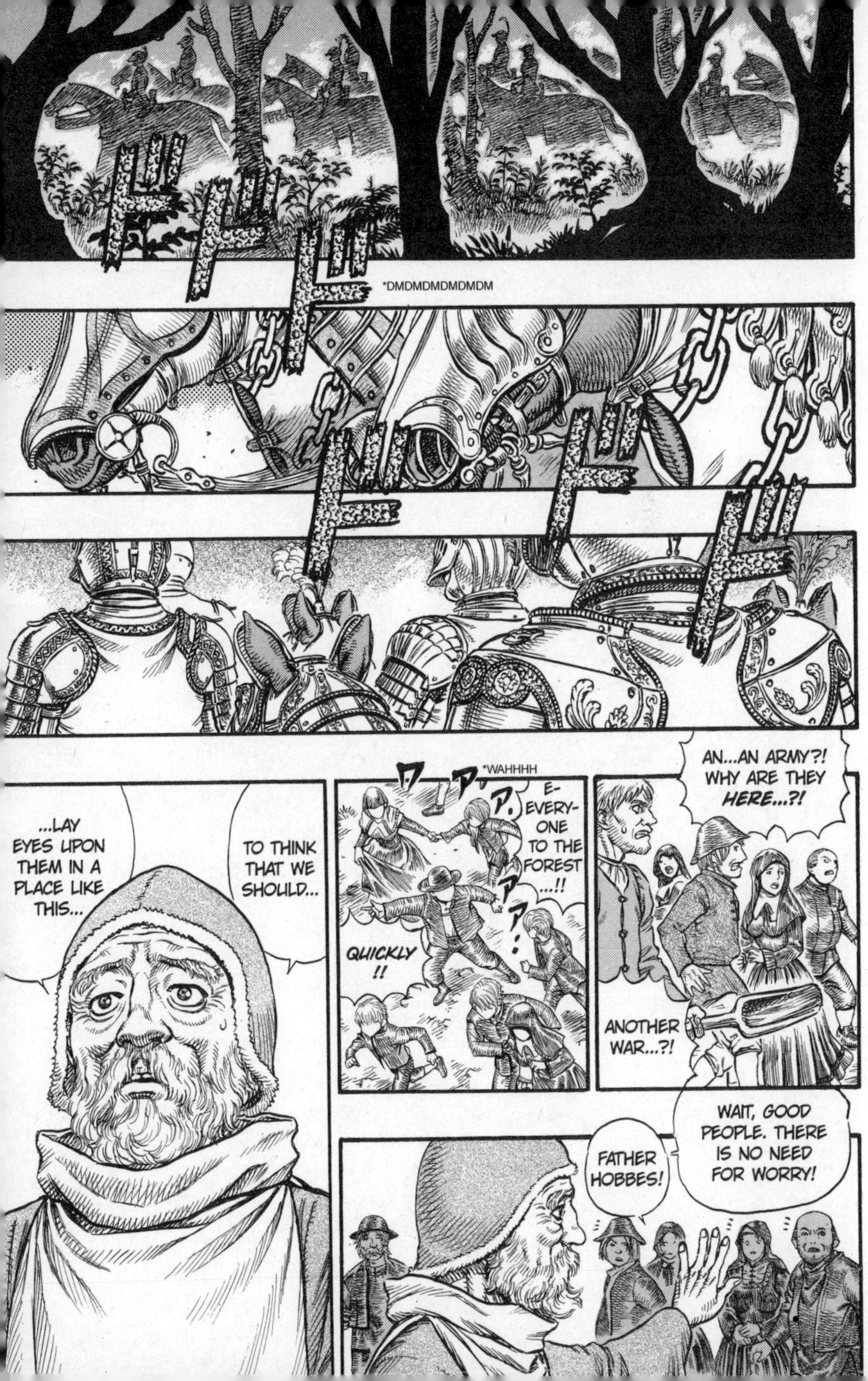
*DMDMDMDMDMDM
AN...AN ARMY?! WHY ARE THEY HERE...?!
ANOTHER WAR...?!
*WAHHHH
E-EVERYONE TO THE FOREST...!!
QUICKLY!!
WAIT, GOOD PEOPLE. THERE IS NO NEED FOR WORRY!
FATHER HOBBES!
TO THINK THAT WE SHOULD...
...LAY EYES UPON THEM IN A PLACE LIKE THIS...

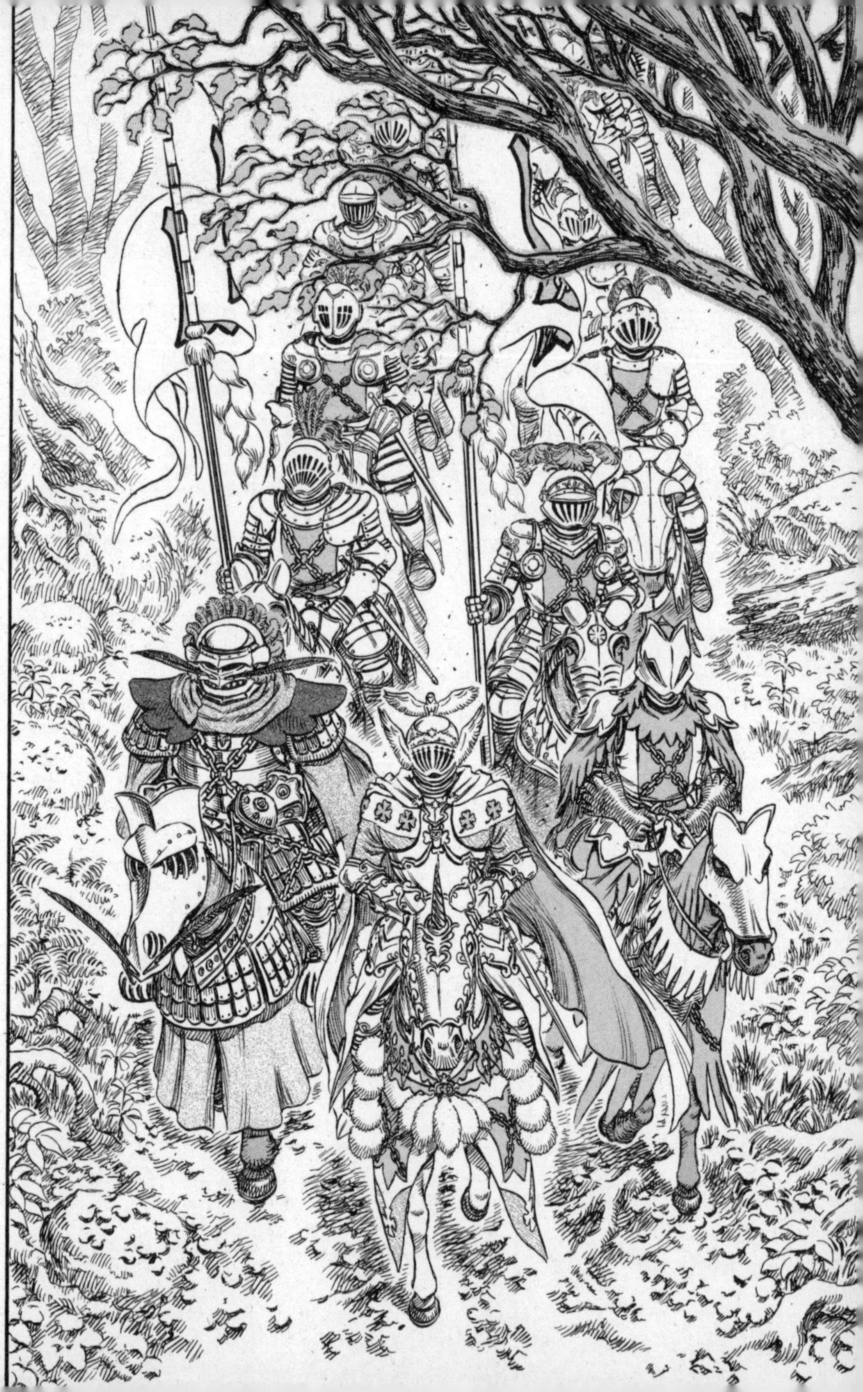

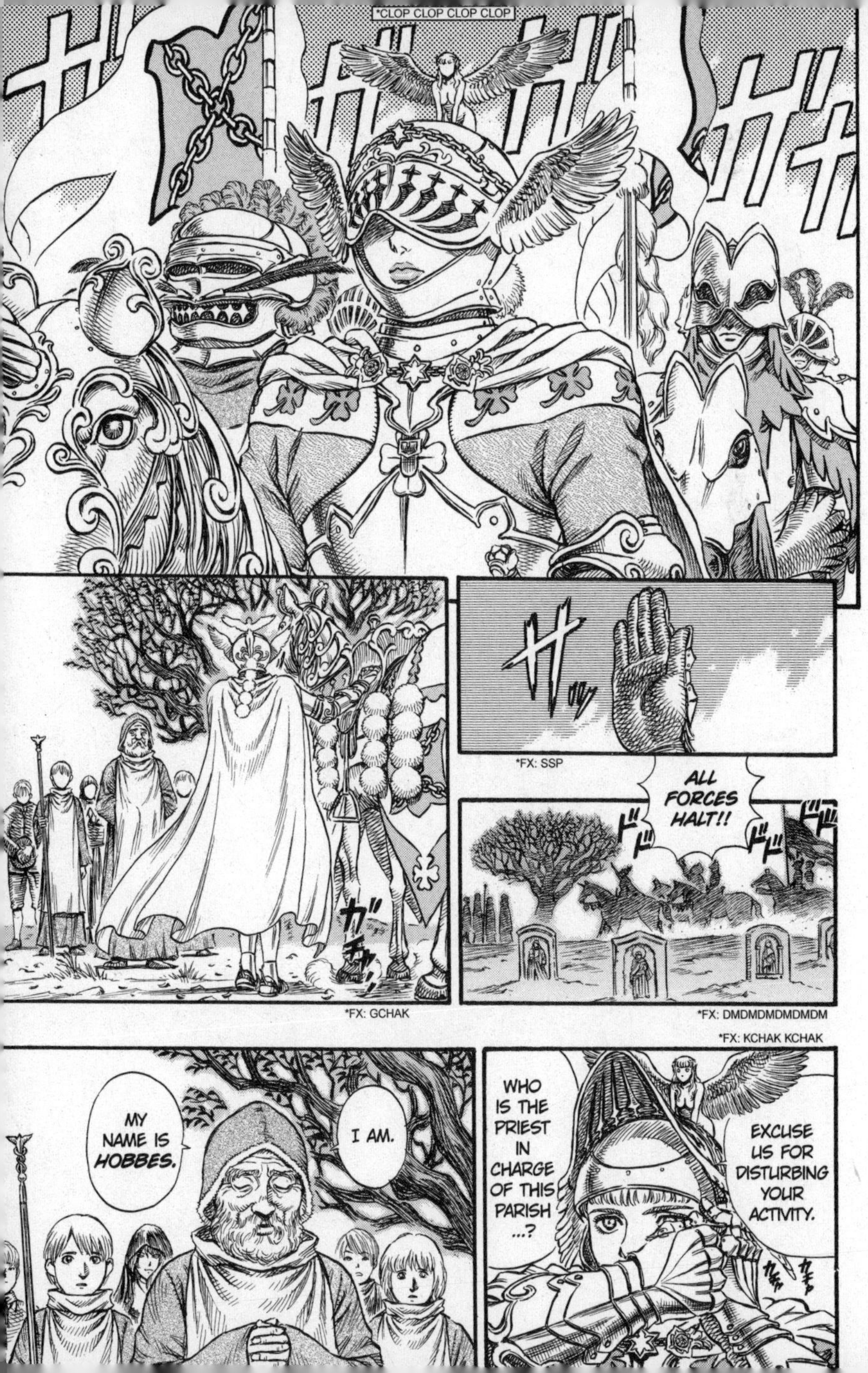
*CLOP CLOP CLOP CLOP
*FX: SSP
ALL FORCES HALT!!
*FX: DMDMDMDMDMDM
*FX: GCHAK
*FX: KCHAK KCHAK
EXCUSE US FOR DISTURBING YOUR ACTIVITY.
WHO IS THE PRIEST IN CHARGE OF THIS PARISH ...?
I AM.
MY NAME IS *HOBBES.*

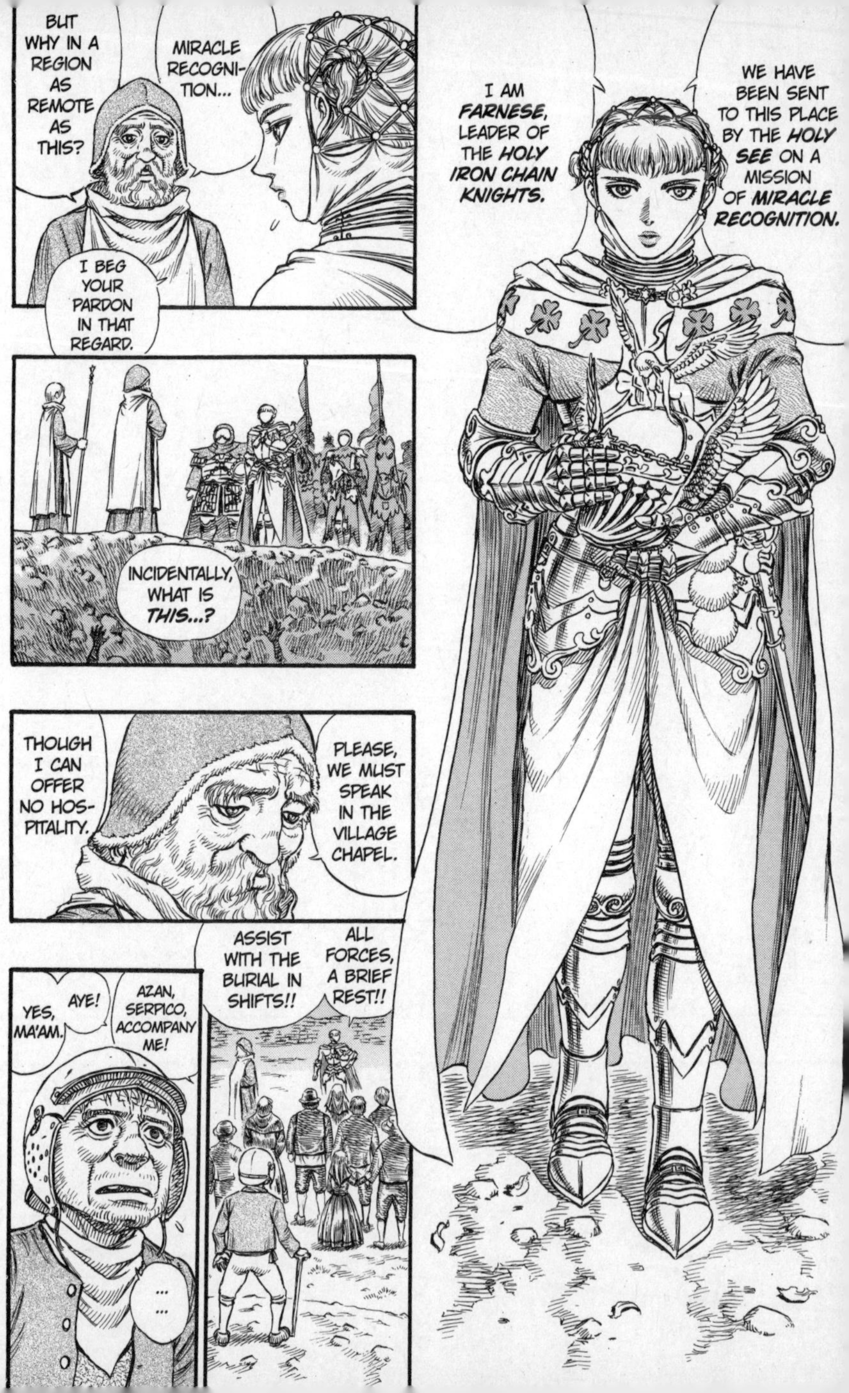

WE HAVE BEEN SENT TO THIS PLACE BY THE HOLY SEE ON A MISSION OF MIRACLE RECOGNITION.
I AM FARNESE, LEADER OF THE HOLY IRON CHAIN KNIGHTS.
MIRACLE RECOGNITION...
BUT WHY IN A REGION AS REMOTE AS THIS?
I BEG YOUR PARDON IN THAT REGARD.
INCIDENTALLY, WHAT IS THIS...?
PLEASE, WE MUST SPEAK IN THE VILLAGE CHAPEL.
THOUGH I CAN OFFER NO HOSPITALITY.
ALL FORCES, A BRIEF REST!!
ASSIST WITH THE BURIAL IN SHIFTS!!
AZAN, SERPICO, ACCOMPANY ME!
AYE!
YES, MA'AM.
... ...

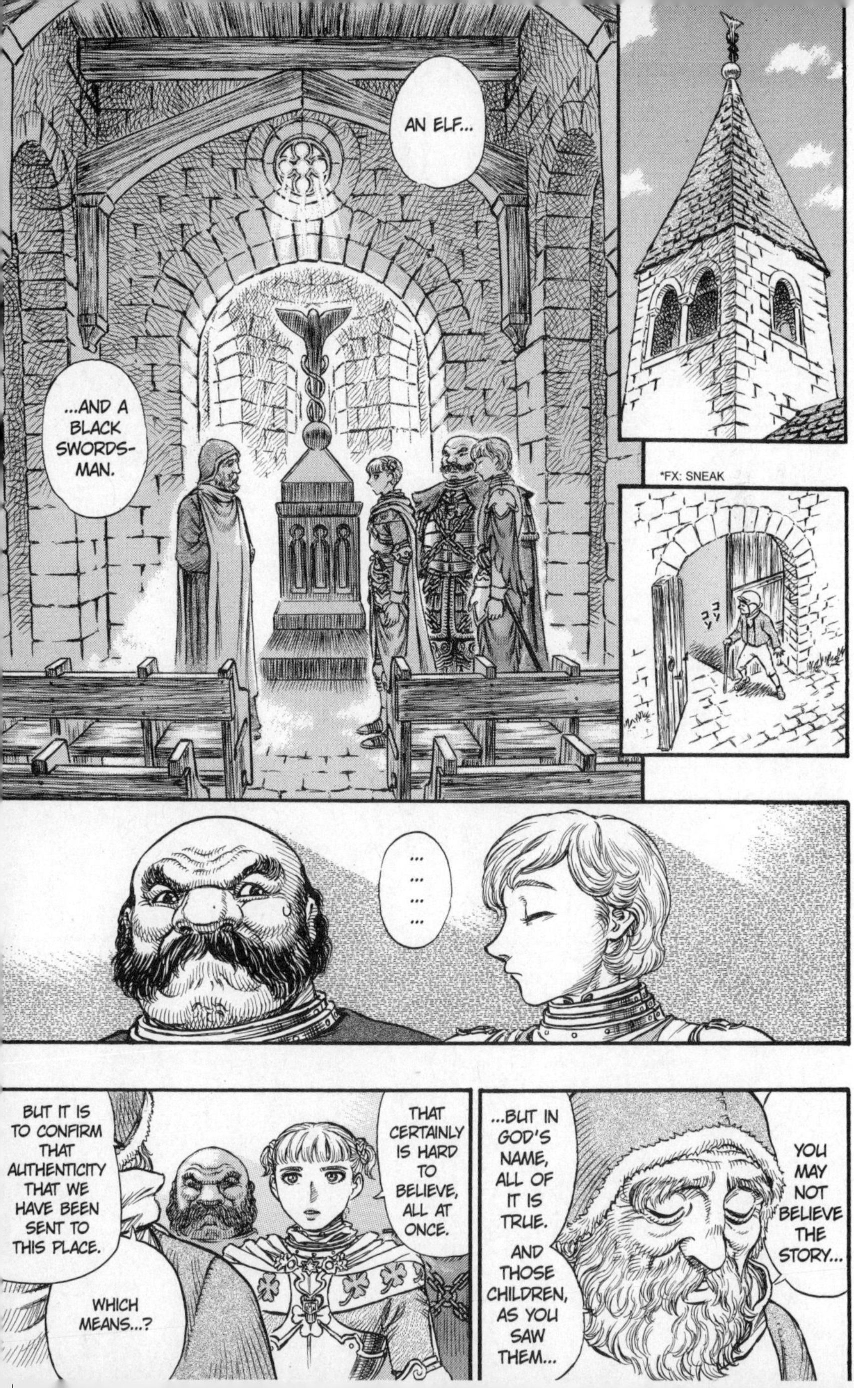
*FX: SNEAK
AN ELF...
...AND A BLACK SWORDSMAN.
... ...
YOU MAY NOT BELIEVE THE STORY...
...BUT IN GOD'S NAME, ALL OF IT IS TRUE.
AND THOSE CHILDREN, AS YOU SAW THEM...
THAT CERTAINLY IS HARD TO BELIEVE, ALL AT ONCE.
BUT IT IS TO CONFIRM THAT AUTHENTICITY THAT WE HAVE BEEN SENT TO THIS PLACE.
WHICH MEANS...?

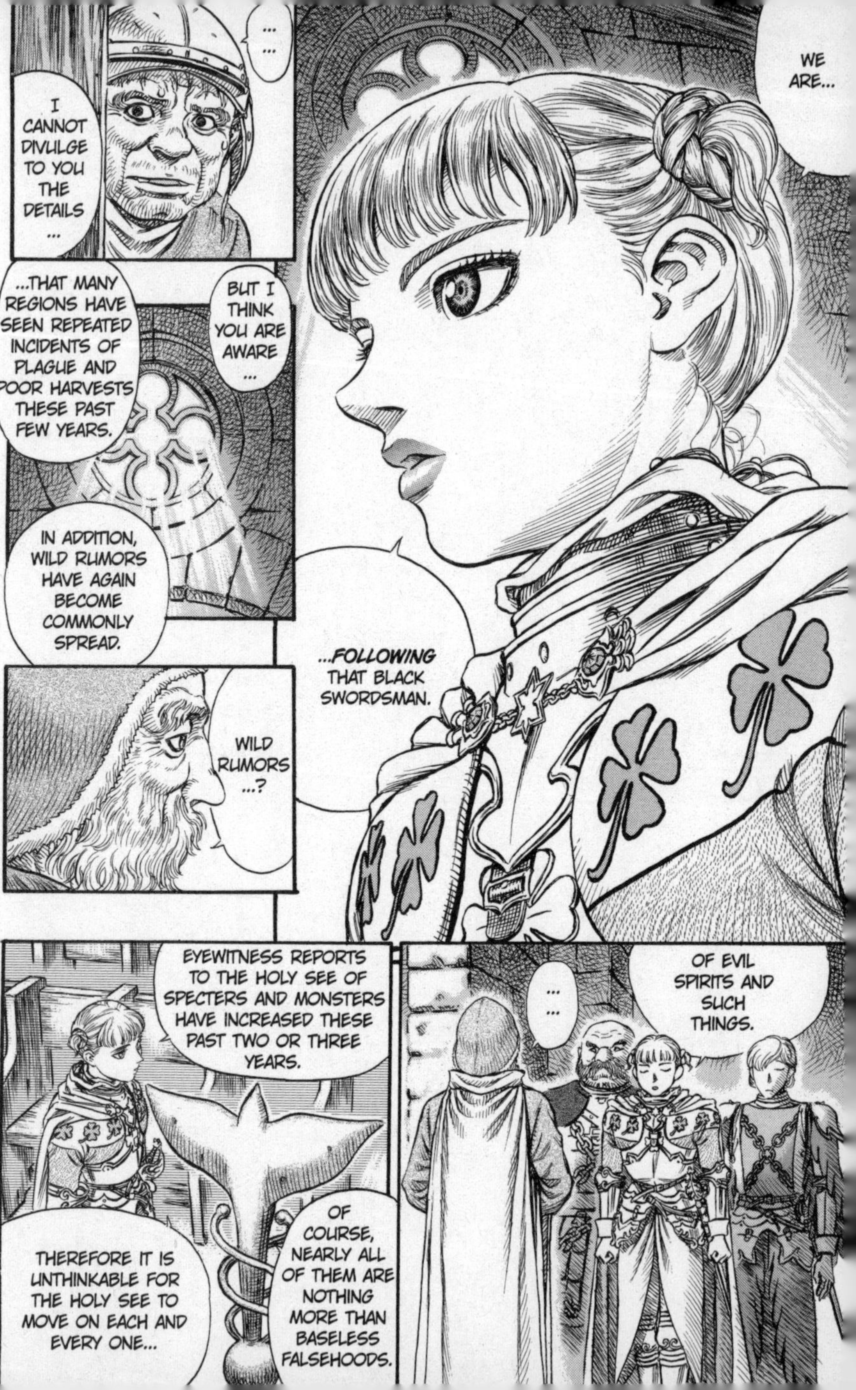
WE ARE...
...FOLLOWING THAT BLACK SWORDSMAN.
......
I CANNOT DIVULGE TO YOU THE DETAILS ...
BUT I THINK YOU ARE AWARE ...
...THAT MANY REGIONS HAVE SEEN REPEATED INCIDENTS OF PLAGUE AND POOR HARVESTS THESE PAST FEW YEARS.
IN ADDITION, WILD RUMORS HAVE AGAIN BECOME COMMONLY SPREAD.
WILD RUMORS ...?
OF EVIL SPIRITS AND SUCH THINGS.
......
EYEWITNESS REPORTS TO THE HOLY SEE OF SPECTERS AND MONSTERS HAVE INCREASED THESE PAST TWO OR THREE YEARS.
OF COURSE, NEARLY ALL OF THEM ARE NOTHING MORE THAN BASELESS FALSEHOODS.
THEREFORE IT IS UNTHINKABLE FOR THE HOLY SEE TO MOVE ON EACH AND EVERY ONE...

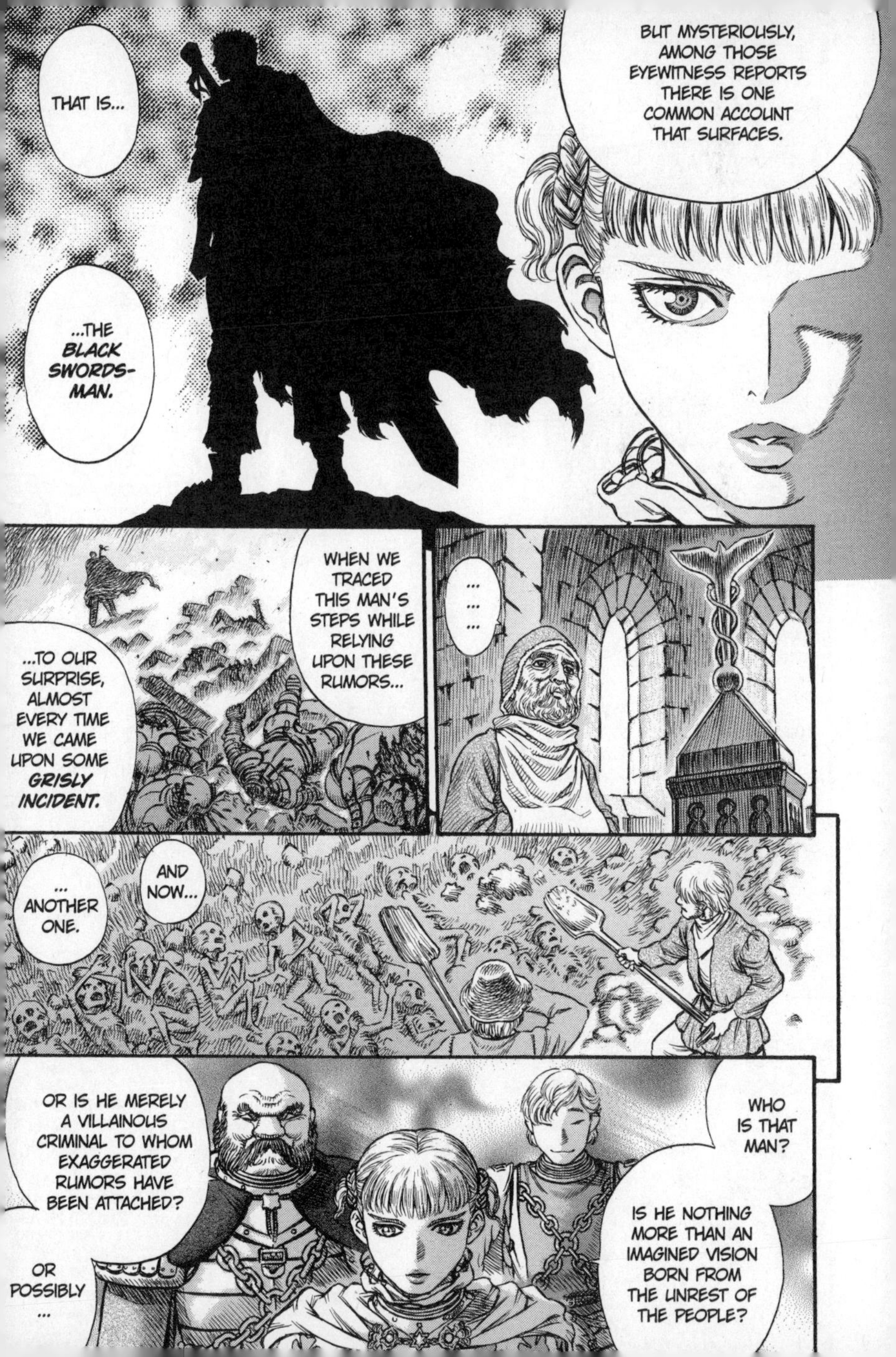
BUT MYSTERIOUSLY, AMONG THOSE EYEWITNESS REPORTS THERE IS ONE COMMON ACCOUNT THAT SURFACES.
THAT IS...
...THE *BLACK SWORDSMAN.*
... ...
WHEN WE TRACED THIS MAN'S STEPS WHILE RELYING UPON THESE RUMORS...
...TO OUR SURPRISE, ALMOST EVERY TIME WE CAME UPON SOME *GRISLY INCIDENT.*
AND NOW...
... ANOTHER ONE.
WHO IS THAT MAN?
IS HE NOTHING MORE THAN AN IMAGINED VISION BORN FROM THE UNREST OF THE PEOPLE?
OR IS HE MERELY A VILLAINOUS CRIMINAL TO WHOM EXAGGERATED RUMORS HAVE BEEN ATTACHED?
OR POSSIBLY ...

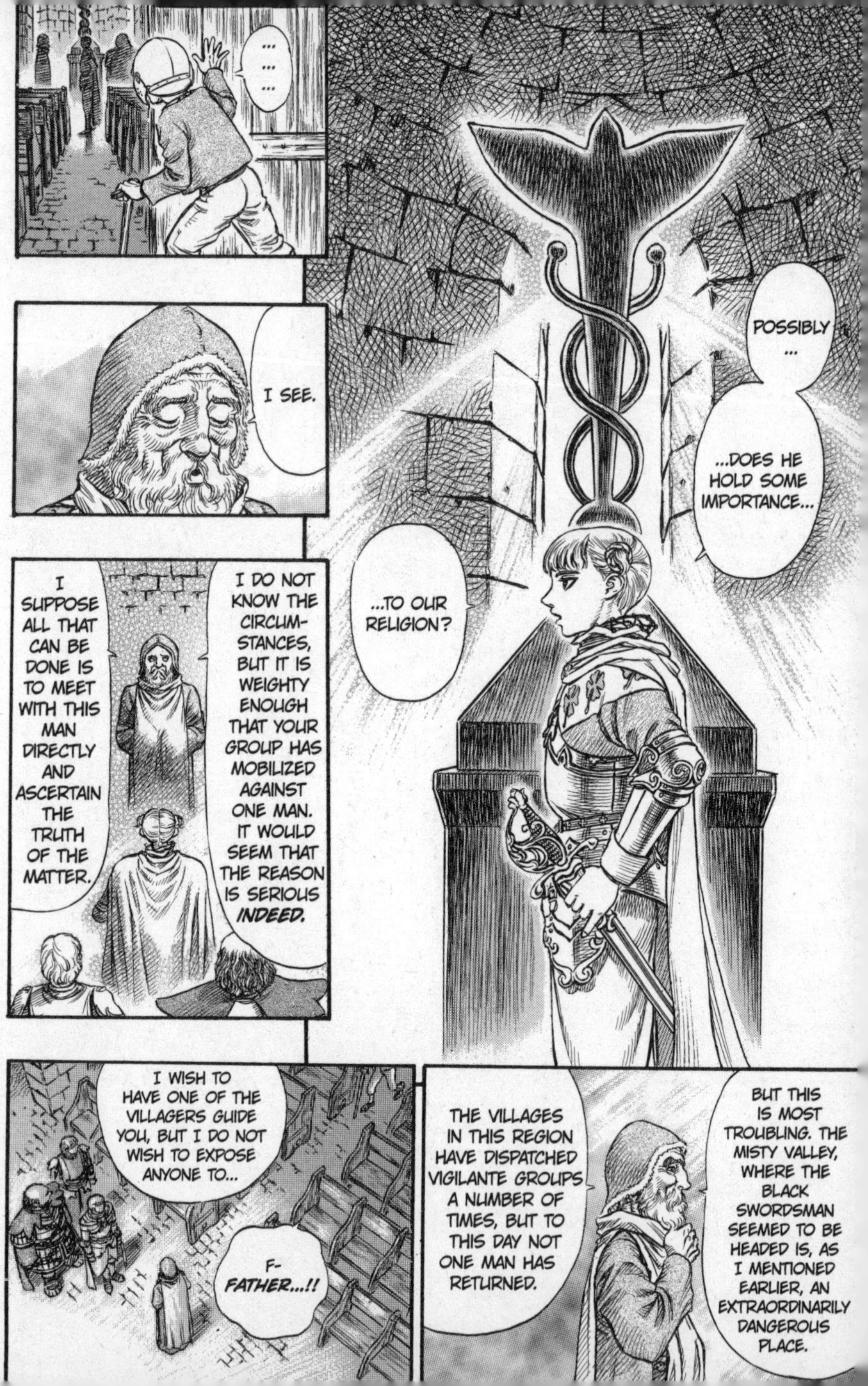

POSSIBLY ...
...DOES HE HOLD SOME IMPORTANCE...
...TO OUR RELIGION?
...
...
...
I SEE.
I DO NOT KNOW THE CIRCUM-STANCES, BUT IT IS WEIGHTY ENOUGH THAT YOUR GROUP HAS MOBILIZED AGAINST ONE MAN. IT WOULD SEEM THAT THE REASON IS SERIOUS *INDEED.*
I SUPPOSE ALL THAT CAN BE DONE IS TO MEET WITH THIS MAN DIRECTLY AND ASCERTAIN THE TRUTH OF THE MATTER.
BUT THIS IS MOST TROUBLING. THE MISTY VALLEY, WHERE THE BLACK SWORDSMAN SEEMED TO BE HEADED IS, AS I MENTIONED EARLIER, AN EXTRAORDINARILY DANGEROUS PLACE.
THE VILLAGES IN THIS REGION HAVE DISPATCHED VIGILANTE GROUPS A NUMBER OF TIMES, BUT TO THIS DAY NOT ONE MAN HAS RETURNED.
I WISH TO HAVE ONE OF THE VILLAGERS GUIDE YOU, BUT I DO NOT WISH TO EXPOSE ANYONE TO...
F- *FATHER...!!*

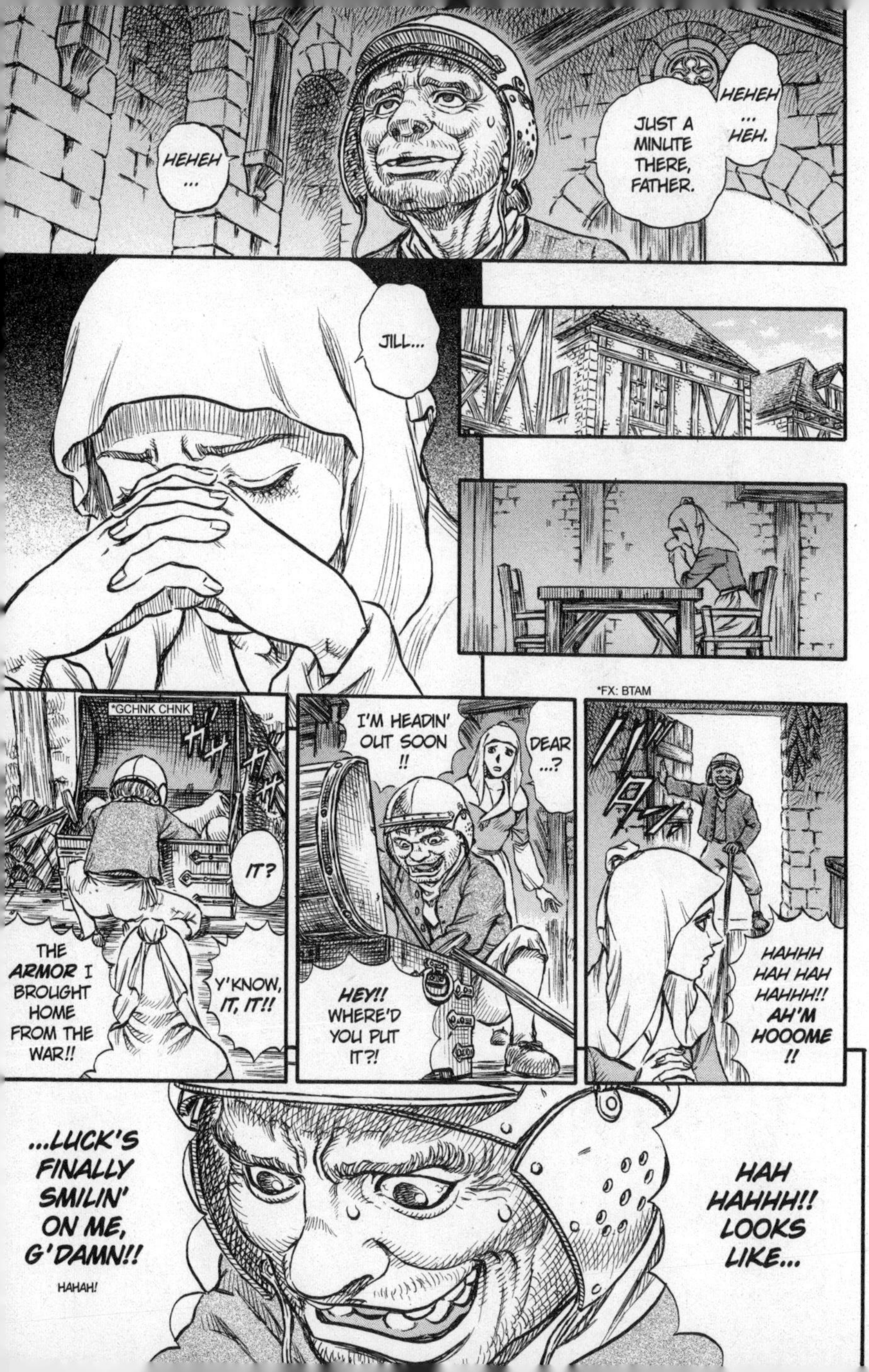
HEHEH ... HEH.
JUST A MINUTE THERE, FATHER.
HEHEH ...
JILL...
*FX: BTAM
HAHHH HAH HAH HAHHH!! AH'M HOOOME !!
DEAR ...?
I'M HEADIN' OUT SOON !!
HEY!! WHERE'D YOU PUT IT?!
*GCHNK CHNK
IT?
Y'KNOW, IT, IT!!
THE ARMOR I BROUGHT HOME FROM THE WAR!!
HAH HAHHH!! LOOKS LIKE...
...LUCK'S FINALLY SMILIN' ON ME, G'DAMN!!
HAHAH!

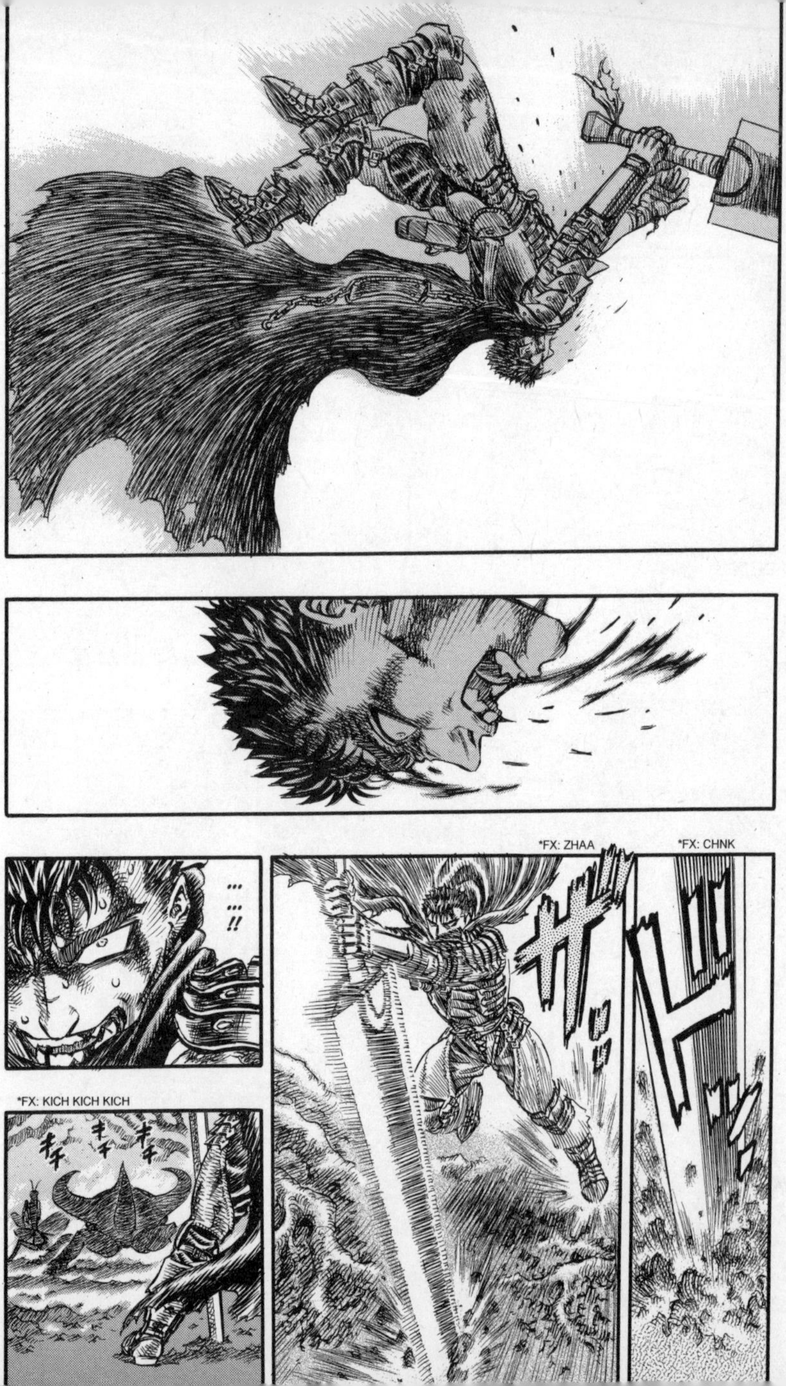
*FX: CHNK
*FX: ZHAA
......!!
*FX: KICH KICH KICH

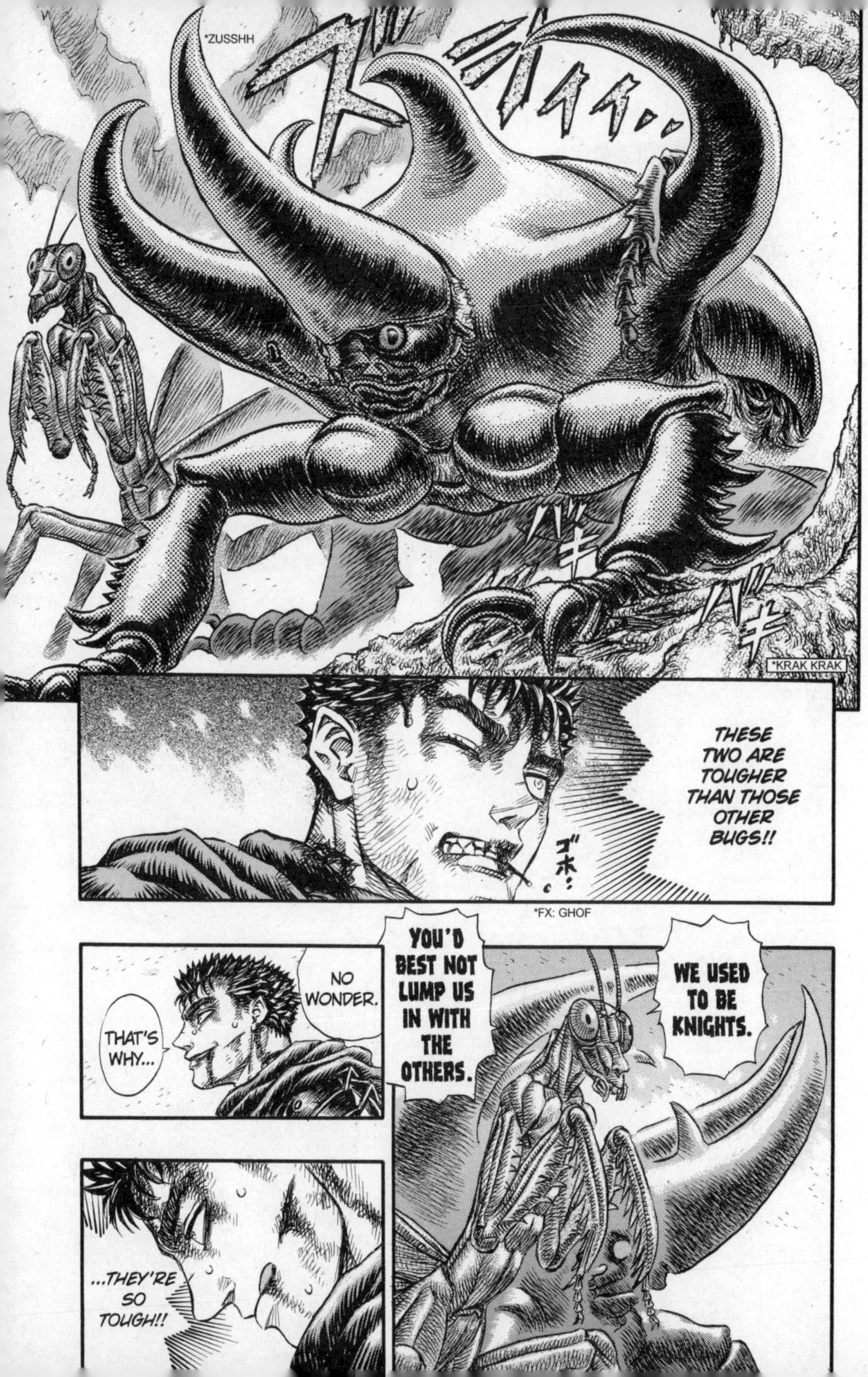
*ZUSSHH
*KRAK KRAK
THESE TWO ARE TOUGHER THAN THOSE OTHER BUGS!!
*FX: GHOF
WE USED TO BE KNIGHTS.
YOU'D BEST NOT LUMP US IN WITH THE OTHERS.
NO WONDER.
THAT'S WHY...
...THEY'RE SO TOUGH!!

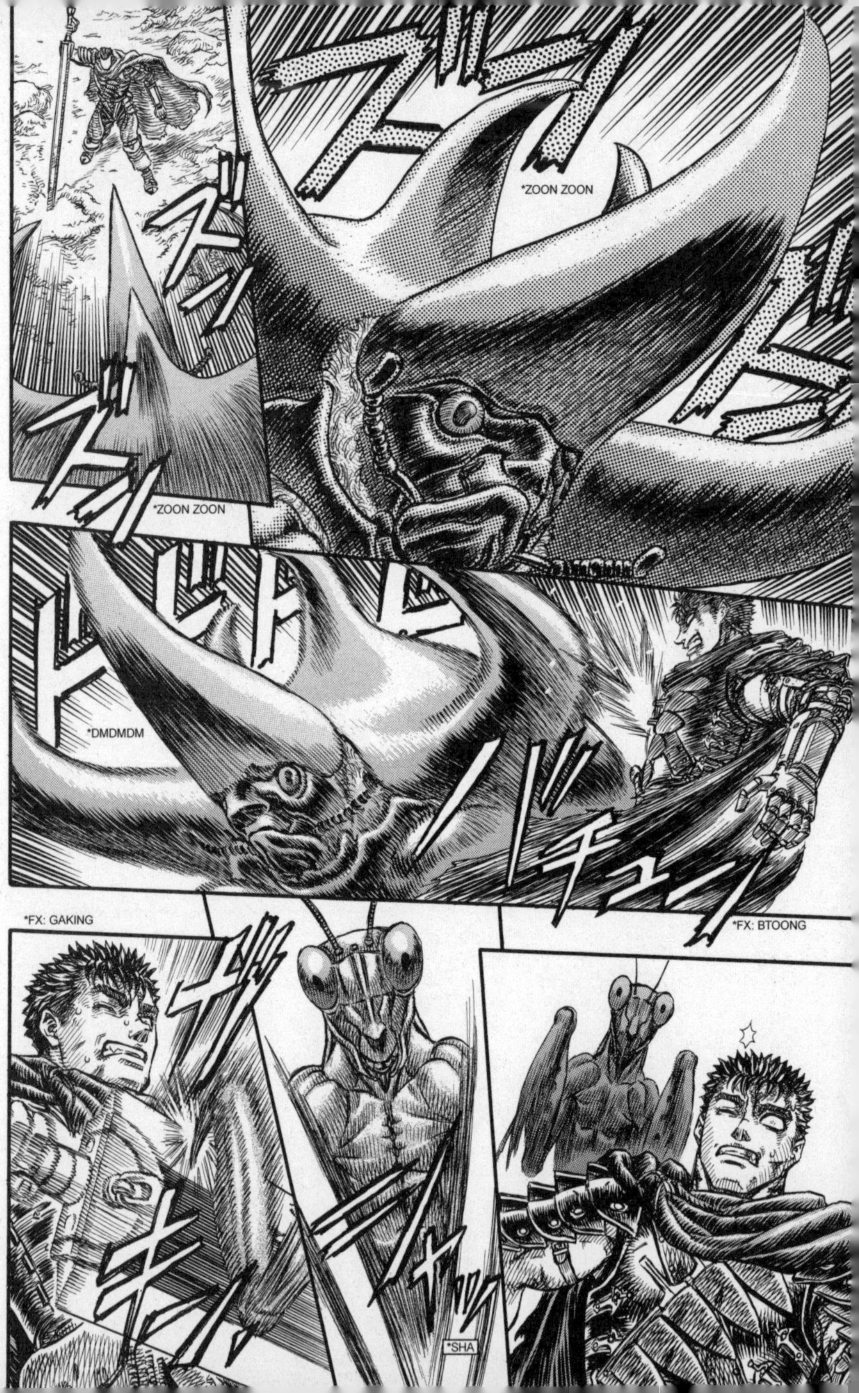
*ZOON ZOON
*ZOON ZOON
*DMDMDM
*FX: BTOONG
*SHA
*FX: GAKING

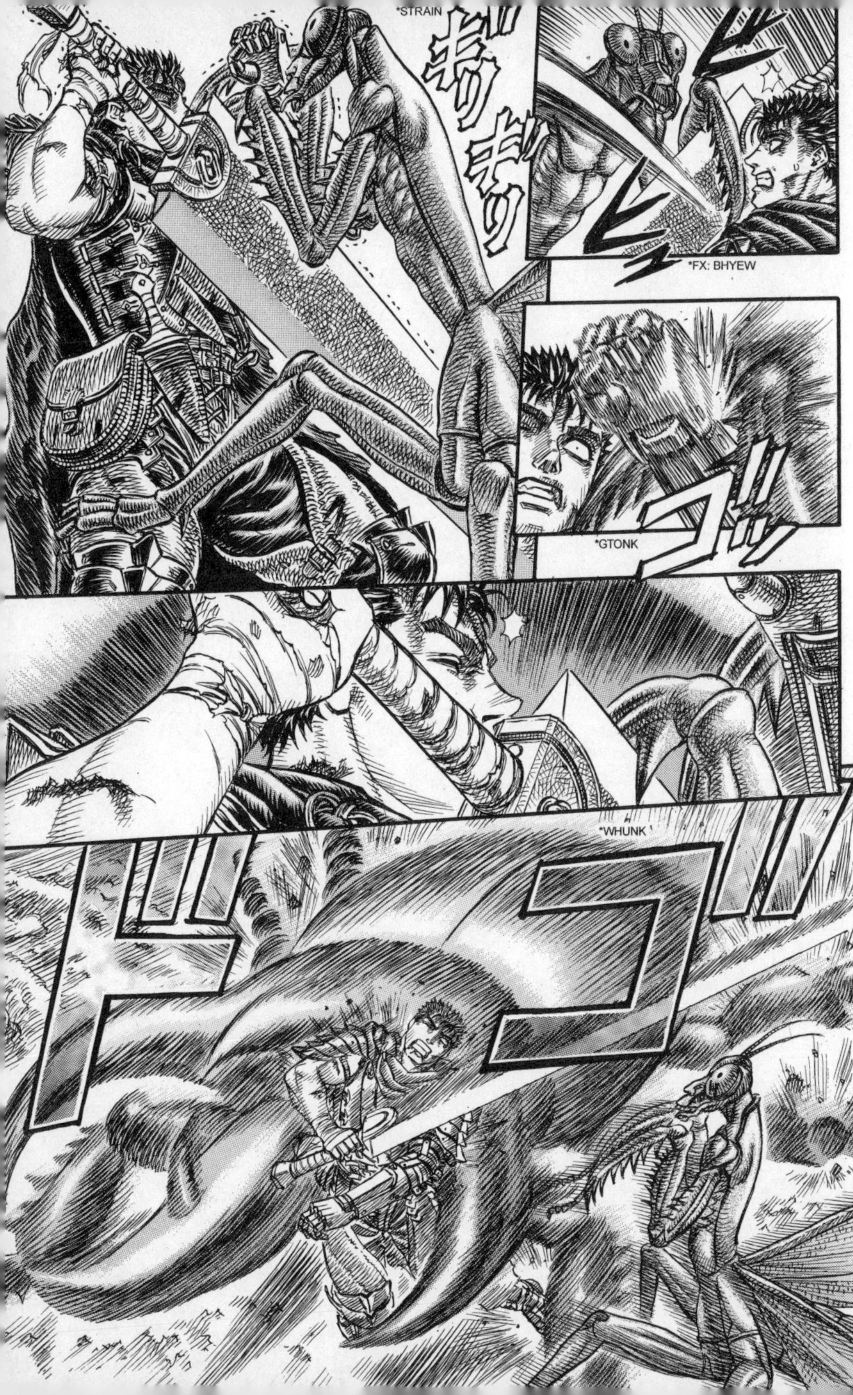

*FX: BHYEW
*GTONK
*STRAIN
*WHUNK

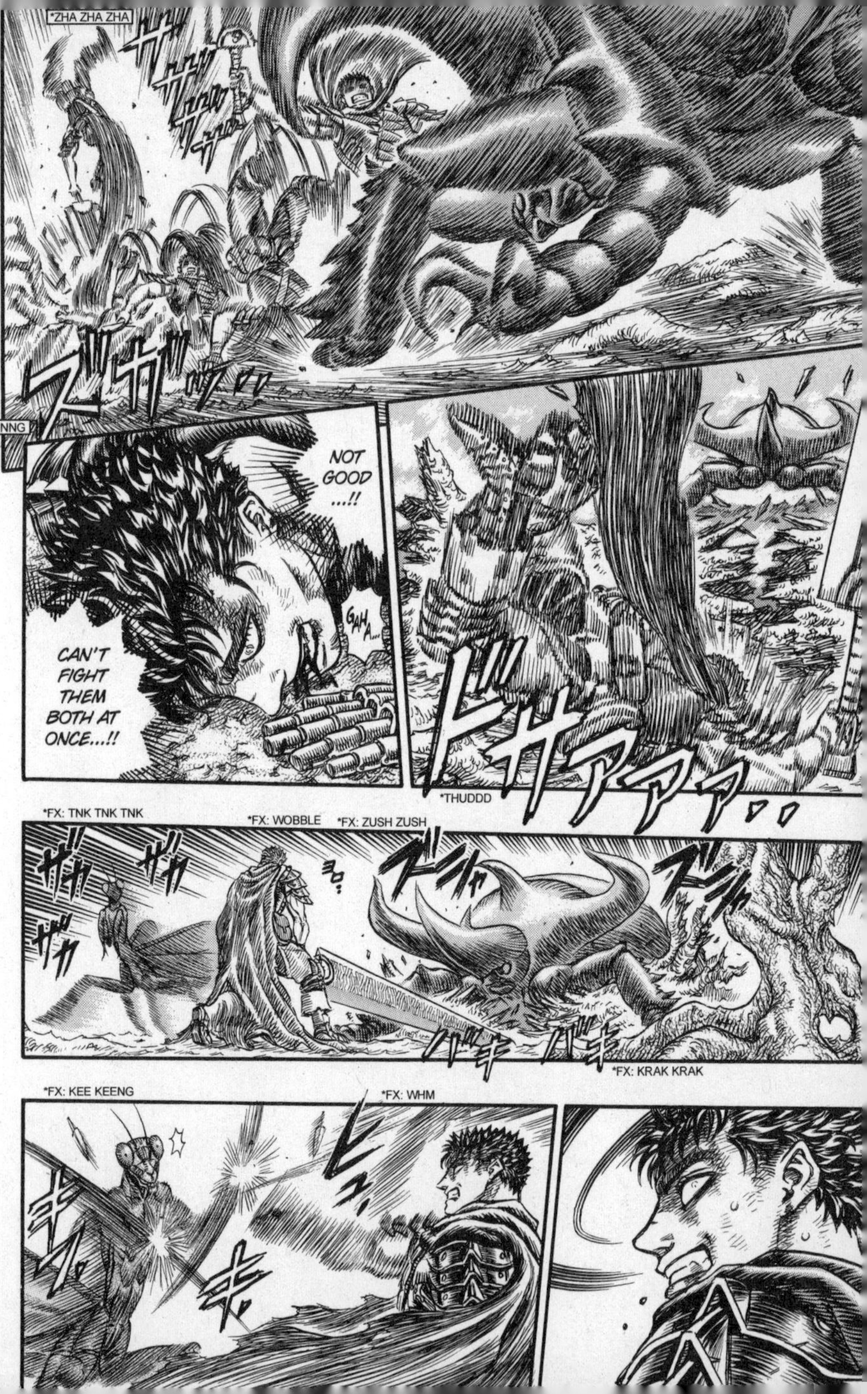
*ZHA ZHA ZHA
*CHNNNG
*THUDDD
NOT GOOD ...!!
GAHA...
CAN'T FIGHT THEM BOTH AT ONCE...!!
*FX: ZUSH ZUSH
*FX: KRAK KRAK
*FX: WOBBLE
*FX: TNK TNK TNK
*FX: WHM
*FX: KEE KEENG

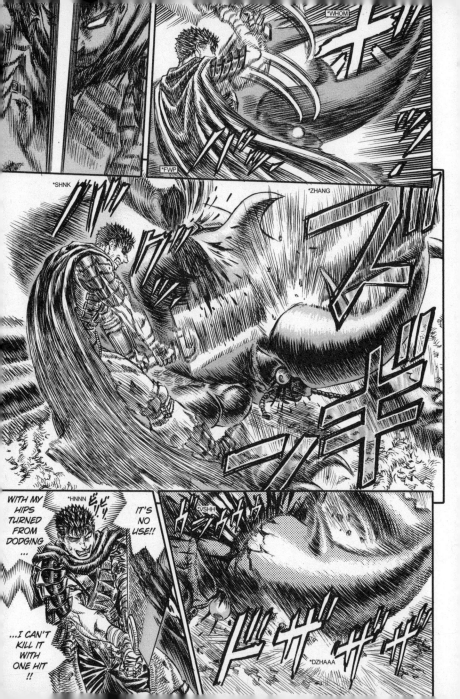

*WHOM

*FWP

*SHNK

*ZHANG

WITH MY
HIPS
TURNED
FROM
DODGING
...

*HNNN

IT'S
NO
USE!!

*VSHH

...I CAN'T
KILL IT
WITH
ONE HIT
!!

*DZHAAA

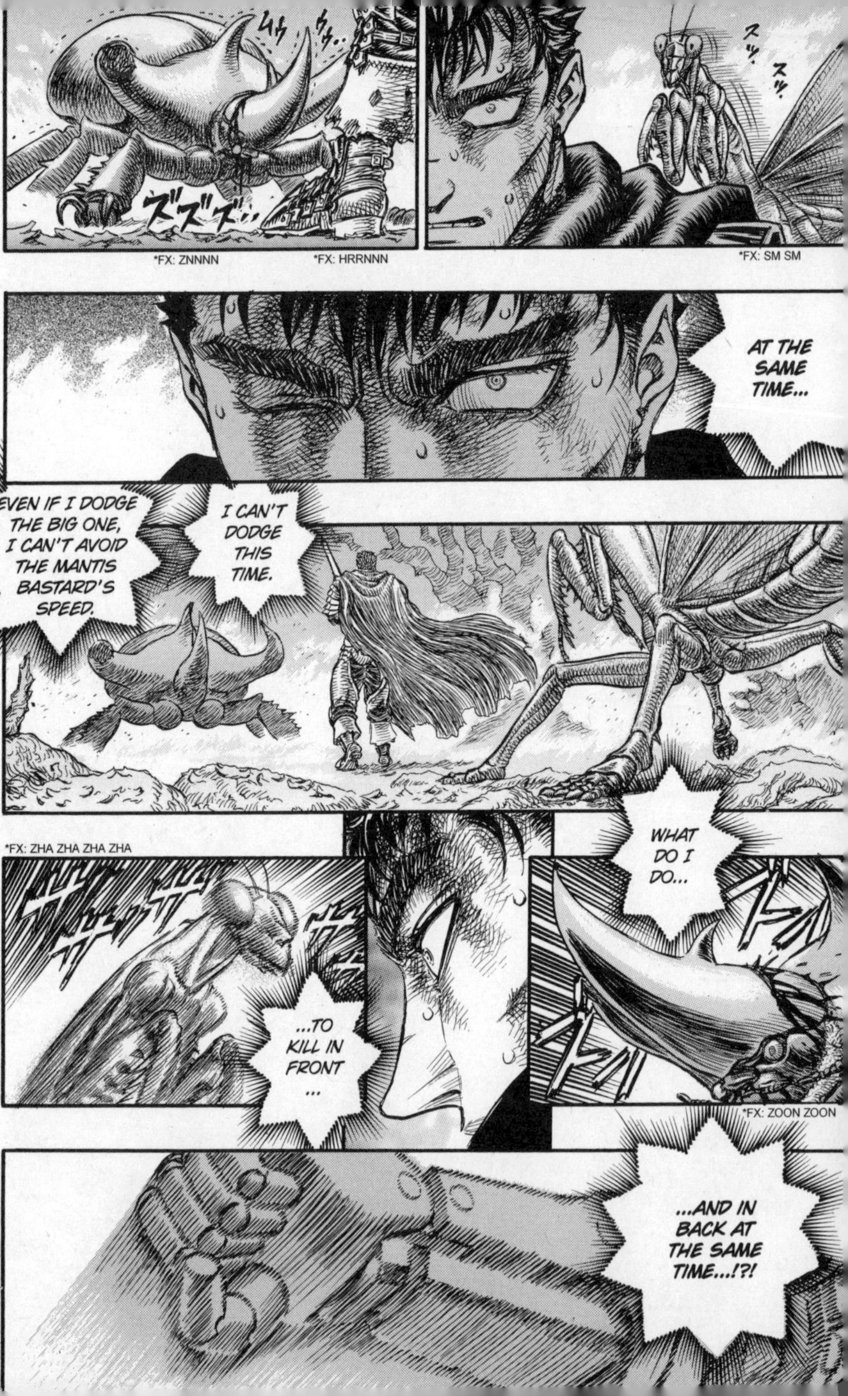
*FX: SM SM
*FX: HRRNNN
*FX: ZNNNN
AT THE SAME TIME...
I CAN'T DODGE THIS TIME.
EVEN IF I DODGE THE BIG ONE, I CAN'T AVOID THE MANTIS BASTARD'S SPEED.
WHAT DO I DO...
*FX: ZOON ZOON
...TO KILL IN FRONT ...
*FX: ZHA ZHA ZHA ZHA
...AND IN BACK AT THE SAME TIME...!?!

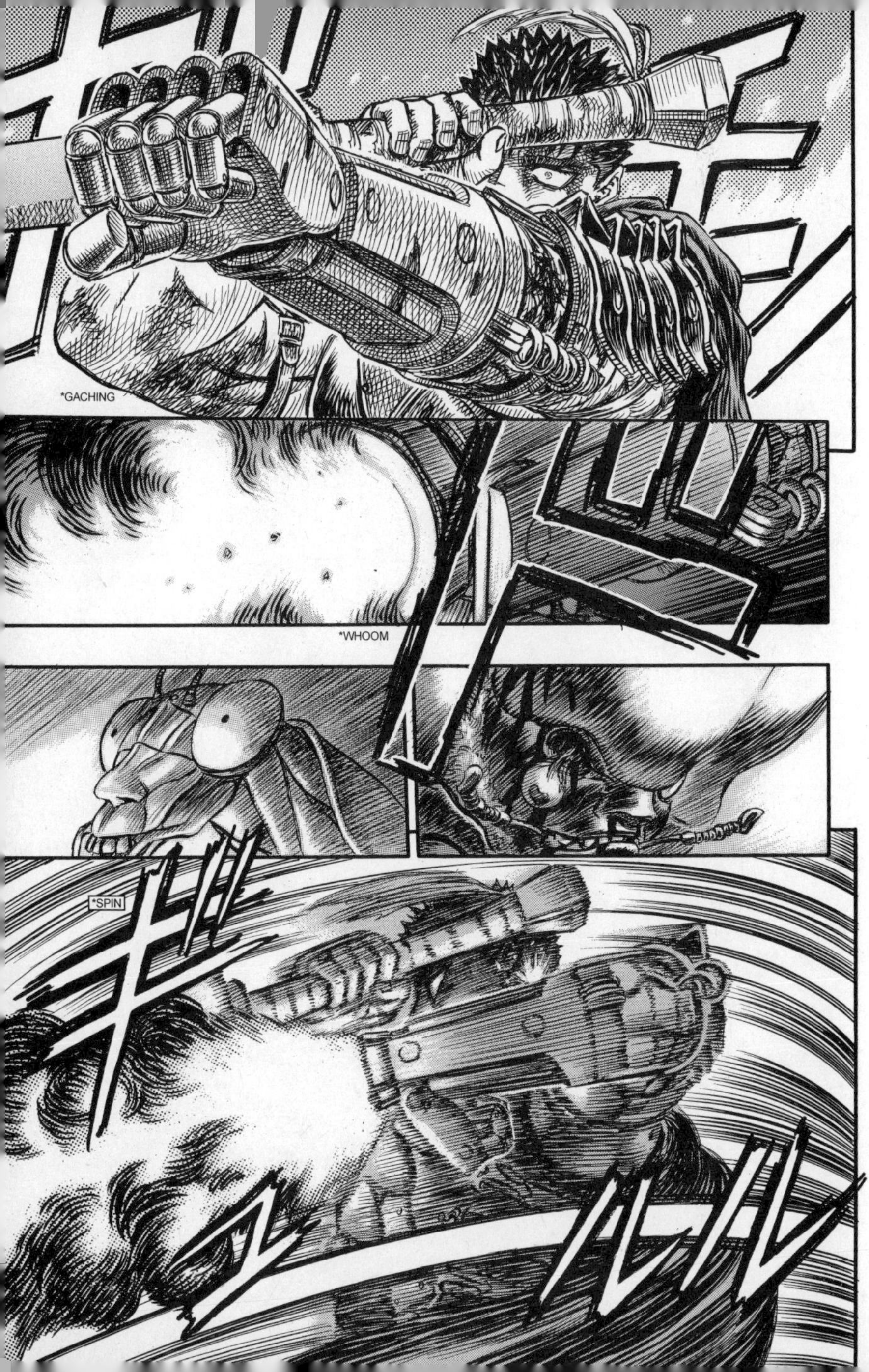
*GACHING
*WHOOM
*SPIN

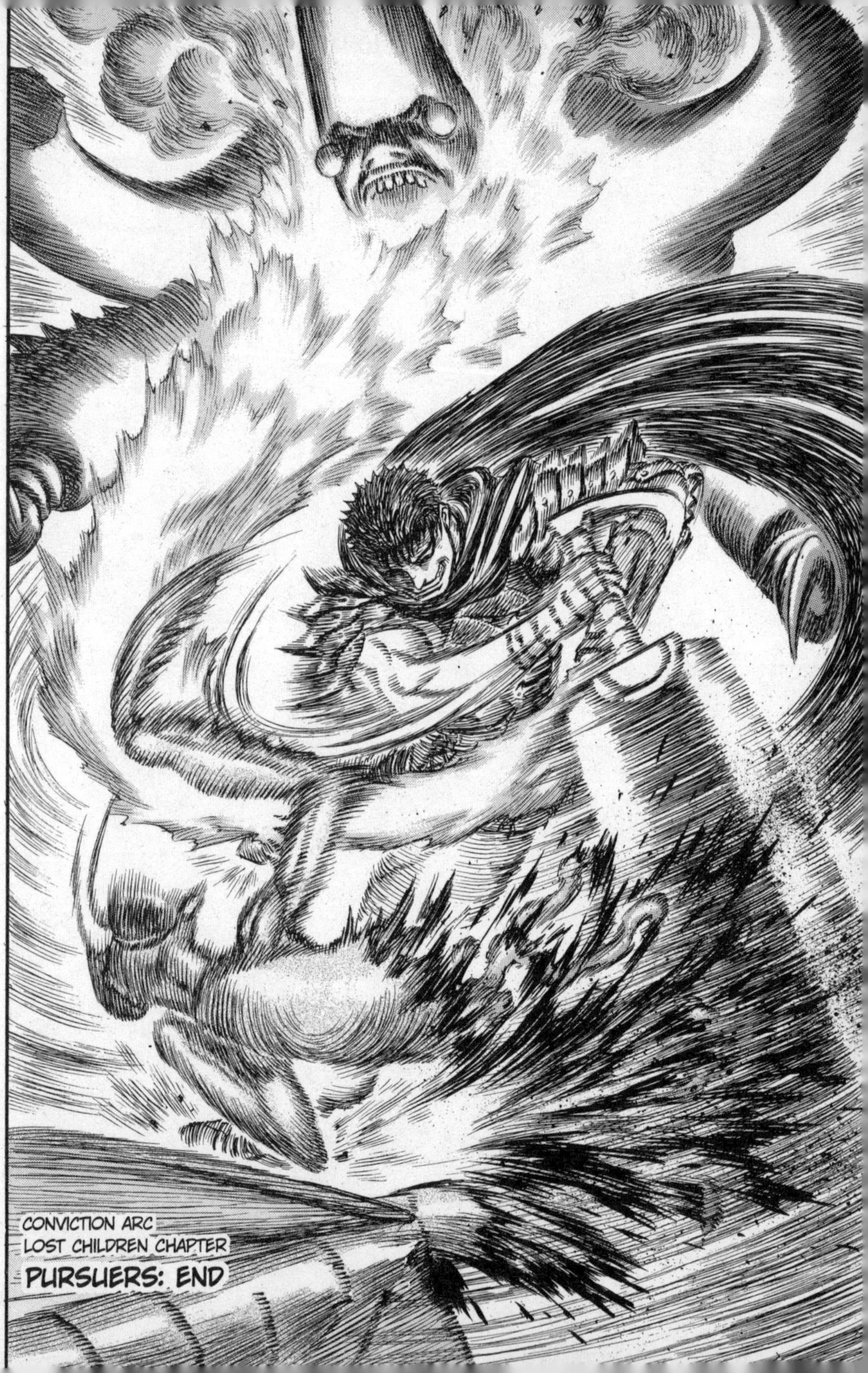
CONVICTION ARC
LOST CHILDREN CHAPTER
PURSUERS: END

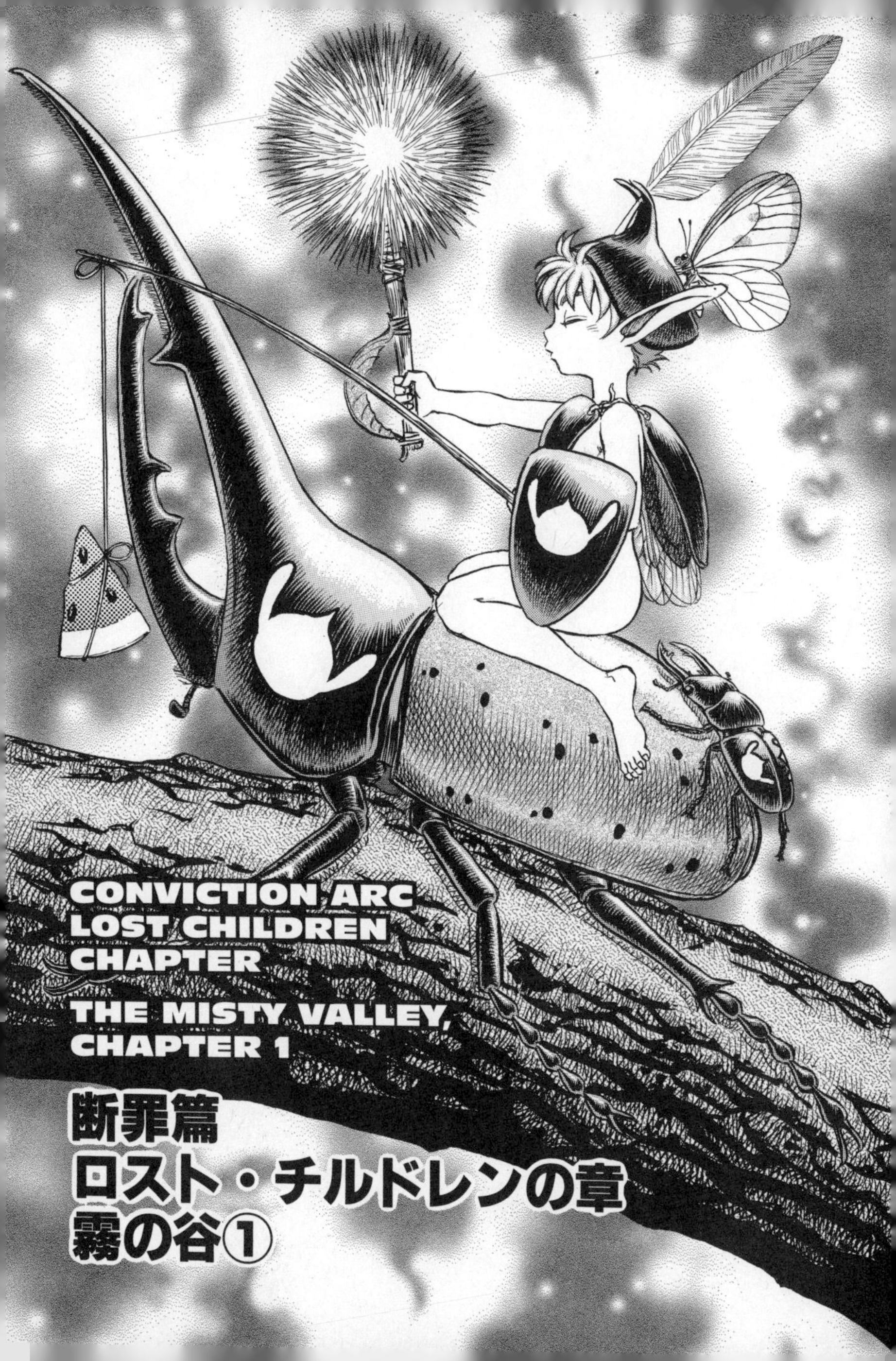
CONVICTION ARC
LOST CHILDREN CHAPTER
THE MISTY VALLEY, CHAPTER 1
断罪篇
ロスト・チルドレンの章
霧の谷①

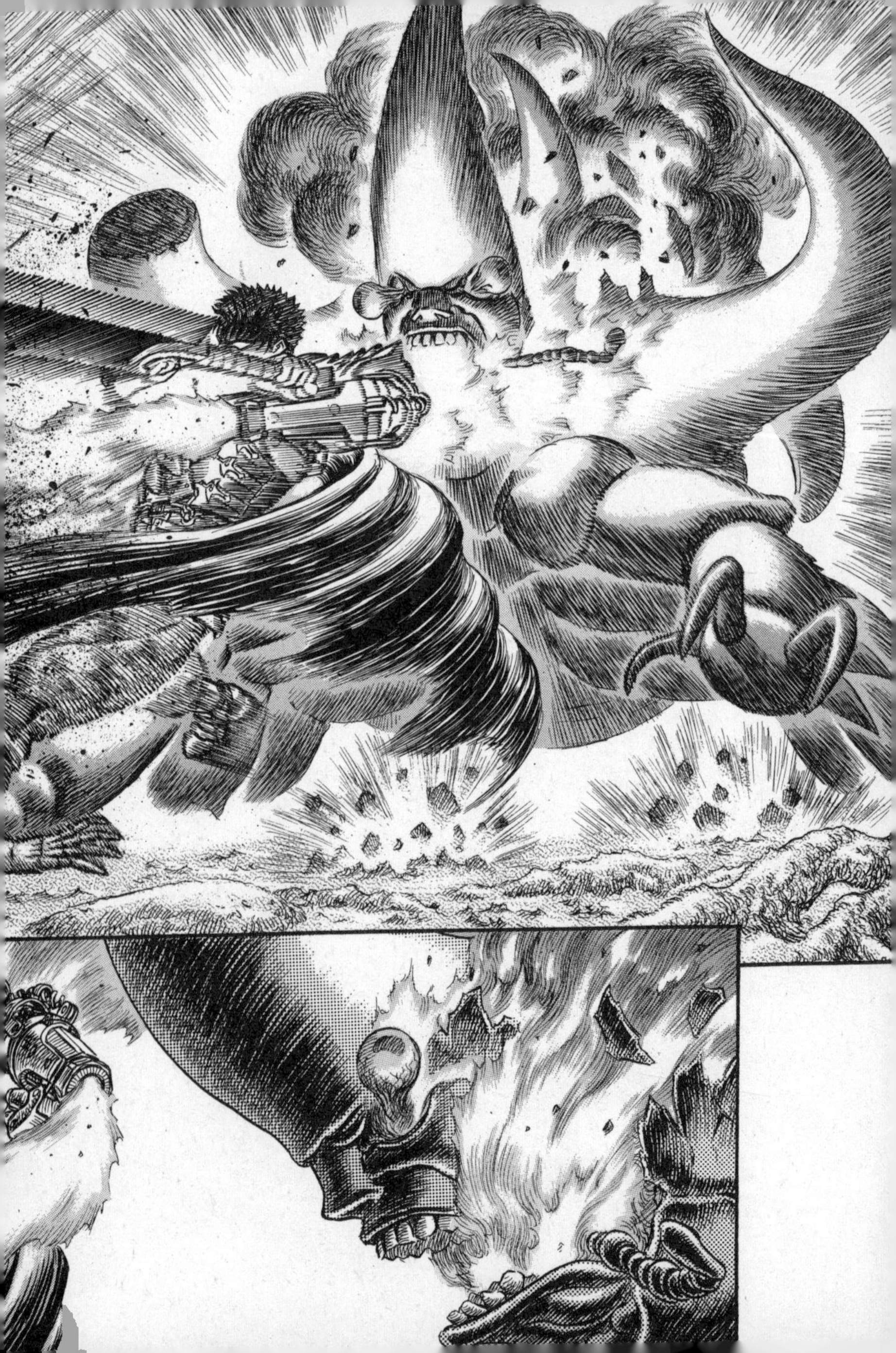

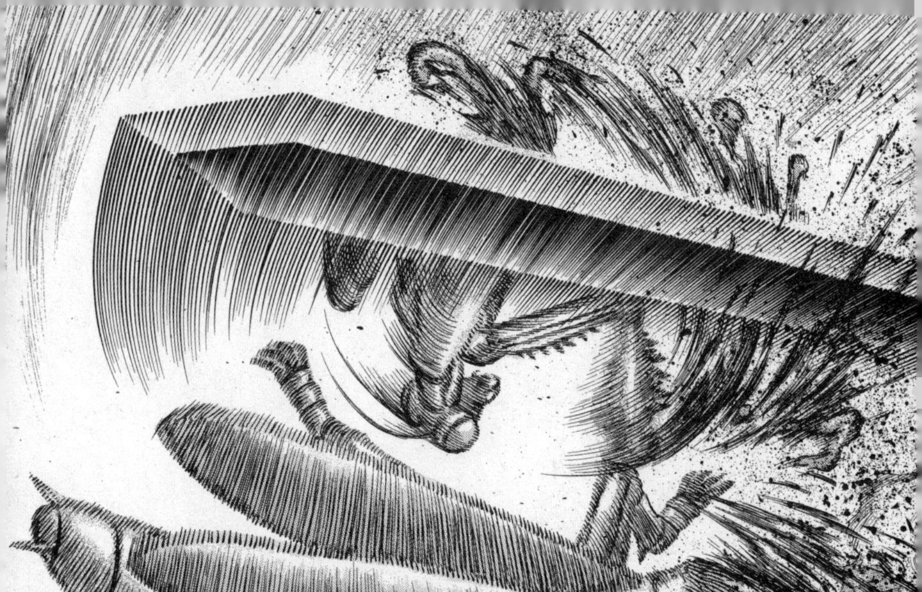
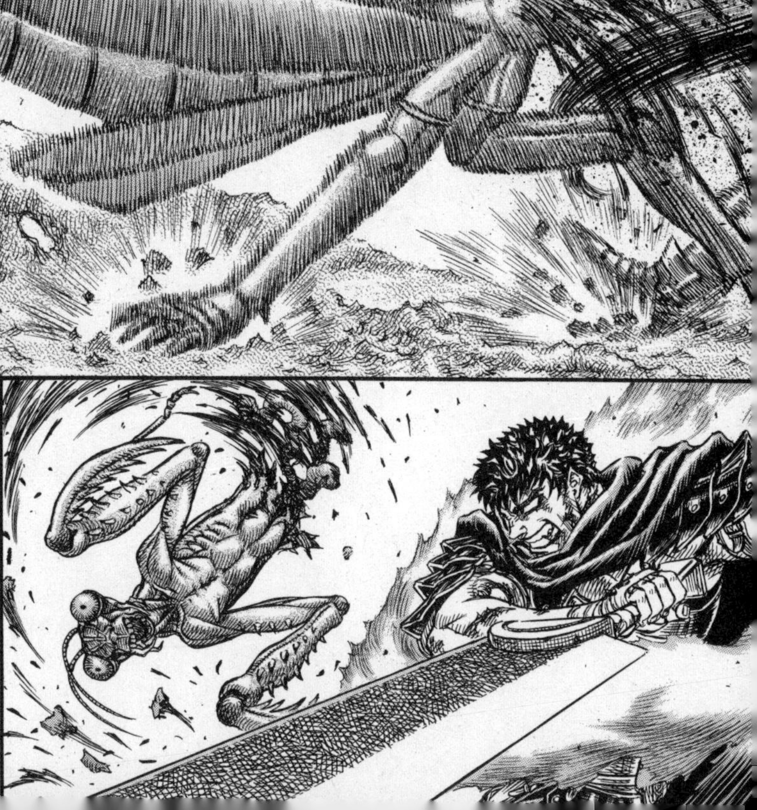

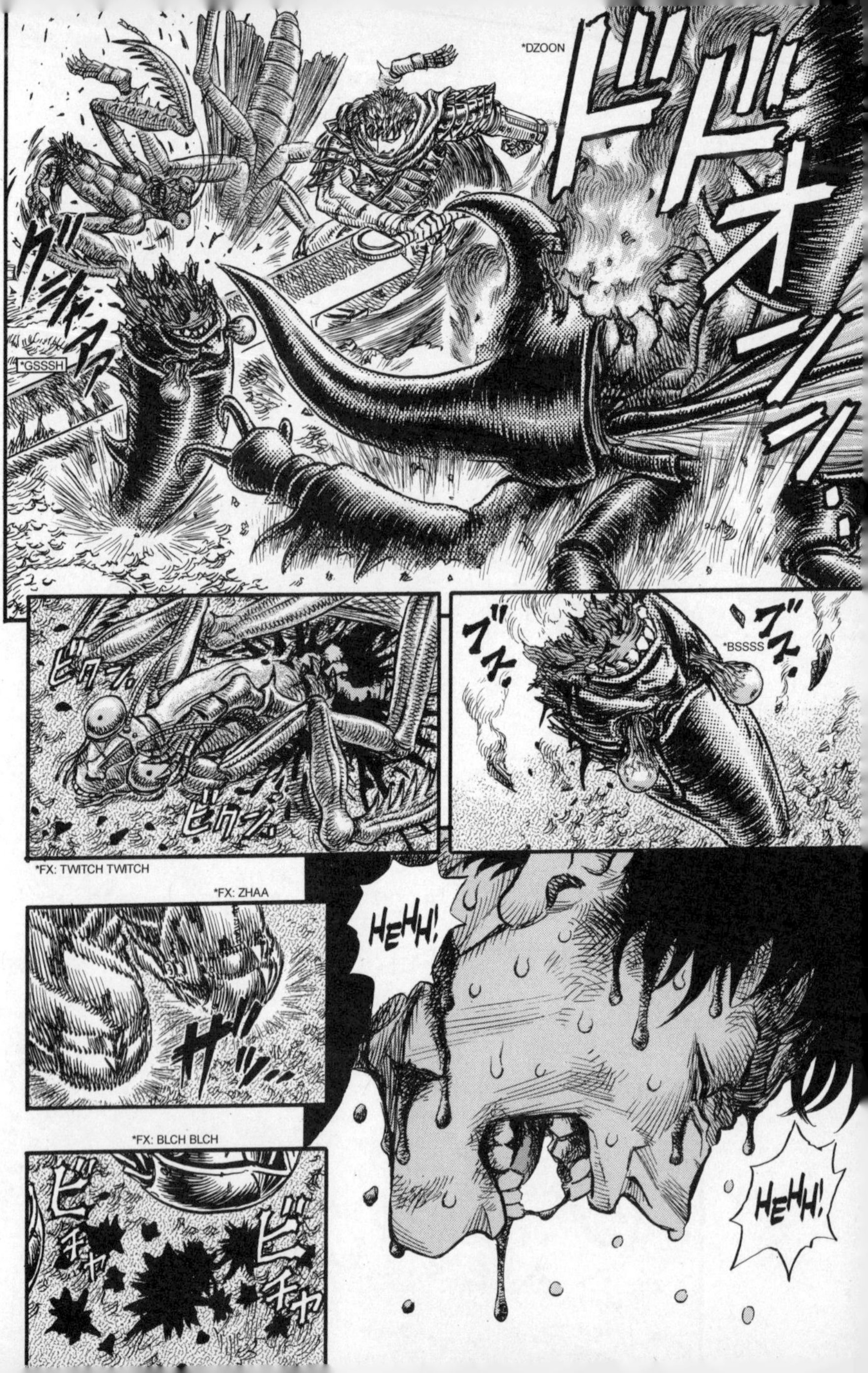
*DZOON
*GSSSH
*BSSSS
*FX: TWITCH TWITCH
HEHH!
HEHH!
*FX: ZHAA
*FX: BLCH BLCH

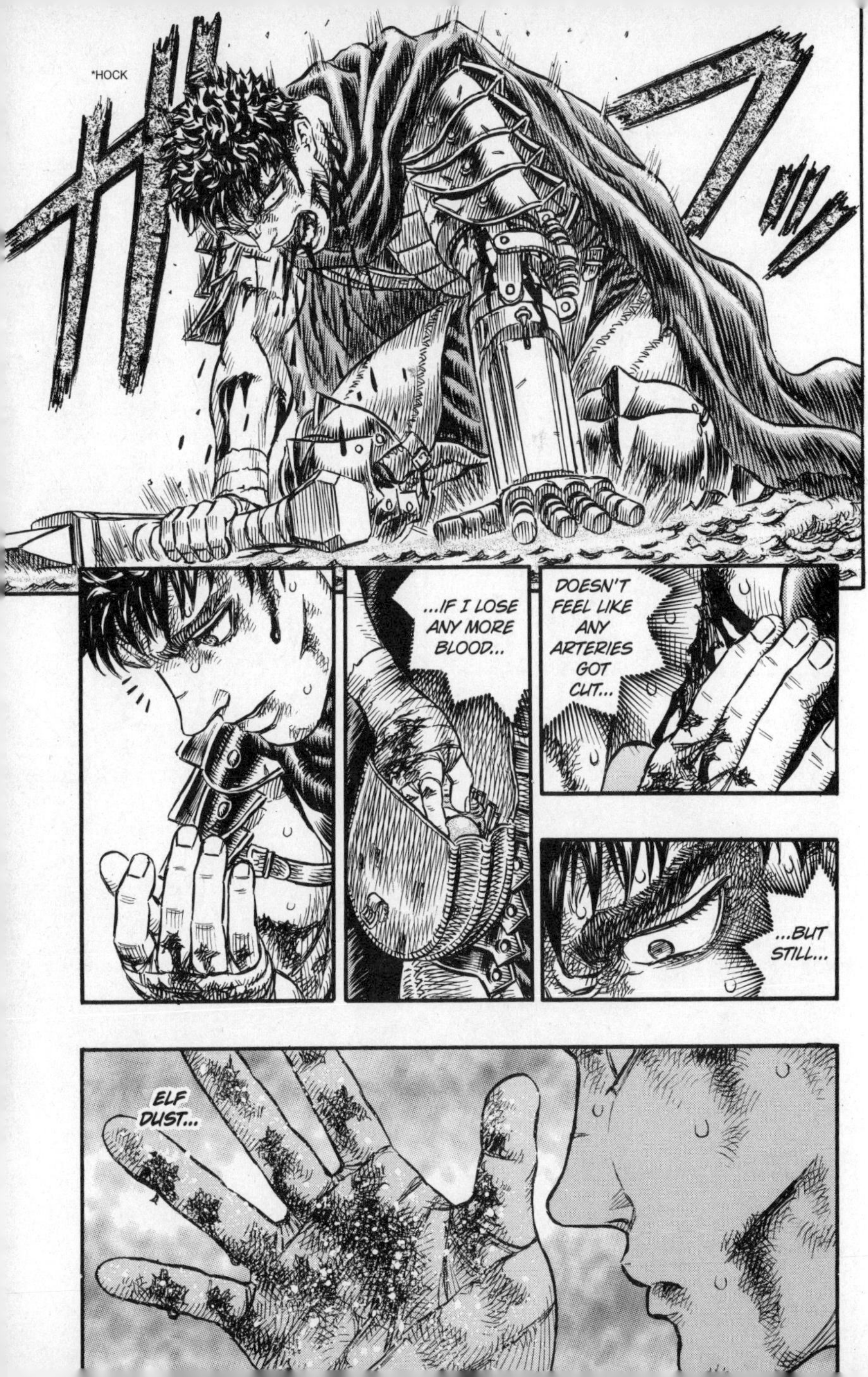
*HOCK
DOESN'T FEEL LIKE ANY ARTERIES GOT CUT...
...BUT STILL...
...IF I LOSE ANY MORE BLOOD...
ELF DUST...

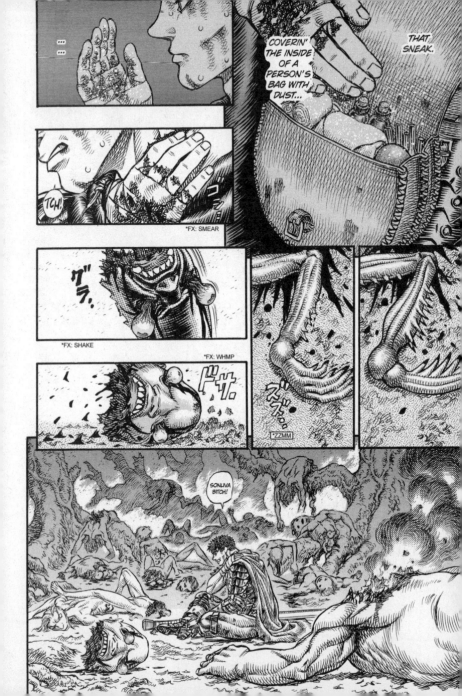

...
...

COVERIN' THE INSIDE OF A PERSON'S BAG WITH DUST...

THAT. SNEAK.

TCH!

*FX: SMEAR

*FX: SHAKE

*FX: WHMP

*ZZMM

SONUVA BITCH!

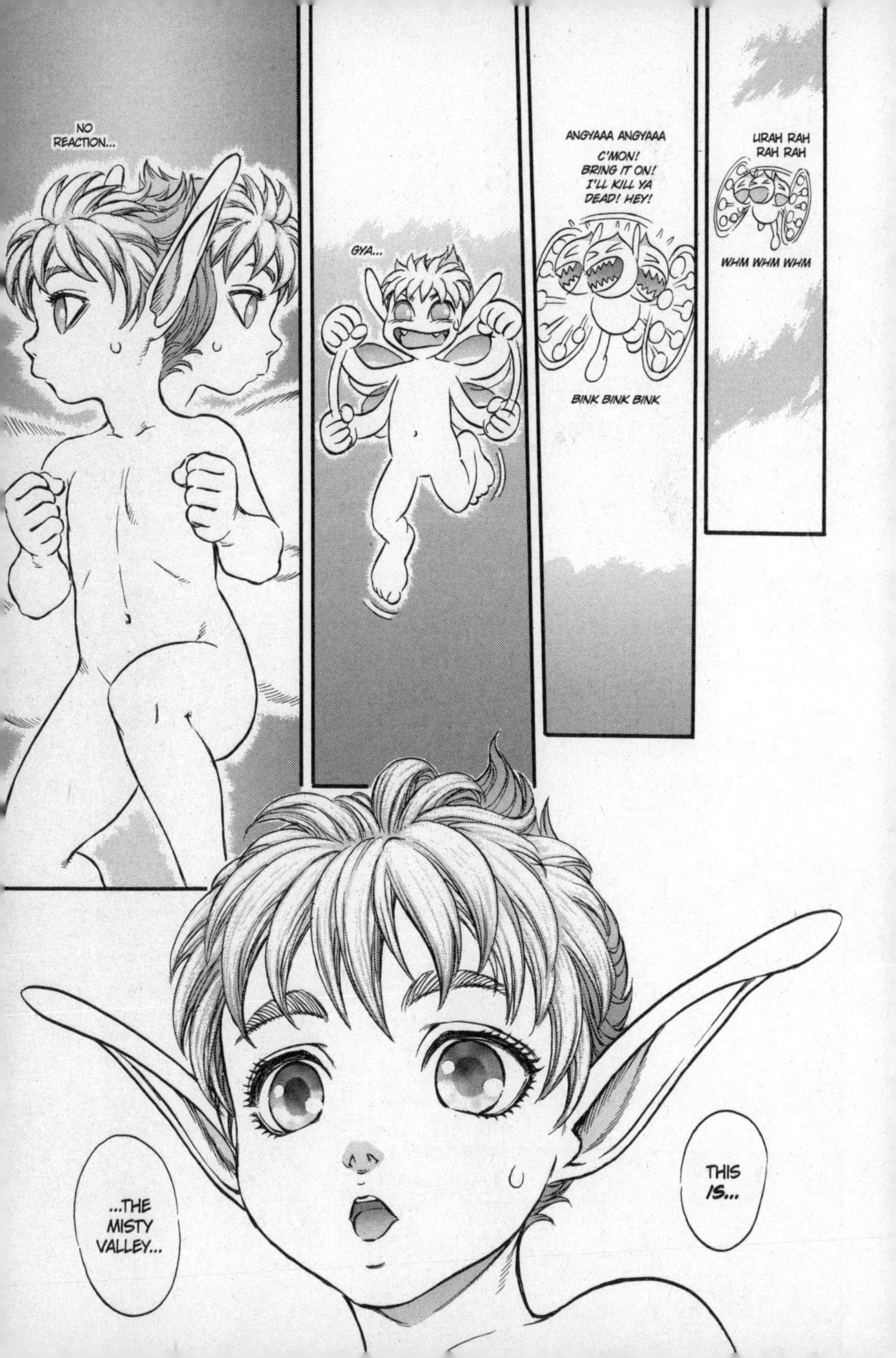

URAH RAH RAH RAH
WHM WHM WHM
ANGYAAA ANGYAAA
C'MON! BRING IT ON! I'LL KILL YA DEAD! HEY!
BINK BINK BINK
GYA...
NO REACTION...
THIS *IS*...
...THE MISTY VALLEY...

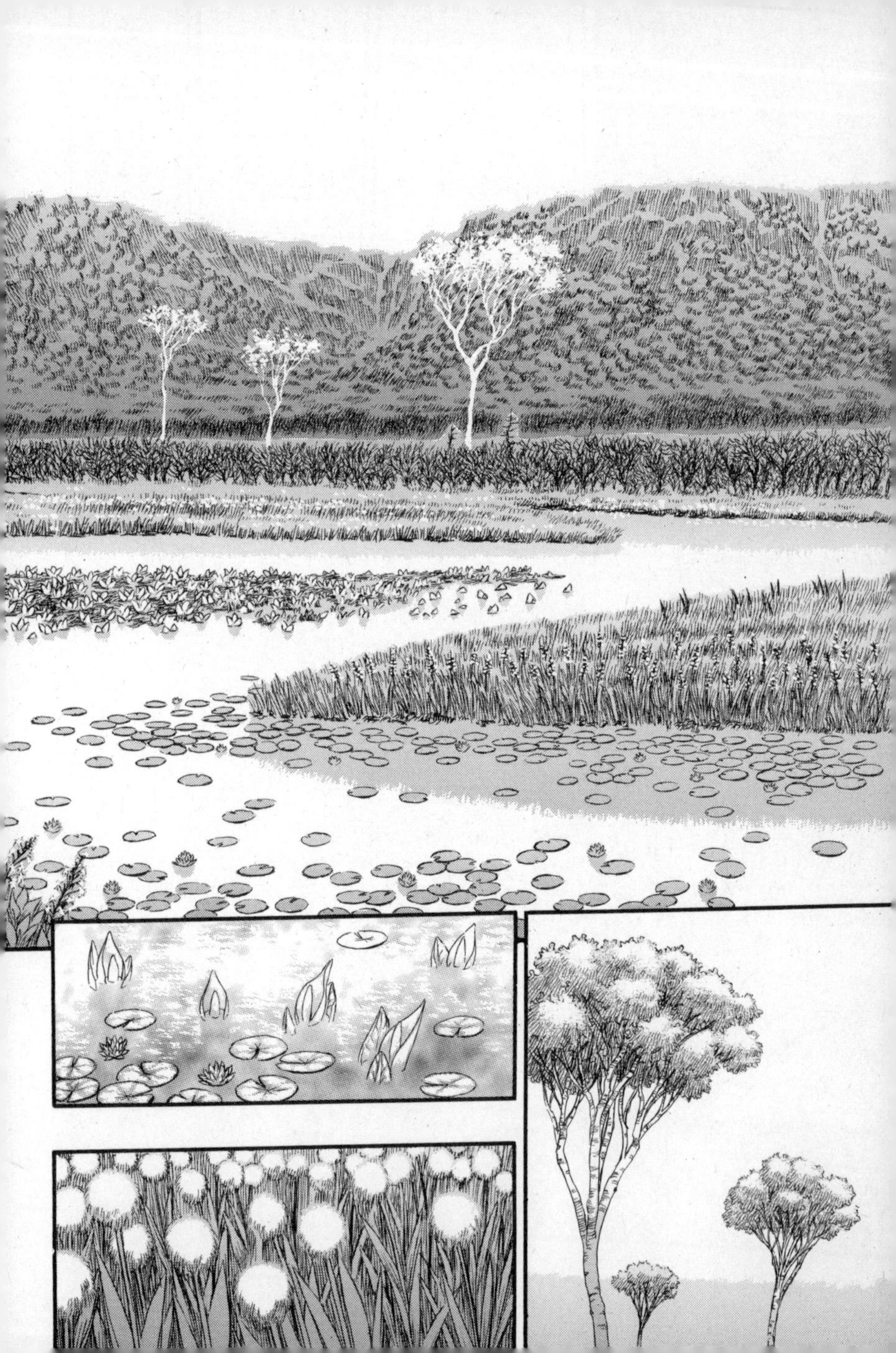

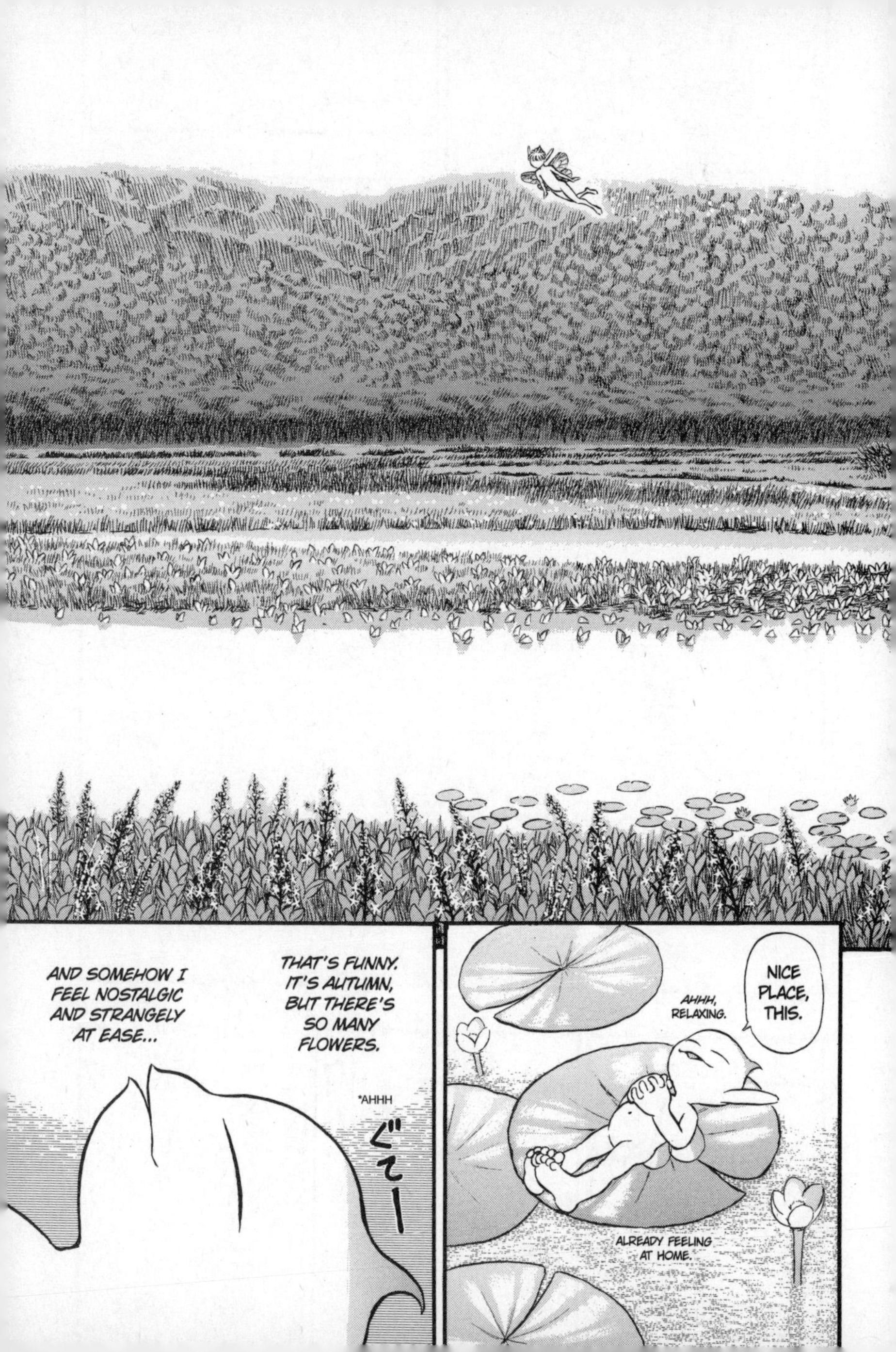
NICE PLACE, THIS.
AHHH, RELAXING.
ALREADY FEELING AT HOME.
THAT'S FUNNY. IT'S AUTUMN, BUT THERE'S SO MANY FLOWERS.
AND SOMEHOW I FEEL NOSTALGIC AND STRANGELY AT EASE...
*AHHH

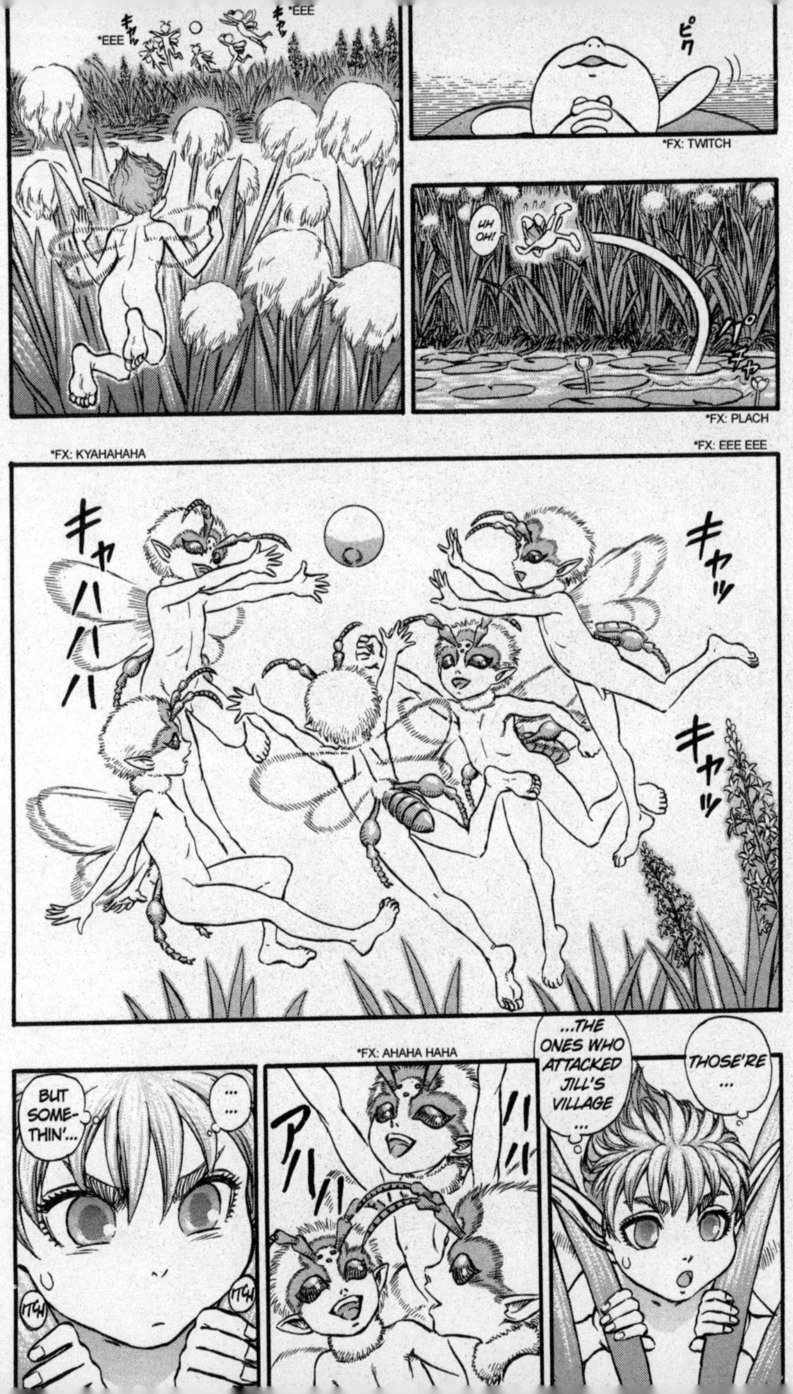
ピク
*FX: TWITCH
UH OH!
パチャ
*FX: PLACH
キャッ
*EEE
キャッ
*EEE
*FX: EEE EEE
キャッ
キャッ
キャハハハハ
*FX: KYAHAHAHA
THOSE'RE ...
...THE ONES WHO ATTACKED JILL'S VILLAGE ...
ハハ
アハハ
*FX: AHAHA HAHA
... ...
BUT SOME-THIN'...
ITCH
ITCH

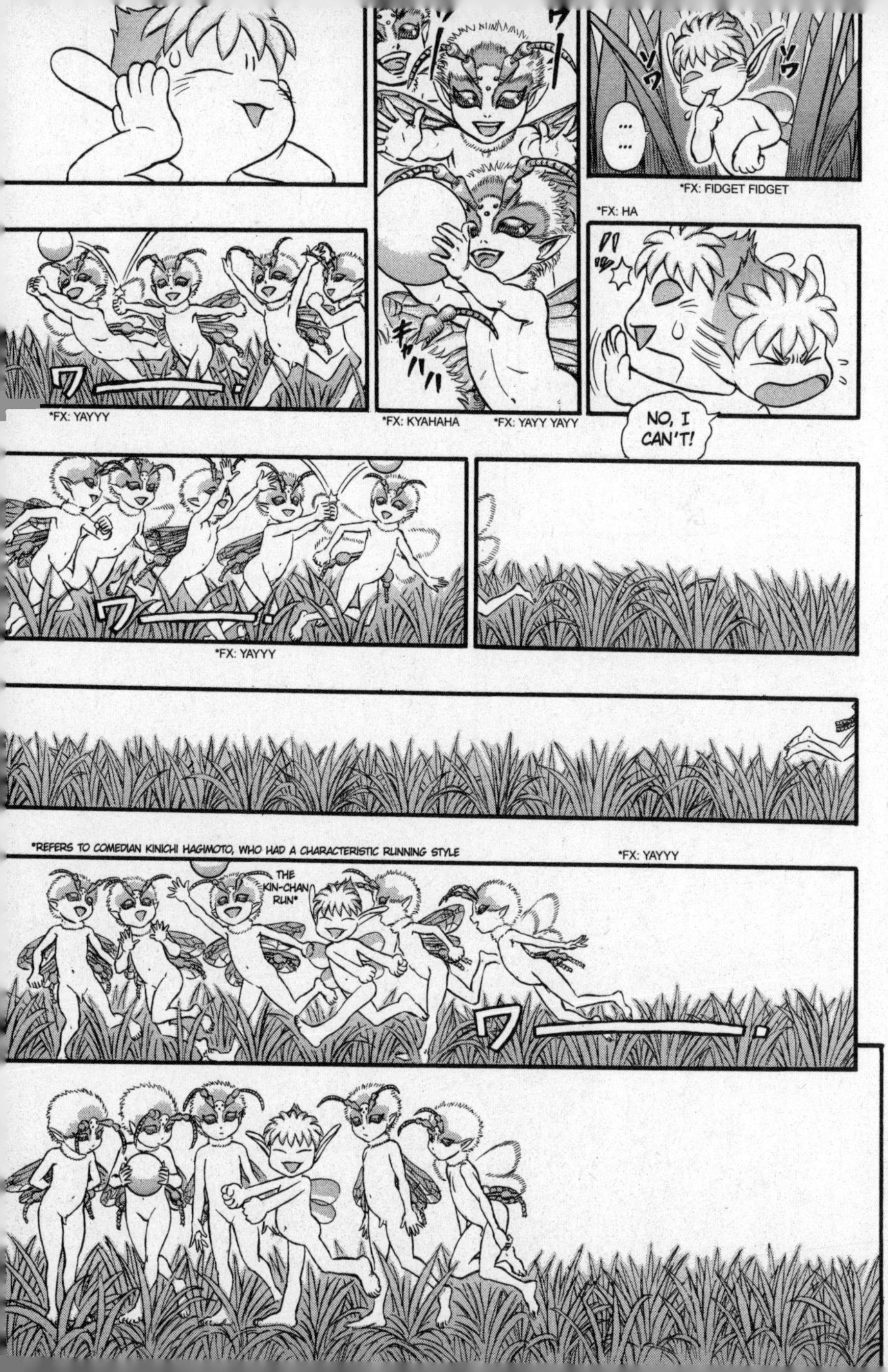

……
……
*FX: FIDGET FIDGET
*FX: HA
NO, I CAN'T!
*FX: KYAHAHA
*FX: YAYY YAYY
*FX: YAYYY
*FX: YAYYY
*REFERS TO COMEDIAN KINICHI HAGIMOTO, WHO HAD A CHARACTERISTIC RUNNING STYLE
*FX: YAYYY
THE KIN-CHAN RUN*

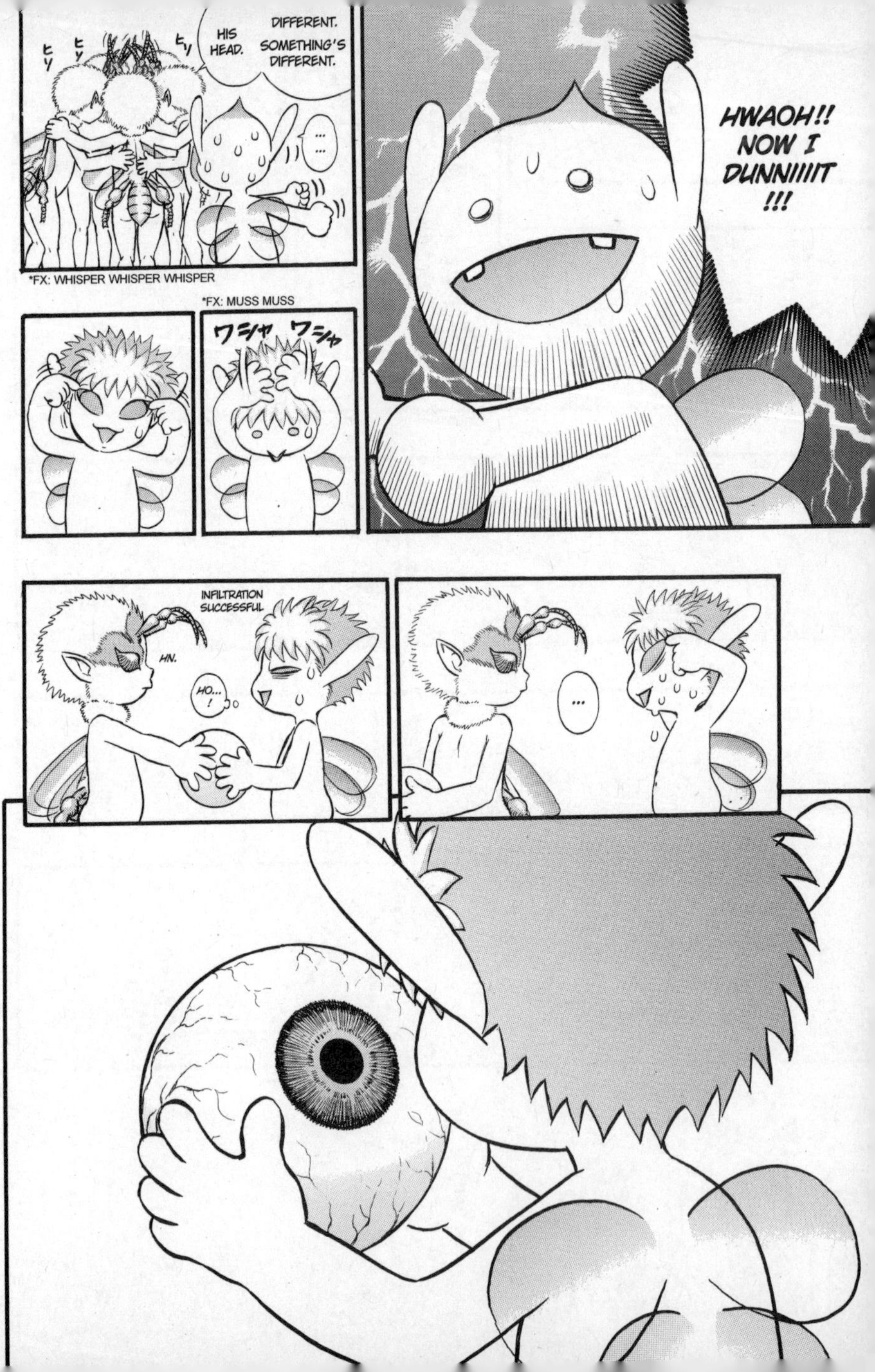

HWAOH!! NOW I DUNNIIIIT !!!
DIFFERENT. SOMETHING'S DIFFERENT.
HIS HEAD.
... ...
ヒソ ヒソ ヒソ
*FX: WHISPER WHISPER WHISPER
ワシャ ワシャ
*FX: MUSS MUSS
...
INFILTRATION SUCCESSFUL
HN.
HO... !

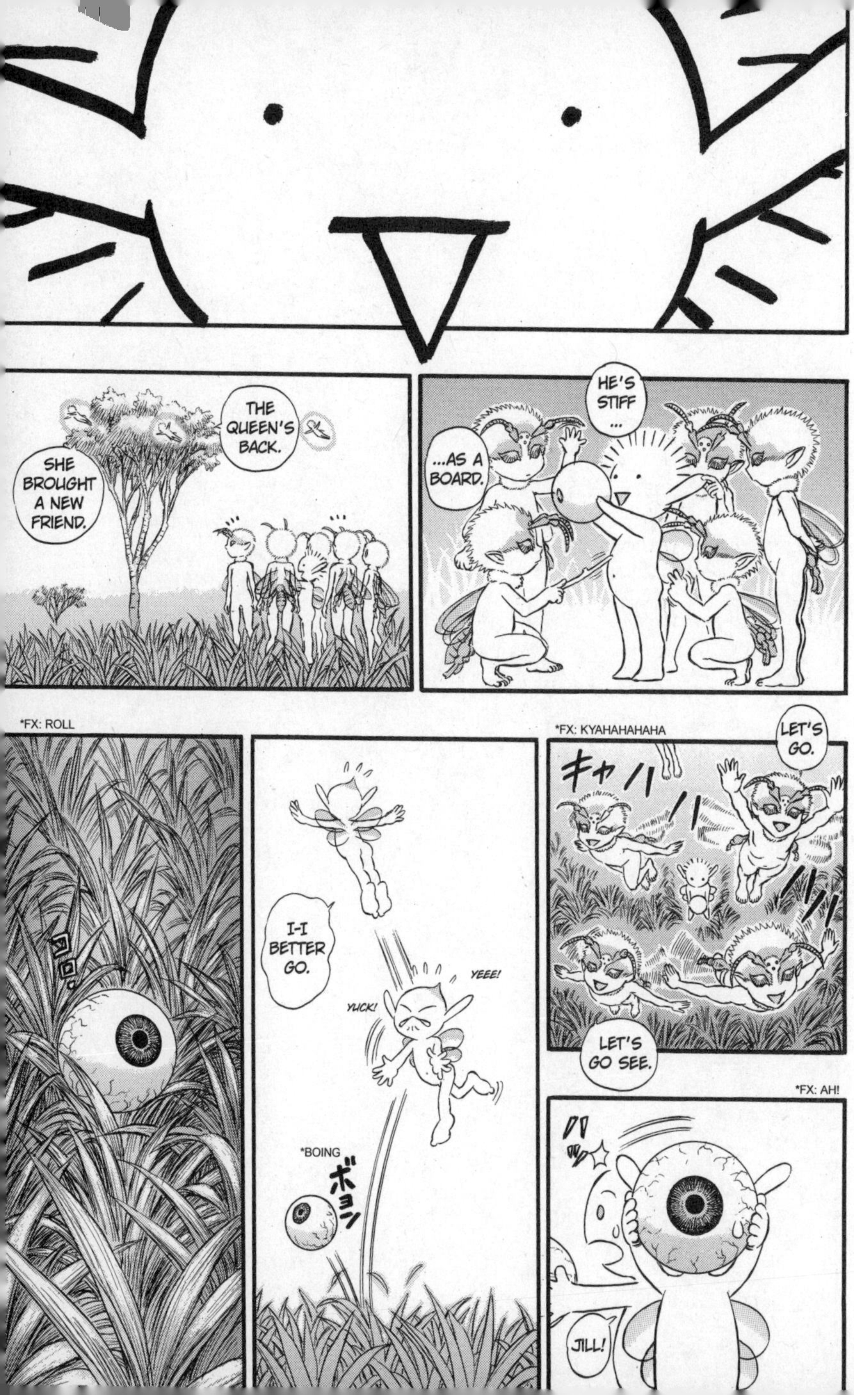
HE'S STIFF ...
...AS A BOARD.
THE QUEEN'S BACK.
SHE BROUGHT A NEW FRIEND.
*FX: KYAHAHAHAHA
LET'S GO.
LET'S GO SEE.
*FX: AH!
JILL!
I-I BETTER GO.
YEEE!
YUCK!
*BOING
*FX: ROLL

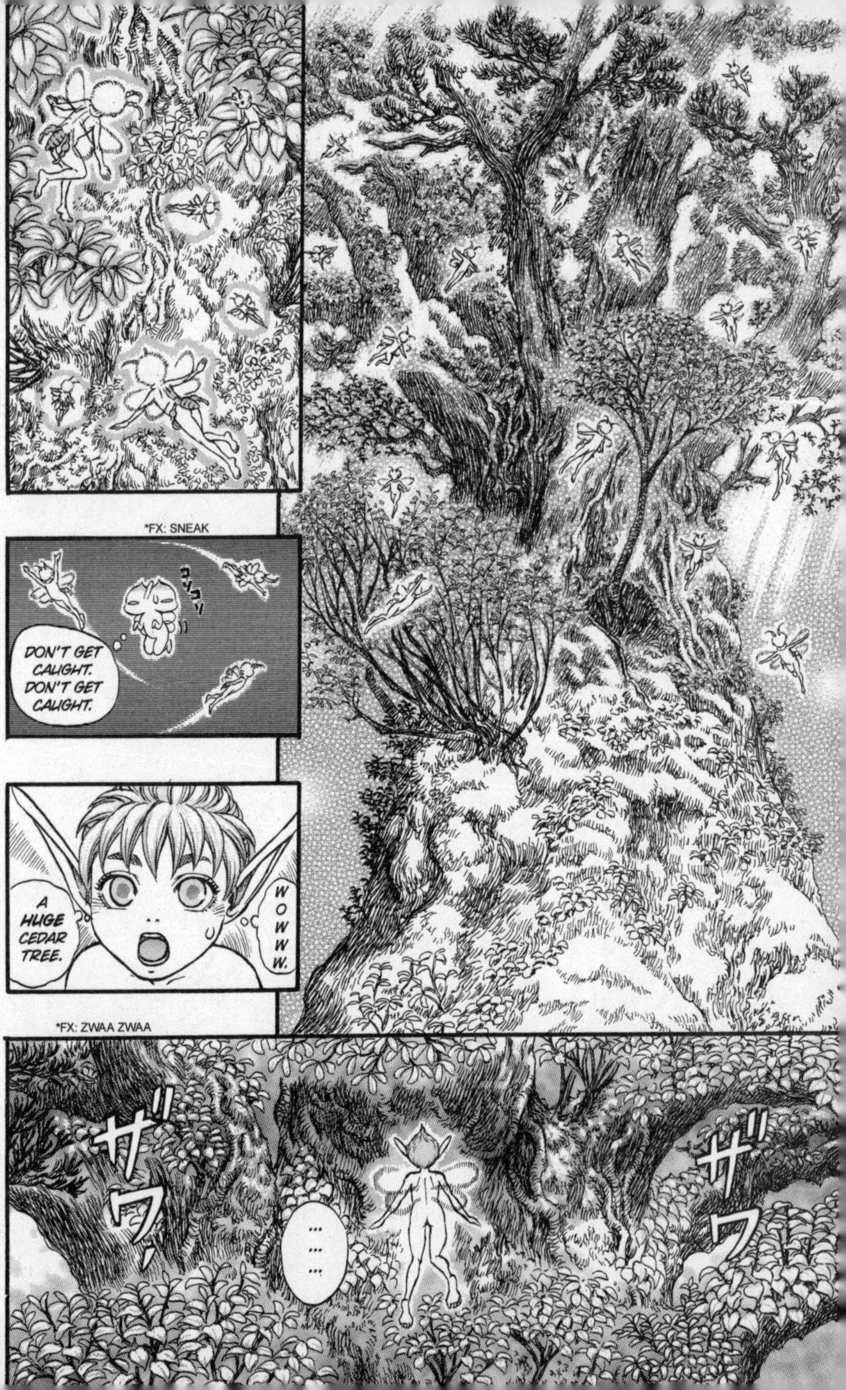
*FX: SNEAK
コソコソ
DON'T GET CAUGHT. DON'T GET CAUGHT.
WOWWWW.
A HUGE CEDAR TREE.
*FX: ZWAA ZWAA
ザワ
... ...
ザワ

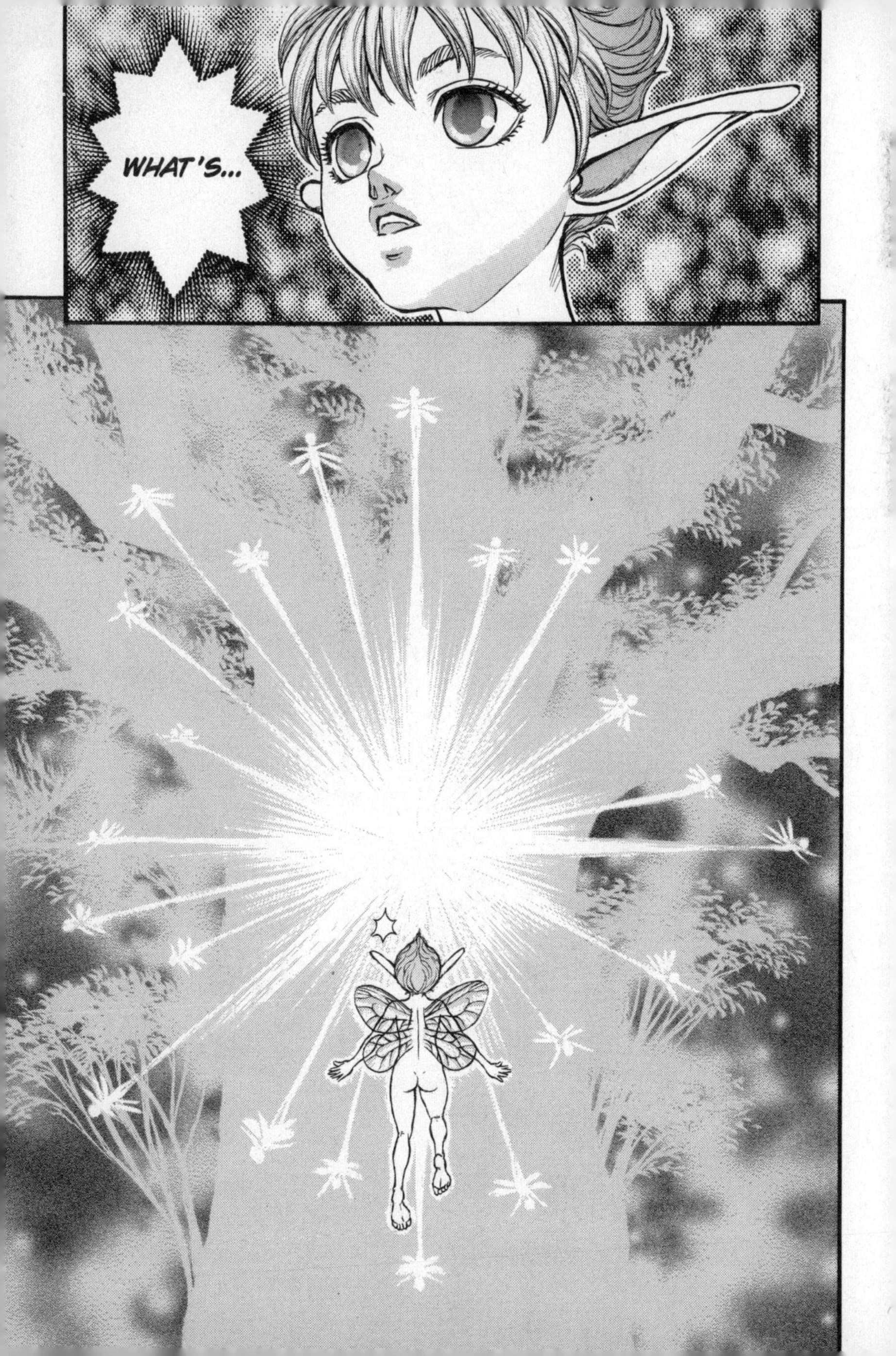
WHAT'S...

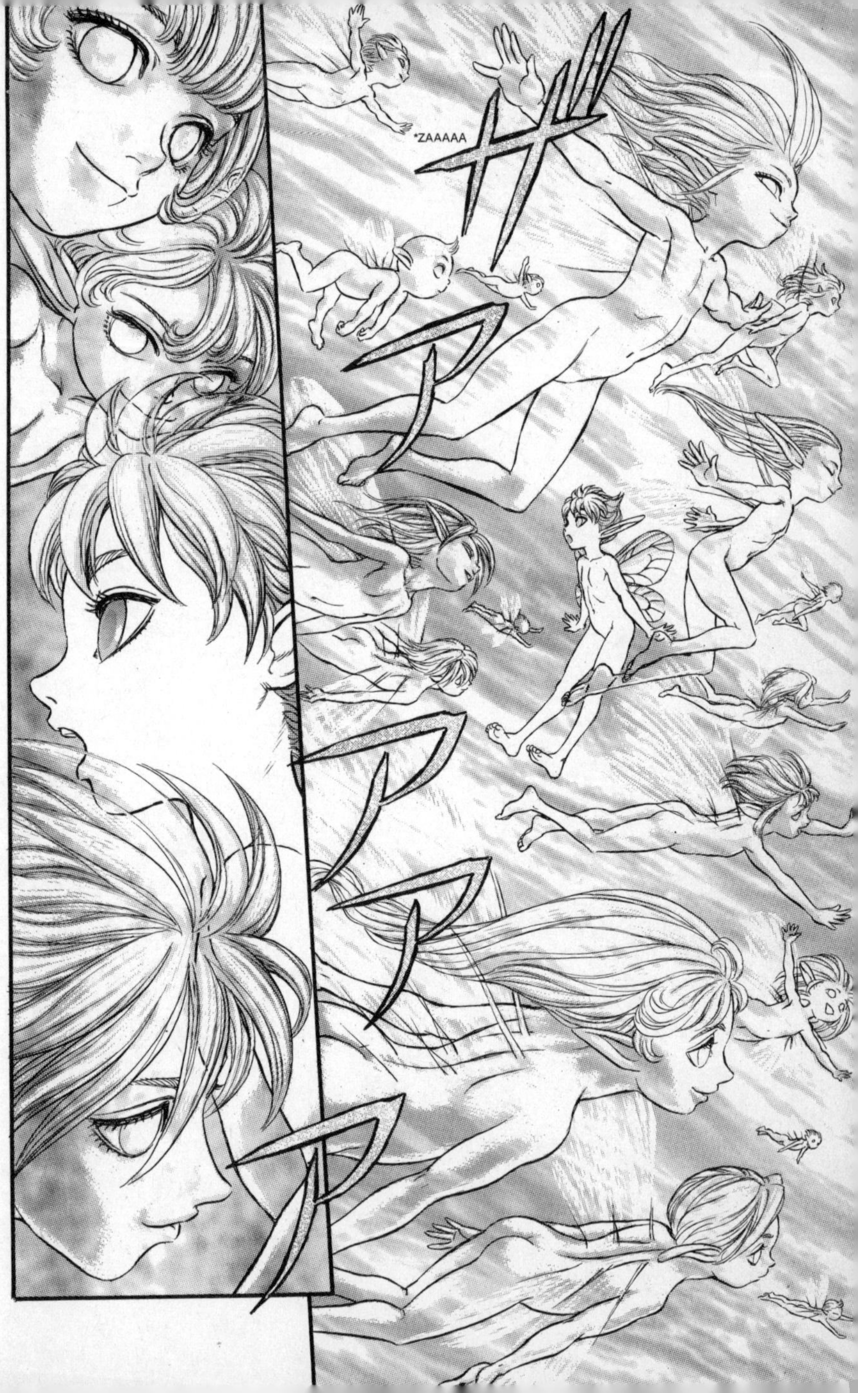
*ZAAAAA

*KSHOOM

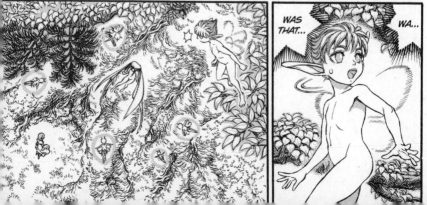

WAS THAT...

WA...

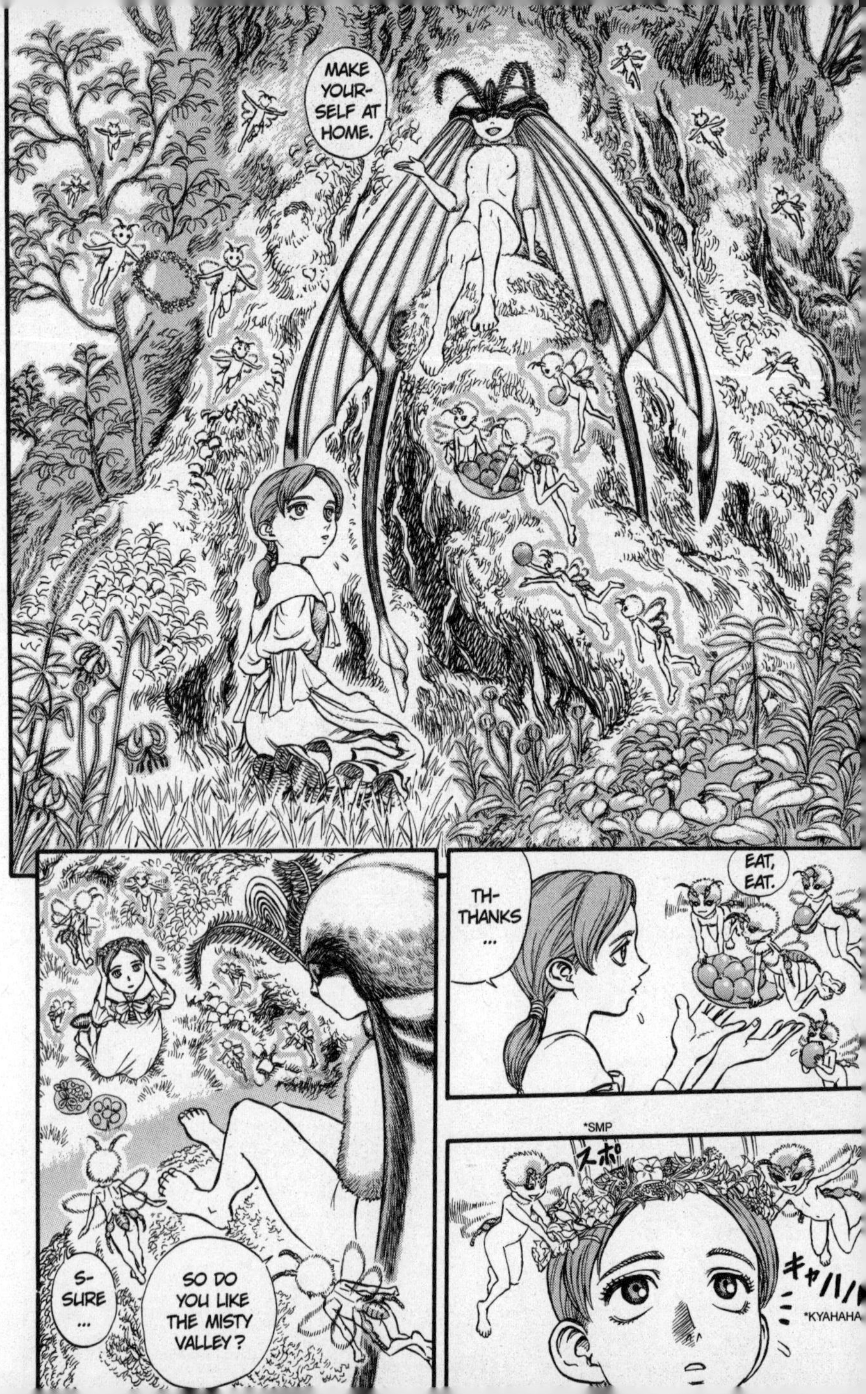
MAKE YOUR-SELF AT HOME.
EAT, EAT.
TH-THANKS ...
*SMP
スポ
キャハハ
*KYAHAHA
SO DO YOU LIKE THE MISTY VALLEY?
S-SURE ...

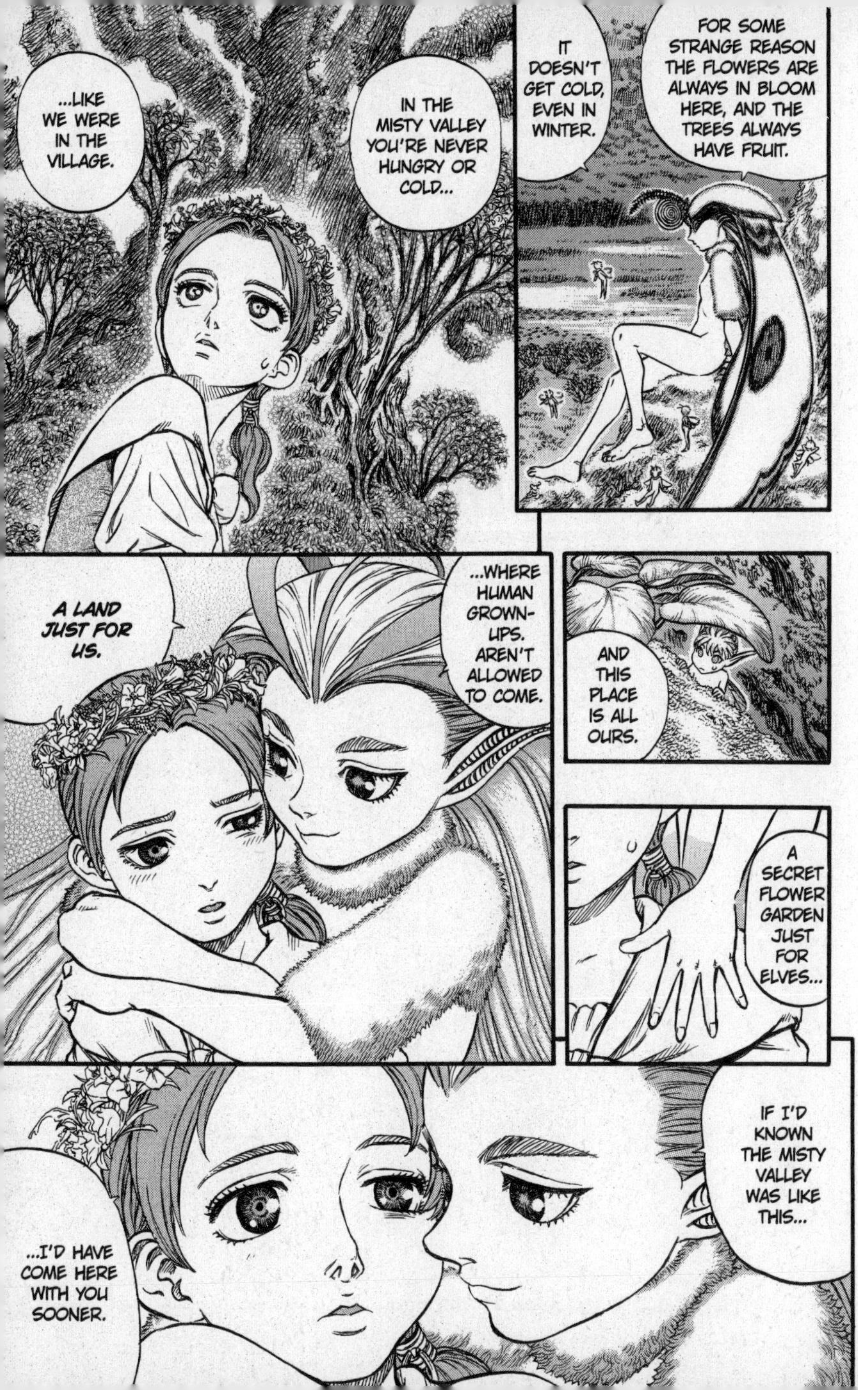
FOR SOME STRANGE REASON THE FLOWERS ARE ALWAYS IN BLOOM HERE, AND THE TREES ALWAYS HAVE FRUIT.
IT DOESN'T GET COLD, EVEN IN WINTER.
IN THE MISTY VALLEY YOU'RE NEVER HUNGRY OR COLD...
...LIKE WE WERE IN THE VILLAGE.
AND THIS PLACE IS ALL OURS.
A SECRET FLOWER GARDEN JUST FOR ELVES...
...WHERE HUMAN GROWN-UPS. AREN'T ALLOWED TO COME.
A LAND JUST FOR US.
IF I'D KNOWN THE MISTY VALLEY WAS LIKE THIS...
...I'D HAVE COME HERE WITH YOU SOONER.

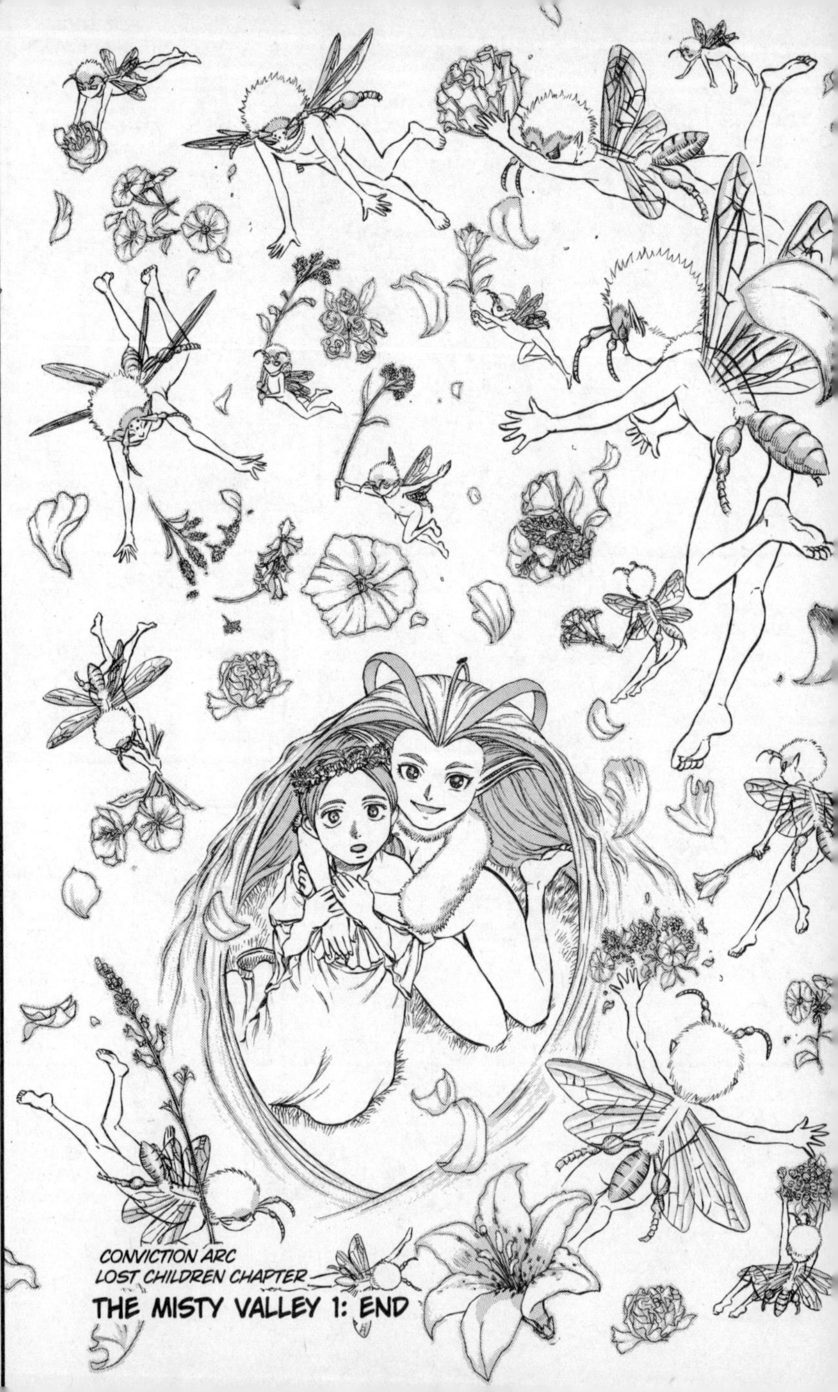
CONVICTION ARC
LOST CHILDREN CHAPTER
THE MISTY VALLEY 1: END

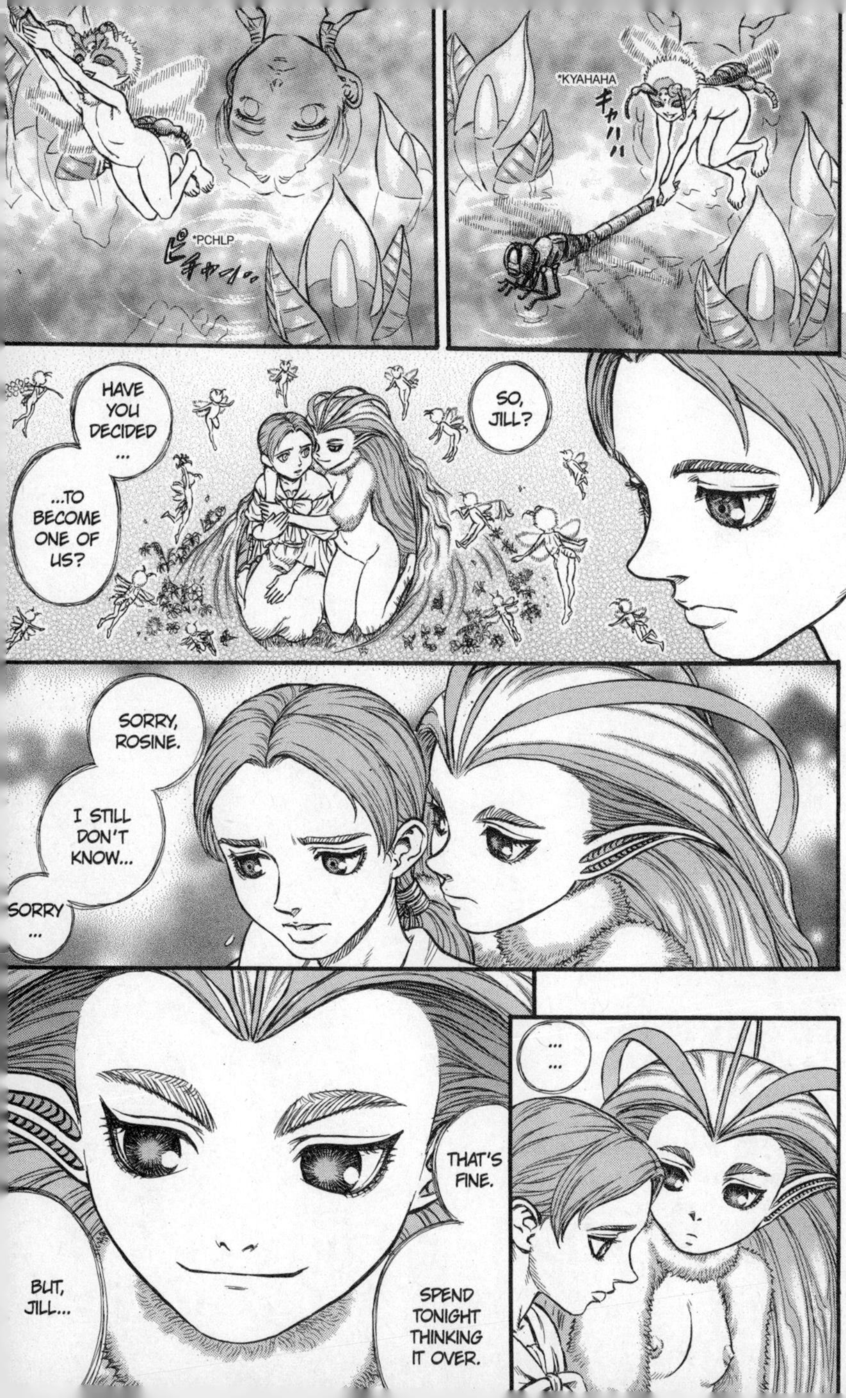
*KYAHAHA
ギャハハ
*PCHLP
SO, JILL?
HAVE YOU DECIDED ...
...TO BECOME ONE OF US?
SORRY, ROSINE.
I STILL DON'T KNOW...
SORRY ...
... ...
THAT'S FINE.
BUT, JILL...
SPEND TONIGHT THINKING IT OVER.

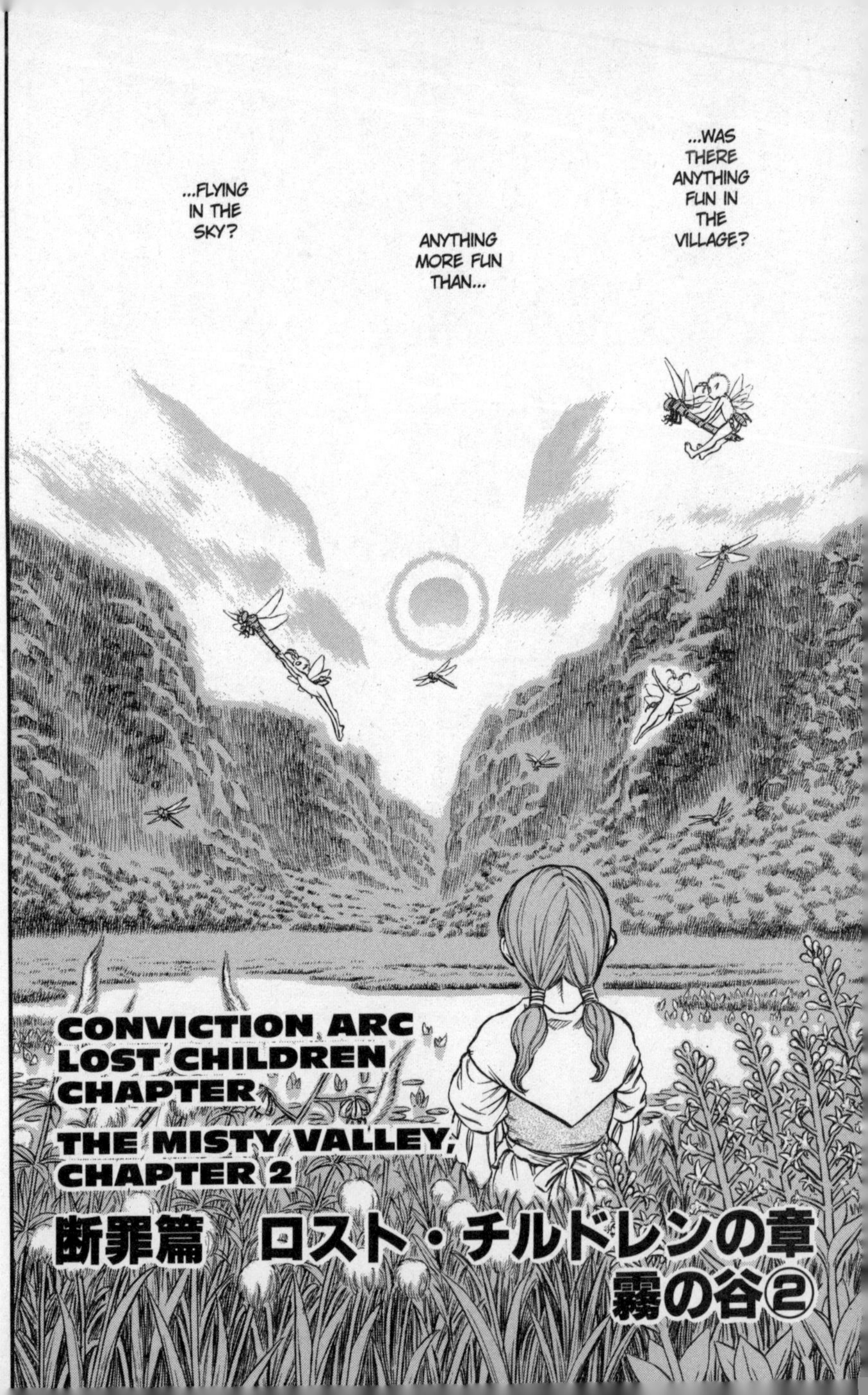
...WAS THERE ANYTHING FUN IN THE VILLAGE?
ANYTHING MORE FUN THAN...
...FLYING IN THE SKY?
CONVICTION ARC
LOST CHILDREN CHAPTER
THE MISTY VALLEY, CHAPTER 2
断罪篇　ロスト・チルドレンの章
霧の谷②

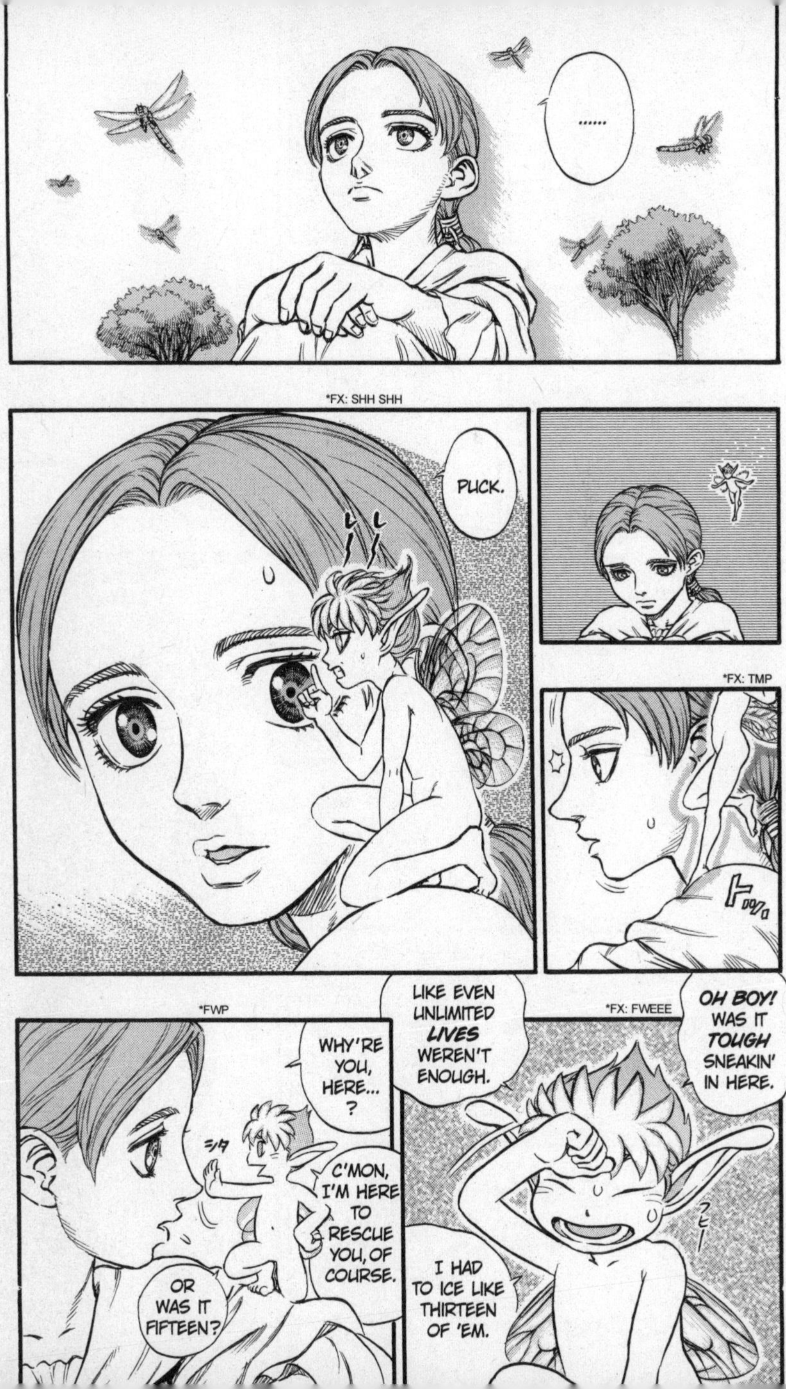
......
*FX: TMP
*FX: SHH SHH
PUCK.
OH BOY! WAS IT TOUGH SNEAKIN' IN HERE.
*FX: FWEEE
LIKE EVEN UNLIMITED LIVES WEREN'T ENOUGH.
I HAD TO ICE LIKE THIRTEEN OF 'EM.
*FWP
WHY'RE YOU, HERE... ?
C'MON, I'M HERE TO RESCUE YOU, OF COURSE.
OR WAS IT FIFTEEN?

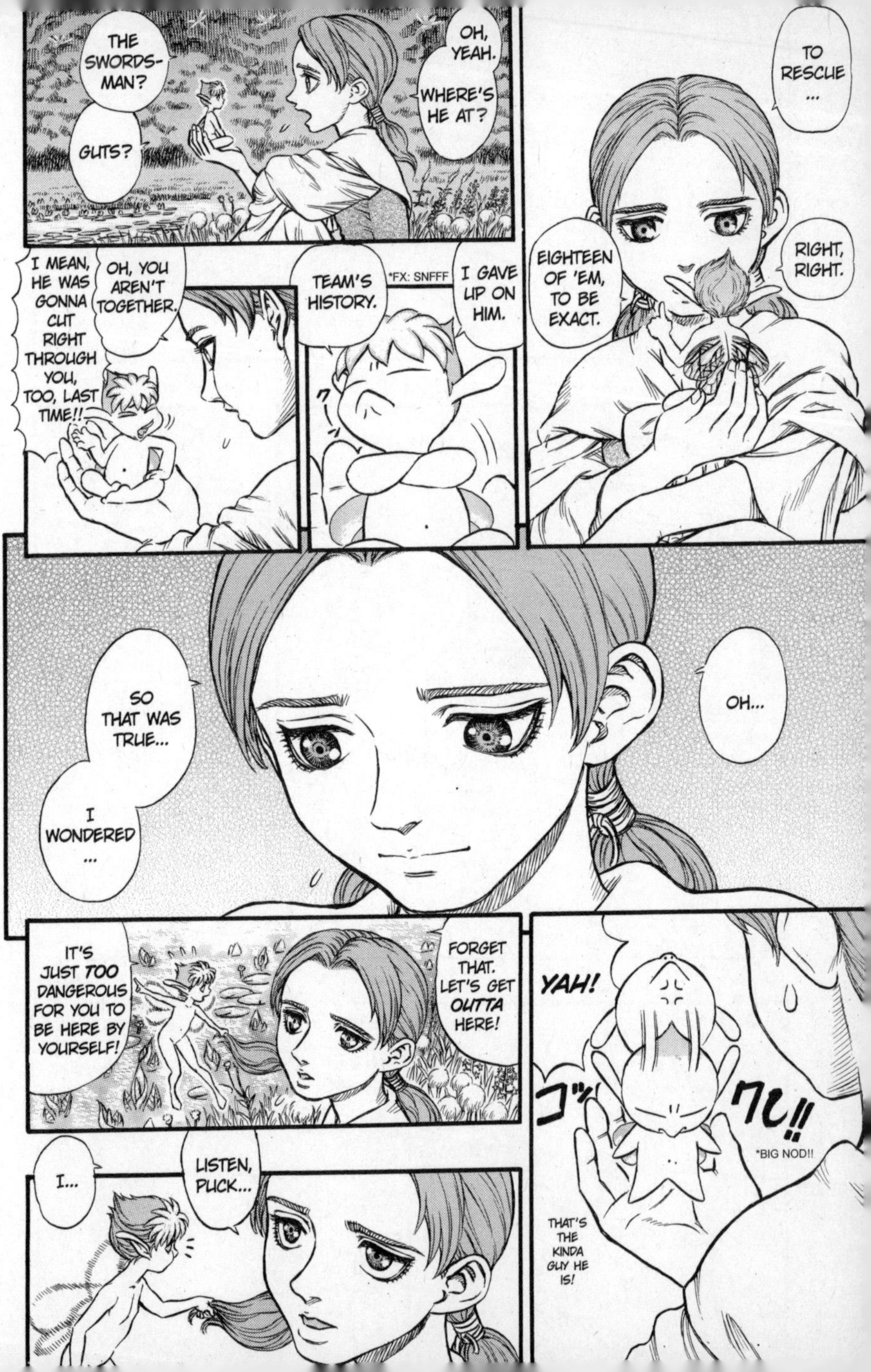
TO RESCUE ...
RIGHT, RIGHT.
EIGHTEEN OF 'EM, TO BE EXACT.
OH, YEAH. WHERE'S HE AT?
THE SWORDS-MAN?
GUTS?
I GAVE UP ON HIM.
*FX: SNFFF
TEAM'S HISTORY.
OH, YOU AREN'T TOGETHER.
I MEAN, HE WAS GONNA CUT RIGHT THROUGH YOU, TOO, LAST TIME!!
OH...
SO THAT WAS TRUE...
I WONDERED ...
YAH!
*BIG NOD!!
THAT'S THE KINDA GUY HE IS!
FORGET THAT. LET'S GET *OUTTA* HERE!
IT'S JUST *TOO* DANGEROUS FOR YOU TO BE HERE BY YOURSELF!
LISTEN, PUCK...
I...

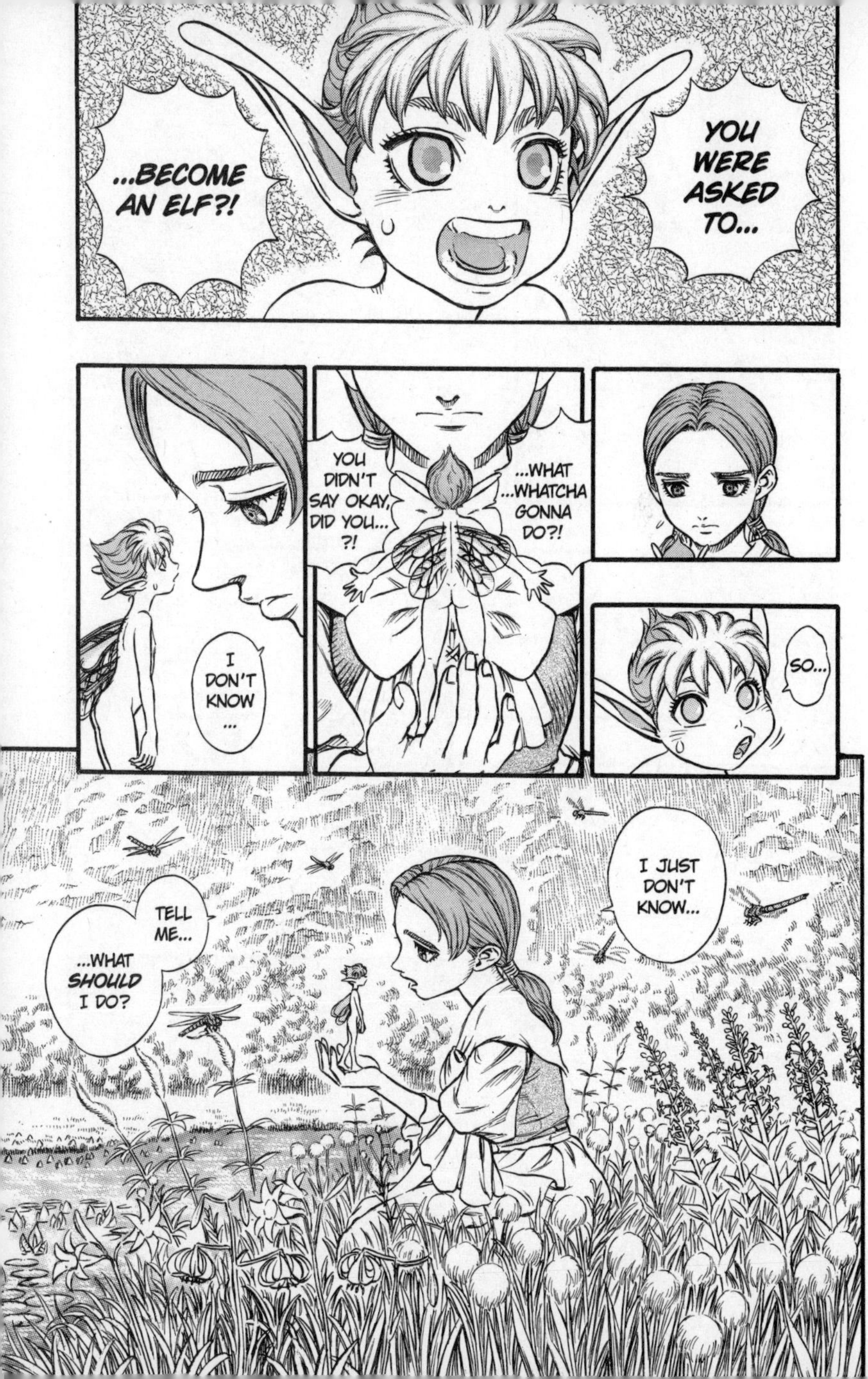
YOU WERE ASKED TO...
...BECOME AN ELF?!
SO...
...WHAT ...WHATCHA GONNA DO?!
YOU DIDN'T SAY OKAY, DID YOU...?!
I DON'T KNOW...
I JUST DON'T KNOW...
TELL ME...
...WHAT SHOULD I DO?

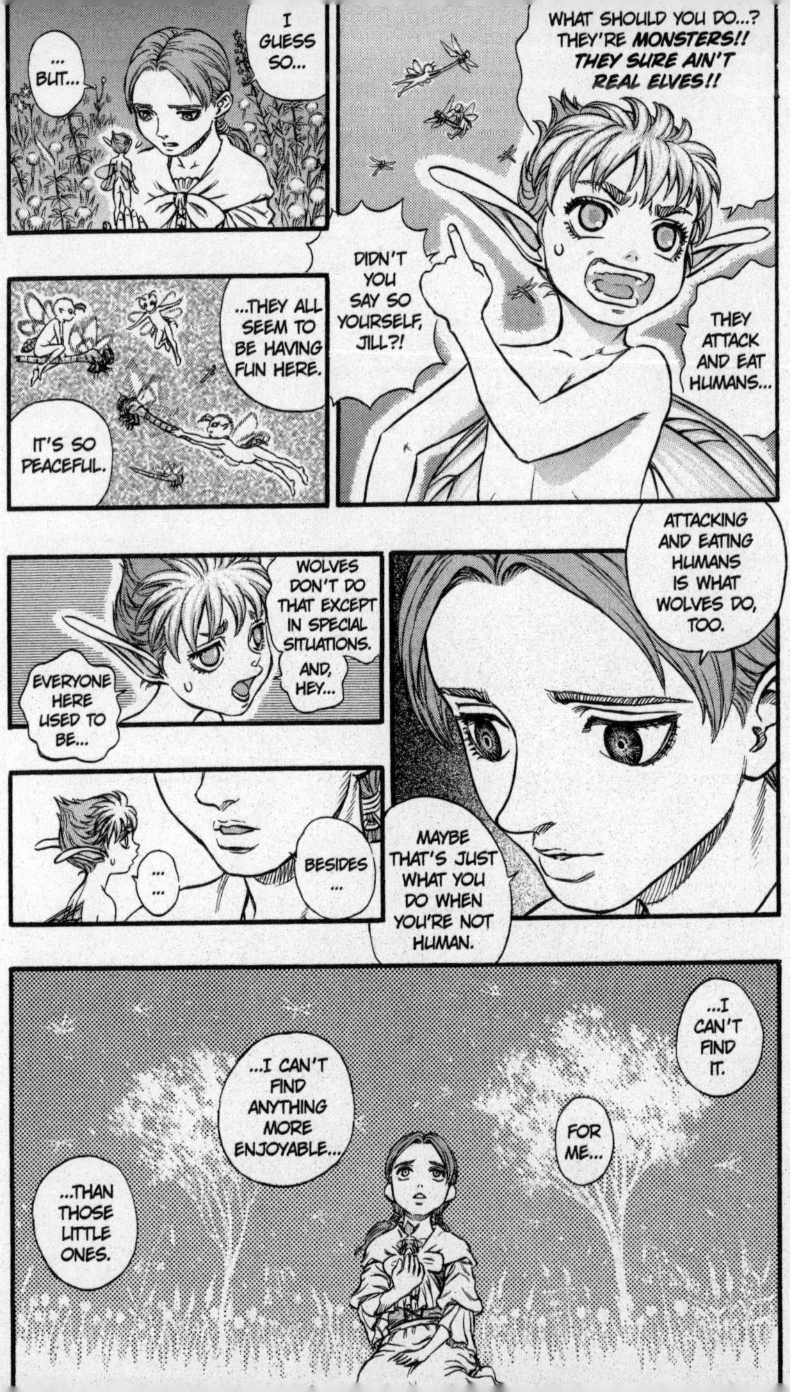
WHAT SHOULD YOU DO...? THEY'RE ***MONSTERS!! THEY SURE AIN'T REAL ELVES!!***
THEY ATTACK AND EAT HUMANS...
DIDN'T YOU SAY SO YOURSELF, JILL?!
I GUESS SO...
... BUT...
...THEY ALL SEEM TO BE HAVING FUN HERE.
IT'S SO PEACEFUL.
ATTACKING AND EATING HUMANS IS WHAT WOLVES DO, TOO.
MAYBE THAT'S JUST WHAT YOU DO WHEN YOU'RE NOT HUMAN.
WOLVES DON'T DO THAT EXCEPT IN SPECIAL SITUATIONS.
AND, HEY...
EVERYONE HERE USED TO BE...
BESIDES ...
... ...
...I CAN'T FIND IT.
FOR ME...
...I CAN'T FIND ANYTHING MORE ENJOYABLE...
...THAN THOSE LITTLE ONES.

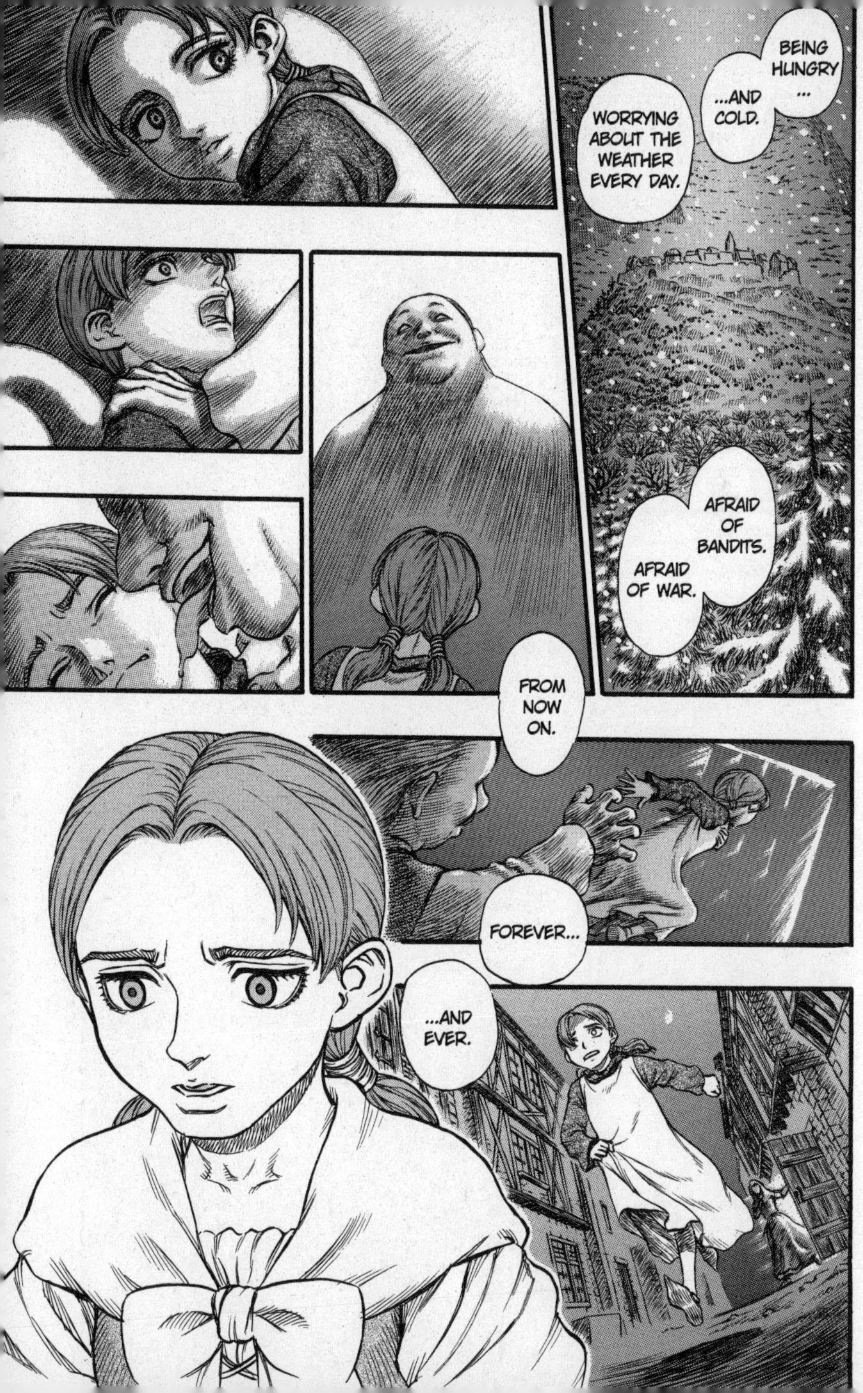
BEING HUNGRY ...
...AND COLD.
WORRYING ABOUT THE WEATHER EVERY DAY.
AFRAID OF BANDITS.
AFRAID OF WAR.
FROM NOW ON.
FOREVER...
...AND EVER.

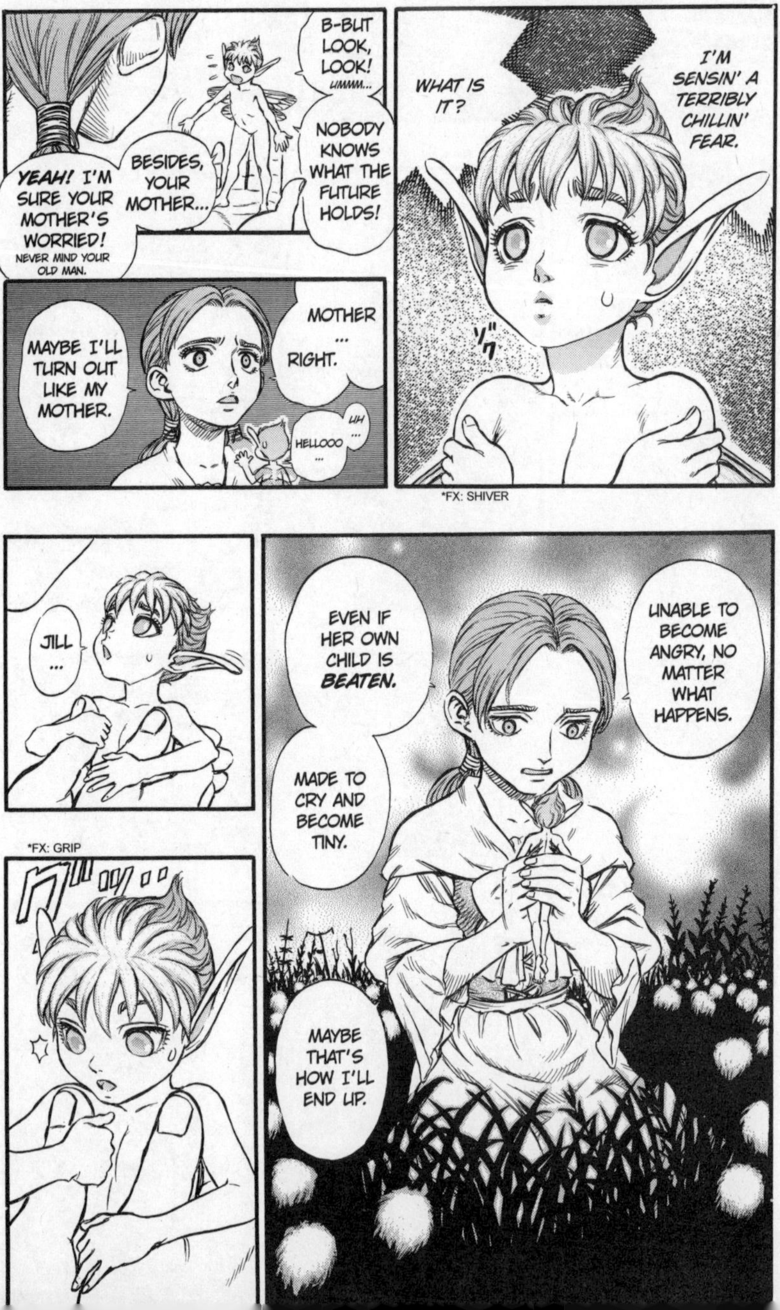

I'M SENSIN' A TERRIBLY CHILLIN' FEAR.
WHAT IS IT?
B-BUT LOOK, LOOK! UMMM...
NOBODY KNOWS WHAT THE FUTURE HOLDS!
BESIDES, YOUR MOTHER...
YEAH! I'M SURE YOUR MOTHER'S WORRIED! NEVER MIND YOUR OLD MAN.
MOTHER ... RIGHT.
MAYBE I'LL TURN OUT LIKE MY MOTHER.
UH ... HELLOOO ...
*FX: SHIVER
UNABLE TO BECOME ANGRY, NO MATTER WHAT HAPPENS.
EVEN IF HER OWN CHILD IS BEATEN.
MADE TO CRY AND BECOME TINY.
MAYBE THAT'S HOW I'LL END UP.
JILL ...
*FX: GRIP

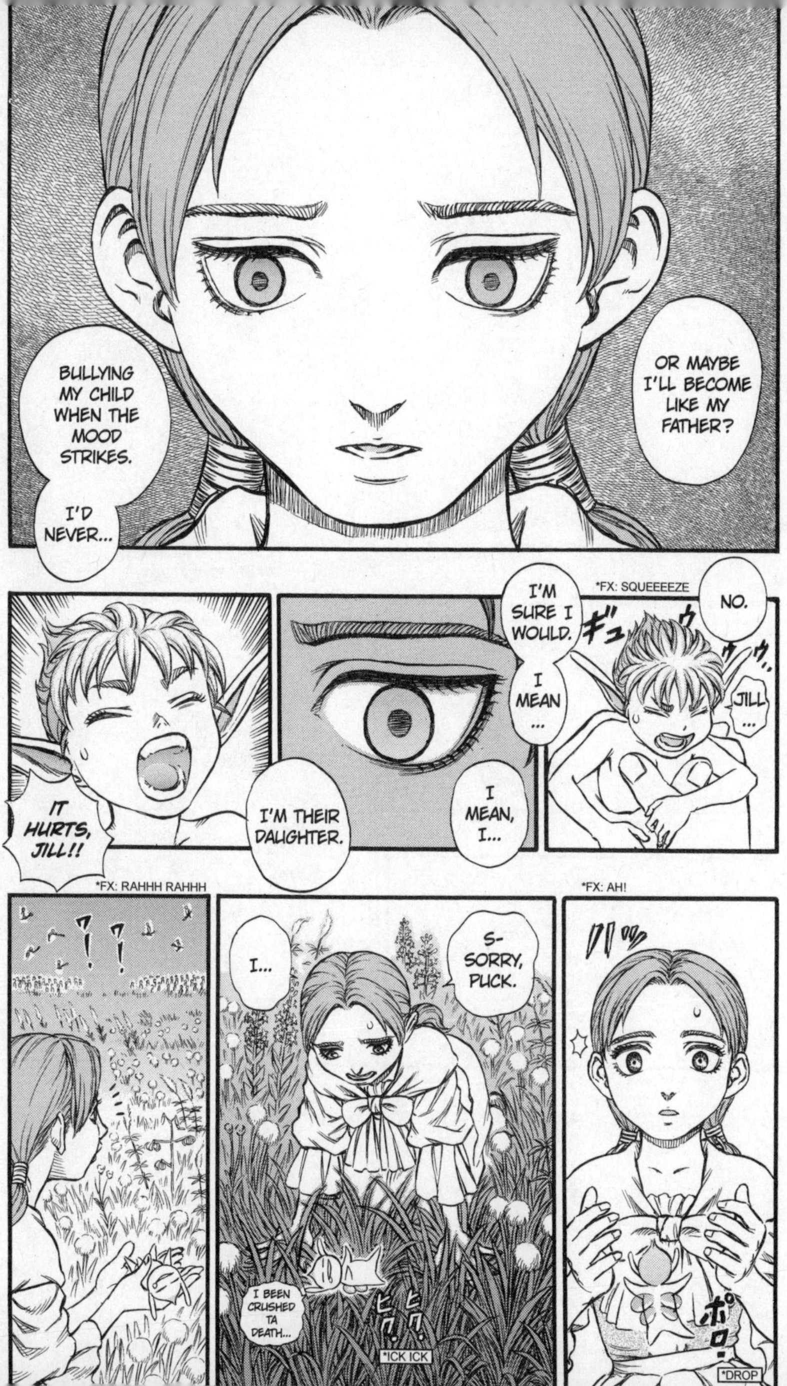
OR MAYBE I'LL BECOME LIKE MY FATHER?
BULLYING MY CHILD WHEN THE MOOD STRIKES.
I'D NEVER...
*FX: SQUEEEEZE
ギュウウウ
NO.
I'M SURE I WOULD.
I MEAN ...
JILL ...
I MEAN, I...
I'M THEIR DAUGHTER.
IT HURTS, JILL!!
*FX: AH!
ハッ
ポロ
*DROP
S-SORRY, PUCK.
I...
I BEEN CRUSHED TA DEATH...
ヒク ヒク
*ICK ICK
*FX: RAHHH RAHHH
ワー！ ワー！

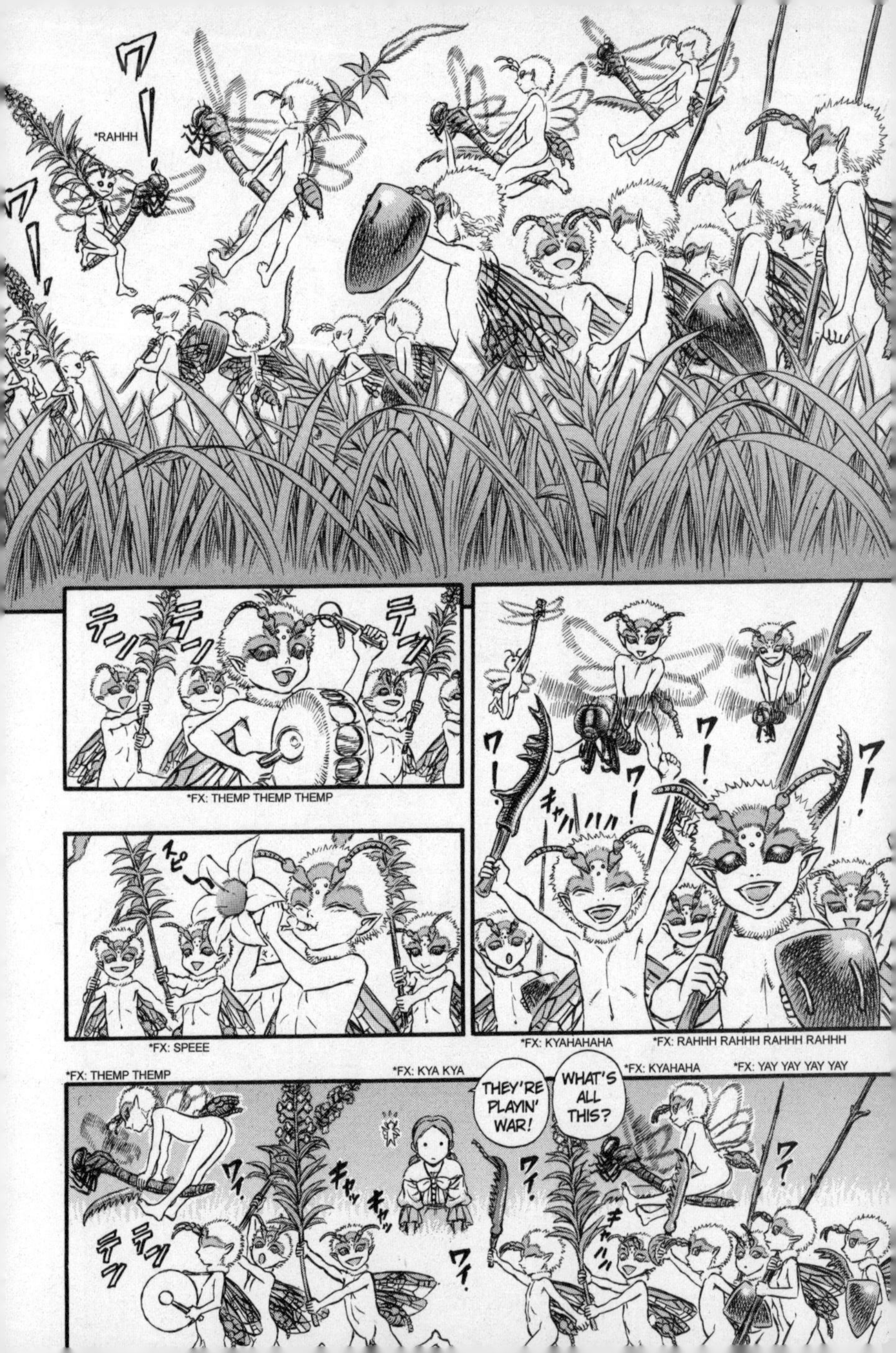
*RAHHH
*FX: KYAHAHAHA
*FX: RAHHH RAHHH RAHHH RAHHH
*FX: THEMP THEMP THEMP
*FX: SPEEE
*FX: YAY YAY YAY YAY
*FX: KYAHAHA
*FX: KYA KYA
*FX: THEMP THEMP
WHAT'S ALL THIS?
THEY'RE PLAYIN' WAR!

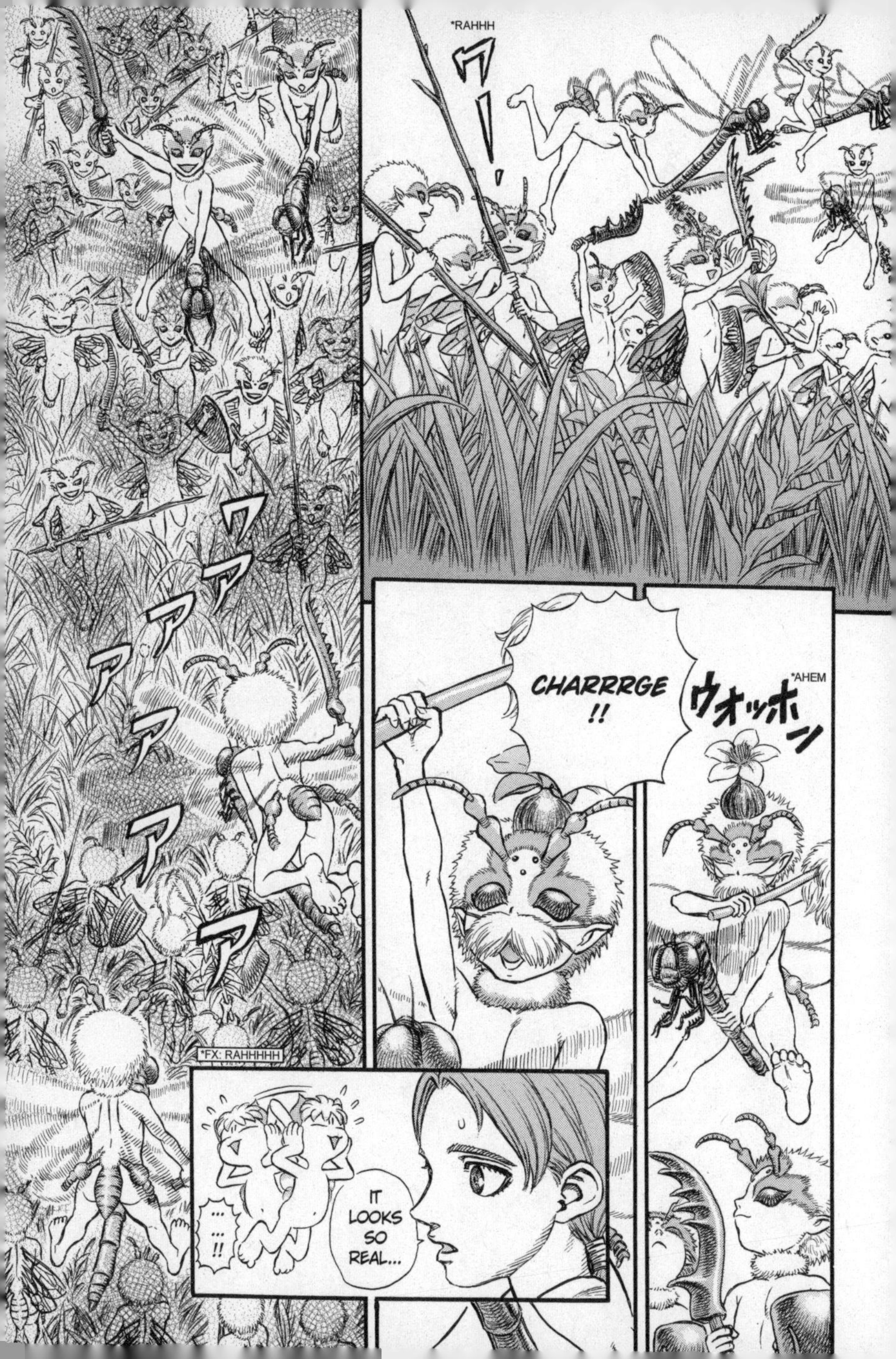
ワー！
*RAHHH
ウオッホン
*AHEM
CHARRRGE !!
IT LOOKS SO REAL...
......!!
ワアアアアアア
*FX: RAHHHHH

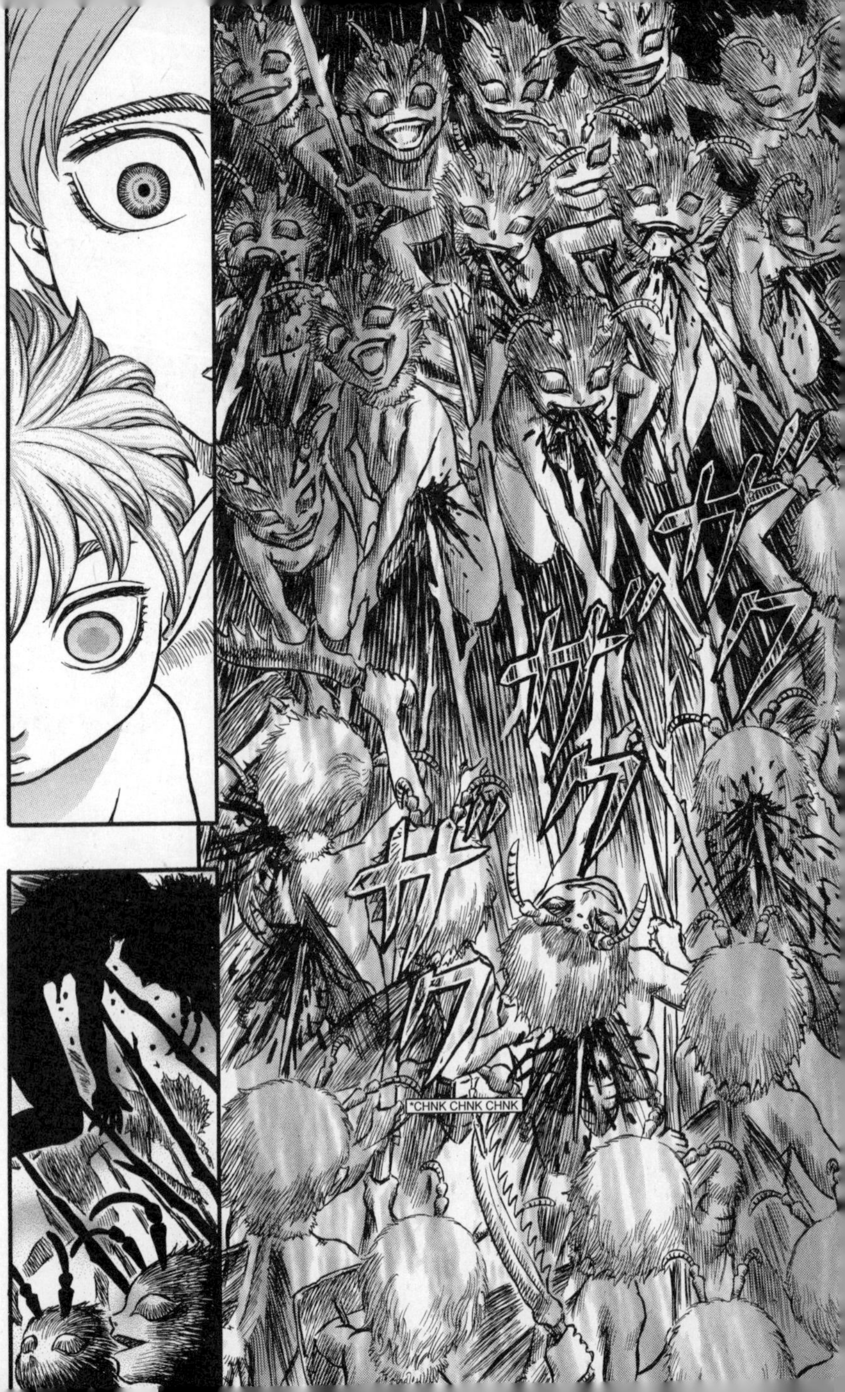
*CHNK CHNK CHNK

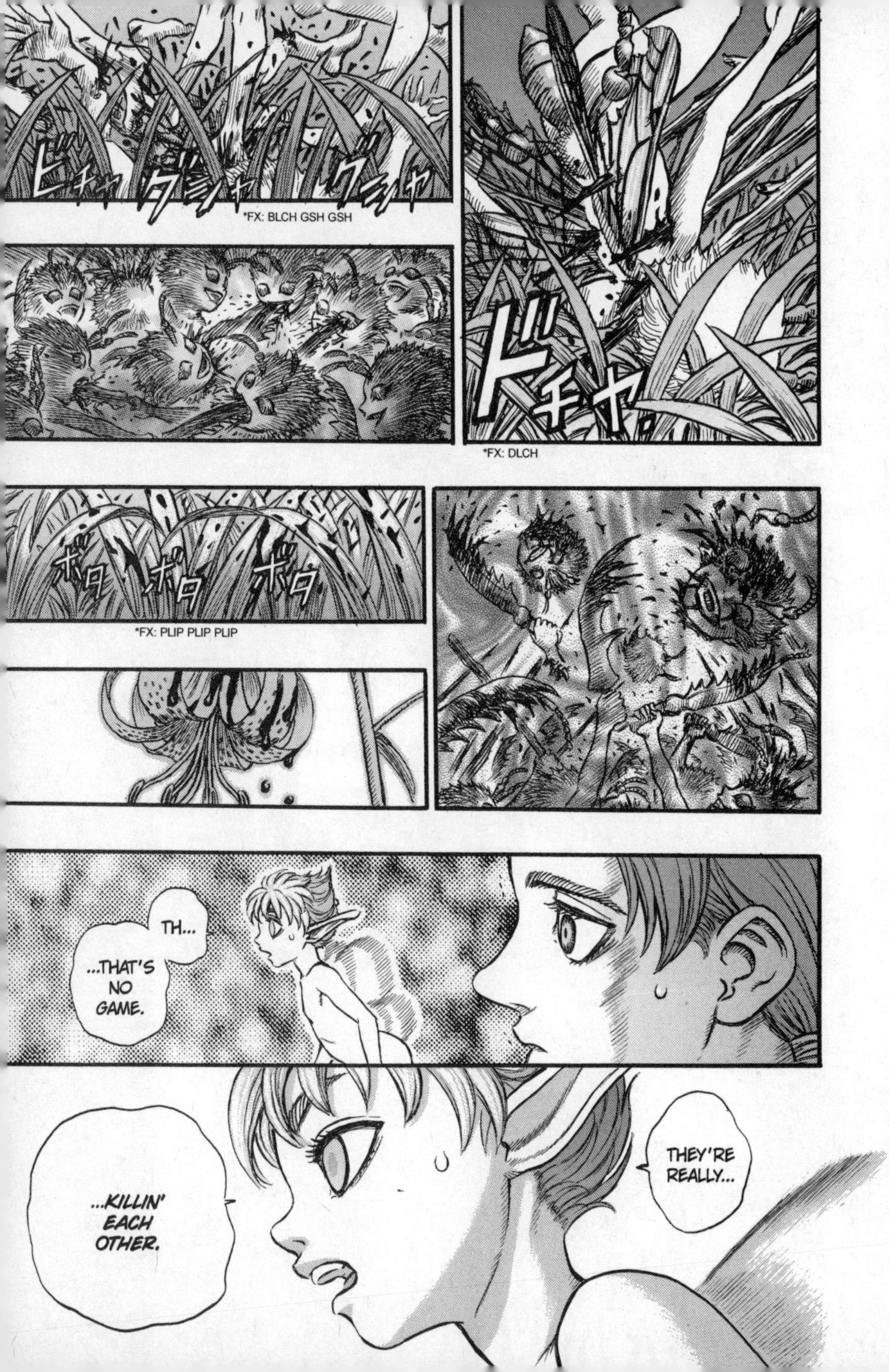
ドチャ
*FX: DLCH
ビチャ グシャ グシャ
*FX: BLCH GSH GSH
ボタ ボタ ボタ
*FX: PLIP PLIP PLIP
TH...
...THAT'S NO GAME.
THEY'RE REALLY...
...KILLIN' EACH OTHER.

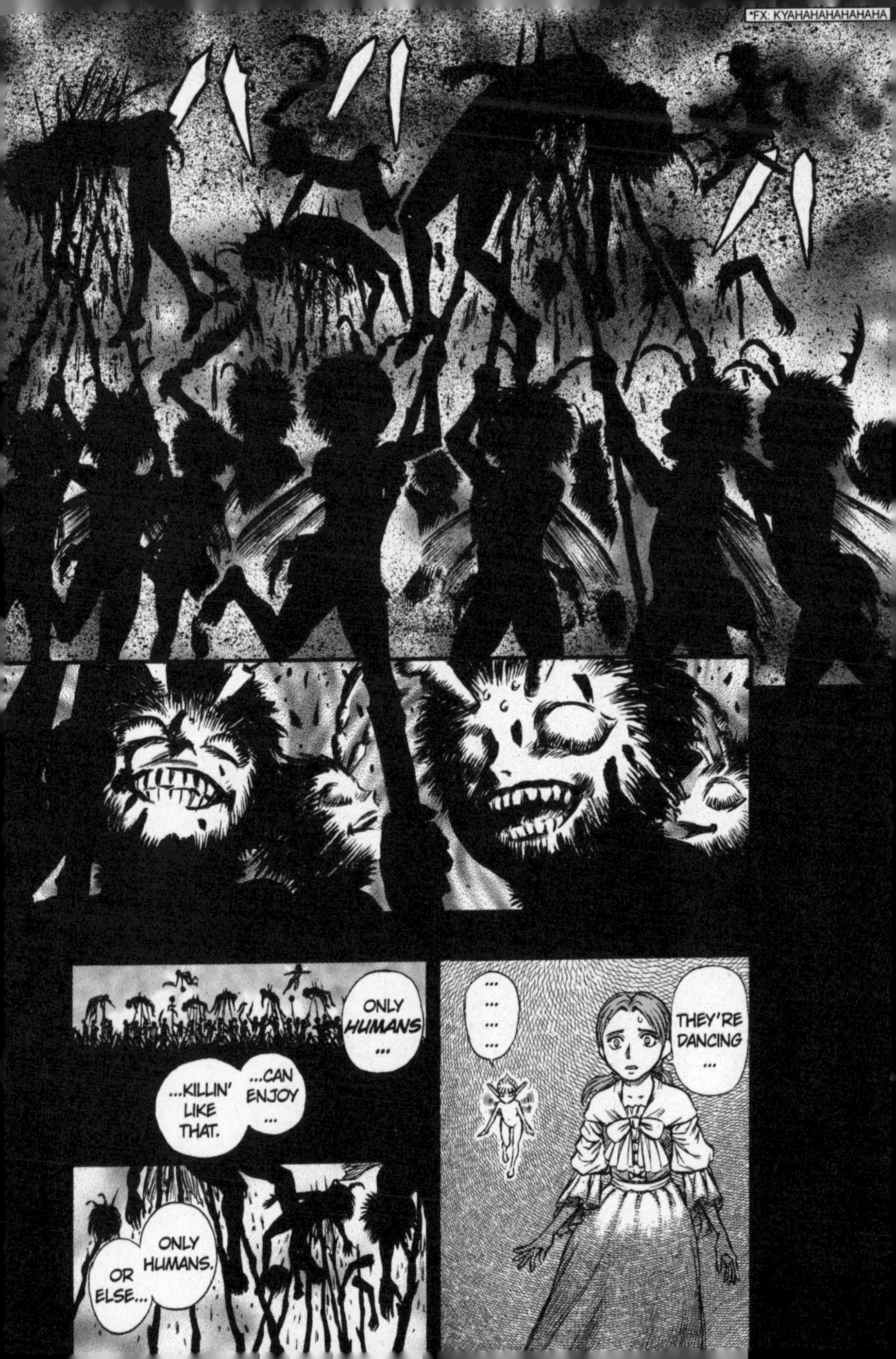
*FX: KYAHAHAHAHAHAHA
THEY'RE DANCING ...
...
...
...
...
ONLY HUMANS ...
...CAN ENJOY ...
...KILLIN' LIKE THAT.
ONLY HUMANS.
OR ELSE...

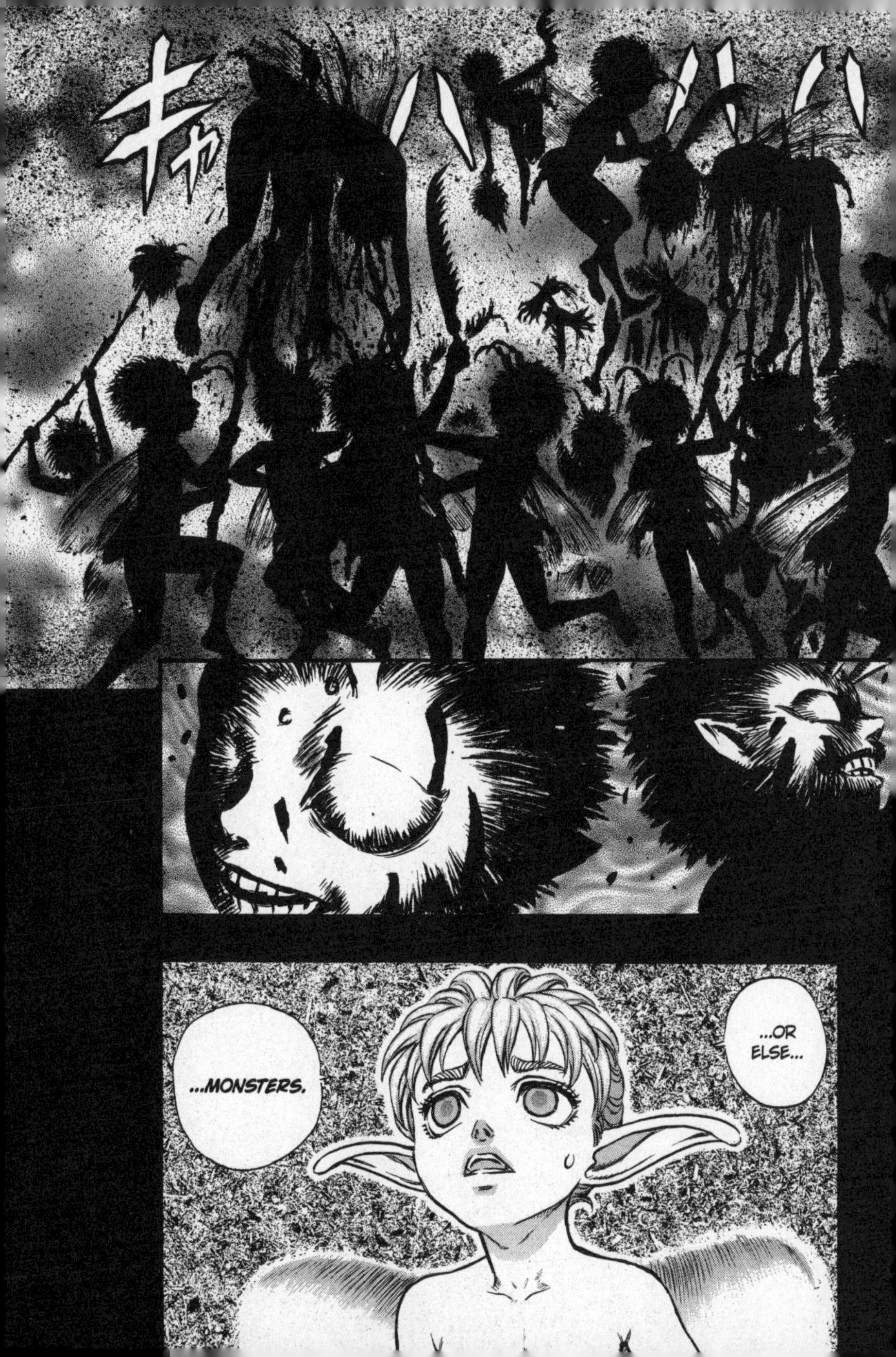
キャハハハ
...OR ELSE...
...MONSTERS.

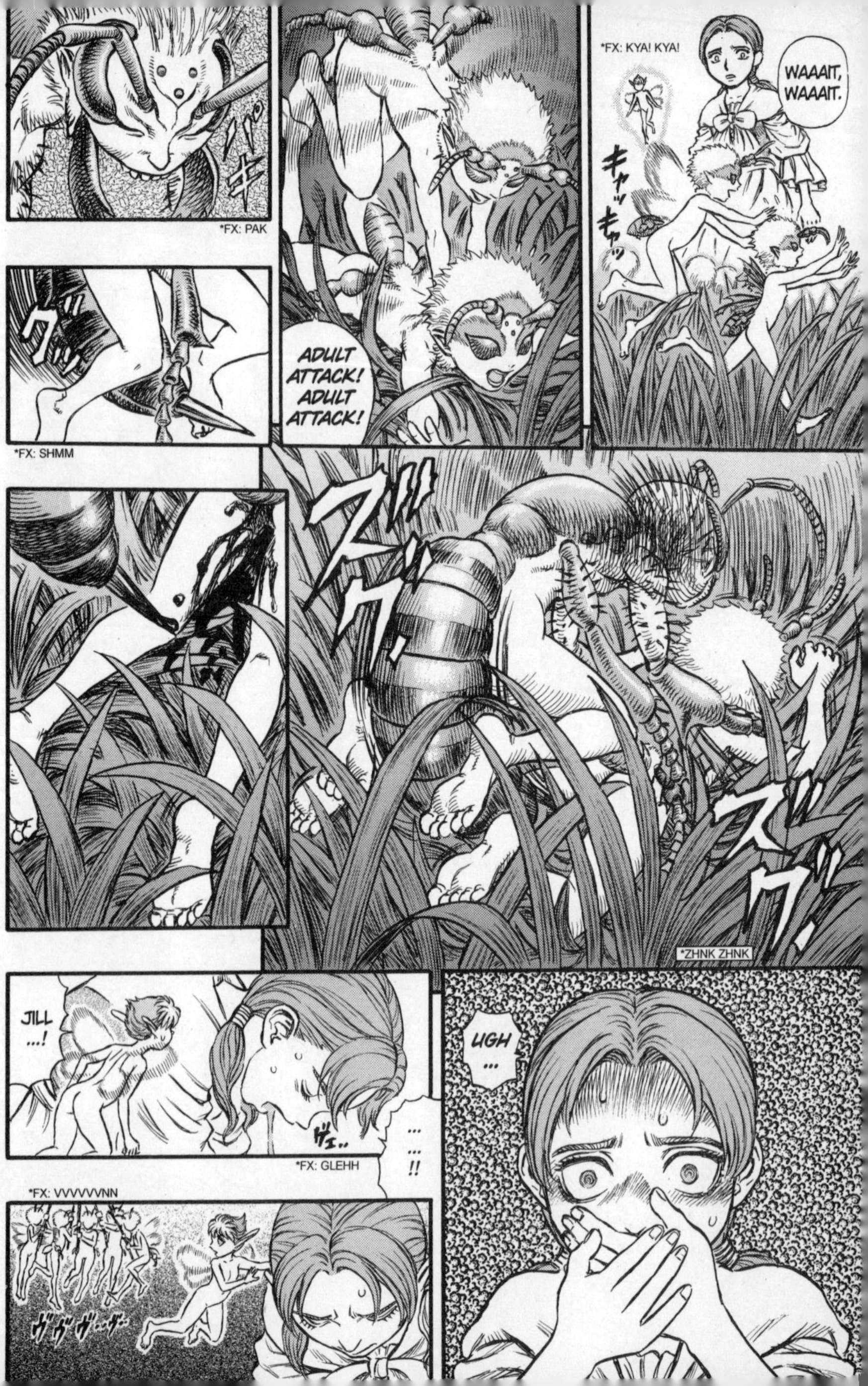
*FX: KYA! KYA!
WAAAIT, WAAAIT.
ADULT ATTACK! ADULT ATTACK!
*FX: PAK
*FX: SHMM
*ZHNK ZHNK
UGH ...
JILL ...!
*FX: GLEHH
... ... !!
*FX: VVVVVVNN

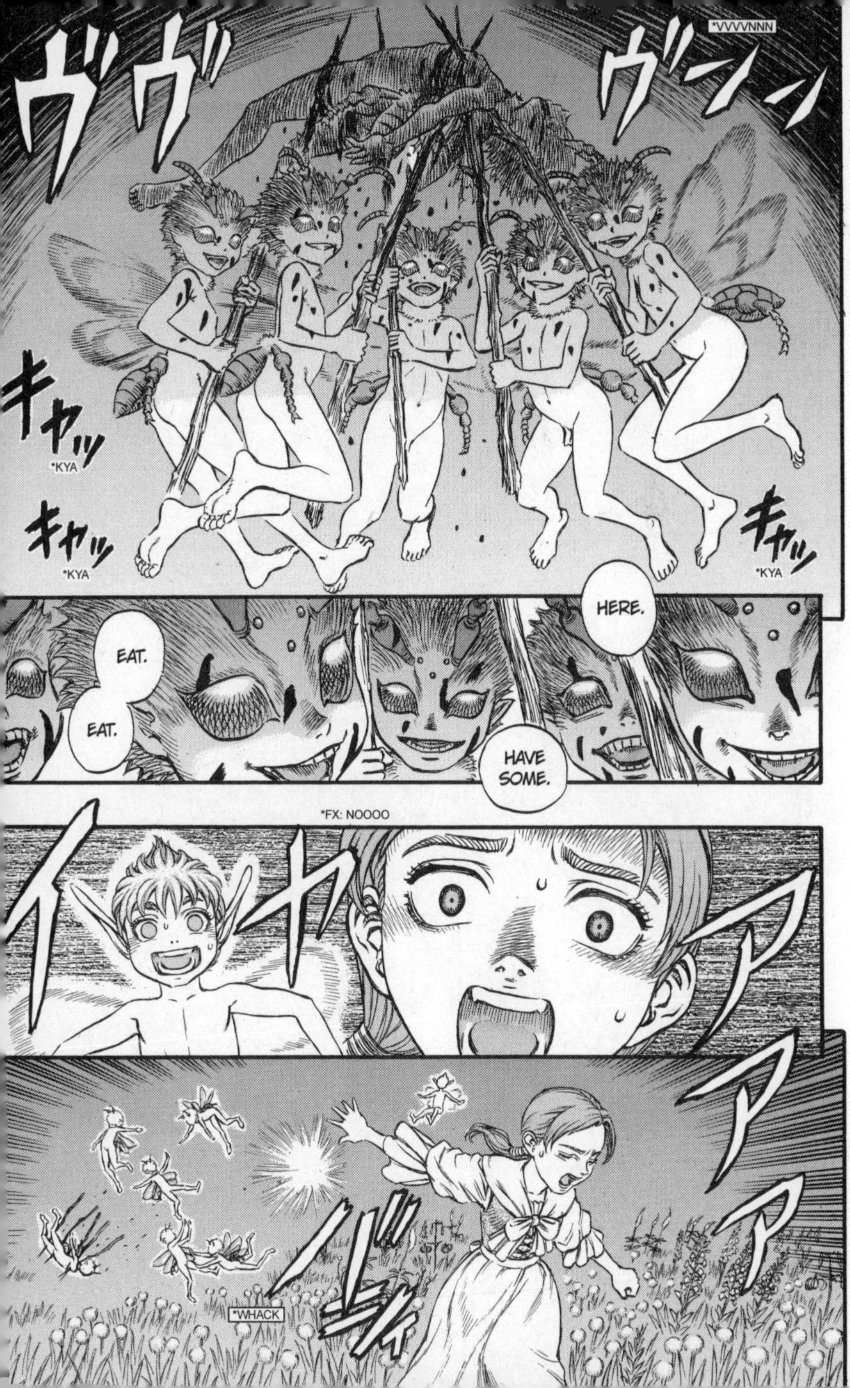
*VVVVNNN
*KYA
*KYA
*KYA
HERE.
HAVE SOME.
EAT.
EAT.
*FX: NOOOO
*WHACK

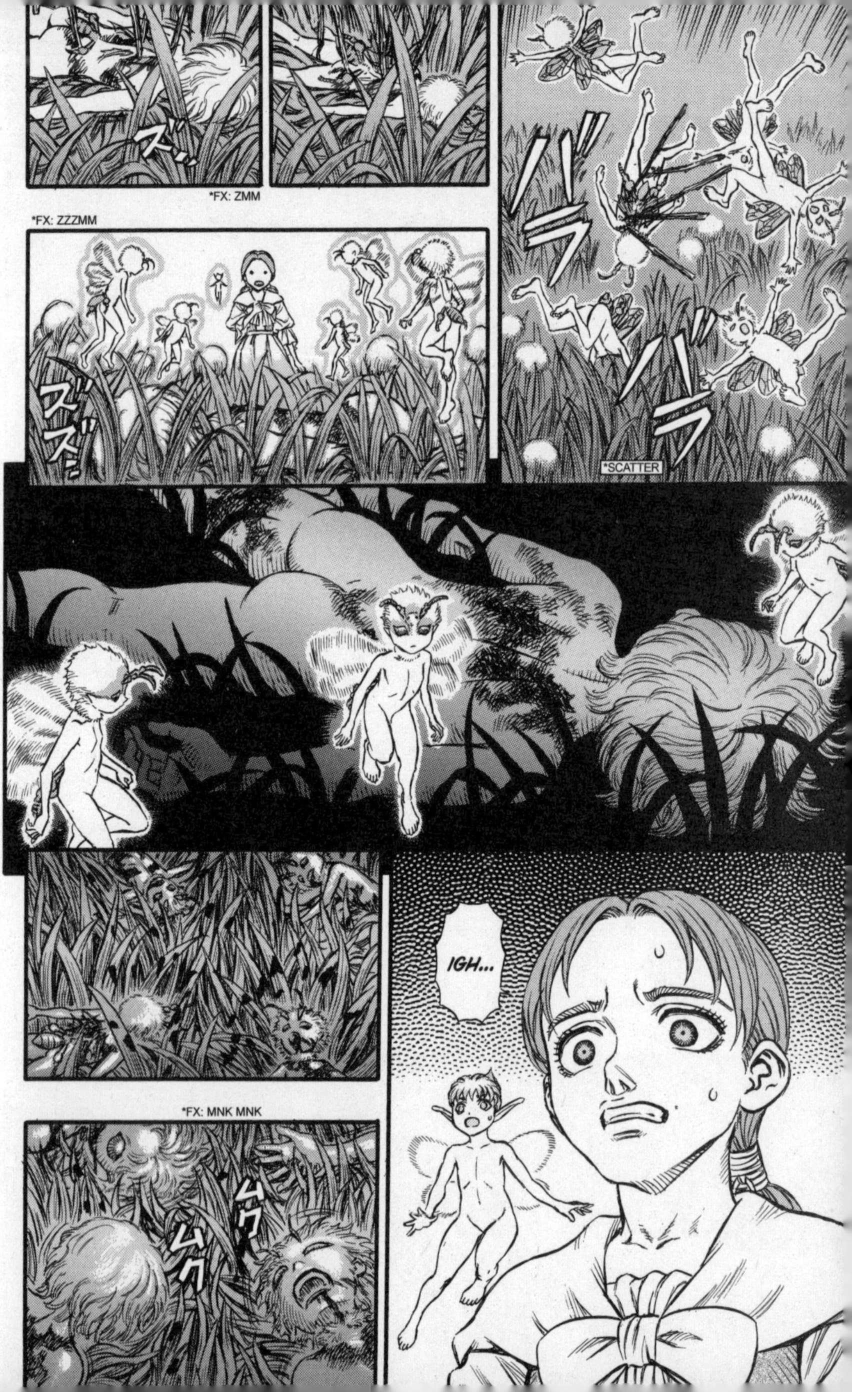
バラ
バラ
*SCATTER
ズ..
*FX: ZMM
ズズズ..
*FX: ZZZMM
IGH...
ムク
ムク
*FX: MNK MNK

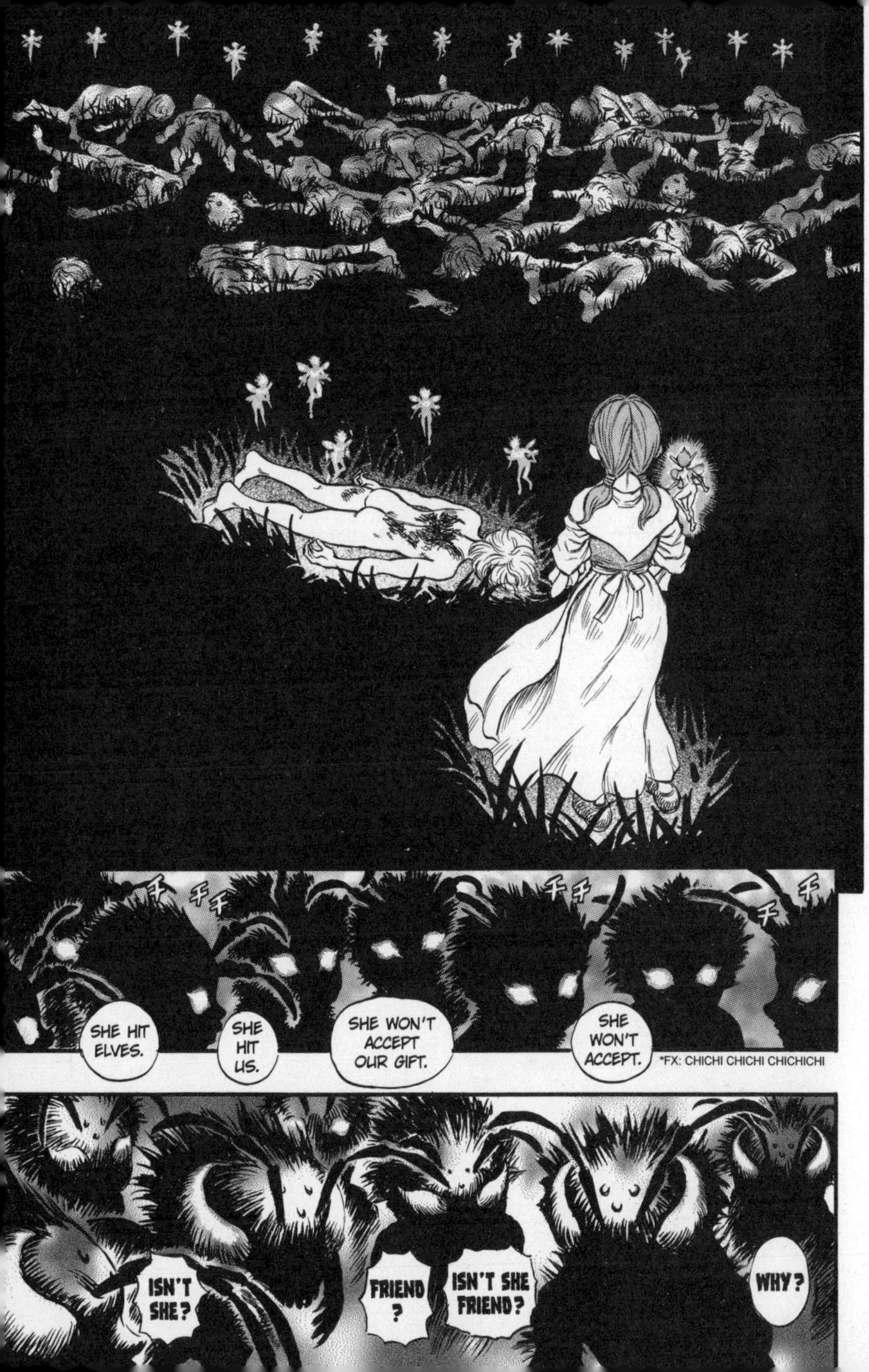
SHE WON'T ACCEPT.
SHE WON'T ACCEPT OUR GIFT.
SHE HIT US.
SHE HIT ELVES.
*FX: CHICHI CHICHI CHICHICHI
WHY?
ISN'T SHE FRIEND?
FRIEND ?
ISN'T SHE?

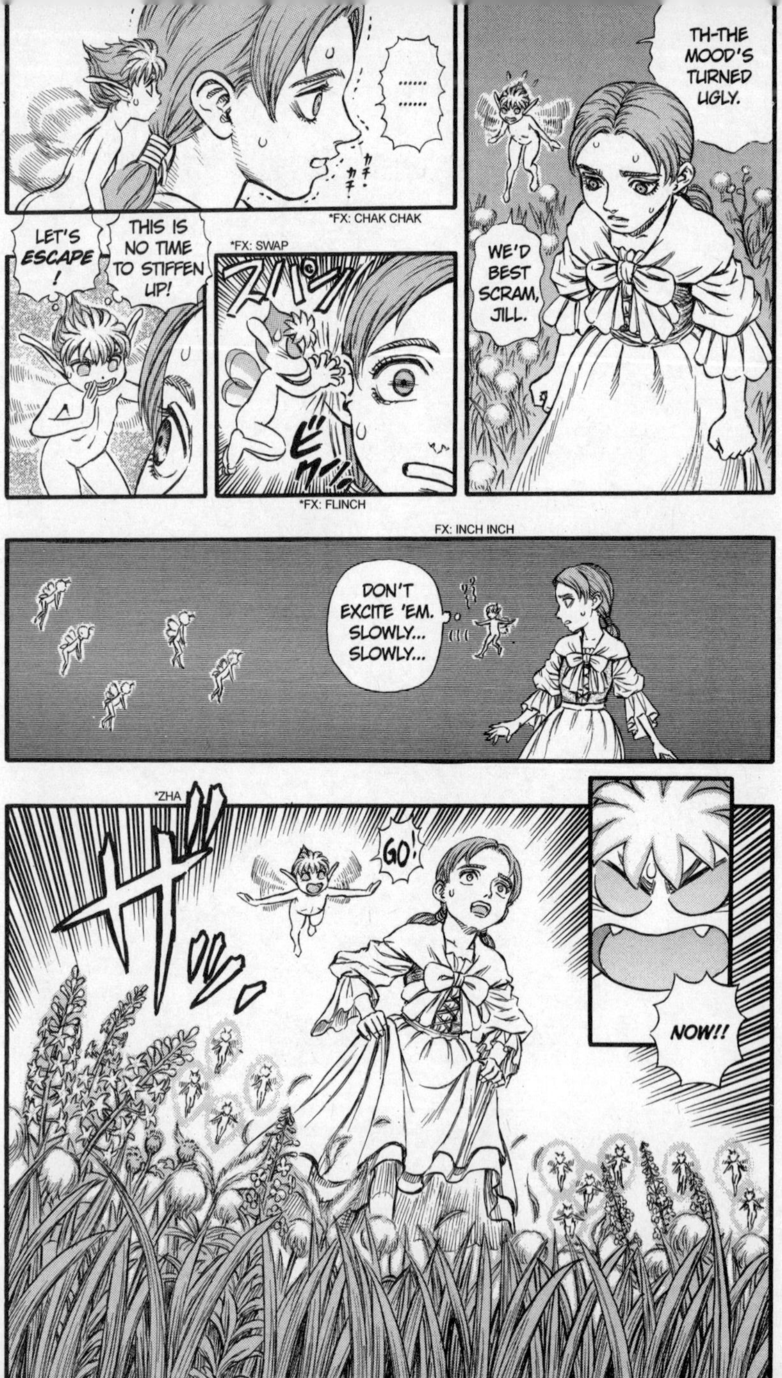
TH-THE MOOD'S TURNED UGLY.
WE'D BEST SCRAM, JILL.
....
カチ カチ
*FX: CHAK CHAK
*FX: SWAP
*FX: FLINCH
THIS IS NO TIME TO STIFFEN UP!
LET'S *ESCAPE*!
FX: INCH INCH
DON'T EXCITE 'EM. SLOWLY... SLOWLY...
NOW!!
GO!
*ZHA

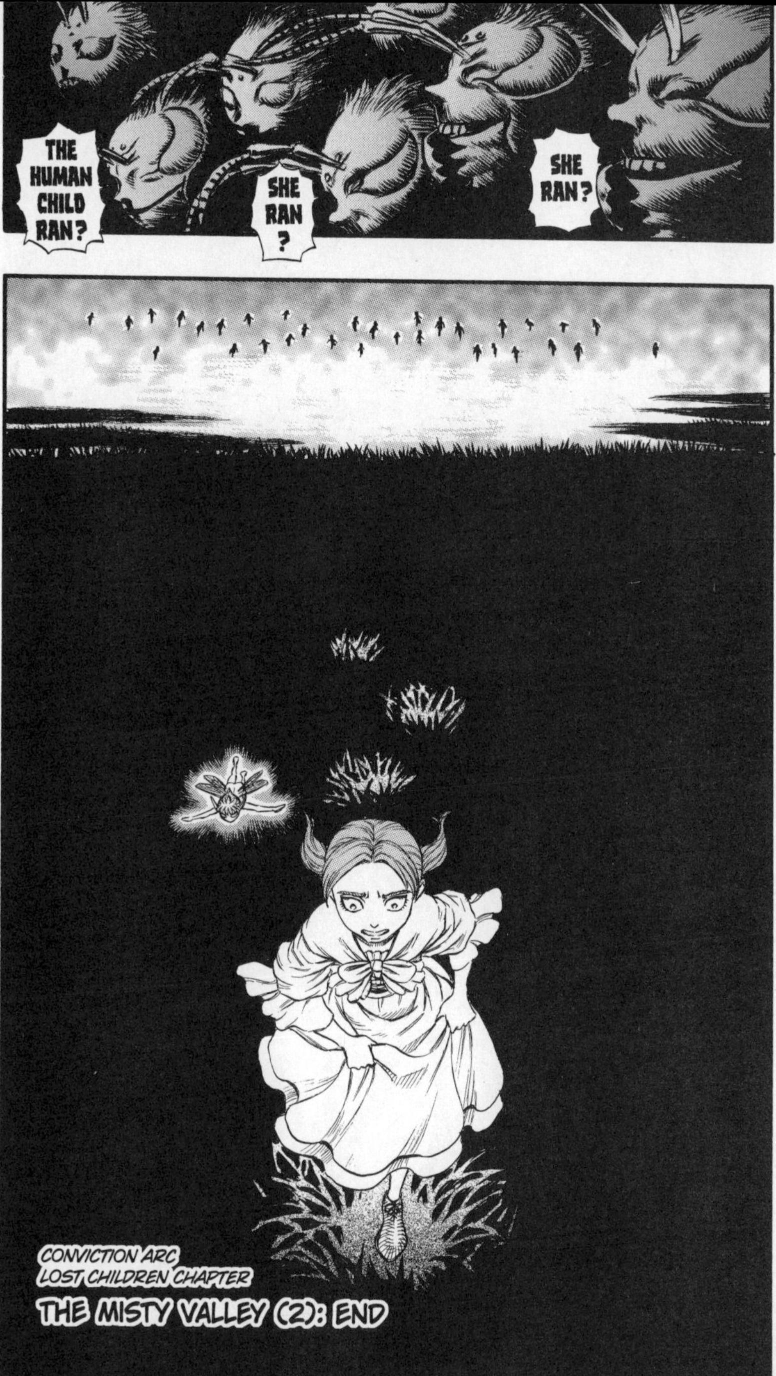
SHE RAN?
SHE RAN ?
THE HUMAN CHILD RAN?
CONVICTION ARC
LOST CHILDREN CHAPTER
THE MISTY VALLEY (2): END

BERSERK

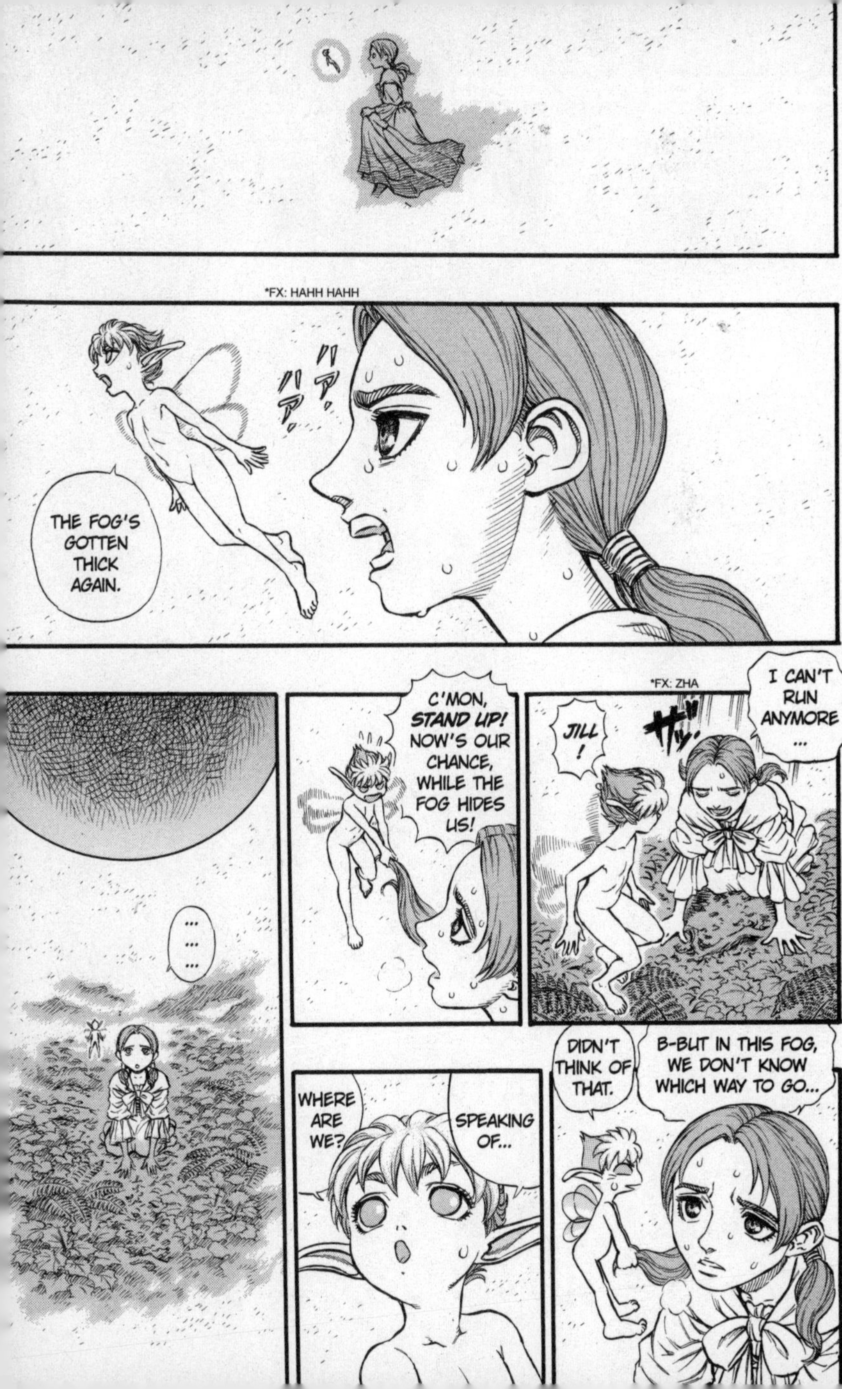
*FX: HAHH HAHH
ハア ハア
THE FOG'S GOTTEN THICK AGAIN.
*FX: ZHA
I CAN'T RUN ANYMORE ...
ザッ
JILL !
C'MON, **STAND UP!** NOW'S OUR CHANCE, WHILE THE FOG HIDES US!
B-BUT IN THIS FOG, WE DON'T KNOW WHICH WAY TO GO...
DIDN'T THINK OF THAT.
SPEAKING OF...
WHERE ARE WE?
... ...

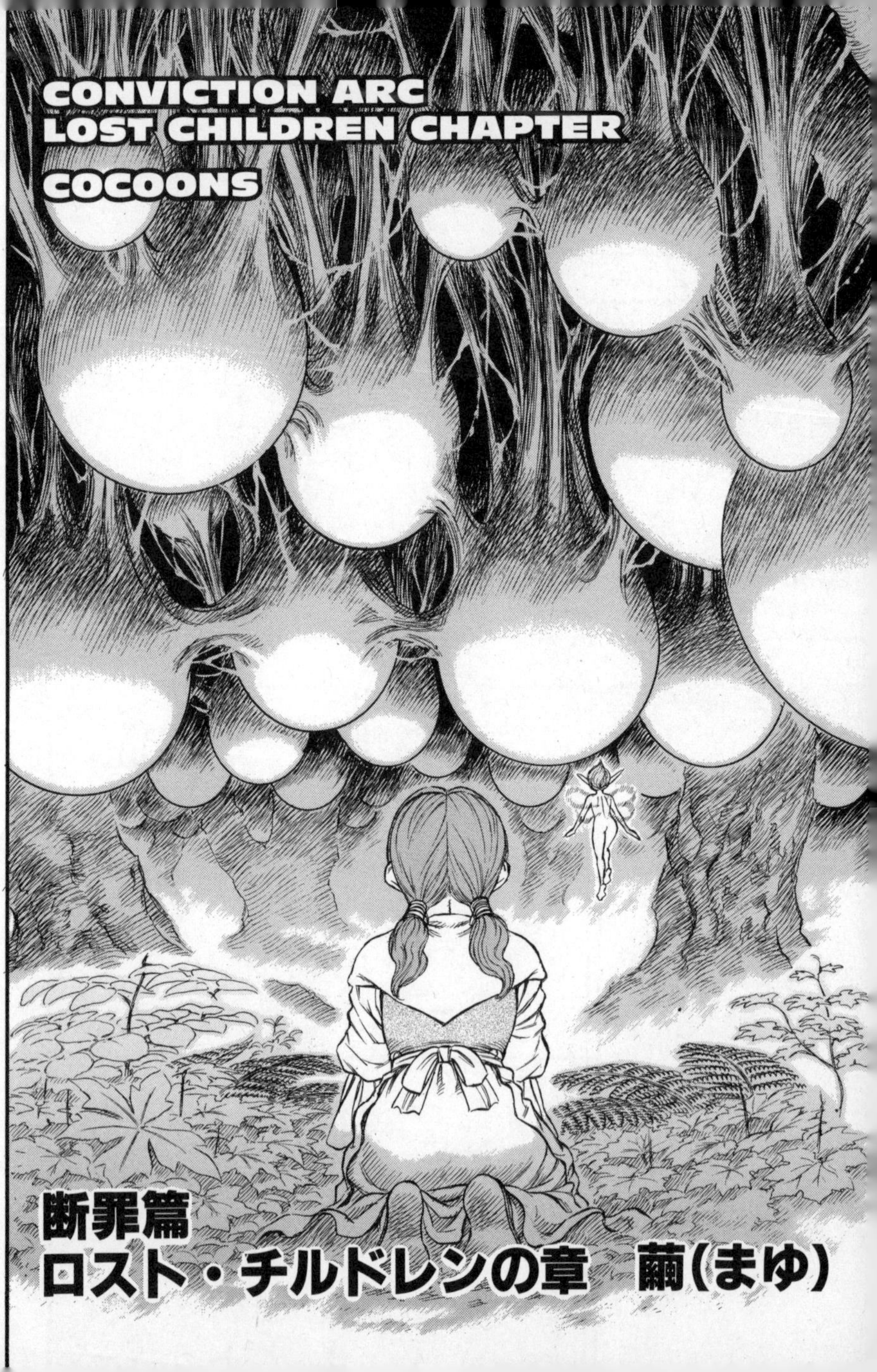
CONVICTION ARC
LOST CHILDREN CHAPTER
COCOONS
断罪篇
ロスト・チルドレンの章　繭(まゆ)

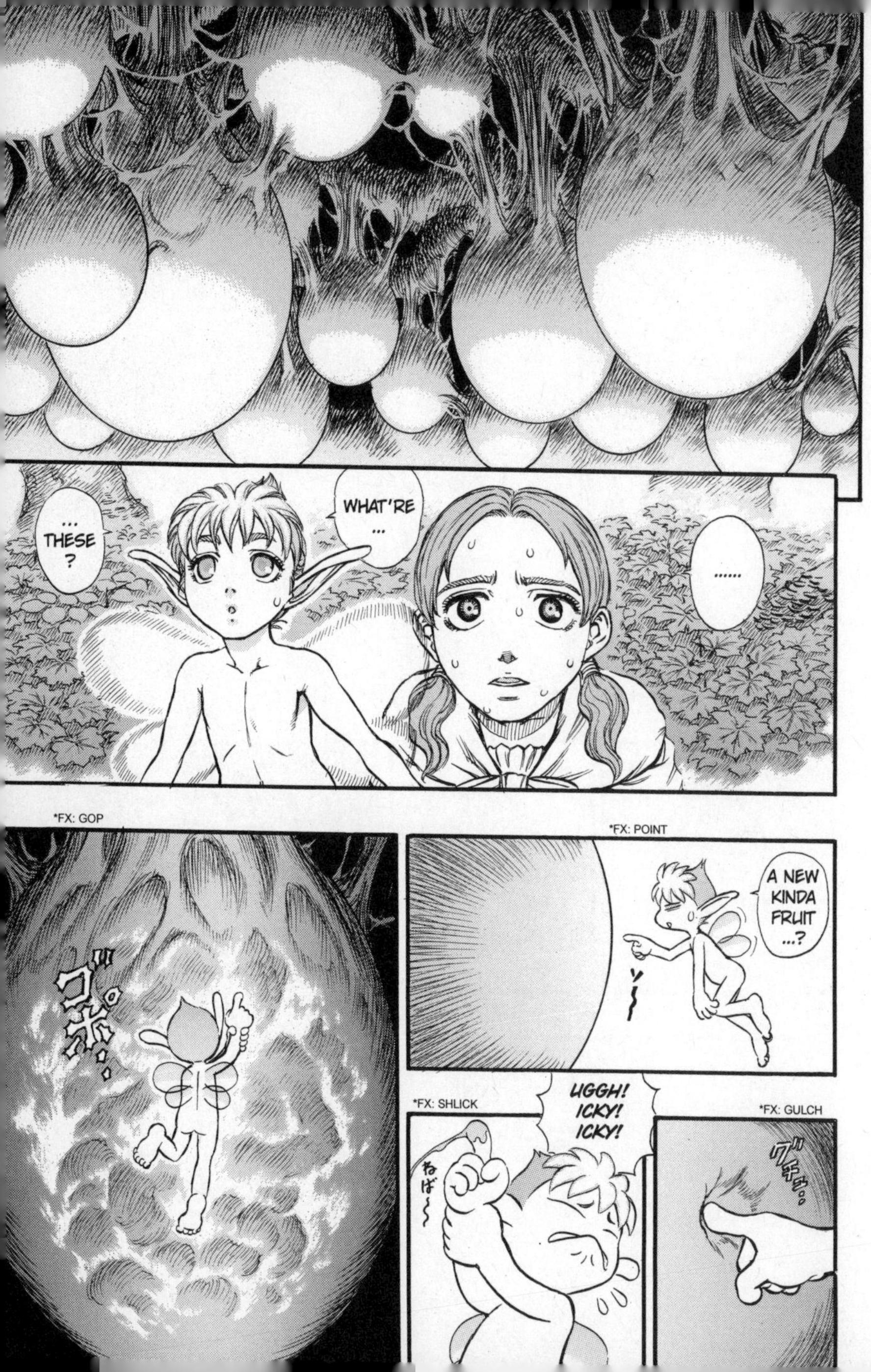
......
WHAT'RE ...
... THESE ?
*FX: POINT
A NEW KINDA FRUIT ...?
*FX: GULCH
*FX: SHLICK
UGGH! ICKY! ICKY!
ねば〜
*FX: GOP

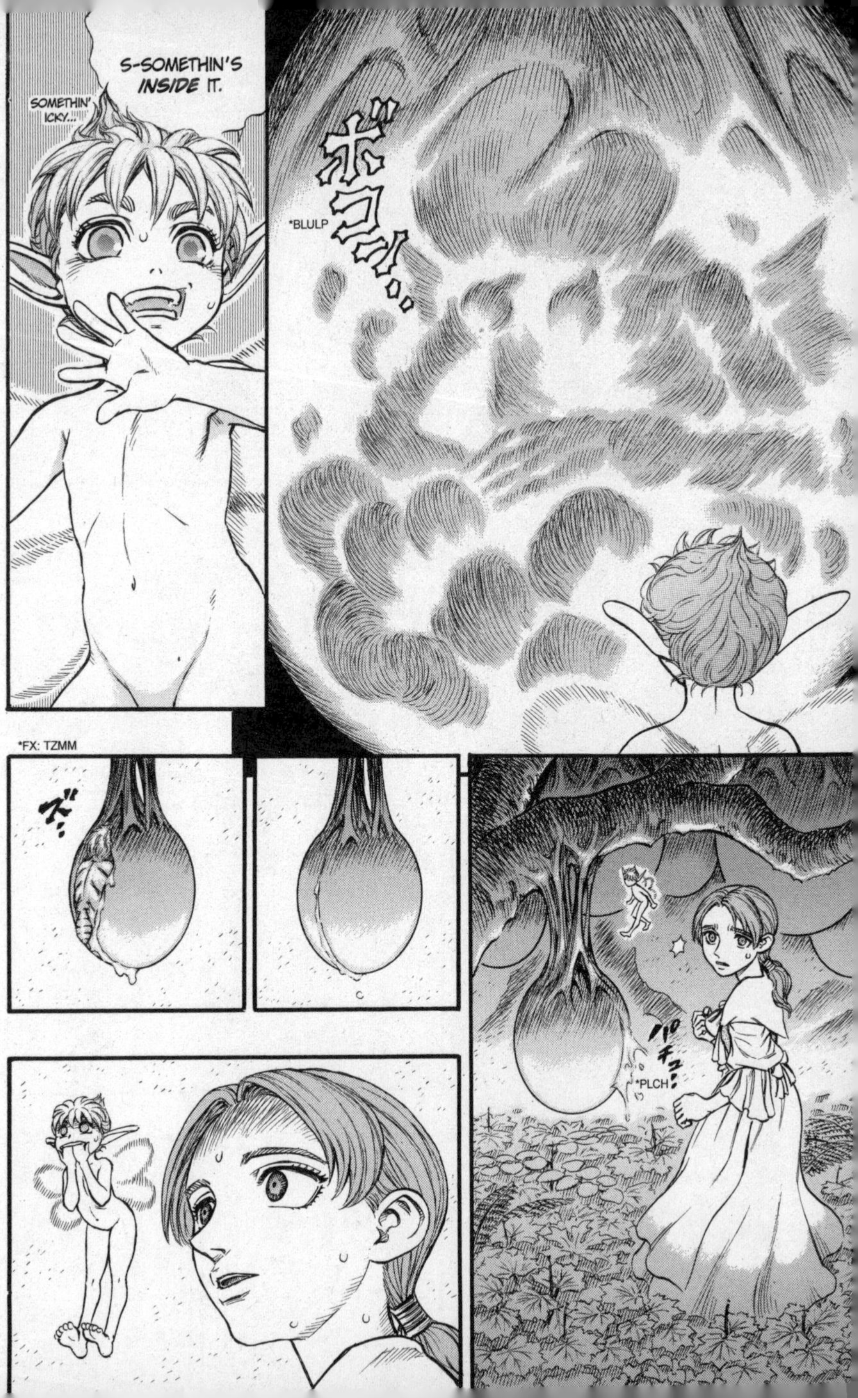
*BLULP
S-SOMETHIN'S INSIDE IT.
SOMETHIN' ICKY...
*PLCH
*FX: TZMM

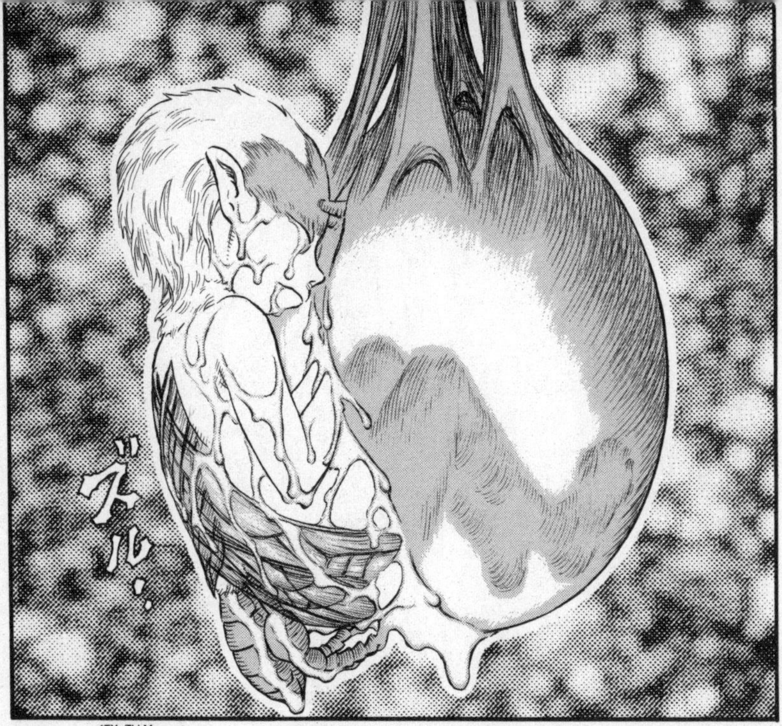
ズル..
*FX: ZLLM

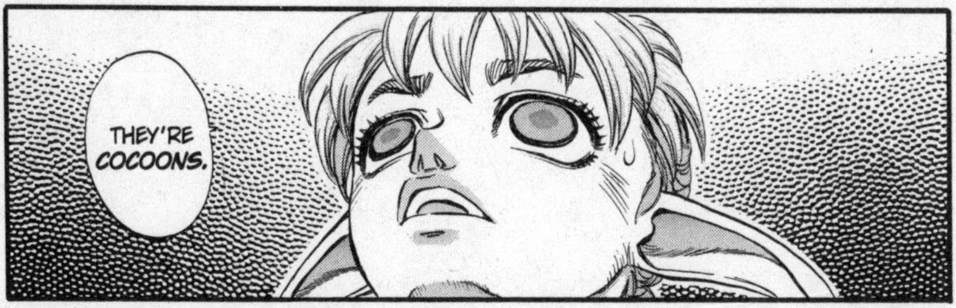
THEY'RE COCOONS.

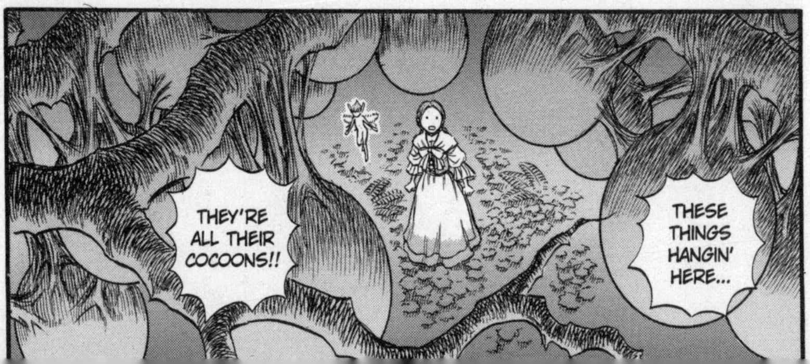
THESE THINGS HANGIN' HERE...
THEY'RE ALL THEIR COCOONS!!

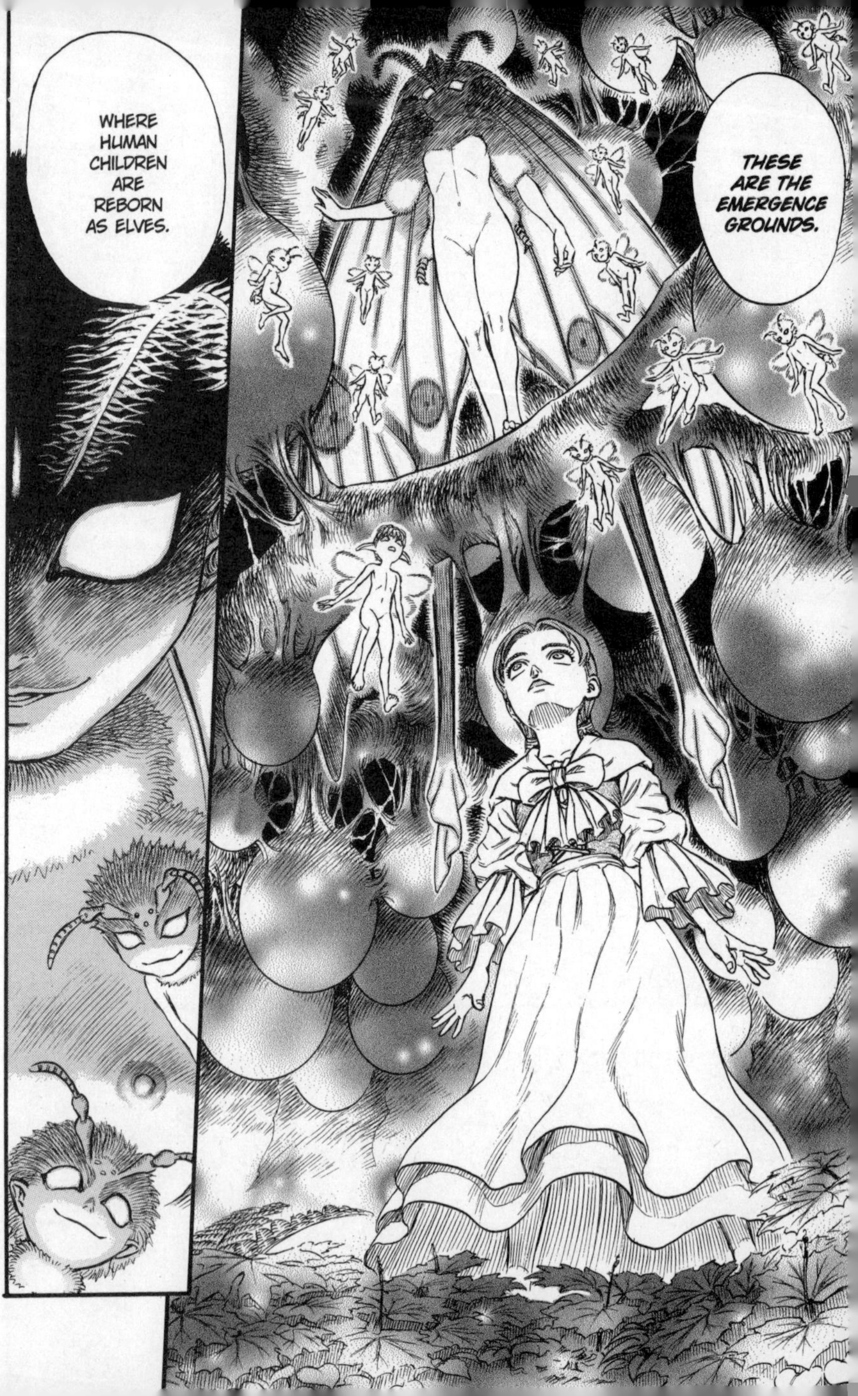
THESE ARE THE EMERGENCE GROUNDS.
WHERE HUMAN CHILDREN ARE REBORN AS ELVES.

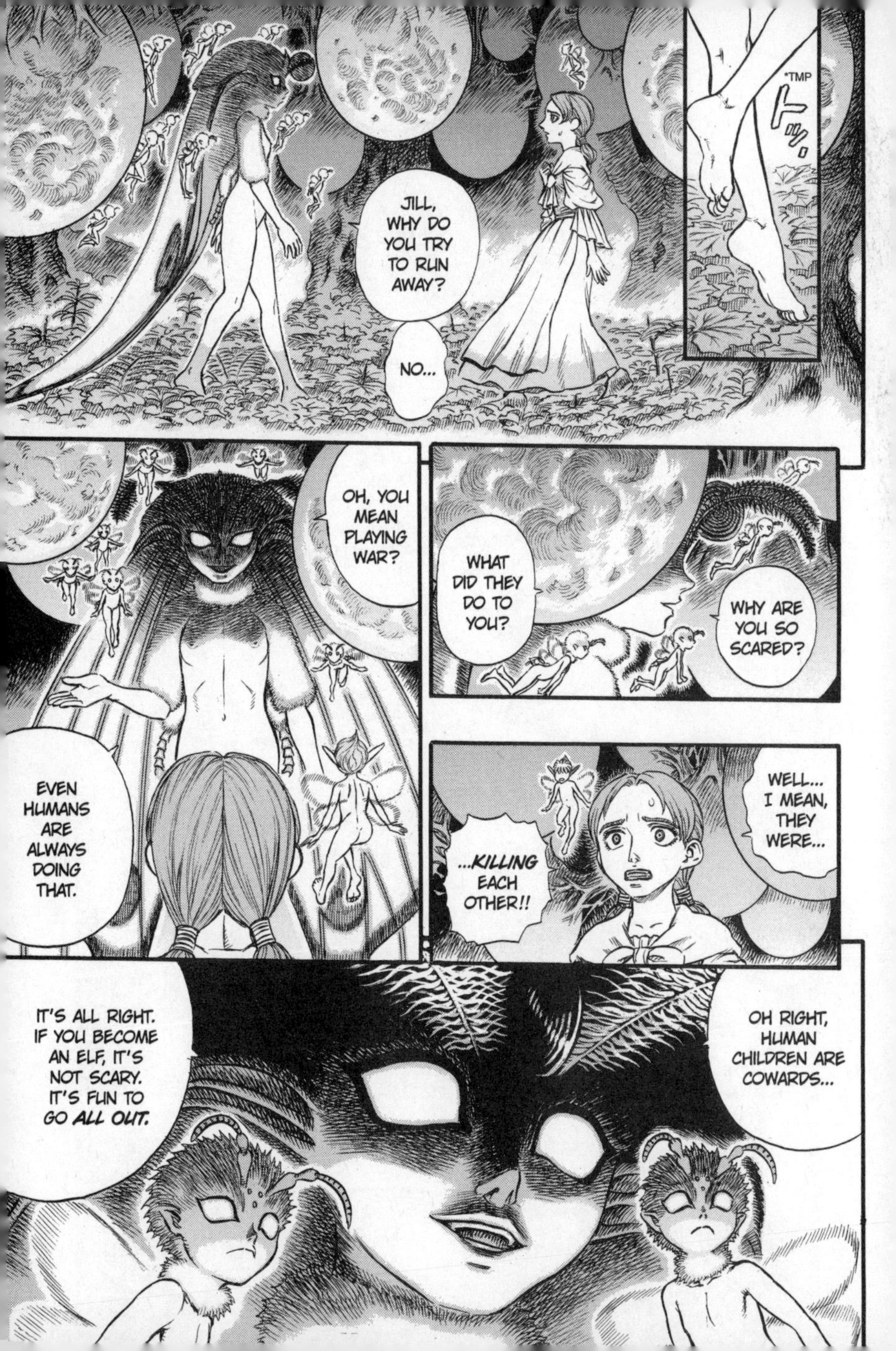
*TMP
トッ
JILL, WHY DO YOU TRY TO RUN AWAY?
NO...
WHY ARE YOU SO SCARED?
WHAT DID THEY DO TO YOU?
WELL... I MEAN, THEY WERE...
...**KILLING** EACH OTHER!!
OH, YOU MEAN PLAYING WAR?
EVEN HUMANS ARE ALWAYS DOING THAT.
OH RIGHT, HUMAN CHILDREN ARE COWARDS...
IT'S ALL RIGHT. IF YOU BECOME AN ELF, IT'S NOT SCARY. IT'S FUN TO GO **ALL OUT.**

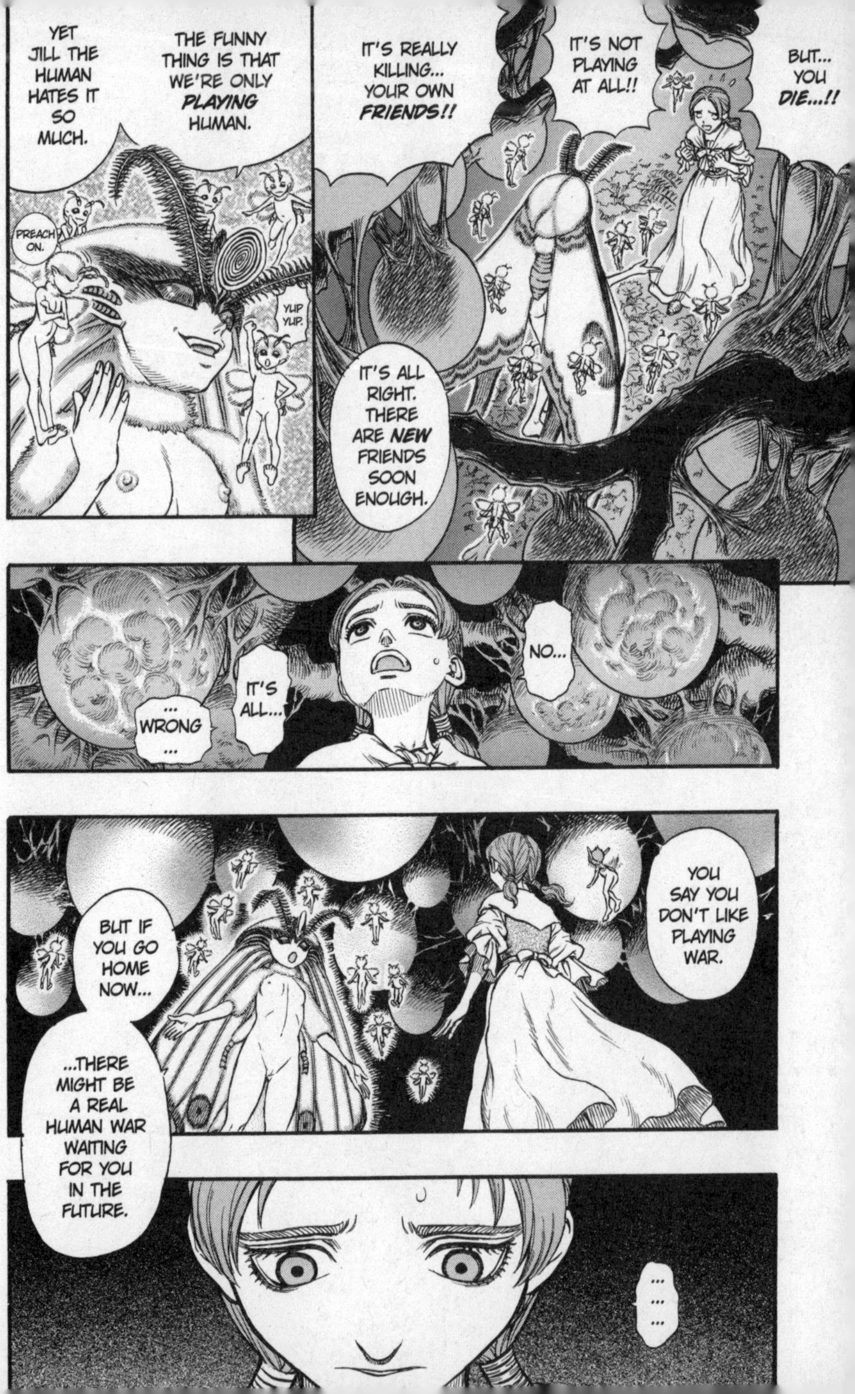
BUT... YOU DIE...!!
IT'S NOT PLAYING AT ALL!!
IT'S REALLY KILLING... YOUR OWN FRIENDS!!
IT'S ALL RIGHT. THERE ARE NEW FRIENDS SOON ENOUGH.
THE FUNNY THING IS THAT WE'RE ONLY PLAYING HUMAN.
YET JILL THE HUMAN HATES IT SO MUCH.
YUP YUP.
PREACH ON.
NO...
IT'S ALL...
... WRONG ...
YOU SAY YOU DON'T LIKE PLAYING WAR.
BUT IF YOU GO HOME NOW...
...THERE MIGHT BE A REAL HUMAN WAR WAITING FOR YOU IN THE FUTURE.
... ...

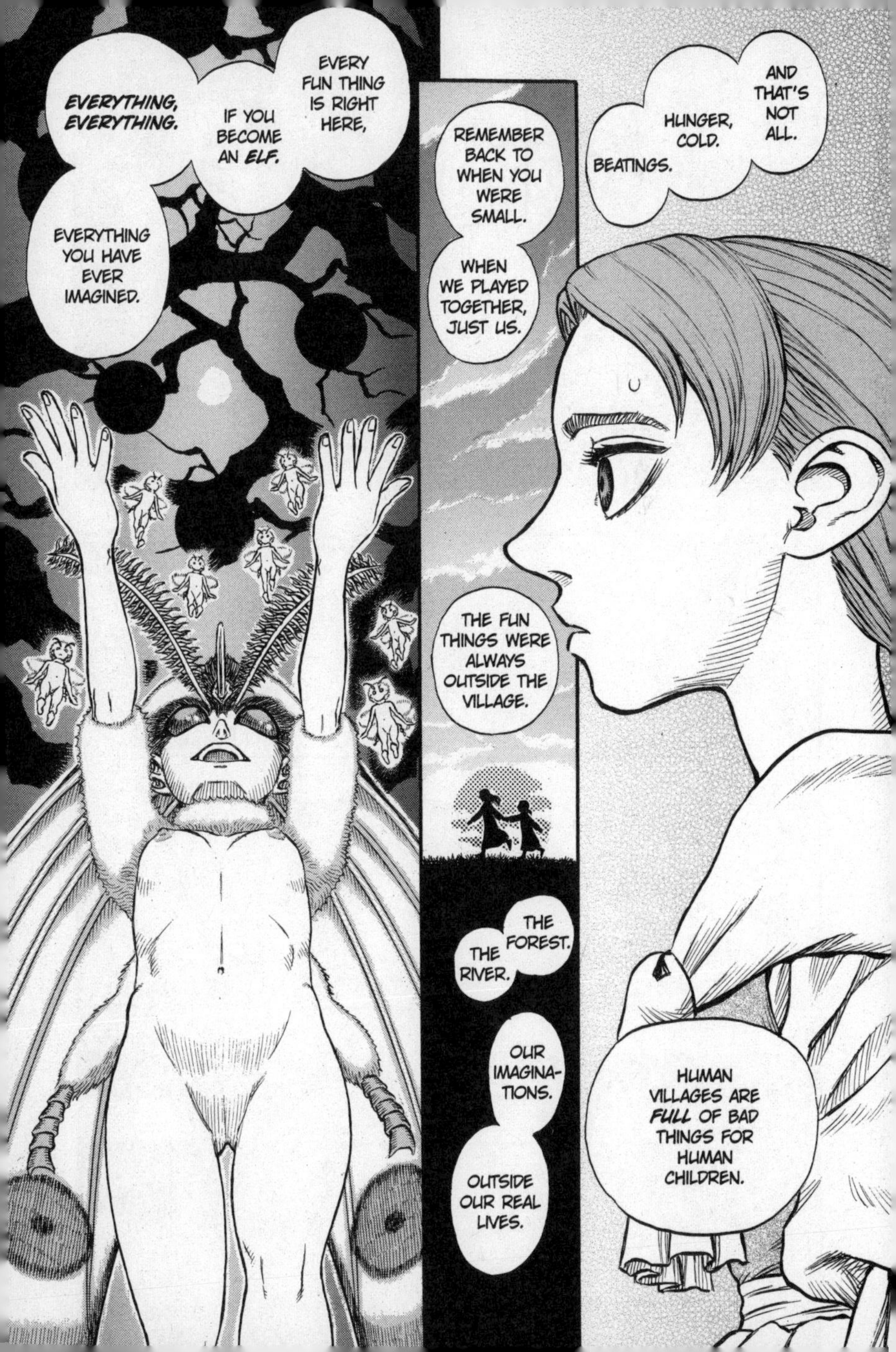

AND THAT'S NOT ALL.
HUNGER, COLD.
BEATINGS.
HUMAN VILLAGES ARE FULL OF BAD THINGS FOR HUMAN CHILDREN.
REMEMBER BACK TO WHEN YOU WERE SMALL.
WHEN WE PLAYED TOGETHER, JUST US.
THE FUN THINGS WERE ALWAYS OUTSIDE THE VILLAGE.
THE FOREST.
THE RIVER.
OUR IMAGINATIONS.
OUTSIDE OUR REAL LIVES.
EVERY FUN THING IS RIGHT HERE,
IF YOU BECOME AN ELF.
EVERYTHING, EVERYTHING.
EVERYTHING YOU HAVE EVER IMAGINED.

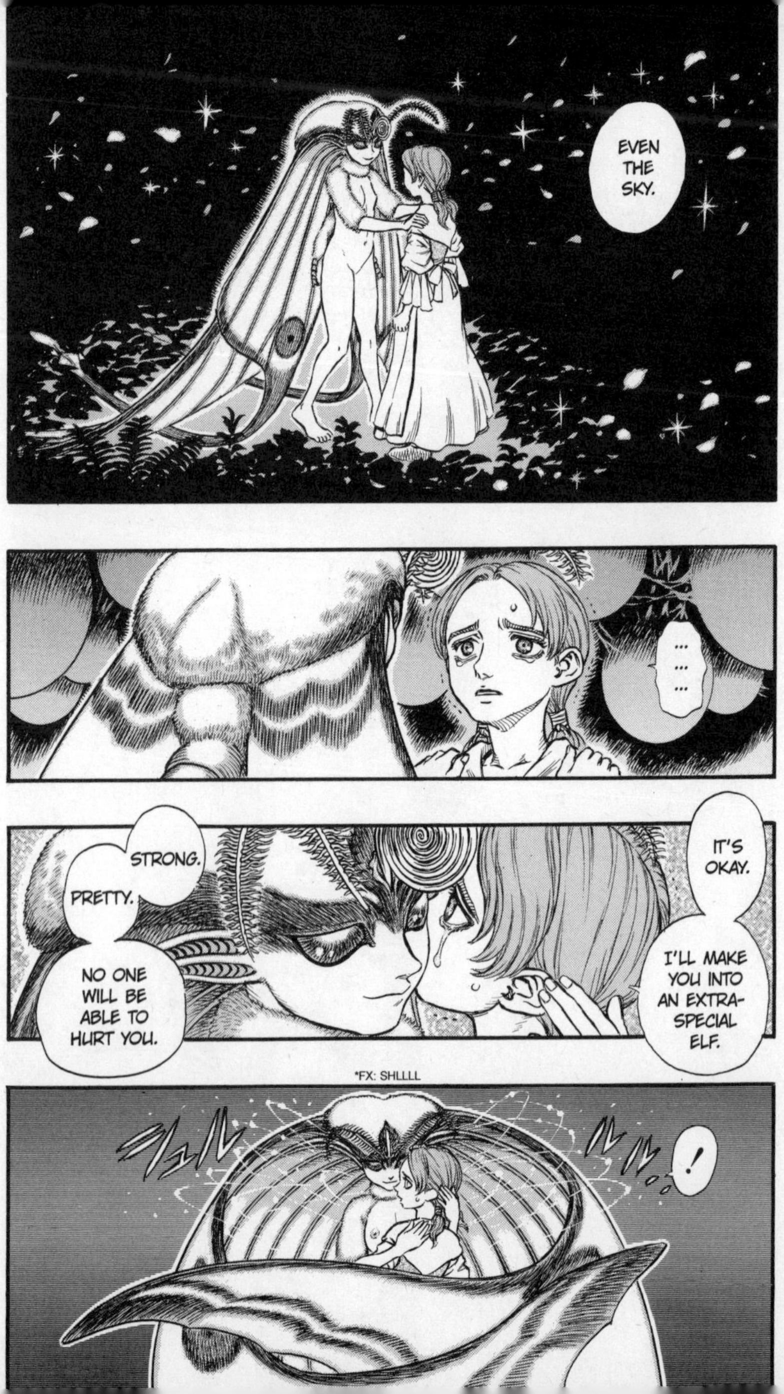
EVEN THE SKY.
......
IT'S OKAY.
I'LL MAKE YOU INTO AN EXTRA-SPECIAL ELF.
STRONG.
PRETTY.
NO ONE WILL BE ABLE TO HURT YOU.
*FX: SHLLLL
!

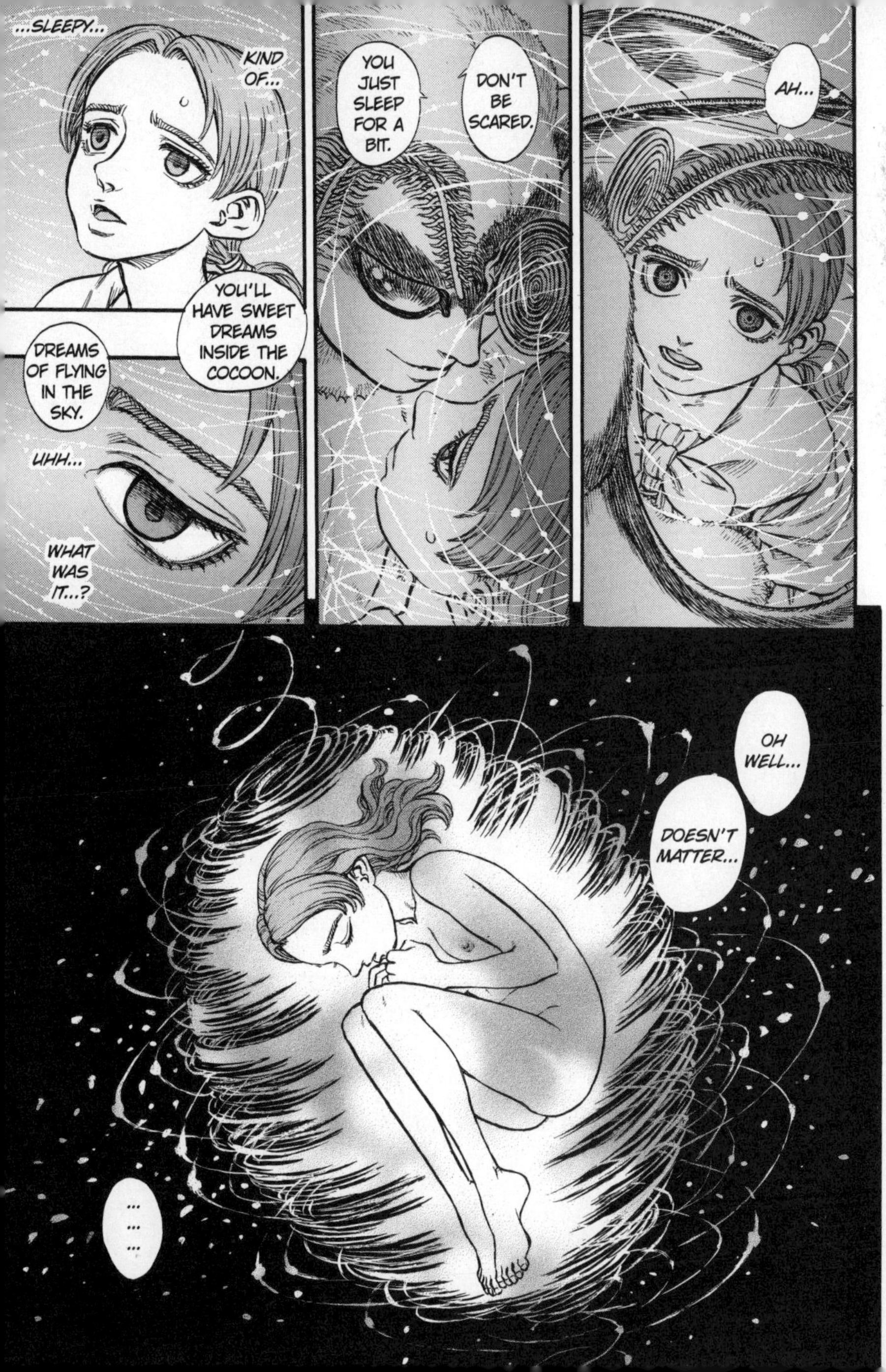
AH...
DON'T BE SCARED.
YOU JUST SLEEP FOR A BIT.
...SLEEPY...
KIND OF...
YOU'LL HAVE SWEET DREAMS INSIDE THE COCOON.
DREAMS OF FLYING IN THE SKY.
UHH...
WHAT WAS IT...?
OH WELL...
DOESN'T MATTER...
... ...

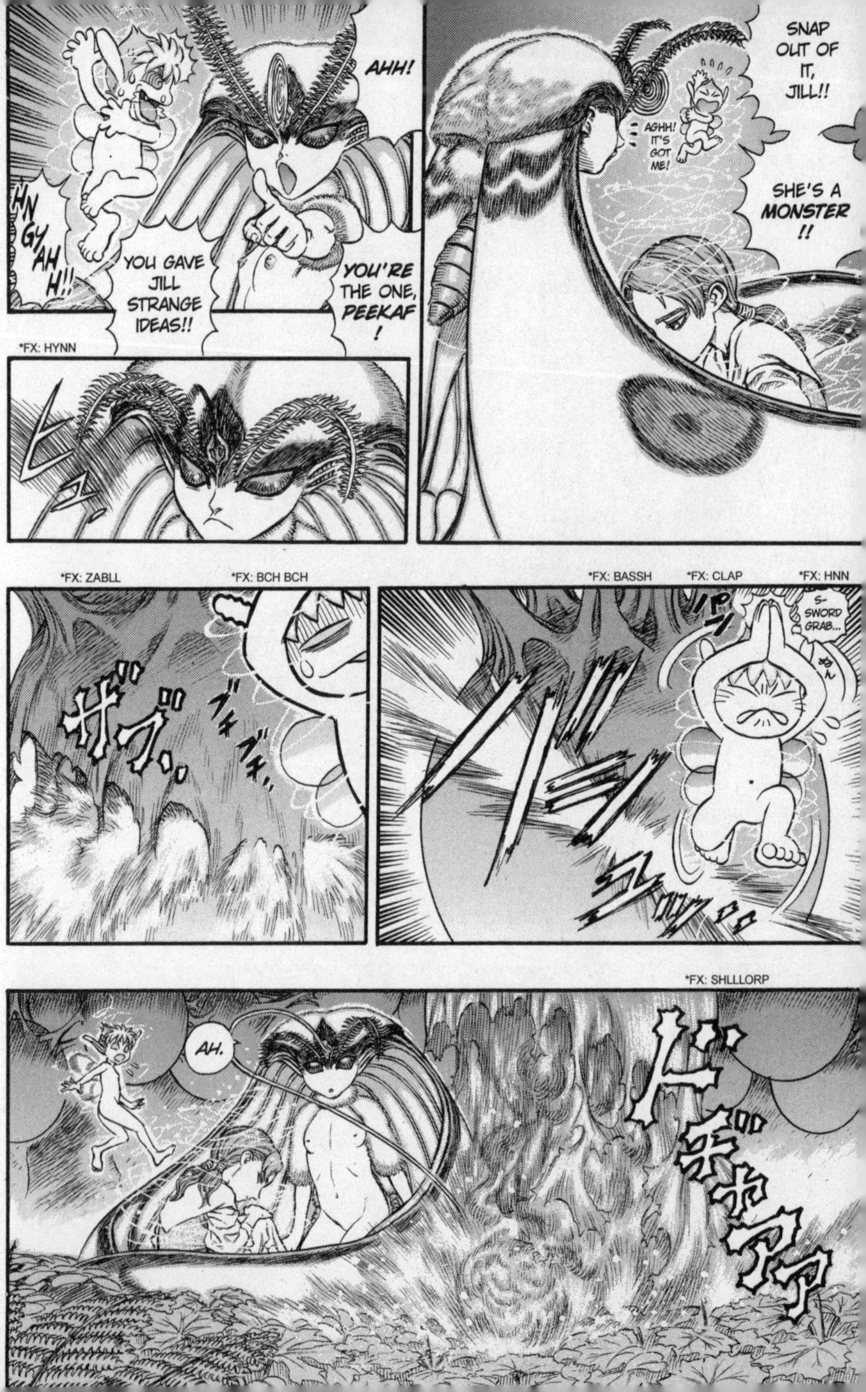
SNAP OUT OF IT, JILL!!
AGHH! IT'S GOT ME!
SHE'S A MONSTER!!
AHH!
YOU'RE THE ONE, PEEKAF!
YOU GAVE JILL STRANGE IDEAS!!
HNGYAHH!!
*FX: HYNN
*FX: BASSH
*FX: CLAP
*FX: HNN
S-SWORD GRAB...
*FX: ZABLL
*FX: BCH BCH
*FX: SHLLLORP
AH.

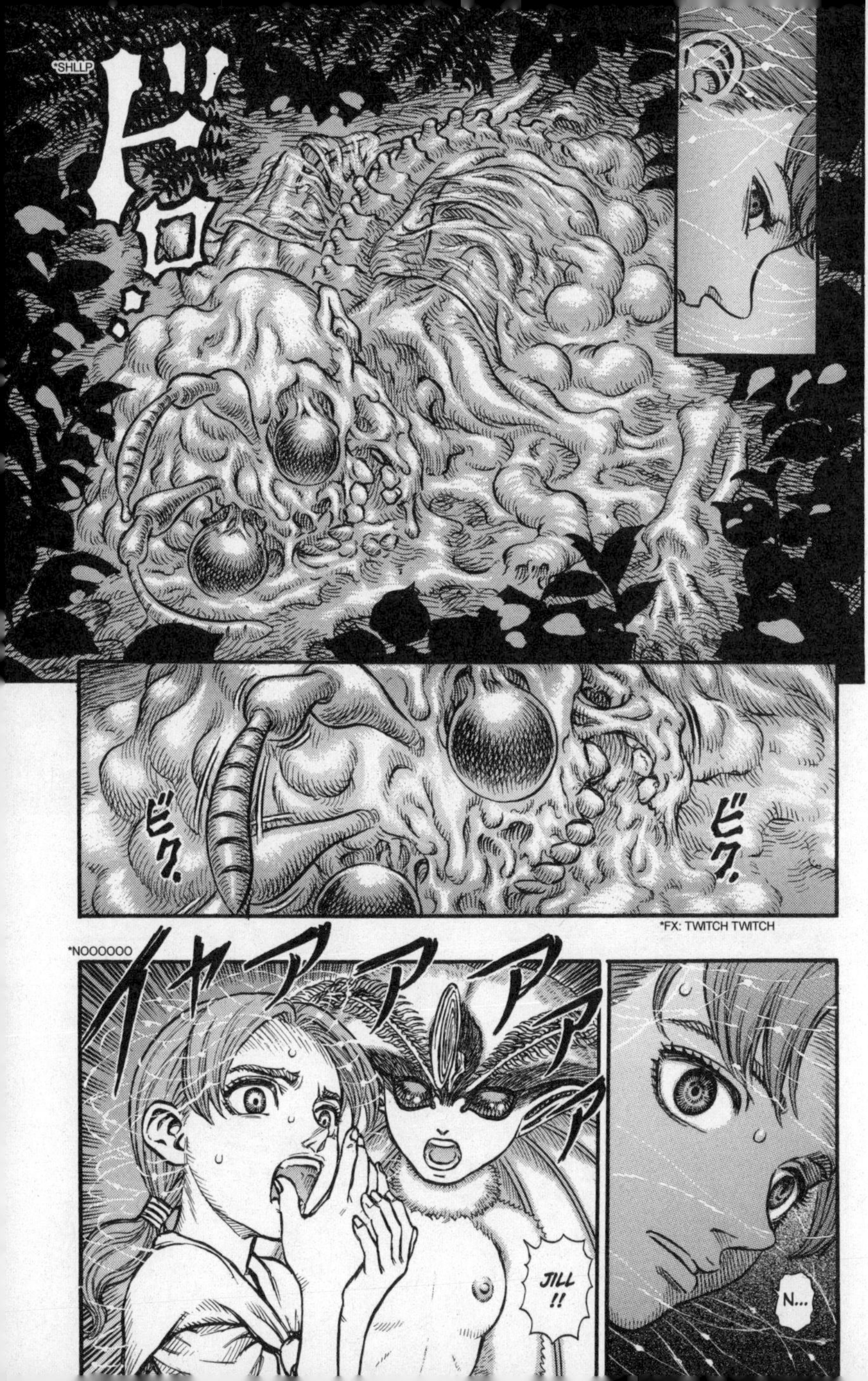

ドロ
*SHLLP
ビク
ビク
*FX: TWITCH TWITCH
N...
イヤアアアアア
*NOOOOOO
JILL !!

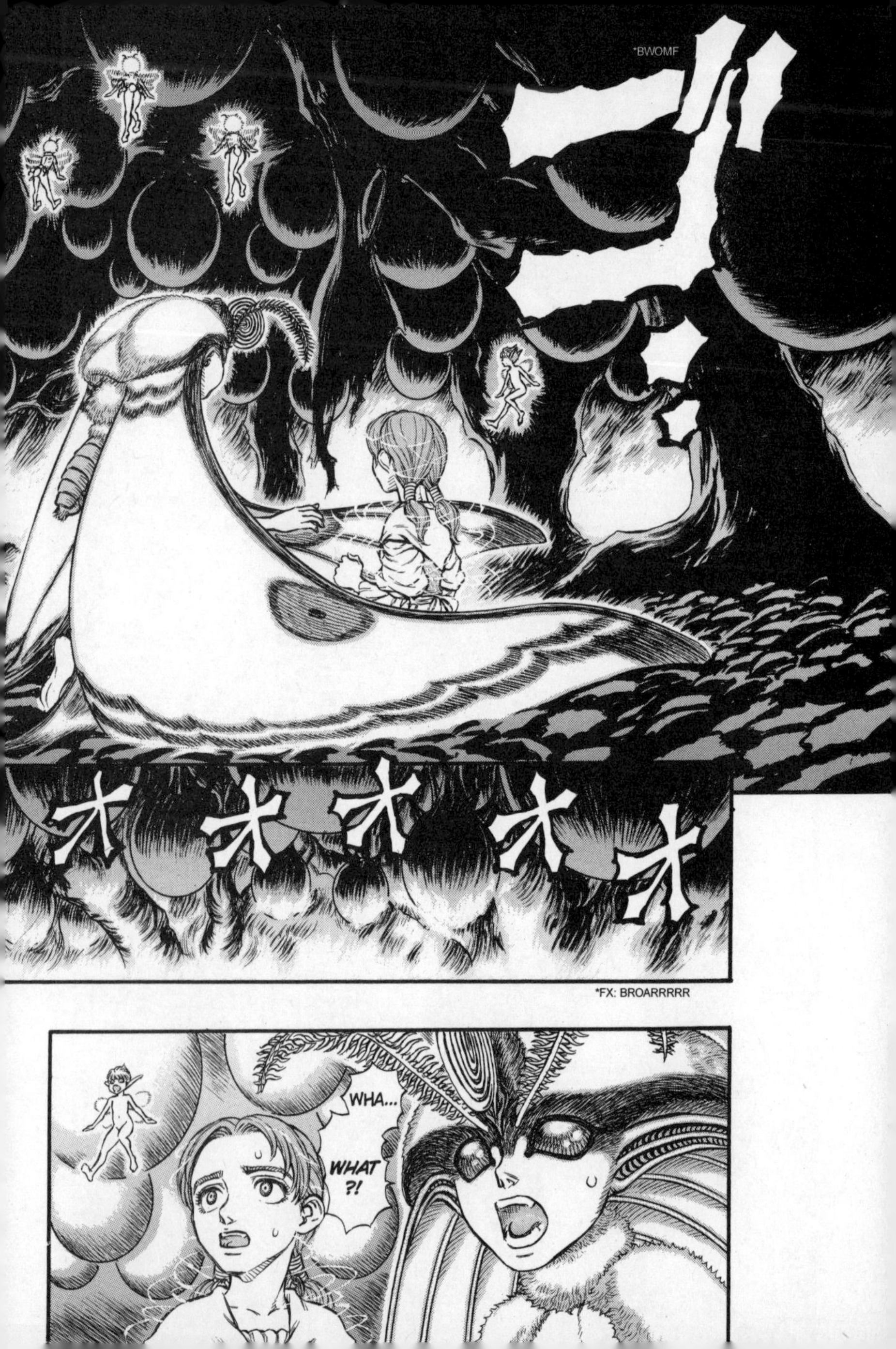
*BWOMF
*FX: BROARRRRR
WHA...
WHAT ?!

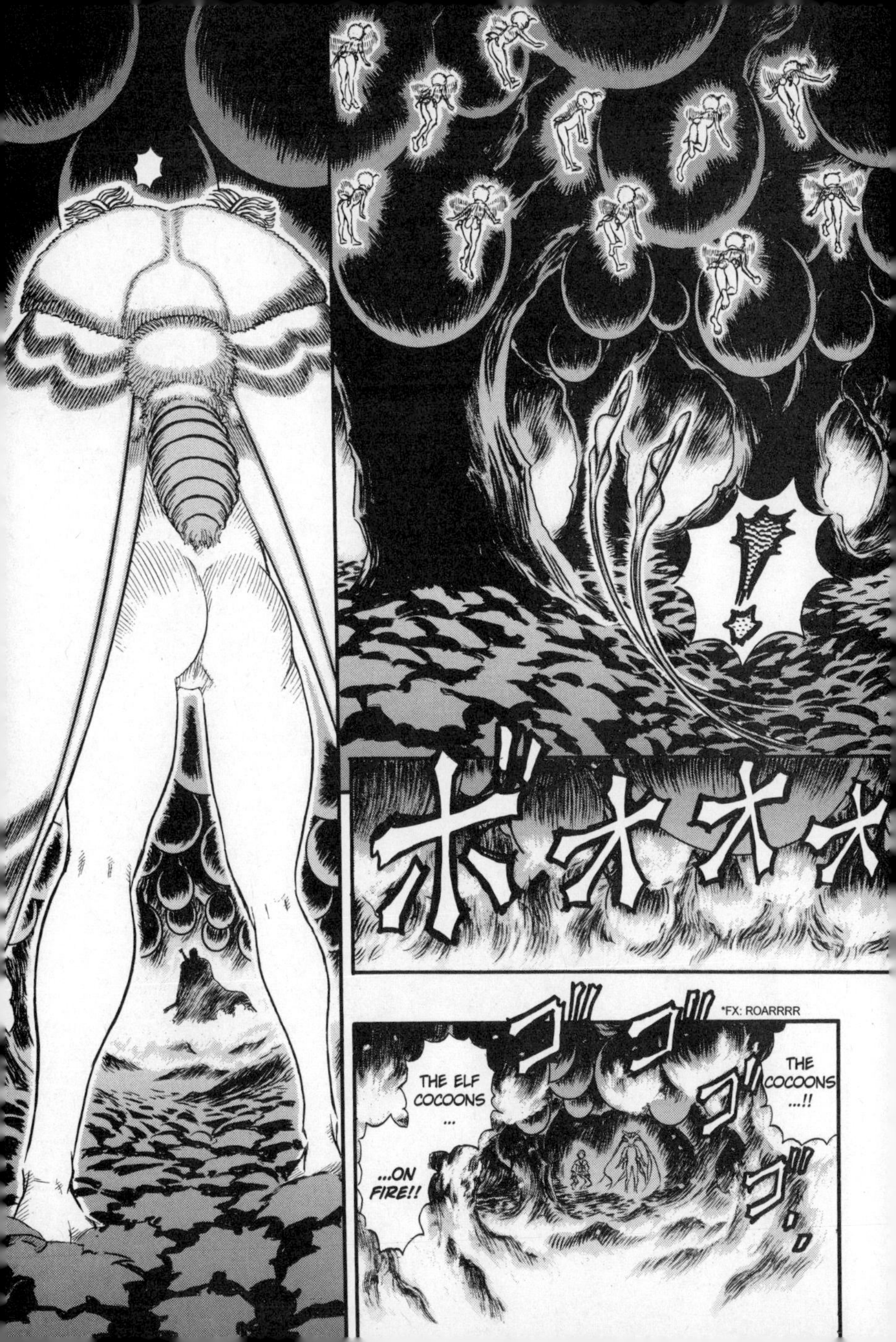
ボオオオ
*FX: ROARRRR
ゴゴゴゴ
THE COCOONS ...!!
THE ELF COCOONS ...
...ON FIRE!!

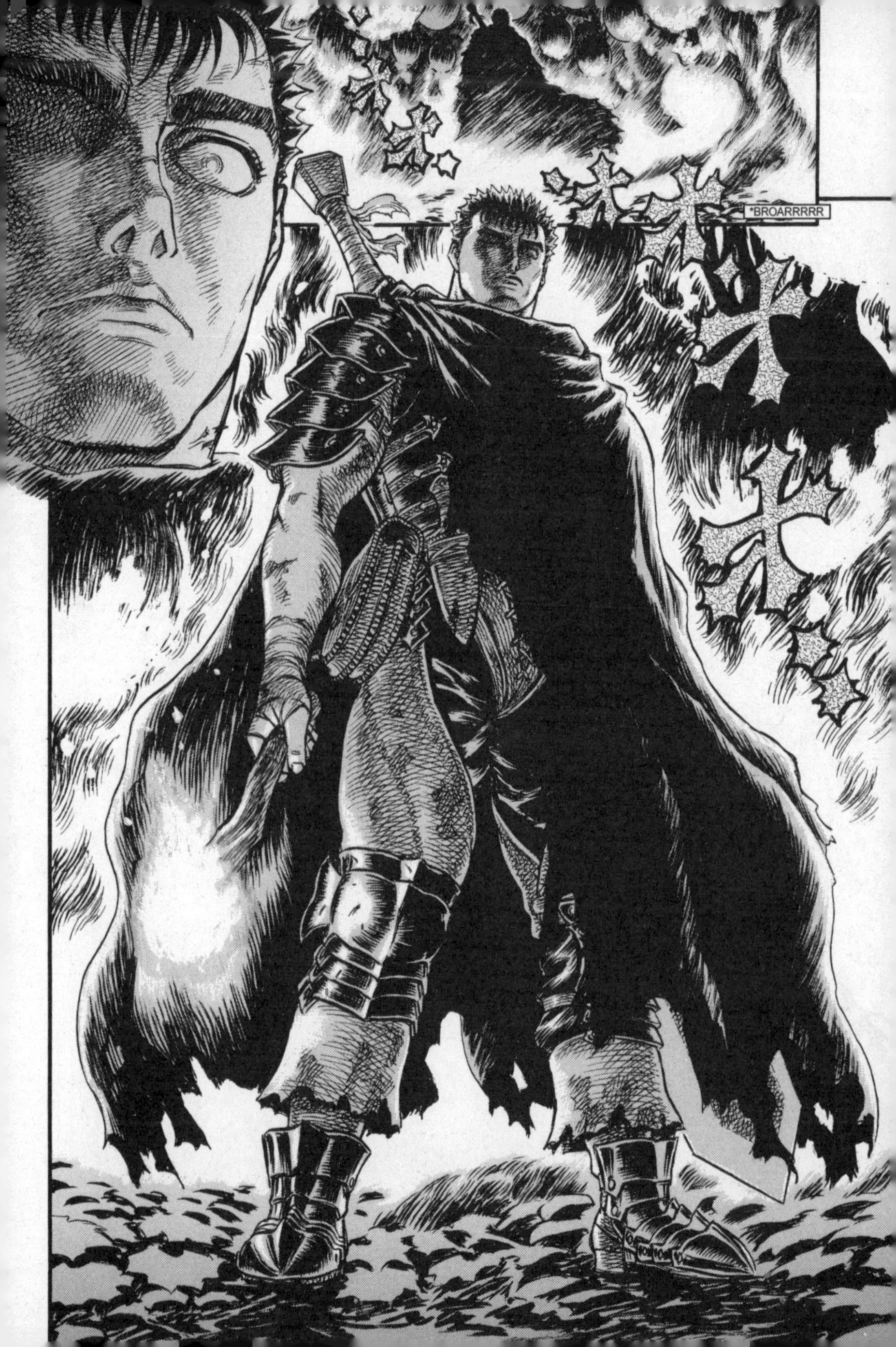
*BROARRRRR

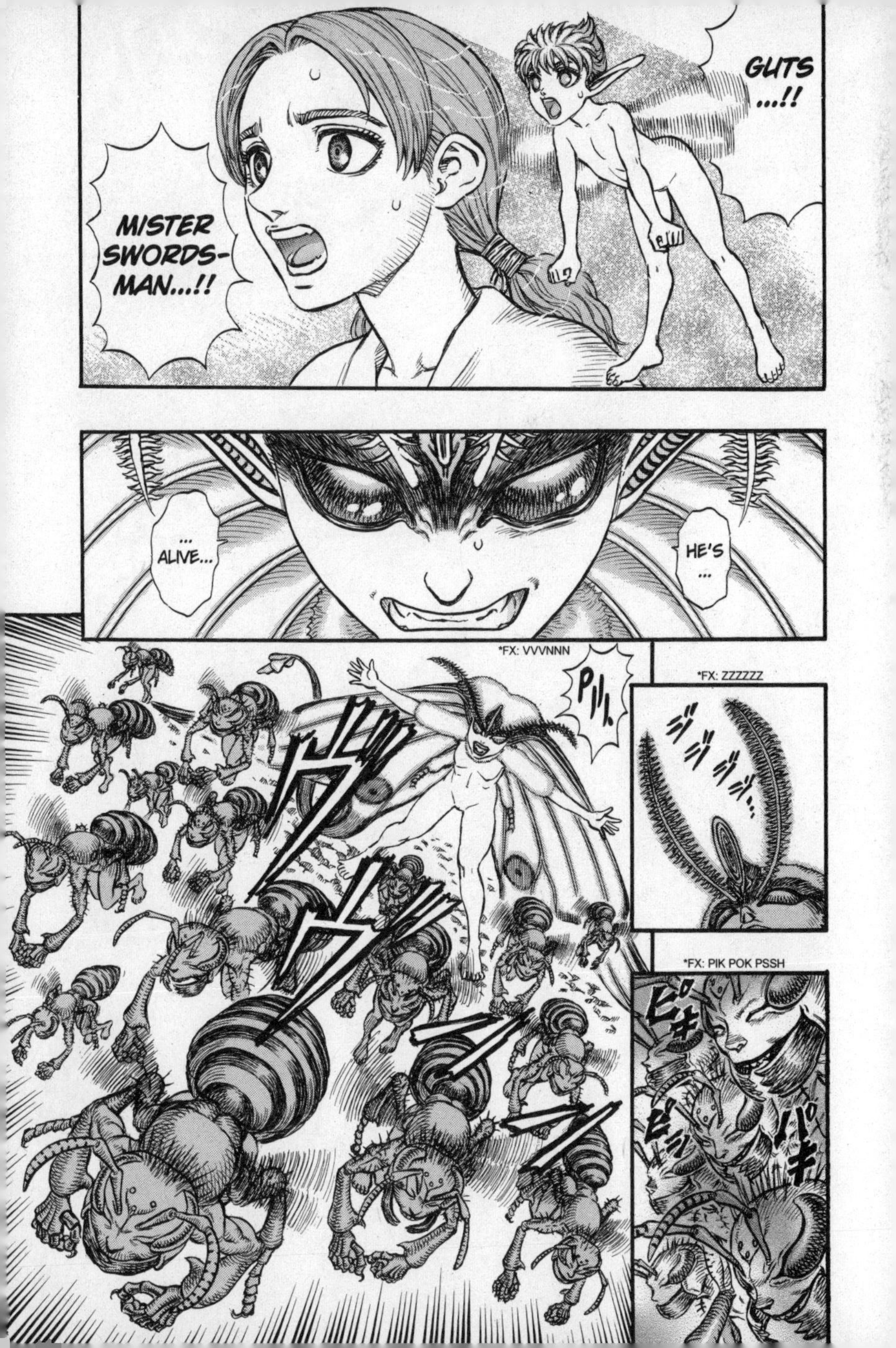
GUTS ...!!
MISTER SWORDS-MAN...!!
HE'S ...
... ALIVE...
*FX: ZZZZZZ
*FX: PIK POK PSSH
*FX: VVVNNN

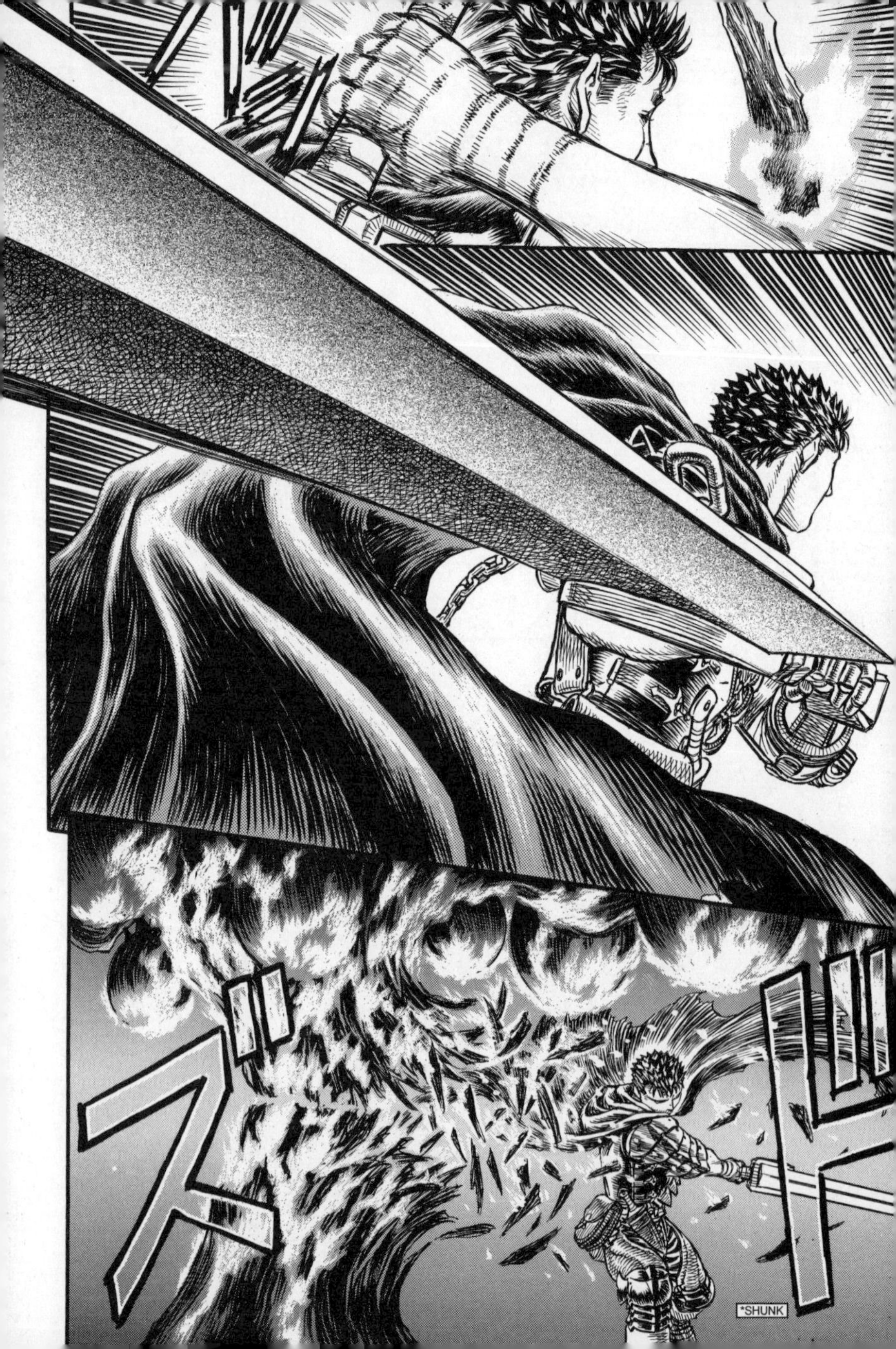
*SHUNK

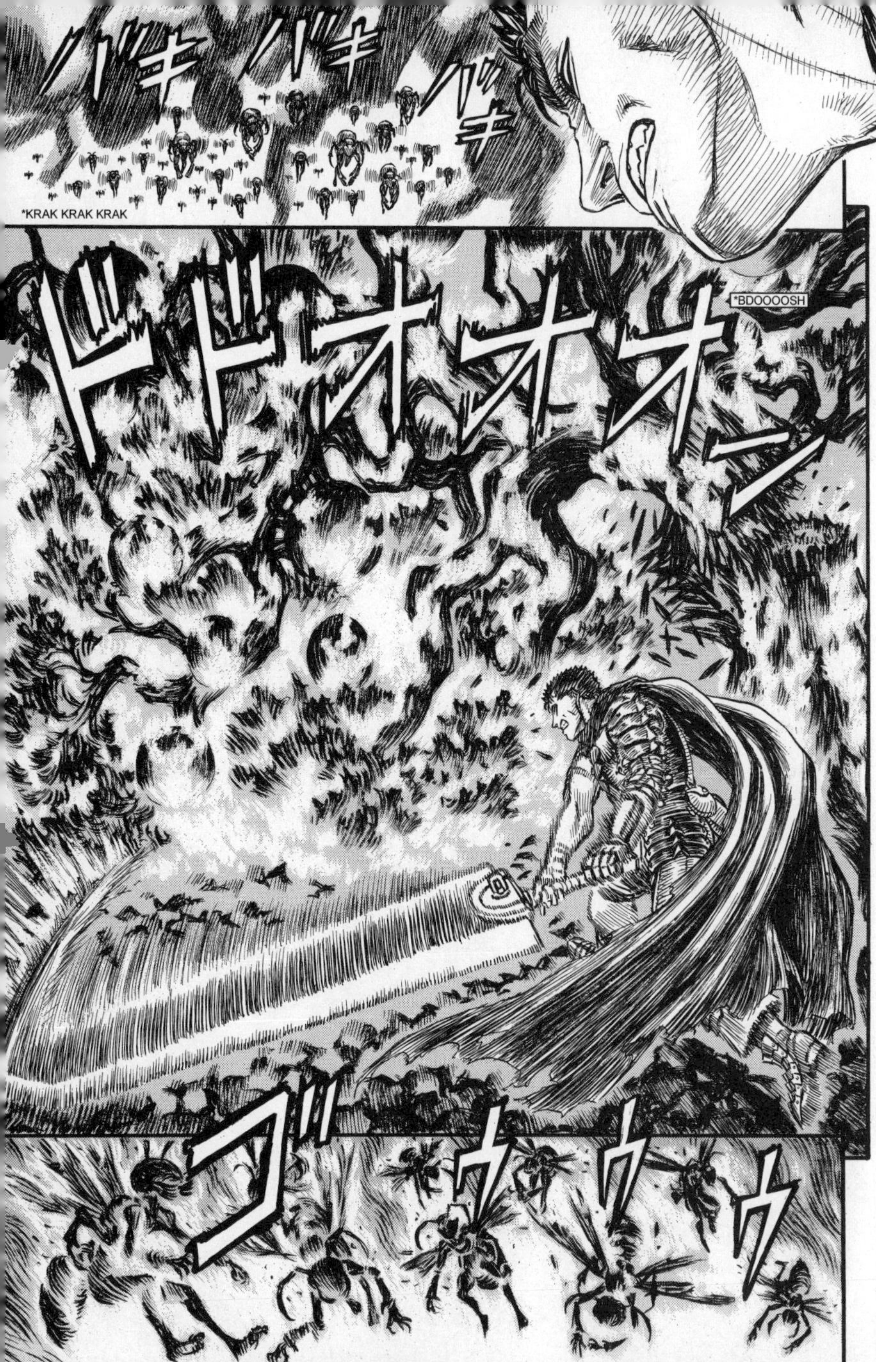

バキ バキ バキ
*KRAK KRAK KRAK
ドドオオオン
*BDOOOOSH
ブウウウ
*FX: FWSSSSH

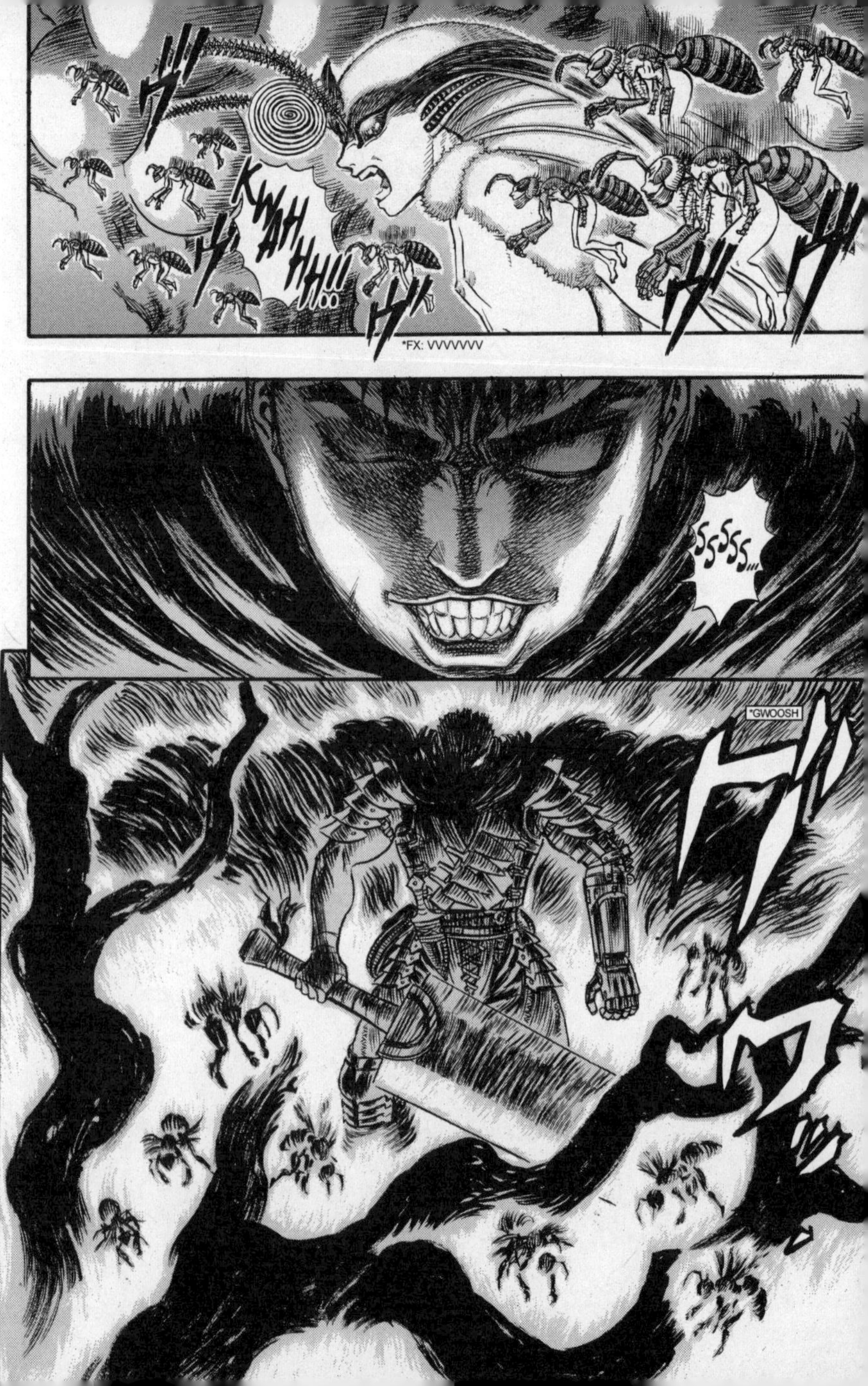
KWAAHHHH!!!
*FX: VVVVVV
SSSSS...
*GWOOSH

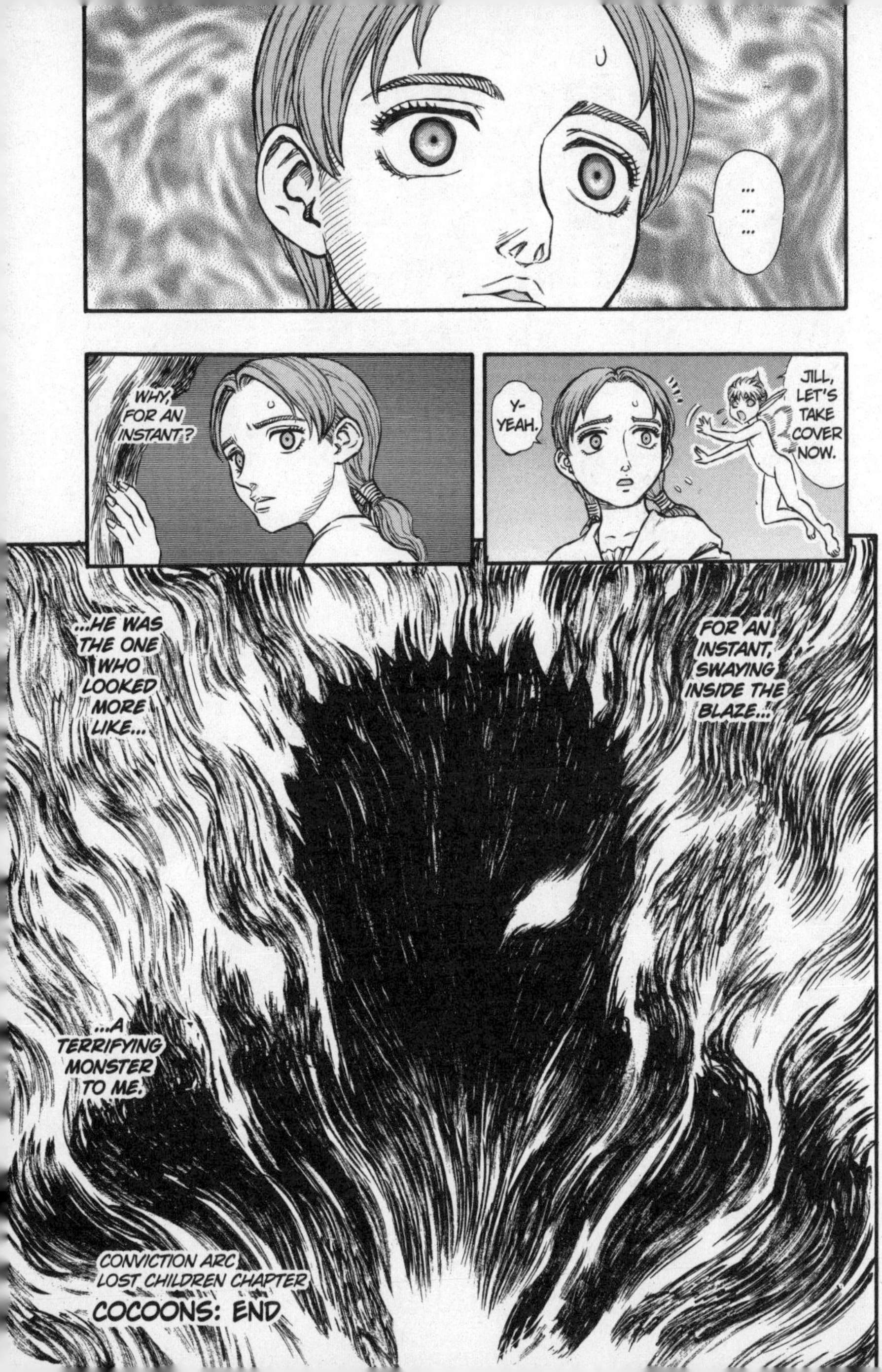
....
JILL, LET'S TAKE COVER NOW.
Y-YEAH.
WHY, FOR AN INSTANT?
FOR AN INSTANT, SWAYING INSIDE THE BLAZE...
...HE WAS THE ONE WHO LOOKED MORE LIKE...
...A TERRIFYING MONSTER TO ME.
CONVICTION ARC
LOST CHILDREN CHAPTER
COCOONS: END

Created by Kentaro Miura, *Berserk* is manga mayhem to the extreme—violent, horrifying, and mercilessly funny—and the wellspring for the internationally popular anime series. Not for the squeamish or the easily offended, *Berserk* asks for no quarter—and offers none!

Presented uncensored in the original Japanese format!

VOLUME 1
ISBN 978-1-59307-020-5

VOLUME 2
ISBN 978-1-59307-021-2

VOLUME 3
ISBN 978-1-59307-022-9

VOLUME 4
ISBN 978-1-59307-203-2

VOLUME 5
ISBN 978-1-59307-251-3

VOLUME 6
ISBN 978-1-59307-252-0

VOLUME 7
ISBN 978-1-59307-328-2

VOLUME 8
ISBN 978-1-59307-329-9

VOLUME 9
ISBN 978-1-59307-330-5

VOLUME 10
ISBN 978-1-59307-331-2

VOLUME 11
ISBN 978-1-59307-470-8

VOLUME 12
ISBN 978-1-59307-484-5

VOLUME 13
ISBN 978-1-59307-500-2

VOLUME 14
ISBN 978-1-59307-501-9

VOLUME 15
ISBN 978-1-59307-577-4

VOLUME 16
ISBN 978-1-59307-706-8

VOLUME 17
ISBN 978-1-59307-742-6

VOLUME 18
ISBN 978-1-59307-743-3

VOLUME 19
ISBN 978-1-59307-744-0

VOLUME 20
ISBN 978-1-59307-745-7

VOLUME 21
ISBN 978-1-59307-746-4

VOLUME 22
ISBN 978-1-59307-863-8

VOLUME 23
ISBN 978-1-59307-864-5

VOLUME 24
ISBN 978-1-59307-865-2

VOLUME 25
ISBN 978-1-59307-921-5

VOLUME 26
ISBN 978-1-59307-922-2

VOLUME 27
ISBN 978-1-59307-923-9

VOLUME 28
ISBN 978-1-59582-209-3

VOLUME 29
ISBN 978-1-59582-210-9

VOLUME 30
ISBN 978-1-59582-211-6

VOLUME 31
ISBN 978-1-59582-366-3

VOLUME 32
ISBN 978-1-59582-367-0

VOLUME 33
ISBN 978-1-59582-372-4

VOLUME 34
ISBN 978-1-59582-532-2

VOLUME 35
ISBN 978-1-59582-695-4

VOLUME 36
ISBN 978-1-59582-942-9

VOLUME 37
ISBN 978-1-61655-205-3

VOLUME 38
ISBN 978-1-50670-398-5

VOLUME 39
ISBN 978-1-50670-708-2

VOLUME 40
ISBN 978-1-50671-498-1

BERSERK OFFICIAL GUIDEBOOK
ISBN 978-1-50670-706-8

BERSERK: THE FLAME DRAGON KNIGHT
Written by Matoko Fukami and Kentaro Miura
ISBN 978-1-50670-939-0

$14.99 EACH!

AVAILABLE AT YOUR LOCAL COMICS SHOP OR BOOKSTORE
To find a comics shop near your area, visit comicshoplocator.com. For more information or to order direct: On the web: darkhorse.com | E-mail: mailorder@darkhorse.com | Phone: 1-800-862-0052 Mon.–Fri. 9 a.m. to 5 p.m. Pacific Time.

DARKHORSE.COM

VAMPIRE HUNTER D

HIDEYUKI KIKUCHI | ILLUSTRATIONS BY YOSHITAKA AMANO

From creator Hideyuki Kikuchi, one of Japan's leading horror authors, with illustrations by renowned Japanese artist Yoshitaka Amano, this series is here printed in an English translation for the first time anywhere!

Volume 1
ISBN 978-1-59582-012-9
$11.99

Volume 2:
RAISER OF GALES
ISBN 978-1-59582-014-3
$11.99

Volume 3:
DEMON DEATHCHASE
ISBN 978-1-59582-031-0
$11.99

Volume 4:
TALE OF THE DEAD TOWN
ISBN 978-1-59582-093-8
$9.99

Volume 5:
THE STUFF OF DREAMS
ISBN 978-1-59582-094-5
$8.99

Volume 6:
PILGRIMAGE OF
THE SACRED AND
THE PROFANE
ISBN 978-1-59582-106-5
$9.99

Volume 7:
MYSTERIOUS JOURNEY TO THE
NORTH SEA PART ONE
ISBN 978-1-59582-107-2
$8.99

Volume 8:
MYSTERIOUS JOURNEY
TO THE NORTH SEA
PART TWO
ISBN 978-1-59582-108-9
$8.99

Volume 9:
THE ROSE PRINCESS
ISBN 978-1-59582-109-6
$8.99

Volume 10:
DARK NOCTURNE
ISBN 978-1-59582-132-4
$8.99

Volume 11:
PALE FALLEN ANGEL
PARTS ONE AND TWO
ISBN 978-1-59582-130-0
$14.99

Volume 12:
PALE FALLEN ANGEL
PARTS THREE AND FOUR
ISBN 978-1-59582-131-7
$14.99

Volume 13:
TWIN-SHADOWED KNIGHT
PARTS ONE AND TWO
ISBN 978-1-59307-930-7
$14.99

Volume 14:
DARK ROAD
PARTS ONE AND TWO
ISBN 978-1-59582-440-0
$14.99

Volume 15:
DARK ROAD PART THREE
ISBN 978-1-59582-500-1
$9.99

Volume 16:
TYRANT'S STARS
PARTS ONE AND TWO
ISBN 978-1-59582-572-8
$14.99

Volume 17:
TYRANT'S STARS
PARTS THREE AND FOUR
ISBN 978-1-59582-820-0
$14.99

Volume 18:
FORTRESS OF
THE ELDER GOD
ISBN 978-1-59582-976-4
$10.99

Volume 19:
MERCENARY ROAD
ISBN 978-1-61655-073-8
$11.99

Volume 20:
SCENES FROM
AN UNHOLY WAR
ISBN 978-1-61655-255-8
$11.99

Volume 21:
RECORD OF
THE BLOOD BATTLE
ISBN 978-1-61655-437-8
$11.99

Volume 22:
WHITE DEVIL MOUNTAIN
PARTS ONE AND TWO
ISBN 978-1-61655-509-2
$11.99

Volume 23:
IRIYA THE BERSERKER
ISBN 978-1-61655-706-5
$11.99

Volume 24:
THRONG OF HERETICS
ISBN 978-1-61655-789-8
$11.99

Volume 25:
UNDEAD ISLAND
ISBN 978-1-50670-163-9
$11.99

Volume 26:
BEDEVILED
STAGECOACH
ISBN 978-1-50670-199-8
$11.99

Volume 27:
NIGHTMARE VILLAGE
ISBN 978-1-50670-927-7
$11.99

AVAILABLE AT YOUR LOCAL COMICS SHOP OR BOOKSTORE

To find a comics shop near you, visit comicshoplocator.com · For more information or to order direct: On the web: DarkHorse.com · Email: mailorder@DarkHorse.com · Phone: 1-800-862-0052 Mon.–Fri. 9 AM to 5 PM Pacific Time.

YASUHIRO NIGHTOW 内藤泰弘
TRIGUN

On the forbidding desert planet of Gunsmoke, a sixty-billion-double-dollar bounty hangs over the head of Vash the Stampede, a pistol-packing pacifist with a weapon capable of punching holes in a planet. Every trigger-happy psycho in creation is aiming to claim Vash dead or alive—preferably dead!—and although Vash is an avowed pacifist, he won't go down without a fight. And when Vash fights, destruction is sure to follow!

TRIGUN OMNIBUS
ISBN 978-1-61655-246-6
$19.99

TRIGUN MAXIMUM OMNIBUS
VOLUME 1: ISBN 978-1-61655-010-3
VOLUME 2: ISBN 978-1-61655-329-6
VOLUME 3: ISBN 978-1-61655-012-7
VOLUME 4: ISBN 978-1-61655-013-4
VOLUME 5: ISBN 978-1-61655-086-8
$19.99 each

TRIGUN: MULTIPLE BULLETS
ISBN 978-1-61655-105-6
$13.99

DarkHorse.com

AVAILABLE AT YOUR LOCAL COMICS SHOP OR BOOKSTORE
TO FIND A COMICS SHOP IN YOUR AREA, VISIT COMICSHOPLOCATOR.COM

For more information or to order direct: On the web: DarkHorse.com
E-mail: mailorder@darkhorse.com
Phone: 1-800-862-0052 Mon.–Fri. 9 a.m. to 5 p.m. Pacific Time.

HELLSING

VOLUME 1:
ISBN 978-1-59307-056-4

VOLUME 2:
ISBN 978-1-59307-057-1

VOLUME 3:
ISBN 978-1-59307-202-5

VOLUME 4:
ISBN 978-1-59307-259-9

VOLUME 5:
ISBN 978-1-59307-272-8

VOLUME 6:
ISBN 978-1-59307-302-2

VOLUME 7:
ISBN 978-1-59307-348-0

VOLUME 8:
ISBN 978-1-59307-780-8

VOLUME 9:
ISBN 978-1-59582-157-7

VOLUME 10:
ISBN 978-1-59582-498-1

$13.99 EACH

AVAILABLE AT YOUR LOCAL COMICS SHOP OR BOOKSTORE!
To find a comics shop in your area, visit comicshoplocator.com.

For more information or to order direct visit DarkHorse.com or call 1-800-862-0052
Mon.-Fri. 9 AM to 5 PM Pacific Time. Prices and availability subject to change without notice.

DARK HORSE MANGA
DarkHorse.com